I0084151

ADDITIONS AND CORRECTIONS

TO THE

W.P.A.

INVENTORY

OF

MEDINA COUNTY, OHIO:

MEDINA

Jana Sloan Broglin

HERITAGE BOOKS
2025

HERITAGE BOOKS

AN IMPRINT OF HERITAGE BOOKS, INC.

Books, CDs, and more—Worldwide

For our listing of thousands of titles see our website
at
www.HeritageBooks.com

Published 2025 by
HERITAGE BOOKS, INC.
Publishing Division
5810 Ruatan Street
Berwyn Heights, MD 20740

Copyright © 2025 Jana Sloan Broglin

(Originally Titled)
INVENTORY OF THE COUNTY ARCHIVES OF OHIO

Prepared by
The Ohio Historical Records Survey Project
Division of Community Service Programs
Works Projects Administration

No. 52. MEDINA COUNTY (MEDINA)

Columbus, Ohio
The Ohio Historical Records Survey Project
April 1942

All rights reserved. No part of this book may be reproduced or
transmitted in any form or by any means, electronic or mechanical,
including photocopying, recording or by any information storage and
retrieval system without written permission from the author, except
for the inclusion of brief quotations in a review.

International Standard Book Number
Paperbound: 978-0-7884-4704-4

Foreword v
Preface
         Preface 2nd edition . . . . vii-viii
         Preface 1st edition . . . . ix-x
List of Abbreviations, Symbols, Explanatory Notes . . . . . xi-xiii
Historical Sketch . . . . xv-xxiv
Governmental Organization and Records System . . . . . xxv-lxiv
Housing, Care, and Accessibility of Records . . . . lxv-lxxi

County Offices and Their Records

County Commissioners 1-28
         Journals. Reports. Improvements. Miscellaneous. Aid for
         the blind. Relief administration.
Recorder 29-50
         Real property transfers; deeds; leases; mortgages; liens;
         registered lands; plats and surveys. Personal property
         transfers. Corporations and partnerships. Licenses and
         grants of authority. Fiscal accounts. Miscellaneous.
Clerk of Courts 51-68
         Dockets and records of trials. Jury and witness records.
         Motor vehicles. Licenses and commissions. Partnership
         records. Elections. Naturalization. Fiscal accounts.
         Miscellaneous.
Court of Common Pleas 69-87
Supreme Court 88-91
Court of Appeals 92-101
         District court. Circuit court. Court of appeals.
Probate Court 102-127
         Calendar and dockets. Court proceedings. Wills. Estates:
         appointments, bonds and letters; inventories,
         appraisements, and sale bills; schedule of debts; accounts
         and cost bills. Inheritance tax. Assignments. Record of
         dependents. Naturalization. Vital statistics: births and
         deaths; marriages. Licenses. Fiscal accounts. Reports.

Juvenile Court................................. 128-132
Probation department 133-136
Aid to dependent children...................... 137-141
Jury Commissioners 142-143
Grand Jury................................... 143-145
Petit Jury.................................... 146-147
Prosecuting Attorney 148-153
Coroner..................................... 154-156
Sheriff...................................... 157-171
Dog Warden 172-173
Auditor 174-219

Property transfers. Maps and plots. Tax Records: tax appraisements; tax returns; tax duplicates and abstracts; assessments; tax exemptions; additions and deductions; utilities; delinquent taxes. Business administration of office: appropriations; orders; general accounts; special accounts; warrants and vouchers. Licenses. Bonds: official; debenture bonds. Reports. Statements. Miscellaneous. Weights and measures.

Treasurer.................................... 220-238

Tax records: duplicates and assessments; additions and deductions; tax stamps; receipts; delinquent taxes; collections; inheritance tax. Fiscal accounts: cashbooks and ledgers; warrants and orders. Bonds. Miscellaneous.

Budget Commissioners.......................... 239-240
Board of Revision............................. 241-245
Trustees of the Sinking Fund 246-247
Board of Elections 248-253

Journal. Records of elections. Miscellaneous.

Board of Education............................ 254-260

Minutes. Reports. Miscellaneous.

Board of Health.............................. 261-266

Minutes. Vital statistics and communicable diseases. Miscellaneous.

Tuberculosis Hospital.......................... 266

Superintendent of the County Home. 267-274
    Minutes. Case records. Financial accounts. Miscellaneous.
Children's Home. 274
Board of County Visitors 275-276
Soldiers' Relief Commission 277-279
    Minutes. Applications.
Soldiers' Burial Commission 280-281
Blind Relief Commission 282-284
Board of Aid for the Aged 285-288
County Engineer. 289-306
    Surveys, maps, and plats: surveys and field notes; plats
    and maps; roads; ditches. Specification and contracts.
    Accounts. Miscellaneous.
Medina Metropolitan Park District. 307
Agricultural Conservation Association. 308-310
Agricultural Society 311-315
Agricultural Extension Service. 316-318

Bibliography. 319-324
List of County Officials 325-336
Addresses and Websites 337-339
Index to Inventory Entries. 341-344

The Historical Records Survey Program

Sargent B. Child, National Director
Willard N. Hogan, Regional Supervisor
Lillian Kessler, State Supervisor
Ruth Sloan, District Supervisor

Division of Community Service Programs

Florence Kerr, Assistant Commissioner
Mary Gillett Moon, Chief Regional Supervisor
Ruth Neighbors, State Director
Marion Wilson, District Director

WORK PROJECTS ADMINISTRATION

Howard C. Hunter, Commissioner
George Field, Regional Director
Carl Watson, State Administrator
Frank T. Miskell, District Manager

Sponsors

The Ohio State Archaeological and Historical Society
The Board of County Commissioners of Medina County:

Grant G. Chidsey
Elno Stauffer
Charles Fuller

The *Inventory of the County Archives of Ohio* is one of a number of bibliographies of historical materials prepared throughout the United States by workers on the Historical Records Survey Program of the Work Projects Administration. The publication herewith presented, an inventory of the archives of Medina County, is number 52 of the Ohio series.

The Historical Records Survey Program was undertaken in the winter of 1935 to 1936 for the purpose of providing useful employment to needy unemployed historians, lawyers, teachers, and research and clerical workers. In carrying out this objective, the project was organized to compile inventories of historical materials, particularly the unpublished government documents and records which are basic in the administration of local government, and which provide invaluable data for students of political, economic, and social history. Up to the present time more than 1700 guides, inventories, and indexes have been issued by the Survey throughout the nation. The archival guide herewith presented is intended to meet the requirements of day-to-day administration by the officials of the county, and also the needs of lawyers, businessmen, and other citizens who require facts from the public records for the proper conduct of their affairs. The volume is so designed that it can be used by the historian in his research in unprinted sources in the same way he uses the library card catalog for printed sources.

The inventories produced by the Historical Records Survey Program attempt to do more than give merely a list of records – they attempt further to sketch in the historical background of the county or other unit of government, and to describe precisely and in detail the organization and functions of the government agencies whose records they list. The county, town, and other local inventories for the entire county will, when completed, constitute an encyclopedia of local government as well as a bibliography of local archives.

The successful conclusion of the work of the Historical Records Survey Program, even in a single county, would not be possible without the support of public officials, historical and local specialists, and many other groups in the community. Their cooperation is gratefully acknowledged.

The Survey Program was organized by Luther H. Evans, who served as director until March 1, 1940, when he was succeeded by Sergeant B. Child, who had been Field Supervisor since the inauguration of the Survey. The Survey Program operates as a nationwide series of locally sponsored projects in the Division of Community Service Program, of which Mrs. Florence Kerr, Assistant Commissioner, is in charge.

Howard C. Hunter
Commissioner

2nd Edition

In 1929 after the stock market crash along with the Great Depression which followed, President Herbert Hoover and his successor Franklin D. Roosevelt formulated relief projects, the most successful was the Work Projects Administration (WPA). Established in 1935, the WPA was the largest of the many programs developed during Roosevelt's "New Deal." In 1939, the agency's name was changed to Work Progress Administration, and continued as such until its demise in 1943.

The Federal Writers' Project, a division of the WPA (known as Federal Project Number One), created jobs for many unemployed librarians, clerks, researchers, editors, and historians. The workers went to courthouses, town halls, offices in large cities, vital statistics offices and inventoried records. Besides indexing works, many records were transcribed. One of these many projects was the *Inventory of the County Archives* which has benefitted genealogists and historians. The inventories listed the records, either by volumes or file boxes and years per record type, within the office. Although the WPA oversaw this project, the information for each volume of records may differ significantly by the information submitted.

This project was to encompass all of Ohio's 88 counties although approximately 30 of these inventories have been located while others may not have been done or are lost. Medina County was one of the counties that had a draft copy only. Contact was made with Lauren Kuntzman, the manager of the Medina Library's Family History & Learning Center, located at 210 South Broadway Street, Medina, Ohio. She graciously allowed copying of the library's copy. Thank you, Lauren.

PREFACE

2nd Edition

The information herein is verbatim from the original document except for obvious spelling errors. (Please note wording is contemporary to the time). Records listed may have met the requirement for retention and have been destroyed as per the records retention act, while other records are considered permanent. (*See:* **https://codes.ohio.gov/ohio-revised-code**) Ohio Revised Code, sections 149.31 and 149.34). Records considered "open" to the public, such as lunacy, idiotic, and juvenile cases when made, may be "closed" due to a revision of state laws. However, the records may be opened to family members with adequate proof of lineage.

The addresses and website section of this edition list an up-to-date location guide to each office mentioned.

NOTE: Many entries on the following pages were very light and difficult to read. Words that are unknown are marked (illegible).

Jana Sloan Broglin
Fellow, Ohio Genealogical Society
Swanton, Ohio
2025

1st Edition

The Historical Records Survey of the Work Projects Administration began operation in Ohio in February 1936. The Project was organized and operated by the district supervisors of the Writers' Project until November 1936 when it became an independent part of the Federal Project No. I. With the termination of the Federal Projects in September 1939, the Ohio unit became the Ohio Historical Records Survey Project, sponsored by the Ohio State Archaeological and Historical Society.

The purpose of the Survey in Ohio has been the preparation of complete inventories of the records of the state and of each county, city, and other local governmental units. *The Inventory of the County Archives of Ohio* will, when completed, consist of a set of 88 volumes numbered according to the position of the county name in an alphabetical list of Ohio counties. Thus, the inventory herewith presented for Medina County is number 52. The inventory of the state archives and of municipal and other local records will constitute a separate publication.

The principle followed in the inventory of the county records has been to place a record in the office of origin rather than in the office of deposit. The records are arranged with those of the executive branch of government first, followed by law enforcement, fiscal, and miscellaneous agencies. Minor agencies are placed in the general arrangement according to constitutional or statutory responsibility to a major subdivision. The legal development of each office or agency has been treated in a prefatory section preceding the inventory of the records of the office. Although a condensed form of entry is used, information is given as to the limiting dates of all extant records, the contents of individual series, and the location of records in courthouse, statehouse, or other depository.

The Ohio Historical Records Survey was inaugurated in Medina County in May 1936. Since July 1940, the project has been under the administrative and technical supervision of Dr. Ruth Sloan. The wholehearted cooperation of the county officials with

1st Edition

the project workers has meant much in the thoroughness and completeness of the result. The board of county commissioners of Medina County, serving as contributing cosponsor, made possible the publication of this volume. For the accuracy of the inventory the project personnel, under the direction of Miss Zelda Brown in Medina County, is entirely responsible. The local and historical essays were written in Summit County under the technical direction of Mr. Robert L. Rousomanoff. Advice and assistance were rendered by the state office staff under the supervision of Miss Winifred Smith, Project Technician.

The various units of the *Inventory of the County Archives of Ohio* are issued in mimeographed or printed form for free distribution to the state and local public officials and public libraries in Ohio, and to a limited number of libraries outside the state. Requests for information concerning particular units of the *Inventory* should be addressed to the Ohio Historical Records Survey Project, Room 216, Clinton Building, Chestnut and High Streets, Columbus, Ohio.

Lillian Kessler
State Supervisor
Ohio Historical Records Survey Project

Columbus, Ohio
April 1, 1942

adm. .... administration
Arch................................. Archaeological
Art. .... Article
bdl. .... bundle
bull. .... bulletin
CCC........................ Civilian Conservation Corps
centiorari .... to be more fully informed
cf. .... (confer) compare
chap(s).. chapter(s)
comp. .... compiler
Const. .... Constitution
demurrer .... a challenge to a particular
claim that is made in court case
ed(s). .... editor(s)
et al. .... (et alii), and others
(et) passim .... and here and there
ex officio .... as a result of one's status or position
ex rel. .... (*ex relations*) at the instance of
et seq. .... and following
fee simple .... full and irrevocable ownership
G. C. .... General Code
habeas corpus .... protection against illegal imprisonment
Hist.................................... Historical
ibid. .... the same reference
loc. cit. .... (*Loco citato*) in the place cited
N.P. .... no place of publication shown
nolle prosequi .... notice of abandonment by a plaintiff
or prosecutor of all or part of a suit or action
n.s. .... new series
O.L. .... *Laws of Ohio*
op. cit. .... (*opere citato*) in the work cited
posse comitatus...................... a group of citizens
called upon to assist the sheriff
R. .... River
rep. .... reporter

R.S. . . . . Revised Statutes
sec(s) . . . . section(s)
sic . . . . thus, following copy
supersedeas . . . . a stay of enforcement of
a judgement pending appeal
U.S.C.A. . . . . United States Code Annotated
v. . . . . versus
vol(s). . . . . volume(s)
W.P.A. . . . . Works Progress/Project Administration
writ . . . . a formal, legal document, a decree
x . . . . by
— . . . . current, to date
4-H . . . . (Four-H)

Each chapter or section of the second part of this volume consists of (1) an essay describing the legal status and functions of one department of county government and (2) an inventory of the records of that department.

Each record constitutes a separate entry. Entries are arranged under topical headings and subheadings.

Every entry sets forth, insofar as applicable, the following:

Entry number. Entries are numbered consecutively throughout the inventory.

The exact title as it appears on the record or if the record has no title a supplied title in brackets. If the title of the record is non-descriptive, misleading, or incorrect, an additional title (in capitals and lower-case letters), also enclosed in brackets, has been supplied.

Dates show inclusive years or parts of years covered by the record. Breaks in dates indicate that the record is missing or was not kept between dates shown. A dash in place of the final date indicates an open record. If no current entries have been made the date of the last entry is noted. Where no statement is made that the record was discontinued at the last date shown, it could not be definitely established that such was the case. Where no comment is made on the absence of prior and subsequent records, no definite information could be obtained.

Quantity. Given in chronological order wherever possible.

Labeling. Numbers and letters within parentheses indicate labeling on volumes, file boxes, or other containers.

Variations in title. The current or most recent title is used but significant variations are shown with dates for which each was used.

Change of agency. Occasionally a record is discontinued as a county record and kept by some other agency.

Description. A statement of the nature and purpose of the record and of what the record shows. As the contents of a record may vary over a period of time the description may differ somewhat from the record at any one period. Wherever feasible,

changes in content are shown with dates. In map and plat entries
the names of author and publisher and the scale, are omitted only
when not available.

Arrangement. Records said to be alphabetically arranged
are frequently alphabetized only as to initial letter of the surname.
This is true especially where there is a secondary arrangement.

Indexing. Self-contained indexes are described in the entry.
Separate indexes constitute separate entries with cross references
to and from the record entry.

Nature of recording. Changes are indicated with dates.

Condition. No statement is made if good or excellent.

Number of pages. Averaged for the series.

Dimensions show size of volumes, maps, file boxes, or
other containers and are expressed in inches in every instance. The
dimensions of volumes are given in order of height, width, and
thickness; of file boxes in order of height, width, and depth.

Location. Rooms referred to are in the county courthouse
unless some other building is specified.

Title-line cross references are used to complete series
where a record is kept separately for a period of time or in other
records for different periods of time. They are also used in all
artificial entries which are made to show, under their proper office,
records kept in the same volume or file with records of another
office. In both instances, the description of the master entry shows
the title and entry number of the record from which the cross
reference is made. Dates shown in the description of the master
entry are for the part or parts of the record contained therein, and
are shown only when they vary from those of the master entry.
Artificial entries show only title, dates, and description.

Separate third-paragraph cross references from entry to
entry, are used to show prior, subsequent, or related records which
are not a part of the same series. If, however, both entries are under
the same department which contain records logically belonging
under that heading but which have been classified under an equally
appropriate heading.

Medina County, in northeastern Ohio lies upon the broad summit of the watershed between Lake Erie and the Ohio River, and is bounded on the north by Cuyahoga, on the east by Summit, on the south by Wayne, and on the west by Ashland and Lorain Counties. It has an area of 435 square miles[1] and a population of 33,034.[2] The county seat is at the city of Medina.

The surface of the county, due to glacial movement, is undulating, the level land having a greater area than the ridge formations. The soil consists in general of clay and gravelly loam, and is well adapted for grazing purposes. The geological structure is made up chiefly of the Mississippian and Pennsylvanian formations, which consists, in the order of relative abundance, of sandstone and shale, limestone, clay, coal, conglomerate, and iron ore.[3] Although the geology suggests a large mineral content the county has never possessed a great abundance of minerals. Some coal is still mined in the Wadsworth region, while considerable areas have produced oil and natural gas.[4]

The area of the county is about equally divided between the glacial plain and the glacial plateau, the village of Medina being just at the division line.[5] The drainage of the land runs northward into Rocky River, westward into Black River, and southward through Killbuck and Chippewa Creeks, the latter two important tributaries of the Tuscarawas and Muskingum system.[6] The source of Black River was originally a swamp of 2000 acres in Harrisville Township. Chippewa is the only lake in the county.

---

1. Simeon D. Fess, ed., *Ohio Reference Library* (Chicago and New York, 1937), III, 120.

2. U. S. Bureau of the Census, *Sixteenth Census of the United States, 1940, Population*, series P-2a, 19.

3. *Report of the Geological Survey of Ohio* (Columbus, 1938), series IV, bulletin 39, 4265.

4. Fess, *op. cit.*, 180, 182.

5. *Ibid.*, 180.

6. *Ibid.*

Prehistoric settlers here were not as numerous as in other counties, but some remnants of their civilization have been found. Evidences of five mounds and one enclosure prove the one-time presence of the Asiatic Mound Builders.[7]

The land now comprising Medina County was traversed almost exclusively by the Wyandot Indians, although a few Delawares were scattered throughout the region. There is no evidence that Indians ever established permanent residence in Medina, and it is very probable that the locality was merely visited by hunting parties. Before the War of 1812, it was the custom of the Indians to meet every fall at Cleveland, from which they paddled into the interior for the winter's hunting and fishing. On these trips they occasionally pitched temporary wigwams in the Medina area, usually near Chippewa Lake and Harrisville. The early white settlers found them fairly friendly, but had little occasion to deal with them. A few friendly Wyandots remained along Center Creek as late as 1882.[8]

After the Revolutionary War, Connecticut ceded to the United States her claims in the northwest with the exception of the so-called Western Reserve. For the sufferers from British raids during the Revolution she set aside the tract of 500,000 acres known as the Fire Lands, and decided to sell the remaining territory. The tract was sold in 1795 to the men who comprised the Connecticut Land Company, and the southern boundary of Medina was surveyed a part of the south line of the Western Reserve in 1807, and the land company divided the area by range and townships, distributing it to their shareholders.[9]

---

7. W. K. Moorehead, "Report of Field Work in Various Portions of Ohio," *Ohio Archaeological and Historical Quarterly*, XI, (1899), 197.
8. W. H. Perrin, J. H. Battle, and W. A. Goodspeed, *History of Medina County and Ohio* (Chicago, 1881), 217.
9. Fess, *op. cit.,* 181.

It was not until 1811, however, that settlements were started, the first homes being made by Joseph Harris in Harrisville, 1811, and Justin Warner in Liverpool the same year. Moses Demming also settled at Liverpool.[10] The War of 1812 delayed further migration, and it was not until 1814-1815 that active settlement began. The first permanent settler in Medina Township was Zenas Hamilton and very soon afterwards Rufus Ferris, Timothy Doane, and Joseph Northrop also settled there.[11] Medina Village was surveyed and platted in 1818 but not incorporated until 1835.[12] Permanent settlements in other townships were made the following years: Brunswick, 1815; Guilford, 1817; Granger, 1816; Wadsworth, 1814; Hinckley, 1824; Litchfield, 1830; Sharon, 1816; Montville, 1820; Westfield, 1817; Spencer, 1832; York, 1832; Lafayette, 1832; Chatham, 1833; and Homer, 1833.[13] The early settlers for the most part came from New England, but in Homer, Spencer, and Liverpool Townships, in the western part, a large number of Pennsylvania Germans made the first settlements, and gave their character to that region.

Pioneer life was typical of other settlements of that day. Communication was difficult because the homes were scattered. Cleveland was the nearest post office, and days were spent making the long and arduous trip for supplies and mail.[14] Looming large in the early animals of the county is the great Hinckley Hunt, held December 24, 1818, to eliminate some of the wild animals which ravaged the livestock. About 600 hunters from Medina and Cuyahoga Counties participated. The "line of battle" was formed with Cuyahoga County as the north line, Bath, Granger, and adjacent towns on the south line, and Medina, Brunswick, and Liverpool as the west line.

---

10. N. B. Northrop, *Pioneer History of Medina County* (Medina, 1861), 7.
11. Henry Howe, comp., *Historical Collections of Ohio* (Columbus, 1891), II, 458.
12. Fess, *op. cit.,* 181
13. *Ibid.*, 180.
14. Northrop, *op. cit.,* 8.

At a prearranged signal soon after sunrise the hunters converged upon a given point in Hinckley Township, driving the game into large clearing, after which the best marksman ascended the trees and began the methodical killing. The quarry killed included 300 deer, 21 bears, and 17 wolves, besides lesser games slain in the process of driving the quarry into the desired spot.[15]

The great inter-county sleigh ride was a sporting event to determine which county could muster the greatest number of sleighs with teams of four or more horses. Summit emerged as the winner in the first ride, on March 15, 1856, with a total of 171 sleighs, defeating Cuyahoga and Medina, whose showing consisted of 151 and 140 sleighs, respectively. Three days later, however, Medina, with a contingent of 182 sleighs, journeyed to Akron and rested the flag from Summit. The events were always accompanied by an abundance of good food, strong drink, and hilarity. The sleigh ride gained so much attention that it was publicized in a British newspaper.[16]

Medina County was formed February 12, 1812, and attached to Portage.[17] It was organized as an independent county in January 1818.[18] The territory was set up as a rectangle, about 20 miles from north to south and about 40 miles from east to west. The Eastern tier of townships was cut off when Summit County was formed, while 14 townships were taken away in the creation of Lorain, Ashland, and Huron Counties.

Eighteen townships in the original county were Norton, Copley, Bath, Richfield, Wadsworth, Granger, Hinckley, Guilford, Montville, Medina, Brunswick, Westfield, Liverpool, Harrisville, Grafton, Sullivan, Penfield, and Huntington.[19]

---

15. A. R. Webber, *History of Hinckley* (Elyria, 1933), 2-3.
16. W. A. Duff, *History of North Central Ohio* (Topeka - Indianapolis), I, 158; Howe, *op. cit.*, 470.
17. *Laws of Ohio*, X, 122.
18. *Ibid.*, XVI, 69.
19. Northrop, *op. cit.,* 11.

The first court was held January 1818 in an old barn near the present courthouse, with Judge Tod of Trumbull, Judge Brown of Wadsworth, and Judge Welton of Richfield as presiding officers.[20]

There were very few roadways during the counties early years. The Indian trails from Sandusky to Tuscarawas and that from Wooster to Chippewa Lake where the only ones before 1818, except for rough trails cut by the pioneers. Medina became a station on the Cleveland to Worcester stage highway, and shortly thereafter, the western terminus of the old Portage Road.[21] The Ohio Canal in 1827 supplemented the roads and made possible the opening of markets for the wheat and other products of Medina which had hitherto been grown only for local flour or animal feed.

The county was late in obtaining railroad facilities. It was not until 1864 that the Erie Railroad built a line across the southern corner of the county through Wadsworth, and in 1870 other railroad facilities were provided by the Baltimore and Ohio.[22] In 1871, the Lake Shore and Tuscarawas Valley Railroad extended its line through Medina, and soon thereafter the Akron, Cleveland, and Youngstown branch of the New York Central Line put Medina on its route. The railroads are now supplemented by 15 state roadways, two United States highways, and several intercity and interstate bus lines.

Medina has always been predominantly agricultural. It is one of a group of counties, led by Portage, which formed the greatest potato growing center in Ohio. Corn, wheat, and oats have been staple crops for over a century, and Medina also ranks among the leaders in the dairying industry.[23]

_____

20. Harriet T. Upton, *History of the Western Reserve* (Chicago and New York, 1910), I, 371.
21. Fess, *op. cit.,* 181.
22. Fess, *op. cit.,* 182.
23. *Ibid.*

In 1930 there were 2674 farms in Medina, with a total acreage of 278,400. Of these, 1,877 were under full ownership, 254 were under part ownership, 36 were under managers, and 507 under tenancies.[24] Crop production for that year included 558,333 bushels of corn, 357,429 bushels of wheat, 51,274 tons of hay, and 196,587 bushels of potatoes.[25] Vegetable production for the same year had a total value of $144,132.[26] The dairy industries yielded the following output 8,779,533 gallons of milk, 83,878 pounds of butter, and 5,157 gallons of cream.[27]

Early manufacturing developed in Wadsworth, Medina, Seville, and Lodi. Those towns all developed the normal quota of small manufacturing establishments, especially flour mills and small machine shops, but the county is not part of the iron and steel district.[28] Present manufacturing is restricted to the three leading towns. Wadsworth is the industrial center, manufacturing matches, valves, locomotive appliances and lubricators. Medina manufactures building materials and furnaces, but is more famous as the home of the Root bee culture and honey products, the distinctive industry developed by Amos I. Root. Honey producers and bee men have turned to Medina for instruction and most of their supplies and equipment for the apiary industry. Root wrote articles describing his experiences with bees and, about 1869, began the manufacturer of hives and supplies. Out of this developed the largest factory in the world specializing in equipment and supplies. He was also the author of works on bee culture. Lodi, once a favorite hunting ground of the Indians, is the chief distributing center for dairy products and vegetables.

----

24. U. S. Bureau of the Census, *Fifteenth Census of the United States, 1930, Agriculture*, II, pt. i, 404-405.
25. *Ibid.*, 434-435.
26. *Ibid.*, 440-441.
27. *Ibid.*, 462-463.
28. Fess, *op. cit.,* 182; Howe, *op. cit.,* 463.

The village of Leroy, not a manufacturing center, is widely known as the home of the Ohio Farmers Insurance Company, a $5,000,000 corporation which has developed the community into one of the cleanest and most pleasant little villages in this part of the country.

No history of the county would be complete without mention of the military service rendered to the county by its citizens in the Civil War. Company K of the Ohio 8th regiment and companies B and E of the Ohio 42nd regiment were composed almost entirely of Medina men, while companies I and G of the same regiment contained 12 and 20 Medina men, respectively.[29] James A. Garfield was colonel of Company G. It is estimated that the county furnished 1550 men, but an accurate count is impossible because of their incorporation into so many different commands.

Religion has always been a dominating influence. In 1817, Rufus Ferris organized a religious Society in Medina Township and obtained the services of Reverend Roger Royce Searle, an Episcopalian rector from Connecticut, who conducted the first public services.[30] In the same year Episcopalians, Congregationalists, and Methodists gathered in Liverpool for regular non-sectarian church meetings.[31] During the 1880s denominational representation in the county was as follows: in Wadsworth there were Episcopalians, Lutherans, Congregationalists, Baptists, and members of the Church of God. In Medina were Episcopalians, Methodists, Disciples, Baptist, and Catholics. In Lodi were Congregationalists, Methodists, and Episcopalians.[32] There are 77 active churches in the county at present, including the following denominations: Methodists, Universalists, Lutherans, Baptists, Catholics, Congregationalists, Mennonites, Presbyterians, Evangelicals, Wesleyan Methodists, Brethren, Missionary Alliance Members, Disciples of Christ, and Seventh Day Adventists.

---

29. Upton, *op. cit.,* 387-388.
30. *Ibid.,* 369.
31. *Ibid.,* 380.
32. Howe, *op. cit.,* 369, 380

The early schools were the usual subscription type, the settlers contributing small amounts of money for the teachers, who were not as a rule trained for their positions. The first schools were founded at Medina and Brunswick in 1817, and were taught by Eliza Northrop and Sarah Tilton, respectively. The total enrollment seems to have been about 14 for Medina and 18 for Brunswick.[33] Other important dates in Medina's educational history are 1835 and 1839, which marked the establishment of the Sharon and Wadsworth academies, two leading educational institutions in the county during the 19th century.[34] Academies were also established at Hinckley, Granger, Sharon, Seville, York, Lafayette, Litchfield, Chatham, Lodi, and Spencer.[35]

Medina's present-day schools are typical of the great advancement made in county education throughout the state, and have invariably maintained the standards of learning which have been set up by the state department of education. From 1914 to 1931, school consolidation programs were adopted which eliminated many of the old one-room school houses. There are now 13 combination high and grade schools, one junior high school, and four elementary schools under the jurisdiction of the county board of education, operated by a personnel of 183 teachers and superintendents. The figures above do not apply to Wadsworth and Medina, which are Exempted Village districts.

Banks were not established until 1857, when Harrison G. Blake founded the Phoenix National Bank at Medina. In 1892, the savings Deposit Bank of Medina also came into existence.[36] The more recent institutions are the Citizens Bank and the First National, both in Wadsworth; the Lodi State Bank of Lodi; the Farmers Savings Bank, Spencer, Ohio; Seville State Bank, Seville, Ohio; the Sharon Center Banking Company, Sharon, Ohio; and the Phoenix National and Savings Deposit Bank of Medina.

---

33. Upton, *op. cit.,* 387-388.
34. *Ibid.,* 387; Fess, *op. cit.,* 182.
35. Perris, Battle, and Goodspeed, *op. cit.,* 289.
36. Duff, *op. cit.* 195.

National prominence has been achieved by several natives of this county. Edith W. Thomas and Harriet Gleason have gained recognition in poetry, their work having been published in various national magazines. Professor John S. Runyan contributed greatly to American Education by his work on phonetics and pronunciation, and was called upon to aid in the preparation of an edition of Webster's Dictionary. Russell A. Alger was widely known as a general in the Civil War, United States senator from Michigan, and Secretary of War under William McKinley and Theodore Roosevelt. Another well-known political figure from Medina was George R. Nash, one time leader of the republican party in Ohio and Governor during the administration of McKinley.[37]

Politically, the county has always leaned toward the Whig and Republican platforms. Up to 1830, the party lines had not been rigidly drawn, and a candidate relied upon his personal popularity rather than party of allegiance. The Anti-Masonic tenants found a fairly large support here, but this sentiment was not hedged in by any party lines. Democrats and their opponents, whether Whigs or Federalists, subscribed to both sides of the question, and it was never brought forward publicly as a political issue. The internal improvements and tariff issues introduced by Henry Clay, caused a temporary crystallization of party lines, as Medina had been hampered by the lack of transportation facilities, and this question struck the inhabitants as having a practical side. After a temporary fluctuation of party power, the Whigs assumed control.[38]

The Anti-Slavery controversy had considerable effect in Medina. A society had been organized as early as 1833, which published numerous pamphlets strongly anti-slavery, while Medina delegates were prominent at the statewide convention held in Licking County in 1836.[39]

---

37. Upton, *op. cit.,* 389; Duff, *op. cit.,* 462.
38. Perrin, Battle, and Goodspeed, *op. cit.,* 230-231.
39. Robert Price, "The Ohio Anti-Slavery Convention of 1836," *Ohio Archeological and Historical Quarterly*, LV (1936), 173-187.

At home the radical anti-slavery movement of the whigs assumed control and it seemed that the question would cause a party split, but the radicals destroyed opposition to its policies and the party again had unified control.[40] During the 20th century Medina shifted to the Democratic side in only two instances, the election of Woodrow Wilson in 1916 and Franklin D. Roosevelt in 1936. Republicans have invariably dominated county government even in such years.

During the 1880s there were six newspapers in the county. The *Banner*, independent organ founded in 1886, was edited by James Cory at Wadsworth, also the home of the *Enterprise*, an independent edited and published by John Clark. The *Times*, also independent, was published in Seville by C. C. Day. The *Review*, Republican sheet organized in 1886, was published in Lodi by H. E. Bassett. The *Republican Gazette and News,* established in 1832, was published in Medina by Green and Neil, and the *Sentinel*, founded at Medina in 1883, was a Democratic weekly published by M. R. Dorman.[41] Four of these papers are still being published. The old *Gazette and News*, now the *Gazette,* is edited and published by M. H. Baldwin. The *Sentinel* is edited by A. M. Long. The Wadsworth *Banner*, now the *Banner Press,* is edited and published by Nellie M. Harter. The Lodi *Review* is edited by Harold L. Harrington. The Wadsworth *News*, edited by John Miller is the only new paper in the county, being founded in 1924.[42]

40. Ferrin, Battle, and Goodspeed, *op. cit.,* 232.
41, Howe, *op. cit.,* 460, 473.
42. H. W. Ayer and Sons, *Directory of Newspapers and Periodicals, 1941* (Philadelphia, 1941), 749, 751, 761.

The county as a political institution and as a subdivision of the state for purposes of political and judicial administration is of ancient origin.[1] In a form substantially similar in all general features and functions, it has existed in England since early times, and in America since its settlement. As the tide of migration moved westward, following the American Revolution the institutions of the seaboard states were transferred to the newer west, undergoing such alteration as best suited frontier conditions.[2]

The earliest provision for the organization of counties in what is now the state of Ohio was contained in the ordinance of 1787, by which the governor of the Northwest Territory was directed to "lay out the parts of the district in which the indian [sic] titles shall have been extinguished into counties and townships subject however to such alterations as may thereafter be made by the legislature."[3] The organization of county government, therefore, began before the organization of the state and before the adoption of a state constitution. Prior to statehood nine counties were organized. The first county lines were drawn in 1788.[4] The last county lines were altered in 1888, exactly 100 years later.[5]

The establishment of local government in the Northwest Territory was one of the first concerns of Governor St. Clair. The ordinance of 1787 furnished the framework, but details of institutions had to be constructed.

1. Edward Channing, *A History of the United States* (New York, 1905), I, 512-519.
2. Beverley W. Bond, Jr., *The Civilization of the Old Northwest: A Study of Political, Social, and Economic Development, 1788-1812.* (New York, 1934), 58-59.
3. Clarence Edwin Carter, ed. and comp., *The Territorial Papers of the United States* (Washington, 1934), II, 44.
4. *Ibid.*, III, 279.
5. *Laws of Ohio*, XXXV, 418; Randolph Chandler Downes, "Evolution of Ohio County Boundaries," *Ohio State Archaeological and Historical Quarterly*, XXXVI (1927), 449.

All county officials, under the provisions of the ordinance, were made appointive by the governor. St Clair, the former resident of Pennsylvania, in providing for local administration depended in a large part upon the Pennsylvania Code, which in some instances, was altered to meet the needs of pioneer communities.[6]

The provisions for local administration were, for the most part, simple and effective. In each county the court of general quarter sessions of the peace, composed of three or more justices of the peace, served as the fiscal and administrative board of the county, estimating county expenditures, appointing tax commissioners, and providing for highway and bridge construction.[7] By the end of the decade the court was authorized to enter into contracts for building or repairing the county jail and the courthouse.[8] Other county officials appointed during the territorial period included sheriff, coroner, recorder, treasurer, a license commission, and justices and clerks of the various courts.[9]

---

6. The governor and judges were given power to "adopt and publish in the district such laws of the original states" as they thought necessary and these laws were to remain in force unless disapproved by Congress. In many cases the governor and judges had not adopted laws of the original states, as the ordinance stipulated, but had passed measures that conformed in spirit. Since there was some question of the legality of these laws St. Clair, in 1795, after the lower house of Congress disapproved of the laws passed at the legislative session of 1792, called a legislative session to revise the territorial code. The commission, after sitting for three months, completed Maxwell's Code, named in honor of the printer, W. Maxwell. Few changes were made in the Maxwell Code by the territorial assembly which was elected in 1798. Carter, *op. cit.*, II, 43. The minutes of the legislative assembly were reproduced in *Ohio State Archaeological and Historical Quarterly*, XXX (1921), 13-53.

7. Theodore Calvin Pease, comp., *The Laws of the Northwest Territory, 1788-1880* (Illinois State Bar Association Law Series, Springfield, 1925, I), 4, 36, 337; 69-70; 467-468; 74, 77, 453, 456, 485.

8. *Ibid.*, 485.

9. *Ibid.*, 8, 24-25, 61, 68-69, 197.

Officers having been appointed, the next step in the organization of government was the establishment of a system of local courts. Evidence seems to indicate that the judicial system for the county had been carefully planned. The court of common pleas, composed of not less than three or more than five appointed judges, was an inferior court having limited civil jurisdiction.[10] The court of general quarter sessions of the peace, besides serving as the fiscal and administrative board of the county, had jurisdiction in lesser criminal cases.[11] A probate court, composed of a single judge, was given jurisdiction in probate and testamentary matters.[12] In 1795, following St. Clair's revision of the territorial code, circuit courts were established and orphans' courts were instituted.[13]

In the meantime the local government was further developed by the organization of civil townships. The governor and judges adopted a law from the Pennsylvania Code requiring the justices of the court of quarter sessions to divide each county into townships and appoint in each township a constable to serve specifically in the township and in the county, a clerk, and one or more overseers of the poor.[14]

The territory entered the second stage of administration when, in 1798, the population having reached the requisite 5,000 the governor ordered the election of a representative assembly.[15] The system of local government continued as established by the governor and judges, and the transition was achieved without a disturbance of local administration.

---

10. *Ibid.,* 7
11. *Ibid.,* 4-7.
12. *Ibid.,* 9.
13. *Ibid.,* 157, 181-188.
14. Pease, *op. cit.,* 37-41, 338. The system of local governmental administration was the result of sectional compromise, since it combined the county system of the southern and middle states with the elements of the New England town. Dwight G. McCarty, *The Territorial Governors of the Old Northwest: A Study in Territorial Administration* (Iowa City, 1910), 53-54.
15. Carter, *op. cit.,* III, 514-515.

The admission of Ohio as a state did not, in the main, materially affect county organization and administration. The system of local government having been organized by the governor and judges and the legislature of the Northwest Territory, the basic offices were continued. Except for the provision for the election of a county sheriff and a county coroner in each county, two officials of utmost importance in pioneer communities, the continuation was silent on such matters as titles, number, and duties of officials.[16]

It devolved, therefore, upon the legislature to confer powers upon the county. In 1804, the legislature made provision for board of county commissioners, composed of three members elected for a three-year term.[17] The board of county commissioners, supplanting the court of general quarter sessions, became the administrative and fiscal board of the county. In 1803, the legislature recognizing the need for a more adequate system of land records, provided for a recorder to be appointed by the court of common pleas for a seven-year term and for a surveyor to be appointed by the court of common pleas.[18] Another act authorized the appointment of a county treasurer by the associate judges, a later one provided for his appointment by the county commissioners.[19]

The legislature also provided during its first session for a prosecuting attorney to be appointed by the supreme court to prosecute cases on behalf of the state.[20] In 1805, the appointing power was transferred to the court of common pleas.[21]

---

16. *Ohio Const., 1802*, Art. VI, sec. 1.
17. *Laws of Ohio*, II, 158.
18. *Ibid.*, I, 136, 90-93.
19. *Ibid.*, I, 97-98; II, 154.
20. *Ibid.*, I, 50.
21. *Ibid.*, III, 47.

A new office was created in 1820, that of county auditor. The auditor first appointed by the legislature, did as his duty the preparation of the tax duplicate.[22] The county board of revision, the purpose of which was to correct some of the inequalities of assessments, was established in 1825. The first board of revision or equalization, as it is sometimes called, was composed of the county commissioners, the auditor, and the assessors.[23]

The judicial power of the state in matters of law and equity was invested in the supreme court, the court of common pleas, and the justices' courts. The articles of the constitution provided for a court of common pleas to be composed of a president and associate justices. The members of the court, appointed by a joint Ballad of both houses of the general assembly, were to hold court in three judicial circuits into which the state was to be divided by the legislature.[24] The court was assigned common law and chancery jurisdiction in all cases as provided by law.[25] To the court was assigned jurisdiction in probate and testamentary matters and in the appointment of guardians, functions performed during the territorial period by the probate court.[26] Finally, the court was authorized to appoint a clerk.[27]

As the wave of democratic philosophy swept across the county in the 1820s and 1830s there arose a demand not only for an extension of the franchise but also for the election of public officials. Accordingly the auditor became an elective official in 1821, the treasurer in 1827, the recorder in 1829, and the prosecuting attorney in 1833.[28]

---

22. *Ibid.,* XVIII, 70.
23. *Ibid.,* XXXIII, 68-69.
24. *Ohio Const., 1802,* Art. III, secs. 3, 8.
25. *Ibid.,* Art. III, sec. 3.
26. *Ibid.,* Art. III, sec. 5; Pease, *op. cit.,* 9.
27. *Ohio Const.,* Art. III, sec. 9.
28. *Laws of Ohio,* XIX, 116; XXV, 25-32; XXVII, 65; XXXI, 13-14.

While the legislature responded to the general demand for the election of county officials, there arose a further demand for a revision of the constitution which failed to meet the needs of an expanding state. This movement came as a result of dissatisfaction with a judicial system which placed the burden of judicial administration upon four judges who had the task of holding court each year in all the counties.[29] Then, too, there arose demand for the election of all public officials, for the prohibition of charters that granted special privileges, and for limitation on the power of the legislature to create a state debt. In February 1850, the legislature, following a favorable popular vote on the proposition, called for the election of delegates to meet in convention in May. The constitution drafted by the delegates, was approved by special election on June 17, 1851. The constitution of 1851, like the constitution of 1802, failed to provide a definite form of county government and administration. Aside from the constitutional provision for the election of a county treasurer, sheriff, and clerk of courts and recreating the probate court which had existed during the territorial period the organic instrument was silent on the administrative duties of the county.[30] Again all matters pertaining to county government were entrusted to the legislature. While the legislature conferred certain powers upon the county, it was limited by the constitutional provision which required all laws of a general nature to be uniform throughout the state.[31]

---

29. J. V. Smith, rep., *Official Reports of the Debates and Proceedings of the Ohio State Convention . . . held at Columbus, Commencing May 6, 1850, and at Cincinnati, Commencing December 2, 1850* (Columbus, 1851), 597 *et seq.* (Jacob Burnet, *Notes on the Early Settlement of the Northwestern Territory* (Cincinnati, 1847) 356. *See* also the *Ohio State Journal*, December 11, 1840.

30. *Ohio Const., 1851*, Art. X, sec. 3; Art. IV, sec. 16; Art. IV, sec. 7.

31. *Ibid.*, Art. II, sec. 26.

The present administrative organization of Ohio county government presents the picture of extraordinary complexity. Each county quadrennially elects, besides the board of county commissioners, nine administrative officials: The recorder, clerk of courts, probate judge, prosecuting attorney, coroner, sheriff, treasurer, auditor, and the county engineer. For convenience the work of county government may be classified under the following general heads: administration, judicial system, law enforcement, finance and taxation, elections, health, public welfare, and public works.

Administration

The board of county commissioners is the central feature of the present structure of county government. The functions of this board touch either directly or indirectly every other branch and department. The board is the agency in whose name actions for and against the county are brought. This board is empowered to determine certain matters of policy for the conduct of county affairs such as adoption of the budget, establishment of services left optional by law, and the authorization of improvements.[32] Thus, in a limited sense it constitutes the legislative branch of the county. The commissioners, however have no ordinance-making powers. The board also functions as the central administrative body although much of the administration, centered in other elective offices, is beyond its immediate control. The county auditor was originally secretary of the board and still functions as such in a majority of the counties. Later provision of the law permitted the board to appoint its own clerk, thus removing this duty from the auditor.[33]

---

32. G. C. sec. 2421.
33. *Laws of Ohio*, XIX, 147; G. C. sec. 2566.

Judicial System

The constitution of 1851 made significant changes in the composition of the court of common pleas. The judges, here to four appointed by the legislature, were made elective for a term not to exceed five years. For the purpose of electing judges the state was divided into nine districts. Each district was divided into three parts, in each of which one common pleas judge was to be elected. Court was to be held in every district or county within such jurisdiction as should be provided by law.[34] The legislature provided for the districts but left the jurisdiction of the court much as it had been in the earlier years of its existence.[35] The constitutional amendment of 1912 abolished the divisions and subdivisions provided by the constitution of 1851, and authorized the election of one or more common pleas judges in each county.[36]

The judicial system was extended in 1851 by the creation of district courts composed of one supreme court justice and several common pleas judges in each district.[37] For administrative purposes the nine common pleas districts were apportioned into five judicial circuits.[38] The courts were assigned original jurisdiction in the same matters as the supreme court and such appellate jurisdiction as might be provided by law.[39] The district courts, abolished by the constitutional amendment of 1883, were superseded by the circuit courts which were given the same jurisdiction as their predecessors.

---

34. *Ohio Const., 1851*, Art. IV, secs. 3, 4, 10.
35. Willis A. Estrich, *et al*, eds., *Ohio Jurisprudence*, XI, 827-839.
36. *Ohio Const., 1851* (Amendment), Art. IV, sec. 3.
37. *Ohio Const., 1851*, Art. IV, sec. 5.
38. *Laws of Ohio*, L, 69.
39. *Ohio Const., 1851*, Art. IV, sec. 6.

The state was divided into seven circuits. In each circuit three judges were to be elected.[40] the judicial system was again altered in 1912 when, by constitutional amendment, the circuits were renamed courts of appeals.[41] The state is divided into nine appellate districts. There are three judges in each district elected by the people of the districts for a six-year term.[42]

The constitution of 1851 recreated the probate court, which, existing during the territorial period was abolished by the first constitution, its authority and jurisdiction being then vested in the courts of common pleas. Each county has one probate judge elected by the people for a four-year term.[43] By constitutional provision, the probate judge has original jurisdiction in probate and testamentary matters, the appointment of guardians,[44] and the issuance of marriage licenses. An amendment to the constitution of 1912 authorized the common pleas judge, when petitioned by 10 percent of the voters in counties having a population of less than 60,000, to submit to the voters at any general election the question of combining the probate and common pleas courts.[45] This combination exists in Adams, Henry, and Wyandot Counties.

Due to an increased amount of juvenile delinquency, the legislature in 1904 authorized the judges of the court of common pleas, the probate court, and the superior and insolvency courts, where established, to appoint one of their members as juvenile judge to hear cases involving neglected, dependent, and delinquent children. In counties which have a court of domestic relations the judge of that court serves in this capacity. This is the case in Medina County.[46]

---

40. *Ohio Const., 1851*, Art. IV, sec. 6; *Laws of Ohio*, LXXXI, 168.
41. *Ohio Const., 1851*, Art. IV, sec. 6 (Amendment, 1912).
42. G. C. sec. 1514.
43. *Laws of Ohio*, CXVIV, 320; *Ohio Const., 1851*, Art. IV, sec. 7.
44. *Ohio Const., 1851*, Art. IV, sec. 8.
45. *Ibid.*, Art. IV, sec. 7 (Amendment, 1912).
46. *Laws of Ohio*, XCVII, 561-562; G. C. sec. 1532.

Law Enforcement

Closely related to the courts are the agencies of law enforcement in the county. Law enforcement is conducted by four officials: The sheriff, prosecuting attorney, coroner, and the dog warden. These officials are concerned primarily with the enforcement of state laws, and leave the enforcement of municipal ordinances, and, in some instances, of state statutes in urban centers to municipal law-enforcement agencies.

The county sheriff, whose duties have been materially curbed by municipal law-enforcement agencies and the state highway patrol, has as his duty the enforcement of state laws.[47] He serves as custodian of the county jail,[48] and as an executive agent of the courts.[49] It has been estimated that approximately one-half of the sheriff's time is devoted to duties connected with the courts. The sheriff is restricted by lack of scientific equipment which has become essential to law enforcement.[50]

---

47. G. C. sec. 2833. The sheriff's authority extends to all parts of the county, although for obvious practical reasons he rarely makes an arrest in incorporated areas.

48. G. C. sec. 3157.

49. G. C. sec. 2834.

50. *The Reorganization of County Government in Ohio: Report of the Governor's Commission on County Government* (n.p., December 1934), 102 *et seq.* The sheriff system worked admirably in rural communities. From the standpoint of police administration, it is unsatisfactory in areas of dense population. In such areas there is a need for a force of officers whose duty it is, not merely to apprehend law violators, but to prevent the infraction of the law by patrolling the territory. For an interesting discussion of some of the newer problems confronting law-enforcement agencies *see* Donald C. Stone. "The Police Attack Crime," *National Municipal Review,* XXIV (1935), 39-41.

The county prosecuting attorney, the most important agent in the enforcement of criminal law, is directed by law to "inquire into the commission" of crime within the county, and to prosecute on behalf of the state all complaints, suits, and controversies to which the state is a party.[51] In conjunction with the state attorney general, he prosecutes in the supreme court cases arising in the county.[52] He acts also in a civil capacity as legal counsel for the commissioners and other county officials.[53] The prosecuting attorney may institute proceedings against an individual, but as a rule charges must be filed against the offender before action is taken. The prosecuting attorney has certain administrative duties such as serving as a member of the county budget commission and of the board of sinking fund trustees.[54]

The county coroner has the ancient duty of determining the cause of death where death occurs under suspicious circumstances or by unlawful means,[55] the proper distribution of property found on or about the deceased,[56] and the management of the county morgue.[57] It has been suggested by the authorities on county administration that the office be abolished and the duties transferred to a medical examiner appointed by the prosecuting attorney.[58]

---

51. G. C. sec. 2916.
52. G. C. sec. 2916
53. G. C. sec. 2917.
54. *Laws of Ohio*, CXII, 399-400; CVIII, pt. i, 700-702.
55. G. C. sec. 2856.
56. G. C. secs. 2863, 2864.
57. G. C. sec. 2856-1.
58. W. F. Willoughby, *Principles of Judicial Administration* (Washington, 1929), 165-173. According to a recent act, effective June 8, 1937, only a licensed physician or a person who shall have previously served as coroner is eligible to fill the office. G. C. sec. 2856-3.

Another law enforcement agent existing within the county is the dog warden. This official is appointed by and is responsible to the county commissioners. No special qualifications are required for the office. The dog warden has as his duty the enforcement of the sections of the general code "relative to the licensing of dogs, the impounding and destruction of unlicensed dogs, and the payment of compensation for damages to livestock inflicted by dogs." The dog warden and his deputies, in the performance of their legal duties, have the same "police powers" as those conferred by statute upon sheriffs and police.[59] Prior to 1927, the duties now performed by the dog warden were performed by the county sheriff.[60]

Law enforcement in the county is defective in two respects: first, there is little or no coordination between the four agencies of law enforcement, and second, there is little or no responsibility for neglect of duty. Evidence seems to indicate that the present inefficient and antiquated system could be corrected by consolidating all law enforcement agencies into a county department of law enforcement under the immediate supervision of the county prosecuting attorney.[61]

The administration of criminal justice in the county has grown up in a more or less hit or miss fashion and is for the most part not satisfactory and extremely cumbersome. Arrests are made by the sheriff or other police officers, who are theoretically officers of the state, but who are under little or no supervision. The accused person is brought before a local magistrate for a preliminary hearing. In the event the accused is committed, it is necessary, in most cases, to receive an indictment before a grand jury.[62]

59. *Laws of Ohio*, CVIII, pt. i, 535; CXII, 348; G. C. sec. 5652-7.
60. *Laws of Ohio*, CVIII, pt. i, 535.
61. *The Reorganization of County Government*, 1417-122.
62. For a criticism of the administration of criminal justice, *see* Edwin H. Sutherland, *Principles of Criminology* (Chicago, 1934), chap. xiv; Willoughby, *op. cit.,* chaps. xi, xiv, xxvi.

Finance and Taxation

There are three types of financial functions performed by county officers: tax administration, handling of the fiscal affairs of the county, and the trusteeship of funds held for individuals in court procedure. The principal financial authorities are the board of county commissioners, the auditor and the treasurer. The commissioners levy taxes, appropriate funds, and authorize payments.[63] The auditor's primary duties are the keeping of accounts, the issuance of warrants, the valuation of real estate, and the preparation of the tax list.[64] The treasurer collects taxes, receives and has custody of county money, and disburses it upon warrant from the auditor.[65] Other functions relating to county finance are performed by the board of revision, budget commissioners, and board of sinking fund trustees.

During the early years of Ohio history the principal sources of state and county revenue were the general property tax, the poll tax, and the fees received from licenses and permits to engage in certain kinds of business.[66]

A tax law enacted by the first territorial legislature (1799) designated certain types of property as taxable for county purposes. All houses in towns, town lots, and outlots, water and windmills, ferries, cattle, and horses were put on the county tax duplicate.

---

63. G. C. secs. 5630, 5637, 7419.
64. G. C. secs. 2568-2570, 2573, 2583-2589.
65. G. C. secs. 2649, 2649-1, 2656, 2674.
66. An act of 1825 levied a tax on the income of attorneys, physicians, and surgeons for state purposes. Amount of tax was determined by the court of common pleas. Salmon P. Chase, comp., *The Statutes of Ohio and of the Northwestern Territory, 1788-1833.* (Cincinnati, 1833), 1471. This act was repealed in 1852. Maskell E. Curwen, comp., *Public Statutes at Large of the State of Ohio* (Cincinnati, 1853), 1755. The poll tax was perpetually abolished by constitutional authority in 1802. *Ohio Const., 1802*, Art. VIII, sec. 23.

A tax on land, subsequently used also for county purposes, was originally devoted exclusively to the needs of the territorial government. County officials were to assist in the administration of this tax as well as that of the county levy.[67]

In the course of time many additions were made to the original list of taxables. Taxable property came to include a capital employed in merchandising (1826), and by exchange brokers (1825), pleasure carriages (1825), money loaned at interest (1831), and stock in steamboats.[68] In the latter year dividends of bank, insurance, and bridge companies were also made taxable.[69] The first act of a general nature directing the taxation of railroads was passed in 1851.[70] In 1862, a tax on the gross receipts of express and telegraph companies was enacted.[71] A levy on the capital stock of freight lines was authorized in 1896.[72] Subsequent enactments brought into the category of "general property" the possessions of public utilities in general. By such accumulations "property," by the end of the nineteenth century, had become a much more inclusive term than it had been one hundred years earlier.

County agencies became even more useful with the discovery of new tax sources. When, at the turn into the twentieth century the general property tax lost its importance as a revenue source for the state, taxes on inheritance and cigarettes, then later, on gasoline, liquid fuel, liquor, retail sales, malt, and the like, took its place.[73]

---

67. Chase, *op. cit.*, 267-279. Previous acts of 1792 and 1795 were temporary in nature.
68. Chase, *op. cit.*, III, 1517; 1476; *Laws of Ohio*, XXIX, 272-280.
69. *Laws of Ohio*, XXIX, 302-303.
70. Curwen, *op. cit.*, 1647.
71. J. R. Sayler, comp., *The Statutes of the State of Ohio* (Cincinnati, 1876), 301.
72. *Laws of Ohio*, XCII, 89-93.
73. Ohio Tax Commission, *Financing State and Local Government in Ohio, 1900-1932* (mimeographed, Columbus, 1934), 2.

County officials continued to administer the general property tax, which was devoted henceforth to the uses of local governments, but they assisted in the administration of a number of those newer taxes as well.

The assistance rendered by county officials has been equally extensive in the system of issuing licenses and permits. The issuance of marriage licenses began during the territorial period (1788).[74] An act to license merchants, traders, and tavern keepers was passed in 1792.[75] Ferry licenses were authorized in 1799.[76] With the passage of time, one license after another has been required until unlicensed businesses have become something of an exception rather than the rule. Even with the increasing assumption of licensing authority by the state, county officials have continued to issue certain licenses assigned to their jurisdiction long ago.[77]

Under the early laws (1792) county commissioners, appointed to annual terms by the courts of common pleas, were to list the male inhabitants above the age of 18, stocks of cattle, yearly value of improved land, and other property. Valuation of this property was made by township and village assessors, appointed annually by the court of common pleas.[78] These local assessors, who became elective in 1795, were again appointed in 1799.[79] In 1825, property valuation was assigned to a new official the county assessor, also appointed by the court of common pleas.[80] This official became elective in 1827 and was succeeded in turn, in 1841, by township assessors to be elected annually.[81]

---

74. Chase, *op. cit.*, I, 101.
75. *Ibid.,* I, 114-115.
76. *Ibid.,* I, 219.
77. *See* p. [not given]
78. *Laws of the Territory of the United States Northwest of the River Ohio* (Philadelphia and Cincinnati, 1792-1796), II, 17-18.
79. Chase, *op. cit.,* I, 169, 273.
80. *Ibid.,* II, 1477.
81. Curwen, *op. cit.,* 775-779.

In conjunction with these administrators a system of real estate reappraisal was initiated. In 1846, county commissioners were directed to divide their counties into suitable districts and to appoint an assessor for each whose chief function should be to revise the valuation of real property.[82] An act of 1863 made these officers elective and provided for reappraisal every tenth year.[83] This was subsequently changed (1868) to every fifth year and, in 1878, returned to the ten-year interval.[84]

In 1913, the assistance of county officers in tax administration was temporarily dispensed with and their duties were given to state officials. The county was again made an entire assessment district but district (or county) assessors were now to be appointed by the governor. The tax commission (established in 1910) was directed to supervise and direct the assessment of real and personal property.[85] This attempt at unification of authority in a state was partially abandoned, however, in 1915, when assessment was returned to the county auditor and to elected township, village and ward assessors.[86] In 1925, the latter officers were discontinued and the duties of assessment devolved upon the county auditor alone.[87]

The advent of the state tax commission brought no great alteration in the process of assessment. The county remains the basic unit and the county auditor continues to serve as an agent of the state. Though the state commission now assesses certain forms of property, certification is made to the county auditor.

---

82. *Ibid.,* 1269.
83. Sayler, *op. cit.*, 413.
84. *Ibid.,*1641; *Laws of Ohio*, LXXV, 459.
85. *Laws of Ohio*, CIII, 786-787.
86. *Ibid.,* CVI, 246 *et seq.*
87. *Ibid.,* CXI, 486-487. Reevaluation of real estate was required in 1925 and every sixth year thereafter.

For example, public utilities are now assessed by the commission and proportional shares of the revenue are apportioned to the counties which contain such property.[88] Financial institutions report directly to the commission which certifies to each county auditor the assessment of each taxable deposit.[89] Intangible property (defined in 1931) owned by individuals and corporations, not otherwise accepted, is listed and valued by the county auditor. Returns showing more than $500 of taxable income are forwarded to the commission for appraisal and certified by it back to the county auditor.[90] From these certifications of the commission, the personal property list return to him by individuals, and the real estate assessment for which he is personally responsible, the auditor makes up the grand duplicate of real and personal property taxes.

      The county continues to be the basic unit also in the matter of budgeting and the levying of taxes on property. In 1792, the courts of general quarter session were directed to estimate the sums needed to defray the costs of county government, specifying as nearly as possible the purposes for which sums were necessary. This earliest of budgets was to be laid before the governor and judges and approved by the legislature. Special commissioners were to apportion or levy the tax.[91] In 1799, it became the duty of these commissioners to ascertain the probable expenses of the county as well as levy the tax - a duty which continued until refinements in administration were made necessary because of the increasing number of taxing authorities.[92]

---

88. G. C. sec. 5430.
89. G. C. secs. 5411, 5412, 5412-1.
90. *Report of the Governor's Commission,* 75; G. C. secs. 5372-3, 5376, 5377.
91. Chase. *op. cit.,* I, 118-119.
92. *Ibid.,* I, 276, 277.

In order to achieve some systematic arrangement in the county fiscal system, the function of estimating expenses, or budgeting, was consolidated in recent years in the hands of a county budget commission. Since the Ohio legislature, in 1911, established a tax rate limitation, it was necessary to establish a commission vested with authority to reduce the amounts set up in the annual tax budgets when the overlapping districts required more than the aggregate maximum tax rate permits.[93] The county budget commission organized in 1911, was composed, for a time, of the auditor, the mayor of the largest municipality, and the prosecuting attorney. Taxing authorities in the county were directed to submit their budgets to this body through the agency of the auditor.[94] The board was authorized to make adjustments in the budgets, alterations which the taxing authority might appeal to the tax commission. The budget commission, directed in 1911 to certify its action to the auditor, was subsequently instructed by law to make such certification to the various taxing units which should themselves authorize the necessary tax levies and certify them to the auditor.[95] In 1927, the composition of this board was altered when the county treasurer replaced the mayor.[96]

Early appeals against unjust assessments (1792) were heard by judges of the general territorial court, judges of the common pleas court, or justices of the general quarter sessions court.[97] After 1795, petitions for redress were directed to the county commissioners.[98]

---

93. G. C. sec. 5625-3. Since 1934 there has been a limitation of 10 mills on the dollar. G. C. sec. 5625-2.
94. *Laws of Ohio*, CII, 270-272.
95. G. C. sec. 5625-25.
96. *Laws of Ohio,* CXII, 399.
97. *Laws of the Territory of the United States Northwest of the River Ohio*, II, 20-21.
98. Chase, *op. cit.* I, 171.

This appeal agency was superseded, in 1825, by the Board of Equalization, composed of the commissioners, the assessors, and the auditor.[99] This agency continued to function through the following years though occasional changes in personnel were made.[100]

With the reorganization of property administration in 1913, the function of tax revision was taken away from county officers. In each district (county) the tax commission was directed to appoint three persons for the term of three years to form a district board of complaints.[101] An act of 1915 abolished this plan, however, and returned the function of revision to the care of county officials. A board composed of the treasurer, prosecuting attorney, probate judge, and the president of the board of county commissioners, was directed to appoint a county board of equalization.[102] This plan, too, was soon dispensed with. An act of 1917, constituted the county treasurer, auditor, and the president of the board of commissioners as the county board of revision.[103]

The history of tax collection is equally intricate. The fiscal duties of the county treasurer, who now collects the property tax, comprised, in the very early period, only the receipt and custody of revenue funds.

---

99. *Ibid.*, II, 1476-1492.
100. The county surveyor became a member at times, in 1868, for example, Sayler, *op. cit.*, 1642.
101. *Laws of Ohio*, CIII, 790-791.
102. *Ibid*, CVI, 254-255.
103. *Ibid*, CVII, 40; G. C. secs. 5580, 5596, Highest appellate jurisdiction, held originally by the general court and later 1805 by the associate judge of common pleas, was given, in 1825, to a State Board of Equalization composed of the state auditor and one other member from each congressional district. Later these boards were composed of the state auditor and a member from each state senatorial district. With the establishment of the state tax commission that agency was made the body of final appeal. *Laws of Ohio*, III, 111; Chase, *op. cit.*, II, 1481; Curwen, *op. cit.*, 1784; G. C. sec. 5625-28.

The actual collection was performed by other agencies. Due to the fact that in earlier years there were two distinct tax levies - one on land for the territory and later the state, and one on other property for county purposes - tax collections involved a double operation and duplicate officials.

The collectors of the county levy assessed in 1792, were appointed by the judges of the court of common pleas who are empowered to designate the sheriff, constable, or any other suitable Person to perform this function.[104] By an act of 1795, township collectors were appointed by the commissioners and assessors.[105] From 1799 to 1805, taxes for county purposes were collected by county collectors.[106] An act of 1805 designated the township listers as collectors of the county levy, but, in 1806, the commissioners were permitted to appoint a county collector instead if they believed such a course to be expedient. This arrangement remained in force until 1825.[107]

The first statute of a general nature providing for attacks on land for territorial purposes was enacted in 1789. From 1799 to 1803, the collectors of the county tax were to collect the territorial tax also.[108] In 1804, however, the county sheriff was specifically assigned as the collector of the state tax.[109] From 1806 to 1815 the county commissioners were again permitted to use their own discretion as to whether a county or township collector should be appointed.[110] The county collector of the land tax mentioned in the statutes from 1816 to 1825 was, in all probability, the same official who collected the county tax, though due to a lack of definite terminology it is impossible to be certain.[111]

---

104. Chase, *op. cit.*, I, 119.
105. *Ibid.*, I, 171.
106. *Ibid.*, I, 277.
107. *Ibid.*, I, 71, 527; II, 1384-1385.
108. *Ibid.*, I, 270.
109. *Ibid.*, I, 415.
110. *Ibid.*, I, 537, 727; II, 973.
111. *Ibid.*, II, 973, 1370-1371.

In 1825, the arrangement for a separate tax duplicate for state and county purposes was abolished and levies for both were made on the same property. In 1827, the office of county collector, who had performed that function in the intervening two years, was abolished and the treasurer, henceforth to be an elective officer, was given the duty of tax collection[112]

The collection of certain taxes other than that on general property is performed by county agencies. Thus, for example, inheritance taxes, authorized by the legislature in 1894, are computed by the county auditor, adjusted by the probate court, collected by the county treasurer, and distributed to the proper agency by the county auditor.[113] County auditors certified to the tax commission lists of persons licensed to engage in the business of selling cigarettes. County treasurers are the agents of the state treasurer for the sale of cigarette tax stamps.[114] The tax on wines, cordials, and beer is collected by means of the sale of stamps by county treasurers in a manner similar to that employed in collecting the cigarette tax.[115] The tax on brewers' wort and malt is collected in an identical manner.[116]

The dispersal of administrative functions among county agencies is demonstrated more effectively, perhaps, and the issuance of licenses and permits which furnish a source of revenue for both the state and the county. The county auditor has issued, collected, and accounted for dog licenses from 1917 to the present;[117] he has issued, and the treasurer has collected the fees from cigarette (1893—)[118] malt (1933—),[119]

------

112. *Laws of Ohio*, XXV, 25.
113. G. C. secs. 5338, 5341, 5345, 5348-11.
114. G. C. sec. 5894-1 *et seq.*
115. G. C. sec. 6064-42.
116. G. C. sec. 5545 *et seq.*
117. *Laws of Ohio*, CVII, 534.
118. Jay F. Laning, comp., *Revised Statutes of the State of Ohio* (Norwalk, 1905), 1513.
119. G. C. sec. 5545 *et seq.*

peddlers' (1862—),[120] and show licenses (1827—).[121] Hunting and fishing licenses have been issued by the clerk of courts since 1904 and 1919 respectively.[122] In addition, the clerk has issued for the court of common pleas, ferry licenses (1805—),[123] auctioneers' licenses (1818—),[124] and peddlers' licenses (1810-1862).[125] Marriage licenses, issued from 1803 to 1851 by the clerk of courts, since the latter date, have been in the jurisdiction of the probate court.[126]

The establishment of a board of trustees of the sinking fund (1919) was a logical development in county fiscal administration. This board, composed of the auditor, treasurer, and prosecuting attorney, has as its principal function the payment of bonds issued by the county and the investment in bonds of monies credited to the sinking fund. Bonds issued in the process of county borrowing must be recorded in the office of the sinking fund trustees and signed by the auditor, as secretary of the board. The trustees certify to the board of commissioners the rate of tax necessary to provide a sinking fund for the payment of the principal and interest of the bonded indebtedness. The trustees are required to keep a full and complete record of transactions and a complete record of the funded debt of the county.[127]

---

120. Sayler, *op. cit.*, 273; *Laws of Ohio*, LIX, 67-68; G. C. sec. 6347.
121. Chase, *op. cit.*, III, 1582; G. C. sec. 6375.
122. *Laws of Ohio*, XCVII, 474; G. C. (Page and Adams) sec. 1430.
123. *Laws of Ohio*, III, 96; VIII, 107; XXIX, 447. Ferry licenses were issued by the associate judges 1803-1805. *Ibid*, I, 94.
124. Chase, *op. cit.*, II, 1040; G. C. secs. 5868, 5869.
125. *Ibid.*, I, 670.
126. *Ibid.*, I, 354; *Ohio Const., 1851*, Art. IV, sec. 8.
127. G. C. sec. 2976-18 *et seq.*

Elections

During the first nine decades of Ohio history the county sheriff was charged with the duty of announcing the time and place of holding elections, providing ballot boxes, ballots and other supplies, and the township trustees were directed by law to serve as judges of the elections.[128] This system continued, with slight alterations designed to facilitate the conduct of elections in Municipal centers until 1892. At that time there were created the offices of state supervisor of elections and deputy state supervisors of elections with duties prescribed for the conduct and supervision of all elections in the state.[129] The secretary of state, designated as the state supervisor of elections, was authorized and instructed to appoint four deputy supervisors for each county, who, in turn, appointed in all precincts for judges and two clerks of elections.[130]

Under the present election laws, provision is made for a chief election officer, a board of elections in each county, and judges and clerks in each precinct. The board of elections in each county consists of four qualified electors in the county, the members of which are appointed by the Secretary of State, two of such members being appointed on the first day of March in the even-numbered years to serve a four-year term.[131]

128. *Laws of Ohio*, I, 76-77; III, 331-332; VII, 113; XXIX, 4; L, 312.
129. *Laws of Ohio*, LXXXIX, 455. This act, however, did not apply to the election of school directors.
130. *Ibid.*, LXXXIX, 455. In 1870 each township, exclusive of the territory embraced within the limits of a municipal corporation which was divided into wards, composed an election precinct. *See ibid.*, LXVII, 46. An act of 1891 proved for the division of precincts in which 500 or more votes had been polled. *See ibid.*, LXXXVIII, 464.
131. G. C. secs. 4785-6, 4785-8. *See also* p. 223.

In making appointments to the membership of the board, equal representation is given to the political party polling the highest and the next highest number of votes for the office of governor in the last preceding state election. In this connection provision is made for the party recommendation of persons for such appointments.[132]

Under the early election laws the canvassing board was composed of the clerk of the court of common pleas and two justices of the peace called by him to his assistance.[133] This practice continued until 1892, when the board of state supervisors of elections succeeded to the duties formerly performed by both the clerk of the court of common pleas and the county sheriff. The sheriff, however, continues to announce the time and place of holding elections in the county until January 1, 1930, when the board of elections assumed this historic duty.[134] The duty of canvassing the returns, under the present statutes, is performed by the board of elections. The board in each county is required, within five days after each general or special election, to canvass the returns and to prepare abstracts of the votes cast.[135] This certified copy of the abstract is to be transmitted to the Secretary of State, and another copy filed in the office of the board.[136] The board is required also to prepare and transmit to the president of the senate a separate abstract of the returns of election of governor, lieutenant governor, secretary of state, auditor of state, and attorney general.[137]

---

132. G. C. sec. 4785-9. Under election law, it is the duty of the Secretary of State to appoint persons so recommended, unless he has reason to believe that such persons would not be competent members of the board.

133. *Laws of Ohio*, I, 83; III,336-337; VII, 119-120; XXIX, 49; L, 316; LXI, 68; LXXXII, 30.

134. G. C. sec. 4785-5; *Laws of Ohio*, LXXXIX, 455; CXIII, 307; The election laws of Ohio were revised and recodified by an act of the general assembly, passed April 5, 1929. *Laws of Ohio*, CXIII, 307-413.

135. G. C. secs. 4785-152, 4785-153.

136. G. C. sec. 4785-153.

137. *Ohio Const. 1851*, Art. III, sec. 3; G. C. sec. 4785-154.

Health

Prior to 1919, the county had few responsibilities regarding health administration. With the development of urban centers with congested areas the problem of health administration was brought to the attention of the legislature. Prior to the enactment of the present health code in 1919, jurisdiction in matters of health was vested in the cities, villages, and townships. Under the act of 1919, all villages and townships in the county were combined into a general health district under the supervision of a board appointed by the advisory council composed of the mayors of villages and chairman of township trustees. Each city in the district is organized as a separate health district. Two general health districts or a general health district and a city health district located within such a district may combine.[138] All physicians are required to report communicable diseases to the district health commissioners who imposed quarantines.[139]

The legislature has placed on the county the burden of responsibility in the treatment of tuberculosis. Any county, regardless of its size, may employ nurses, operate clinics, and care for patients in private, municipal, or county sanitariums. Any county having a population of 50,000 or more inhabitants may, with the consent of the state department of health, erect and operate sanitariums, and two or more counties may form districts for the same purpose. The sanitariums are operated by the county commissioners or special boards appointed by the county commissioners.[140]

---

138. *Laws of Ohio*, CVIII, pt. i, 238; CVIII, pt. ii,1085-1086.
139. *Laws of Ohio*, CVIII, pt. ii, 1088-1089.
140. G. C. secs. 3148-1 pt. ii, 3148-3.

Besides establishing sanitariums for the treatment of tubercular patients, counties are authorized to operate general hospitals. The county hospital is operated by a board appointed by the county commissioners.[141] Evidence seems to indicate that the county is the proper unit for hospital administration.

Public Welfare

The administration of Public Welfare is one of the most complex and one of the most expensive functions of county government. The administration of institutional and outdoor relief is delegated to eight boards and commissions operating independently and with little regard for efficiency.

The administration of the county home is vested in the county commissioners and a superintendent appointed from a list of names of persons eligible under civil service regulations.[142]

Although provision was made for the institutional care of the county's indigent as early as 1816, it was not until after the conclusion of the War between the States when hundreds of Ohio children were left homeless, that the legislature enacted measures for the care of dependent children.[143] Prior to the act of 1865, the trustees of the poor house were authorized to apprentice dependent children. The administration of the children's home is vested in a board of trustees, appointed by the county commissioners, and a superintendent appointed by the board of trustees.[144]

The board of county visitors, and agency for the examination of county institutions, was created by the general assembly in 1882. Until 1906, the board was appointed by the court of common pleas and after that date by the probate judge.[145]

---

141. G. C. secs. 3127 to 3138-4.
142. G. C. secs. 2522, 2523.
143. *Laws of Ohio*, III, 276; VIII, 223-224.
144. G. C. secs. 3081, 3084. (illegible).
145. *Laws of Ohio*, LXXIX, 107; XCVIII, 28; G. C. sec. 2971.

The board consists of six persons appointed for terms of three years.

In 1886, counties were required by law to provide relief for indigent soldiers and sailors and their indigent wives, children, and parents.[146] Soldiers' relief is administered by the commission consisting of three persons appointed by the court of common pleas for terms of three years. This commission, in turn, selects township and ward committees.[147]

In 1884, the legislature made provision for a soldiers' burial commission in each county.[148] The administration of soldiers' burials is vested in a commission consisting of two persons in each township and ward appointed by the county commissioners.[149]

Counties maintain a system of pensions for the needy blind. Prior to 1880, blind relief was administered in the county by the probate judge (1904 - 1908), by a blind relief commission appointed by the probate judge (1908 - 1912) and by the county commissioners (1913 - 1936). [150] The present system originated in 1936, when the legislature accepted the provisions of the Federal Social Security act. Blind relief is financed by federal, state, and local funds and is administered in the state by the Ohio Commission for the Blind and in the county by the county commissioners, whose decisions are subject to review by the Ohio Commission for the Blind.[151]

---

146. *Laws of Ohio*, LXXXII, 433-434.
147. G. C. secs. 2930-2931.
148. *Laws of Ohio*, LXXXI, 146-147.
149. G. C. sec. 2950.
150. *Laws of Ohio*, XCVII, 393-394; XCIX, 56-58; CIII, 60.
151. *Ibid.*, CXVI, pt. ii, 195-200.

Prior to 1932, the county confined its relief activities to the institutional care of the indigent. Outdoor relief, except for those persons lacking a legal settlement, was provided and administered by the townships and cities. With the coming of the economic depression the resources of the municipalities and townships proved inadequate for financing relief activities. Accordingly, in 1932, the legislature conferred on all counties the authority to care for the poor in their own homes. Funds for such purposes were provided by the issuance of bonds and by diversion of gasoline taxes for financing such services. While the state relief commission, created for administering state relief, is required to pass up on local relief budgets, the county relief offices, administered by the county commissioners, provide relief services in the county.

Today old age pensions are relieving the counties of the increased burdens of institutional relief. This system, originating in 1933, provides for persons 65 or more years of age. No person may be granted a pension if the net value of his property is in excess of $3,000 or his annual income is in excess of $480.[152] The old age pension system is financed by state and federal funds and is administered by a division of the department of public welfare through county boards of aid for the aged.[153] Under the provision of the initial act, the county commissioners served as ex-officio members of the board of aid for the aged in the county. Since May 1, 1937, the chief of the division has been required by law to appoint an advisory board in each county consisting of five members. This board, appointed for a two-year term, succeeded to the duties formerly performed by the county commissioners.[154]

---

152. *Laws of Ohio*, CXV, pt. ii, 421-429; CXVI, pt. ii, 86-88, 216-221; G. C. sec. 1359-2.
153. *Ibid.*, CXV, pt. ii, 431-439
154. G. C. sec. 1359-12.

Aid to dependent children, although provided for by the legislature, in 1913, in the form of mothers' pensions, assumed a new significance, when, in 1936, the legislature accepted the provisions of the Federal Social Security Act. Aid to dependent children is financed by federal, state, and local funds. The administration of the act and the state is delegated to the department of public welfare and in Medina County to the judge of the court of domestic relations serving as juvenile judge.[155]

Public Works

The responsibility for the administration of public works in the county rests with the board of county commissioners, the county engineer, and the sanitary engineer. The county commissioners, since the inauguration of county government, have had the responsibility for the authorization and financing of public works. With the immense development of highway improvement, occasioned by the introduction of automobiles and trucks as means of transportation, public works became one of the most important functions of the county commissioners and consequently the county engineer, who, during the first 120 years of his office, had as his principal duty the surveying of lands, received new duties and responsibilities with respect to the construction of roads, culverts, ditches, and in most cases bridges.[156] Within the last two decades the township roads, under the joint authority of the county and the township trustees, have been gradually absorbed by the county and state systems of highways.[157]

---

155. *Laws of Ohio*, CXVI, pt. ii, 188-196.
156. *Ibid*, XCVIII, 245-247; CVIII, pt. i, 497.
157. The centralization of highway construction was guaranteed under the road law of 1915. The township trustees, at one time one of the most important agencies in local highway construction, have become a local improvement board with powers to authorize but not to supervise road construction. *Laws of Ohio*, CVI, 589-594.

The Ohio counties were formed to meet the needs of rural pioneer communities with a population spread relatively uniformly over the entire state. Recent decades have brought remarkable changes. Many sections of the state have become thoroughly industrialized, and as a result of the change, have been forced to deal with such problems as housing, health, sanitation, police administration, scientific transportation, and sewage disposal. These problems with which the county organization has been unable to cope are rapidly taking the forms of city problems.

The census of 1930 shows that the 1,201,455 persons in Cuyahoga County 900,429 were in Cleveland, of the 361,055 persons in Franklin County 290,564 were in Columbus, of the 589,356 persons in Hamilton County 541,160 were in Cincinnati, and that of the 347,709 persons in Lucas County 290,718 were in Toledo. It is not strange, therefore, that demands were made for a reorganization of the county government to eliminate the waste and confusion occasioned by overlapping jurisdiction of county and municipal functions.[158]

In view of the growth of large cities and the confusion occasioned by the conflict of county and municipal powers, there has been an attempt to work out a more satisfactory relationship between the two organs of local government. This took the form of a constitutional amendment, which, defeated in 1919, was placed on the ballot in 1933 by initiative petition and adopted by the electorate. The amendment provides:

---

158. U. S. Bureau of the Census, *Fifteenth Census of the United States, 1930, Population,* III, pt. ii, 518, 520, 521, 525. C. A. Dykstra, "Cleveland's Effort for City-County Consolidation," *Nat. Mun. Review,* VIII (1919), 551-556.

"The General Assembly shall provide by general law for the organization and government of counties, and may provide by general law alternative forms of county government. No alternative form shall become operative in any county until submitted to the electors thereof and approved by a majority of those voting thereon under regulations provided by law. Municipalities and townships shall have authority, with the consent of the county, to transfer to the county any of their powers or to revoke the transfer of any such power, under regulations provided by general law, but the rights of initiative and referendum shall be secured to . . . every measure . . . giving or withdrawing such consent."[159]

The constitutional amendment of 1933 altered the status of the county. Where the status of the county was formally fixed by statute it is now subject to local determination in the same matter as municipalities.

The arguments advanced in favor of the system fall under three heads:

1. It makes possible a different form of government for urban centers where political, social, and economic conditions differ from those of rural counties.

2. It promotes efficiency and economy by the elimination of duplicate officers and employees.

3. It promotes efficiency by the centralization of power and responsibility.[160]

---

159. *Ohio Const. 1851*, (Amendment, adopted November 7, 1933), Art. X, sec. 1.

160. *The Ohio State Journal*, October 9, 1933; C. A. Dykstra, *loc. cit.*

A commission on county government was appointed by Governor White in 1933 to formulate optional plans of county government for submission to the legislature.[161] Accordingly, in 1935, the commission submitted to the legislature ten bills embodying its recommendation as to matters of county reorganization. The major bills authorized three optional forms of county government, subject to adoption by the local electorate: (1) a county manager plan, (2) the elective plan, (3) the appointing executive plan.[162] Of the ten bills presented, two became laws. One of these authorized the transfer to the county of any local governmental activity by voluntary agreement between the county and a local subdivision within the county. This measure, of course, opened the way for the consolidation of such functions as welfare, law enforcement, and sewer construction which need unification in counties having a large urban population.[163] The other act authorizes the charter county to take over welfare administration, noninstitutional relief, and park construction.[164]

While the amendment offers an opportunity for the improvement of local government in counties in which large municipalities have developed, no use has been made of the provision.[165] At present Franklin County with a population of 361,055 has essentially the same type of county government as Vinton County with the population of 10,287.[166]

---

161. R. C. Atkinson, "County Home Rule Development in Ohio," *Nat. Mun. Review,* XXIII, (1934), 235.
162. R. C. Atkinson "Ohio– Optional County Legislation," *Nat. Mun. Review,* XXIV, (1935), 228.
163. *Laws of Ohio,* CXVI, 102-104.
164. *Ibid.,* CXVI, 132-135.
165. Home rule charters were submitted to the voters in Hamilton, Cuyahoga, Lucas, and Franklin Counties. Advocates of home rule attributed the defeat of these measures to politicians who saw in the scheme the destruction of the spoils system. See R. C. Atkinson, "Ohio-County Charter Elections," *Nat. Mun. Review,* XXIV, (1935), 702-703.
166. U. S. Bureau of the Census, *Fifteenth Census of the United States, 1930, Population,* III, pt. ii, 520, 531.

While unsuccessful attempts have been made to correct some of the defects of county administration in areas containing large urban populations, little consideration has been given to rural counties where, on account of a constant decline in population, the old governmental organization has become unduly expensive and ill-suited to the needs of the population. This is particularly true in the counties located in the southeastern and northwestern portions of the state where the population has steadily declined since 1880. There is a question as to whether the services of modern government in such counties can continue to be maintained without the consolidation of contiguous territory for purposes of administration. The Ohio constitution, from its beginning in 1802, has contained a restriction upon the legislature regarding the minimum area of counties. None could be formed with less than 400 square miles–or reduced below that size.[167] With the development of modern means of transportation and communication this area is ridiculously small. The combination for administrative purposes of sparsely populated counties, having common social and economic interest would eliminate waste, overhead, and duplication of personnel.

Governmental service is constantly requiring the employment of better trained officials. Evidence seems to indicate that only by enlarging the size of the administrative area to make possible the specialization in work, can the requisite degree of training and skill be secured in the performance of public service.[168]

---

167. *Ohio Const. 1851,* Art. II, sec. 30; *Ohio Const. 1802,* Art. VII, sec. 3.
168. Cf. H. Eliot Kaplan, "A Personal Program for County Service," *Nat. Mun. Review,* XXV, (1936), 596-600.

The relation of the county to the state is also a matter of importance. As a result of radical changes in economic life, matters which were at one time a purely local interest and concern have become of state-wide importance. During recent years the old type of county organization has proved inadequate to meet the needs of modern civilization. Recognition of this fact is found in the steady growth of state control of such matters as public accounting, health and welfare administration, and law enforcement.

At the same time the county has definitely supplanted the township as the administrative unit. This is particularly noticeable in the substitution of the general health district for the township district, and the transfer of tax assessment to the township assessors to the county auditor. The county-state administration of highway maintenance and public welfare has been affected. Although many deplore the passing of the little red schoolhouse, the substitution of the county school district to the township area has resulted in better educational advantages for children residing in rural areas.

It is significant that modern invention has removed the necessity for the rural administrative units of such small proportions. The transfer of power from the smaller to the larger unit has arisen out of the desire for better service and economy. Little remains to justify the retention of the township.

Records System

It has been the duty of most officials since the beginning of county government to keep a record of the business of their offices. Differences in population between counties, however, forced a wide variance in the recording as evidenced by the fact that several types of records were kept in the same book in some counties, and in others were kept in separate books. As indicated in detail in the office essays, preceding the records of each office, the legislature eventually prescribed not only what records were to be kept, but also the content. In this field there was a remarkable advance following the adoption of the constitution of 1851. Such legislation assured some uniformity in the county records system.

There are three county officials whose work consists mainly in the preparation and custody of records: the recorder, the clerk of courts, and the judge of the probate court. All three have some part in the recording of documents and instruments affecting the title of property and of other documents presented for record. The last two have as their principal duty the keeping of court records; the clerk of court serves as clerk of both the court of common pleas and the court of appeals, and the probate judge maintains the records of his own court.

It is the duty of the county recorder to copy, index, and file documents authorized to be recorded in his office. The system of recording is prescribed in detail by law. In most counties recording is done by typewriter with considerable use of printed forms. The photographic method of copying is in use in Clark, Cuyahoga, Hamilton, Lucas, Montgomery, and Summit Counties. Deeds, mortgages, plats, and leases must be copied into separate books, and indexed by direct and reverse indexes.[169] The recorder is required, also, to prepare daily an alphabetical index to such instruments.[170]

The principal records of the clerk of courts are prescribed by statute. They include an appearance docket, a trial docket, an execution docket, a journal, and a complete record of proceedings, a system of indexes, and a file of original papers.[171] The clerk is responsible for a variety of non-judicial records work of which the filing and indexing of automobile bills of sale was the major item. The bill of sale law was repealed by an act effective January 1, 1938, requiring the clerk to issue certificates of title to motor vehicles in triplicate and to file a duplicate of the certificate.[172]

---

169. G. C. secs. 2757, 2764.
170. G. C. secs. 2764, 2766.
171. G. C. secs. 2878, 2884, 2885.
172. G. C. sec. 6290-6.

At present the clerk of courts acts as the agent of the state for the sale of hunting, trapping, and fishing licenses,[173] and also issues auctioneers' and ferry licenses.[174]

The office of the probate court performs the following services: the recording of miscellaneous instruments, including marriage licenses[175] and certificates of physicians, surgeons, and nurses which authorize them to practice their profession in the state.[176] The court record system of the office, originating in 1853 and continued by the probate code of 1931, is prescribed by statute and involves the proper keeping of papers in each case and copying materials in appropriate record books.[177]

Few records are prescribed for the law-enforcement agencies. The county sheriff is required by law to keep at least three books; a foreign execution docket,[178] a cashbook,[179] and a jail register.[180] Indexes, direct and reverse, to the foreign execution docket were required in 1925.[181] The system of recording is prescribed by statute. The county coroner's records consist of two: a report of findings in cases of unlawful death,[182] and an inventory of articles found on or about the body of the deceased.[183] Such records are required by law and the contents of the records minutely prescribed.

---

173. G. C. secs. 1430, 1432.
174. G. C. secs. 5868-5869, 5947-5950.
175. *Ohio Const. 1851,* Art. IV, sec. 8.
176. *Laws of Ohio,* XCII, 45-47; XCIX, 499; CVI, 193.
177. *Ibid.,* CXIV, 321-322.
178. G. C. sec. 2837.
179. G. C. sec. 2839.
180. *Laws of Ohio,* XLI, 74; G. C. Sec. 3158.
181. *Laws of Ohio,* CXI, 31.
182. G. C. sec. 2857.
183. G. C. sec. 2859.

The number and type of records kept by county prosecuting attorneys vary widely. In some counties the records of the prosecuting attorney are kept on standard forms and include such records as grand jury docket, a grand jury testimony record, and a criminal court docket. In Medina County the grand jury records are kept by the county clerk of courts. The prosecuting attorney keeps a criminal docket and files criminal records under four classifications: pending, disposed, inactive, and liquor cases. The civil records are classified as pending cases, disposed cases, foreclosures of tax liens, tax claims, opinions on schools, and letters relative to county bank deposits. However, in many counties of the state no records or files are kept and individual memoranda are disposed of by the incumbent. Since the prosecuting attorney is vested with large discretionary powers, there is need of special records and files. Such records according to authorities on judicial administration should include, among others, a permanent record of the names and addresses of witnesses, the deputy or division handling the case, and the reason for failure to prosecute, and the reason for which a *nolle prosequi* was asked and granted.

The records of the financial agencies of county government are prescribed by statute. Although records were kept in the earlier years, it was not until 1902 that the matter of keeping and the content of such records attracted the attention of the legislature. It was evident that accounts had not only been poorly kept, but there had been little uniformity among the counties of the state. Accordingly, in 1902, the legislature enacted the most important and far-reaching laws on the subject. This act provided for a uniform system of accounting, auditing, and reporting, under the supervision of a newly created bureau of inspection located in the office of the auditor of state. The act further provided for the annual examination of finances of all public offices.[184]

184. *Laws of Ohio*, XCV, 511-515.

The governor's commission on the reorganization of county government, after studying the county records system and noting the illogical combination of administrative, judicial, and financial functions, made the following recommendations:[185]

1. County charters and optional forms of government should provide for the department of records and court service to take over the functions of the recorder and clerk of courts, the non-judicial records work of the probate court, and the functions of the sheriff as a court officer.

2. The issuance of licenses should be transferred from the clerk of courts to the department of finance.

3. Wider use should be made of the photographic process of recording in large counties.

4. Legislation should be adopted permitting the destruction of chattel mortgages and automobile bills of sale after they have ceased to have effect.

5. The requirement of three systems of indexes of cases in the clerk's office should be eliminated from the code and only the index of pending suits and living judgments should be required.

6. Provisions should be made in the rules of common pleas court for service of process by mail and that method should be brought into general use.

---

185. *Reports of Governors Commission,* 186-187. See also R. E. Heiges, *The Office of Sheriff in the Rural Counties of Ohio* (Findlay, 1933), 55-56, 60-61.

Concurrently with the development of a record system, steps were taken to assure the proper restoration of damaged or dilapidated records treating of lands and surveys. The county engineer, when directed by the county commissioners, is required by law to transcribe any and all dilapidated maps and the records of plats and field notes of surveys from the records of the courts of common pleas, auditor, recorder, or other officer in the state where they may be procured.[186] Similarly, the county recorder, when authorized by the county commissioners, is required to transcribe from the records of the counties all deeds, mortgages, powers of attorney, and other instruments of writing, for the sale, conveyance, or encumbrance of lands, tenements, or hereditaments situated within his county.[187]

The large accumulation of county records, occasioned by increasing governmental service, presents a serious problem. It is important, on the one hand, that valuable space in county courthouses and other county depositories not be cluttered up with vast quantities of useless materials. On the other hand, it is more important that every precaution be taken to prevent public officials from destroying valuable public records in order to make space for current business.

Within recent years photography has become an increasingly important aid in archival administration. The Ohio Legislature, following the modern trends in recording, has enacted measures looking forward to the conservation of space in the county courthouses by permitting county officials to destroy records which have been reproduced photographically.

---

186. G. C. sec. 2804.
187. G. C. sec. 2763.

Under this act, passed in 1937, any county official charged with keeping public records may, when the space requires it, have such records copied or reproduced by any photographic process and destroy the original papers. The original records, however, must be preserved until the time for filing legal proceedings based upon the documents shall have elapsed.[188]

While the legislature has attempted to enact legislation looking forward to the conservation of much needed space in county courthouses a significant trend is to be observed in the increasing interest which has been displayed for a department of county archives for all noncurrent records may be properly housed, classified, listed, and made more readily accessible to those interested in consulting them. The arguments advanced in favor of such a system are: (1) that the preservation of county records should be viewed as a distinct function of county government, (2) that the administration of county archives should be under the direction of those qualified to serve efficiently and effectively both the needs of the administration and historians, (3) that the construction of county archives buildings with non-current records would make available more space for current business, which, at present, is seriously curtailed.

In the field of archival administration the state rather than the county, has been the experimental laboratory, and the results have been imminently successful.[189]

---

188. G. C. sec. 32-1.
189. For an interesting and informative article on the administration of state archives, see Charles M. Gates, "The Administration of State Archives," *The Pacific Northwest Quarterly,* XXIX, (January 1938), No. 1; also in *The American Archivist,* I (July 1938), 130-141.

The first courthouse in Medina County was started in 1818 and completed in 1826. It was a two-story rectangular structure with a brick exterior and embellished plaster interior. The contractor was Benjamin Lindsey, who constructed the building at a total cost of $3500.[1]

The present courthouse was erected in 1840 at a cost of $3100.[2] Additions to this structure were made in 1872, 1906, and 1933.[3] It is a red brick building, trimmed in white stone and capped by a clock and cased steeple which gives it an appearance not unlike a place of worship. The interior, including floors, stairways, balustrades, and corridors, are of wood construction.

All of the following records are housed in the county courthouse unless otherwise specified.

County Commissioners. The commissioners occupy two rooms on the north side of the main floor of the courthouse. All of the early records of this office are housed in the north storeroom, while the current volume records are kept in the commissioners' record room, on steel roller shelving along the north wall. Unbound records are kept in steel file cases, along the south wall, auditor's office and aid to dependent children's office. Ventilation and lighting are good, but the office is crowded, with no room for expansion. The records of this office number 46 volumes, 8 file boxes, seven folders, 511 sheets, and one bundle.

Relief Administration. The county relief office is located in the basement. Records are housed in a steel file cabinet and in steel file boxes. Ventilation, lighting, and space are adequate. The records number two volumes and 14 file boxes.

---

1. [Miscellaneous Expenditures and Receipts], 1818-1826.
2. Duff, *op. cit.,* I, 457.
3. *Ibid.*

Due to poor copies, some information may be illegible.

     Clerk of Courts. The clerk occupies four rooms on the north side of the second floor. All early records are kept in the north and south store rooms. The modern records are kept on steel shelves in the record rooms. Only the very current records are kept in the main office. All rooms are well lighted and well ventilated, but are crowded, with no room for expansion. The records number 257 volumes, 43 file drawers, 38 file boxes, 40 cartons, 15 bundles, and one envelope.

     Court of Common Pleas. All early records are kept in the south court room. The modern records for this office are housed in the clerk of courts office and record room. The records number 264 volumes, 3 file drawers, and 3 cartons.

     Supreme Court. These records will be found in the clerk of courts' courtroom and original papers, found with the clerk of courts, will be in the north storeroom. The records number five volumes.

     Court of Appeals. This office keeps its records in the clerk of courts' office and record rooms. The original papers, filed with the clerk of courts, will be found in the clerk of courts' office. The records number 21 volumes, (?) file drawers, 2(?)8 bundles.

     Probate Court. The offices are located on the south side of the first floor, and occupy two rooms and a vault. Early records are housed in the north and south store rooms. More recent volume records are kept in steel file cabinets in the vault. The main and private offices are well lighted and ventilated, and are not crowded at the present time. The vault however is poorly lighted, inadequately ventilated, and crowded, with no room for expansion. The records number 947 volumes, 146 file drawers, two file boxes, three file cabinets, 35 reports, and one cardboard box.

Juvenile Court. The bound records are housed in the offices of probate court and consist of 3 volumes. Original papers filed in juvenile cases are kept in the probate court vault.

Probation Department. This office is located on the southwest side of the second floor and consists of one room. Bound records are kept on steel shelves, along the south wall, while the unbound records are housed in file cabinets and file boxes, along the north and east walls. The records consist of 3 volumes, 6 file boxes, 4 file drawers, and 72 reports.

Aid to Dependent Children. This office is located on the south side of the second floor and consists of one room. Records are housed in file drawers along the west wall in auditor's office. The records consist of 8 file drawers.

Jury Commissioners. Records of this body are kept in the clerk of courts' record rooms and clerk of courts' office.

Grand Jury. Records are housed in the clerk of courts' office, record room, Auditor's office, and north storeroom.

Prosecuting Attorney. The county prosecutor's office is located at 122 East Liberty Street, Medina, Ohio, and consists of one room. Early records are housed in the south storeroom and Auditor's office. The modern records are housed in steel file cases along the north wall of the prosecutor's office. Ventilation and lighting are good, and the office has more than ample space at present. The records number 5 volumes and 2 file boxes.

Coroner. All coroner's records are housed in the offices of the clerk of courts, auditor's office, and south storeroom.

Sheriff. The sheriff occupies one room in the southwest corner of the second floor. The early records are housed in the north storeroom. Volume records are kept on steel shelves along the east wall, while the unbound records are housed in steel file cases along the north wall. The office is well lighted and well ventilated, and is not too crowded. The records number 53 volumes, 1 file box and 800 sheets.

Dog Warden. The dog warden's office is located at the Dog Pound, State Route 162, R. D. 5, Medina, Ohio. Early records are housed in the north storeroom and current records are housed in dog warden's office.

Auditor. The county auditor occupies two rooms on the north side of the first floor. Early records are found in the north and south store rooms. More recent volume records are kept in the main office on steel shelves, while the unbound records are housed in steel file cases. The very current records are kept in the auditor's private office. Ventilation and lighting for the offices are adequate, but the rooms are crowded, with no room for expansion. The records number 798 volumes, 151 file boxes, 278 bundles, 75 cartons, two folders, and 180 sheets.

Treasurer. The office is on the northeast side of the first floor and consists of one room and a vault. All old records are housed in the north and south store rooms. More recent volume records are kept on steel shelves in the vault, while the unbound records are housed in steel file cases, also in the vault. The very current records are kept in the treasurer's office. This office is well lighted and well ventilated, but is crowded, with no room for expansion. The vault is inadequately lighted and ventilated, and is crowded, with no room for expansion. The records number 1629 volumes, one file drawer, 18 file boxes, 2 boxes, 3 cartons, and 106 bundles.

Budget Commissioners. The records for this office are found in the auditor's main office, and number 2 volumes.

Board of Revision. This board keeps its early records in the north storeroom and the current records in auditor's main office. The records number 3 volumes and 2 file boxes.

Board of Trustees of the Sinking Fund. Records for this board are housed in the auditor's main office, and number 1 volume.

Board of Elections. The board occupies one room on the north side of the basement. The early records are housed in the engineers storeroom. The volume records are kept in steel file cabinets along the east wall, while the unbound records are housed in steel file boxes and a file drawer, along the west wall. Lighting and ventilation are good, and the room has ample space at present. The records number 427 volumes, 1 file drawer, 7 file boxes, and 10 rolls.

Board of Education. The office of this board is located in the old Eagles building corner of West Friendship and North Elmwood Streets, Medina, Ohio. The early records are housed in the north storeroom. Most of the records consist of unbound records which are housed in steel file cases and drawers, in the clerk's office. Some volume records are kept in the superintendent's office. The rooms are well lighted and well ventilated, and contain ample space at the present time. The records number 2 volumes, 4 file drawers, 27 file boxes, and 1 box.

Board of Health. The board of health occupies two rooms on the northeast side of the first floor. Volume records are kept in a steel file cabinet along the north wall, while the unbound records are housed in steel file cases, along the west wall. Lighting and ventilation are fair, and the office is not overcrowded at the present time. The records number 5 volumes, 6 file drawers, and 11 file boxes.

Superintendent of the County Home. The records of the county home are housed in the office of the superintendent of the home, which is located at R. F. D. #5, Lafayette Township, Ohio. The early records are located in the Commissioner's Office. Volume records are kept on top of steel file cases, while the unbound records are housed in the same cases, which are located along the south wall. Ventilation, lighting, and space are adequate. The records number 17 volumes, 5 file drawers, and 4 file boxes.

Board of County Visitors. This office keeps no separate records. They may be found in the probate court office.

Soldiers' Relief Commission. Records of this commission may be found in the Soldiers' Relief Commission office, Princess Block, Public Square, Medina, Ohio, and the auditor's main office. The records number 4 volumes and 2 file boxes.

Soldiers' Burial Commission. These records are kept in
the commissioners' office and auditor's main office.

Blind Relief Commission. Records for this office are found
in the auditor's main office and early records are found in the north
storeroom. The records number 1 volume and 1 file box.

Division of Aid for the Aged. This department is located in
the Princess Block, Public Square, Medina, Ohio, and occupies two
rooms. Practically all of the records are unbound and are kept in
steel file boxes, located along the north wall of the secretary's
office. The main office houses no records, as it is used only for
consultations. Lighting, ventilation, and space are adequate for
both rooms. The records number 1 volume and 13 file boxes.

County Engineer. The engineer's office consists of two
rooms in the Southeast corner of the first floor and two rooms and
vault in the north west corner of the basement. Records are housed
in steel file cases along the north wall of his private office and
along the east and north walls of the main office. Ventilation,
lighting, and space are more than adequate. The drafting room is
on the north side of the basement floor. Records are housed in steel
file boxes, along the east and west walls. Ventilation, lighting, and
space are fairly adequate. The engineer's vault is located south of
the drafting room on the basement floor. Volume records are kept
on steel shelves, along the north and west walls, while unbound
records are housed in steel file cases, along the south and east
walls. Ventilation and lighting are good, but the vault is crowded.
Road and bridge records are housed in the engineer's storeroom on
the third floor. The records number 245 volumes, 10 file drawers,
30 file boxes, 458 notebooks, one glass covered and one uncovered
wall chart, 21 pigeon holes, 13 letter files, one folder, 16 bundles,
and 1 wooden box.

Metropolitan Park District Board. This office keeps no
separate records. They may be found in the auditor's main office.

Agricultural Conservation Association. All records for
this association are housed in the Agricultural Conservation Office,
located on the second floor of the Gazette Building, Medina, Ohio,

and consist of 29 file drawers and 28 file boxes.

Agricultural Society. Records for this society are in the custody of Jay V. Einhart, Secretary-Treasurer, Medina County Agricultural Association, R. D. 6, Medina, Ohio. The records number 54 volumes.

Agricultural Extension Agent. This agency occupies two rooms in the northwest corner of the basement. Records are housed in steel file cases, along the north wall. Ventilation, lighting, and space are more than adequate. The records number 12 file boxes.

North Storeroom. This room is located in the northwest corner of the third floor and is used as a depository for a large number of the early county records. Volume records are stacked on wood shelves, located along the south and east walls, while unbound records are housed in cardboard boxes and wooden file boxes, along the north wall. Ventilation and lighting conditions are fair, and the room is not overcrowded. The records number 2021 volumes, 35 file drawers, 30 file boxes, 101 bundles, 120 cartons, 3 boxes, and 391 sheets.

South Storeroom. This room is in the southwest corner of the third floor and is also used for the storage of the early county records. The bound and unbound records are arranged just as they are in the north storeroom (see above). Lighting, ventilation, and space are adequate. The records number 346 volumes, 4 file drawers, 2 file boxes, 3 file cabinets, 8 rolls, and 1 bundle.

The governmental system established in 1802, under the first constitution of Ohio, made no provision for the office of county commissioners and its existence is due entirely to statutory enactment. The board, created in 1804, was the successor of the courts of general quarter sessions, which, during the territorial period served as the representative agent of the county. The board of county commissioners consisted of three members elected for a three-year term.[1] In 1807 the commissioners were made a corporate body vested with the power to sue and be sued.[2] They were required to keep a record of their proceedings, to levy taxes for the support of the county, to appoint a county treasurer, and to supervise the construction of bridges.[3] They were paid on a per diem basis. Moreover, during the same period (1804) they were given the task of constructing courthouses, jails, and offices for the clerk of courts, court of common pleas, sheriff, auditor, and the treasurer.[4] From 1805 to 1820 the commissioners were required to fix the amounts of tavern and ferry licenses and the rates for transportation by ferry.[5] Of these earlier duties the commissioners retain all but those of fixing the amount of tavern and ferry licenses and ferriage rates and that of appointing a county treasurer. However, since 1831 they have been authorized to examine and inspect the accounts of the county treasurer and to examine the condition of county finances.[6]

Besides the duties regarding county building construction and finance, the commissioners were given the task of constructing local highways when so authorized by the legislature.

---

1. *Laws of Ohio*, II, 150.
2. *Ibid.*, V, 97.
3. *Ibid.*, VIII, 45.
4. *Ibid.*, II, 154-157; XXIX, 315.
5. *Ibid.*, III, 96; VIII, 107; XVIII, 170.
6. *Ibid.*, XXIX, 201. *See also* G. C. sec. 2644.

During the first thirty years of Ohio history the duties of the commissioners in this respect were local in nature, but as the system of road construction expanded they were given the additional duty of converting free turnpikes into state roads.[7] During the 1840s and 1850s private companies were authorized by the legislature to construct plank roads.[8] When those companies were caught in the stringency of a financial depression in 1857, the commissioners were authorized to purchase their holdings. If such transactions were made, the transfer signed by the president of the company, was to be deposited with the county auditor.[9] In 1871 the commissioners, although earlier subjected to regulatory measures by the legislature, were prohibited from levying taxes for roads to exceed three and a half mills on the dollar on the taxable property in the county.[10] Later, in 1885, they were authorized to levy taxes not to exceed five mills on the dollar on all taxable property in the county for maintenance of roads which had been damaged by excessive wear or were damaged from other causes.[11]

    With the development of modern means of transportation, scientific principles were applied to road construction and maintenance. Although the county surveyor, now the county engineer, had in earlier years furnished the commissioners with estimates for bridge construction, it was not until the latter part of the 19th century that they were authorized to utilize his scientific knowledge in road construction.[12] At the beginning of the present century the surveyor was directed to appoint a maintenance engineer, with the consent of the commissioners, to supervise the repairing of improved roads in the county.[13]

---

7. *Laws of Ohio*, XLVII, 74.
8. *Ibid.*, XLVIII, 49; L, 282.
9. *Ibid.*, LIV, 198.
10. *Ibid.*, LXVIII, 117.
11. G. C. sec. 7419.
12. *Laws of Ohio*, LXXXIX, 172; XCVIII, 245-247.
13. *Ibid.*, CVIII, pt. i, 497.

Although the county commissioners have never been closely associated with the administration of criminal justice, their earlier duties regarding the construction of county jails qualified them, in the earlier period for additional duties in this respect. During the middle of the 19th century the commissioners of Cuyahoga County were authorized to employ persons on construction work who were confined in the county jails.[14] While this provision was repealed by the criminal code, adopted in 1853, other earlier functions applicable to all counties were continued. Since 1843, the commissioners have provided equipment and fixtures for places of incarceration and food and clothing for prisoners, and have appointed a jail physician.[15] Since 1869, they have been authorized to offer a reward for the detection or apprehension of any person charged with a felony in the county.[16] Since 1892, the commissioners in any county where there is no workhouse may, under certain conditions, release or parole an indigent person confined in the jail.[17] With the extension of modern crime into the rural areas in the form of small town bank robbing, the commissioners were given the duty of furnishing motorcycles to the sheriff and his deputies in an attempt to compete with the high-powered equipment used by modern gangs. One of the latest functions in this respect is the contracting with radio stations for the broadcasting of descriptions of fleeing criminals.[18]

Besides providing for those who have violated the laws, the commissioners were given the duty of caring for persons who, because of poverty or physical or mental defects, became public charges.

---

14. *Ibid.,* XXXVII, 54.
15. *Ibid.,* XLI, 74; LXXXVII, 186.
16. *Ibid.,* LXVI, 321.
17. *Ibid.,* LXXXIX, 408; CXIII, 203.
18. G. C. sec. 2412-1.

Thus, county relief for the indigent, one of the most pressing problems of the 20th century was met in frontier Ohio. As early as 1805 an act, modeled from the territorial law, was passed which was similar to all respects to the poor laws of the 17th century England.[19] Under the early enactments the township trustees were authorized to appoint overseers of the poor. In 1816 the county commissioners were authorized to construct "poor houses" for the care of the county's indigent. As the system developed in succeeding decades the county was made responsible for those who had become permanently disabled, and for paupers who could not be satisfactory cared for except at the county infirmary, now called the county home. Since 1913 they have been authorized, in any county containing a city which has an infirmary, to contract with the director of public safety for the care of the county's indigent.[20]

The township trustees and officials of municipal corporations were made responsible for providing temporary relief to needy residents of the state, or the county, township, or city. In the event any person becomes chargeable to a township in which he had not gained legal residence, it was the duty of the overseers, later the township trustees, to remove him to the township where he was legally settled. With slight alterations, the principles of this system continued until the twentieth century.[21]

Since 1908 the commissioners have been authorized to issue warrants for tax relief of the blind in sums varying from $100 to $400 per year.[22]

---

19. *Laws of Ohio,* III, 272.
20. G. C. Sec. 2419-1.
21. For a study of the administration of relief in Ohio prior to 1934 see Aileen Elizabeth Kennedy, *The Law and Its Administration* (Sophonisba P. Breckinridge, ed., *Social Service Monographs*, No. 22, University of Chicago Press, Chicago, 1934).
22. See p. [not given].

When the blind relief commission was abolished in 1913 its powers and duties were transferred to the county commissioners who were authorized, on evidence furnished by a registered physician or surgeon that the applicant for blind relief might have such disability benefitted or removed by medical or surgical treatment, and with the written consent of the patient, to expend all or part of a year's relief allowance for this purpose.[23]

Six years later, in 1919, this allowance for blind relief was raised to $200 per person per annum, and the county commissioners were authorized to appoint such clerks as they might deem necessary to investigate applications and to serve at the pleasure of the county commissioners.[24]

In 1927 the maximum benefit for blind relief was increased to $400 per person per annum, but in the event of both a husband and wife being blind and both receiving relief, the total maximum benefit for the two was fixed at $600 per annum.[25]

In April 1936 the state accepted the provisions of the Federal Social Security Act approved August 14, 1935, providing federal grants for state aid to the blind, and the legislature designated the Ohio commission for the blind the administration agency in the state, and the county commissioners were made the administration agency in the county. The county commissioners were directed to appropriate from the general fund of the county a sum sufficient when supplemented by federal and state grants to provide for the blind a substance "compatible with decency and health" and if they failed to make such appropriations the attorney general was directed to bring *mandamus* proceedings against them.

_____

23. *Laws of Ohio,* CIII, 60.
24. *Ibid.,* CVIII, pt. i, 421-422.
25. *Ibid.,* CXII, 109.

The act of 1936 provides that those entitled to blind relief are persons not less than eighteen nor more than sixty-five years old, who have lost their sight while residents of the state, and who have resided in the state for a period of five years in the nine years immediately preceding application, the last year of which period shall have been continuous. Applications for blind relief are filed with the county commissioners who are required by statute to list such claims in their order of application in books kept for that purpose. At least ten years prior to action on a claim the applicant files a duly certified statement, including a certificate from a registered physician "skilled in diseases of the eye" stating to what extent the applicant's vision is impaired, and written evidence from two reputable citizens that they know the applicant to be blind and that "he has the qualifications to entitle him to the relief asked." The county commissioners may allow the examining physician a fee not to exceed $5, and may employ an additional physician to examine the applicant. If after such inquiry the county commissioners are satisfied that the applicant is entitled to relief, they are directed by statute to issue an order for such sum as the board finds necessary, not to exceed the maximum fixed in 1927, such sum to be paid monthly from the fund created for that purpose. The ruling of 1913 concerning medical and surgical treatment for applicants remains in effect. Persons whose applications are denied by the county commissioners may appeal to the state commission for the blind which on its own motion may revise any decision of the county commissioners. Both the Ohio commission for the blind and the county commissioners have power to issue subpoenas, compel presentation of papers and examine witnesses.

At least once a year, oftener if directed by the Ohio State Commission for the Blind, the county commissioners must examine the qualifications, disabilities, and needs of all persons on the list of the blind, and may increase or decrease the amount of relief according to the budgetary requirements within the limits fixed by law.

If the county commissioners remove a name from the list of the blind they are required to notify the county auditor and the Ohio State Commission for the Blind as to their actions.[26]

The commissioners of Medina County allowed $600 in the year 1940 for the relief of the needy blind.[27] Benefits were granted to three clients who received from $15 to $30 monthly, according to their needs, which were determined by the investigator appointed by the commissioners.

In addition to furnishing financial aid to the civilian population the commissioners were authorized, in 1886, to levy a tax for the relief of indigent Union soldiers, sailors, or marines of the Civil War, only if such veterans were deceased, for their dependents.[28] In 1919 the provisions of the original act were amended to include all indigent veterans of the World War.[29] The commissioners were authorized also, in 1884, to defray the funeral expenses of any honorably discharged soldier, sailor, or marine who died indigent. Ten years later the provisions of the act were extended to include the mother, wife, or widow of any soldier, sailor, or marine, and war nurses.[30]

The humanitarian duty of caring for the county's dependent and neglected children was delegated to the county commissioners. Since 1866 they have been authorized to establish and maintain children's homes. At the beginning of the present century, when the treatment of children was undergoing a remarkable change, they were authorized to place dependent and neglected children in private homes or institutions where they would receive food, clothing, and medical and dental treatment.[31] The development of the juvenile court system added new responsibilities.

26. *Laws of Ohio,* CXVI, pt. ii, 195-200.
27. Commissioners' Journal. XVII [1936-1941], 509.
28. *Laws of Ohio,* LXXXIII, 232.
29. *Ibid.,* CVIII, pt. i, 633.
30. *Ibid.,* XC, 177
31. *Ibid.,*CIX, 533.

In order to segregate completely juvenile offenders from adults being tried in the regular criminal courts, the commissioners were authorized to provide a separate building, to be known as the "juvenile court."[32]

The unprecedented depression in the third decade of the 20th century proved the antiquated, un-centralized system of relief administration entirely inadequate. As a result of the abnormal unemployment conditions and the crop failures following the drought of 1930, many local subdivisions of the county charged by law to administer support and medical relief to the indigent were unable to discharge their obligations. Accordingly, in 1931, the legislature passed an emergency act authorizing the county, township, and municipal taxing authorities to borrow money and issue bonds for poor relief, providing the state tax commission found that no other funds were available.[33]

During the early months of 1932, the governor, aware of the widespread suffering in the state, called the legislature into special session.[34] At this session the legislature authorized him to appoint a state relief commission composed of five members to study the relief situation. This commission was permitted to cooperate with the national, state, or local relief commission, which, in many counties, had been established and was already functioning. Since the county and township treasuries were depleted, because of the excessive drain caused by the mounting relief load and the steady decline of tax collections, the legislature authorized an excise tax on utilities, for the years 1932-1937, to be used for relief purposes. This state tax was to be allocated to the counties on the basis of population, the tax duplicate, and the value of the utilities property in the county as of 1930. The funds allocated to each county under this act were to be credited to the "county poor relief excise fund."[35]

---

32. *Ibid.,* CXIII, 470.
33. *Ibid.,* XCIV, 11-12
34. See message of the governor to the eighty-ninth general assembly in *Laws of Ohio*, CXIV, pt. ii, 6-8.
35. *Laws of Ohio*, CXIV, pt. ii, 19-20.

The county commissioners were authorized to borrow money for emergency relief and evidence such indebtedness by the issuance of negotiable bonds and notes. Upon submission of such resolution to the state tax commission, the commission was directed to estimate the amount which would probably be allocated to the county from the public utility excise taxes and was directed to calculate the total amount of bonds, the principal and interest on which might be paid out of such estimated allocation. The date of maximum maturity of such bonds was to be on or before March 15, 1938. If, in the year 1932, additional funds were needed for poor relief, the county commissioners were authorized, after the state commission found that no other funds were available, to issue additional bonds in an amount not exceeding one tenth of one percent of the general tax list and duplicate of the county. The maturity date of such additional bonds was to be on or before September 15, 1940.[36]

The proceeds of the sale of such bonds were to be placed in a special fund, denominated the "emergency relief fund." No expenditures were to be made from this fund except in accordance with the method and under the uniform regulations prescribed by the state relief commission, and in no case after December 31, 1933. The county commissioners were authorized to distribute, prior to the first of March 1933, portions of the fund to the political subdivisions of the county, according to their needs for poor relief determined by the county and set forth in such an approved budget. The money distributed to the subdivisions was to be expended to them for poor relief, including the renting of lands and the purchase of seeds for gardening by the unemployed.[37] County poor relief included mothers' pensions, soldiers' relief, temporary assistance to nonresidents, maintenance of a county and a children's home, and work and direct relief. In the townships and municipalities relief was interpreted to be the support of the poor

---

36. *Ibid.*, CXIV, pt. ii, 18-21.
37. *Ibid.*, CXIV, pt. ii, 21-22.

and the burial of persons who died indigent. Each subdivision administering funds under the act was expected to require labor in exchange for relief given to any family in which there resided an able-bodied wage earner.[38]

In the same year the county commissioners were designated as a board to administer the state law providing aid for the aged.[39] In February 1933, the tenure of the state relief commission was extended to March 1, 1935.[40] In the same year the legislature levied an additional stamp tax on the sale of bottled and bulk beer, malt, cosmetics, and toilet preparations to furnish additional funds for emergency relief.[41] The state treasurer was authorized to appoint the county treasurer as his deputy for the purpose of selling tax stamps to be affixed to such articles.[42]

The commissioner's duties regarding poor relief were further extended in 1935. They were authorized to provide non-institutional support, care, assistance, or relief for the indigent in the county.[43] In 1935, the state relief commission ceased to exist by reason of the terms of the act creating it. The legislature, however, passed a measure designed to correlate all emergency poor relief work, activities, and administration with the Federal Emergency Relief Administration which is authorized to administer and direct the distribution and expenditures of federal funds for relief in the state. Accordingly, all powers previously vested in the state relief commission were transferred to the county commissioners, functions, which, under the act, were delegated to the county commissioners. This representative, however, was subjected to such terms and conditions in respect to auditing, examinations, and reports as were directed by the county commissioners and such federal agency.

38. *Ibid.*, CXIV, pt. ii, 17.
39. *Ibid.*, CXV, pt. ii, 431-439.
40. *Ibid.*, CXV, 22.
41. *Laws of Ohio*, CXV, 642, 649; CXV, pt. ii, 5, 22, 83, 177 200, 247, 256.
42. *Ibid.*, CXV, 642.
43. *Ibid.*, CXVI, 571.

The county commissioners were directed to conduct relief activities outside limits of municipal corporations through the township trustees, insofar as practicable, and were to be guided by the recommendations of the township trustees with respect to relieve need in such political subdivisions. Again, as in 1932, the commissioners were authorized, if the state tax commission found that no other means existed to provide funds, to borrow money and issue bonds in the year 1935 to 1936. The maximum maturity date of such bonds as to be on or before March 1, 1944.[45] Other bonds, in addition to those secured by the county's share of the excise tax, might be issued not to exceed one fifth of 1 percent of the general tax list of the county.[46] If the county was unable to issue bonds by reason of the limitation imposed by the constitution,[47] the taxing authority of such subdivision was authorized to submit the question of issuing bonds to the electorate either at a general or special election.[48]

The year 1936 saw the re-creation the state relief commission, consisting of four members appointed by the governor, this body was authorized to serve until January 31, 1937. Again, as in 1932, the commission was directed to study problems of relief, to receive advice from federal, state, and local governmental departments, to cooperate with agencies of the national and local governments and private agencies engaged in administration or financial support of direct or indirect relief, to administer moneys appropriated to the commission for poor relief, to examine the conduct and local governmental agencies in administering relief, and to order the distribution and payment of moneys from state treasury.

---

44. *Ibid.,* The county commissioners recommended to the State Relief Commission in November 1933, the appointment of Gordon Phillips as first director of emergency relief for Medina County.
45. *Laws of Ohio,* CXVI, 571.
46. *Ibid.,* CXVI, 575.
47. *Ohio Const., 1851,* Art. XII, sec. 2.
48. *Laws of Ohio,* CXVI, 578.

The county commissioners were authorized to administer all advances by the state to the relief commission and were directed to operate through duly authorized agencies townships, municipalities, and school districts. Within the appropriations made by the commissioners and subject to the rules and regulations of the state relief commission, the commissioners were instructed to appoint assistants and such other employees as were necessary.[49]

The county commissioners, like the state relief commission, were directed to cooperate with all agencies of the federal, state, and county governments, and with private agencies which were engaged in administering relief or financial support to the needy. It was made the duty of all county, township, and municipal governments administering relief or assistance to dependents to report to the county commissioners, at their request, the names and addresses of all persons to whom they were providing aid and the amount and character of aid given.[50]

The principle of issuing bonds and securing them by the county's share of the utility taxes was continued. Moreover, there was appropriated to the state relief commission the general revenue fund the sum of $3,000,000 which was designated as the "state relief rotary fund." The various counties of the state which had not issued bonds and were now not authorized to do so without the consent of the people, were empowered to obtain an advance from state relief rotary fund in an amount equal to that of the bonds which were permitted to be issued under the provision of this act. If the county failed to repay the total of all advances and interest at two percent before June 1936, the state relief commission was directed to refuse to make further allocations or distributions to the county.[51]

---

49. *Laws of Ohio*, CXVI, pt. ii, 133-148.
50. *Ibid.,* CXVI, pt. ii, 133-148, 240.
51. *Ibid.*, CXVI, 133-148.

In the early months of 1937 the legislature authorized the state relief commission to serve until April 1937. Under this act the county commissioners are authorized to give temporary support and medical relief to nonresidents and to all needy persons possessing legal residence in the county. Funds may be expended for both direct and work relief. However, all persons on relief able and competent to perform labor who refuse to accept private employment under prevailing conditions and prevailing wages, may be dropped from the relief rolls. This ruling does not apply, however, to areas where strikes are prevalent. On the other hand, any person receiving relief in the county is permitted to engage in any business without losing his release status. During the period of such employment, he is required to forfeit the pro rata amount of relief received by him, and is eligible to his former relief status upon the conclusion of such employment.

The county commissioners are required to file with the state relief commission a budget and a detailed statement and plan showing how the funds to be received are to be expended, the purpose for which they are to be used, the nature and kind of work to be carried on, and the number of persons to be aided by such relief. Besides this, the county commissioners must file a complete analysis of their proposed expenditures, together with an estimate of all available resources, including the unencumbered proceeds of any bonds heretofore issued and the amount of bonds which the county commissioners have a right to issue without a vote of the people on the approval of the state commission of Ohio as authorized in 1935.

Of the funds allocated to the county by the state relief commission for direct relief, tax commissioners may, when they believe that the cost of administration may be reduced, reallocate the funds on a percentage basis of relief requirements of the various subdivisions.[52]

The emergency relief measures, passed during the period 1932-1937, gave the counties for the first time a centralized relief administration. All records of this work are located in the relief administration office.

The first relief director of Medina County was appointed by the commissioners in November 1933,[53] when the state relief commission ceased to exist, and the powers previously vested in the state relief commission were transferred, to the commissioners. During the years of the depression two bond issues totally only $45,000 were issued against the excise tax expectancy,[54] the county being easily able to handle its relief load without resorting to the other extraordinary expedience permitted by depression legislation. In the year 1940, the commissioners expended $14,934 for direct relief,[55] maintaining an average monthly role of 110 families.[56]

In addition to other forms of relief the county commissioners provide funds for aid to dependent children.[57] They are required to include in the annual tax budget and amount not less than that computed to yield a levy of 15 one-hundredths of one mill on each dollar of the general tax list of the county. Funds are also provided by the federal and state government. If the commissioners fail to comply with the provisions of the act relative to appropriations, the state department of public welfare is directed to institute *mandamus* proceedings against them.[58]

While control over relief work has become one of the most important phases of the commissioners' work, particularly in recent years, many other responsibilities have been assigned to them. The commissioners, by authority conferred upon them to construct public buildings, were given duties regarding educational advancement. Since 1871, they have been authorized to accept bequests for the construction of county libraries, and since 1923, to issue bonds, after receiving the approval of the voters, for the construction of libraries, or to contract with existing libraries for the use of the people in the county.[59]

---

54. Bond Register, 1932-1937, *see* entry 319.
55. Relief Encumbrance Register, 1940, *see* entry 27.
56. *Ibid.*
57. *See* p. [not given].
58. G. C. secs. 1359-31 to 1359-45; *Laws of Ohio*, CXVI, pt. ii, 188-195.
59. G. C. secs. 2454, 2455; *Laws of Ohio*, CX, 242.

More over, during the same period they were authorized to provide and maintain civic centers in the county and to employ an expert director to supervise and administer them.[60]

Other duties not closely related to the original ones have been added from decade to decade. For example, in 1850 the commissioners were authorized to subscribe for one leading newspaper of each political party in the county and cause them to be bound and deposited with the county auditor as public archives.[61] An amendment to the original act, passed in 1923, provided for the preservation of such newspapers for a period of 10 years, after which they may be removed to the Ohio State Archaeological and Historical Society library.[62] They have been authorized also to promote historical research by appropriating annually a sum not to exceed $100 to defray the expenses of compiling and publishing historical data for historical societies not incorporated for profit.[63]

During the early years of the twentieth century the commissioners were given the duty of providing facilities for county sanitation, which, in previous years had been sadly neglected. In 1917 they were authorized to lay out, establish, and maintain one or more sewer districts within the county. Since 1917 no sewer or sewage treatment works may be constructed outside of any incorporated municipality by any person, persons, firms, or corporations until the plans have been approved by the commissioners.[64]

---

60. G. C. sec. 2457-4.
61. *Laws of Ohio*, XLVIII, 65.
62. *Ibid.*, CX, 4.
63. G. C. sec. 2457-1.
64. G. C. sec. 6602-1; *Laws of Ohio*, CVII, 440.

Then, too, during the same period the commissioners were authorized to provide facilities for the treatment of tuberculosis. In 1908 they were authorized to establish a county tuberculosis hospital and in 1909 to co-operate with the commissioners of other counties for the establishment of a district tuberculosis hospital.[65] Medina County maintains no tuberculosis hospital. Patients are sent to the Edwin Shaw Sanatorium, Akron, Ohio; the Ohio State Hospital for Tuberculosis, Mt. Vernon, Ohio; the Avalon Sanatorium, Mt. Vernon, Ohio; and the Oak Ridge Sanatorium, Green Springs, Ohio. The county pays the maintenance costs of all indigent patients sent to the institutions. Since 1917, the commissioners have been authorized to establish tuberculosis dispensaries and provide by tax levies the necessary funds for their establishment and maintenance.[66]

Finally the county commissioners have acted in a supervisory capacity over other county officials. Since 1850 they have been authorized to compare the annual reports and statements made to them by the prosecuting attorney, the clerk of courts, the sheriff, and the treasurer; take measures to rectify errors, correct discrepancies; and record in their journal the results of such examinations. In 1896, the commissioners were given their present duty of visiting hospitals, detention homes, private asylums, and any other institutions exercising a reformatory or correctional influence over individuals, and reporting on the sanitary conditions and the treatment of inmates.[67] These reports are required to be filed with the county prosecuting attorney and kept open to the inspection and examination of the public.

------

65. *Laws of Ohio*, XCIX, 62; C, 87.
66. G. C. secs. 3148-1, 3153-4, 3153-5.
67. *Laws of Ohio,* CII, 212.

The board of county commissioners offers a typical example of an office, which, designed primarily for an Agricultural Society, has expanded to meet the needs and requirements of modern society. At present the commissioners are elected for a four-year term.[68]

Medina County, being primarily agricultural, has always been extremely conservative in its management. All bonds having so far been paid when due, no refunding of issues has ever been necessary. The county has never exceeded the 10 mill limit.

By the nature of its people and their needs, Medina County tends toward a less complex county government than most. It has no county water supply or sewer system, no county library, no planning commission, and no tuberculosis sanatorium. The county has never built a workhouse, but boards such prisoners in the county jail and occasionally in the workhouse at Dayton, Ohio.[69]

Much of the work of road maintenance and repair is now delegated to the engineer, the responsibility for its performance still rests with the commissioners, who have in their charge the $536 mi of highway, about 400 bridges and about 3,000 culverts of Medina County.[70] Here, as everywhere, upkeep rather than new construction constitutes by far the great part of the work.

---

68. *Ibid.,* CVIII, pt. ii, 1300.
69. Record, Common Pleas, 1940, *see* entry 127.
70. Contract Record [Bridges and Culverts], 1940, *see* entry 465.

Proceedings

1. COMMISSIONERS' JOURNAL
1824—. 18 vols. (1-8). Title varies: Commissioners' Record, 1824-1882, 2 vols.

Record of minutes and proceedings of the board of county commissioners showing date of meeting, receipt of all petitions, including petitions to establish, alter, vacate, or improve roads, bridges, and ditches, actions and orders of the board, purchase of all county property, building and repair of all county buildings, copies of all resolutions passed by the board, appropriations for funds for county offices, itemized accounts of bills approved for payment with date of approval, record of county tax levies, approval of tax rates for county bonds, bids for county funds, receipt of monthly or annual reports of county officials, and all business transactions of Medina County; also includes establishing amounts of yearly wolf bounties, 1818-1830; relief for needy upon application of township trustees, 1818-1854; appointments of superintendent and matron of county home, and annual semi annual reports of county home, 1854—; sheep claims and approval of payment, 1882—; blind relief applications and grants,1900—; proceedings relating to agricultural society,1845—; inspection of and report of condition of county jail,1818-1913; also includes County Officers' Report of Fees and Salaries, 1850-1928, entry 4 and Burial Record of Indigent Soldiers, 1928—. The first commissioners' journal, 1818-1823 was stolen in December 1823, therefore there are no previous records of the journal. Arranged chronologically by dates of meetings. 1824-1850, no index. For separate index, 1851-1914, see entry 2. Self-contained index in each volume1914—, Showing name or subject, date of entry, bills, purpose, and page number. 1824-1922, Handwritten;1923—, Handwritten and typed, some on printed forms. 475 pages. 18 x 13 x 3. 13 volumes, 1824-1922, North storeroom; 5 volumes, 1923— Commissioners' office.

2. GENERAL INDEX [To Commissioners' Journal]
   1851-1914. 6 vols.
Index to Commissioners' Journal, entry 1, showing date of meeting, volume and pages numbers of journal, name of individual or firm, bills allowed, road and ditch contracts, and miscellaneous. Volumes five and six, 1904-1914, show index to proceedings of commissioners' meetings. Arranged alphabetically by names of individuals or firms and chronologically thereunder by dates of meetings. Handwritten on printed forms. Average 475 pages. 18 x 13 x 3. North storeroom.

3. RECORD, MEDINA COUNTY HOME
   1854—. 5 vols. (1-5) Title varies: Directors' Minutes, Medina County Infirmary, 1854-1895, 1 vol.; Record, Medina County Infirmary, 1895-1916, 2 vols.
Record of minutes of the meetings of county infirmary directors, 1854-1913 and of the county commissioners (acting as the board of directors), 1913—, showing date of meeting, names of members present, bills passed for payment, record of all resolutions, sale of stock, crops, expenditures and receipts, and bids on food; also includes the annual and semiannual reports of infirmary directors to county commissioners, showing date of report, present number of inmates registered in institution according to last report, births, deaths, and number discharged since last report, itemized account of receipts and expenditures for period of report, detailed inventory of county property, and date of filing. Arranged chronologically by dates of meetings. Indexed alphabetically by subjects. Handwritten. Average 300 pages. 16 x 11 x 2.5. 1 volume 1854-1895, 2 volumes, 1896-1916, North storeroom; 2 volumes, 1917—, Commissioners' office.

4. COUNTY OFFICERS' REPORT OF FEES AND SALARIES
   1928—. 1 file box. 1850-1928 in Commissioners' Journal, entry 1.
Certified annual statement to county commissioners by county

officers, of salaries paid by each office and fees collected, showing name of office, amount of annual salary, annual amount of fees, sworn statement by and signature of officer making report, date of filing, and signature of auditor; auditor's annual statement, showing total salaries of officials and total fees earned by all offices; prosecuting attorney's annual statement, showing traveling expenses, date of trip, to what place, regarding what matter, and amount; clerk of courts' statement, showing fines assessed in common pleas court, name of defendant, amount assessed, fines collected, and amount paid into treasury; coroner's statement, showing name and address of deceased, date, place, and cause of death, whether accidental, natural, or by violence, amount of fees, and totals. Arranged chronologically by dates filed. No index. Handwritten and typed, some on printed forms. 10 x 4.5 x 14.5. Auditor's office.

5. WEEKLY REPORT OF DOG WARDEN
1927—. 1 file box.

Weekly report of dog warden to county commissioners of all dogs seized and impounded, redeemed, or destroyed, showing date of report, name and address of owner or harborer of dog (if known), breed and description of dog, whether owned or strayed, number of days harbored, date seized, date disposed of, whether redeemed or destroyed, funds collected, and date paid into treasury, file number, date filed, date week ending, and signature of clerk of board of commissioners. Arranged numerically by file numbers. No index. Handwritten on printed forms. 10 x 4.5 x 14.5. Auditor's office.

Public Improvements

Roads

6. JOURNAL [Road District #1]
1903—. 2 vols.

Record of the minutes of meetings of the township trustees of

Medina County organized into a board of road commissioners, showing date of meeting, members present, and record of all transactions, including letting of contract, purchase of materials, road repairing, and issuance of bonds; also includes Ditch Record [Petitions], 1925—, entry 461. Arranged chronologically by dates of meetings. Indexed alphabetically by subjects. 1903-1911, handwritten on printed forms; 1912—, handwritten. Average 450 pages. 18 x 13 x 3. 1 volume, 1903-1911, North storeroom. 1 volume, 1912—, Auditor's main office

7. RECORD OF ROAD LEGISLATION
1920—. 3 vols. (1-3)

A copy of section 2406, General Code of Ohio, including all legislation passed concerning road improvements, all successful bidders on road improvements and their bids, notices of road improvements, proof of publication, and sworn statement, showing name of property owner, date of entry, road identification, section and road numbers, compensation, damages, costs and expenses of said improvements, survey plans, estimates, inspections and examinations in detail, all levies, resolutions concerning sinking funds and bond issues, and signature of publisher. Arranged chronologically by dates entered. Indexed alphabetically by names of property owners showing road and section numbers. Typed. Average 300 pages. 18.5 x 12 x 2.5. Commissioners' office.

8. INTER-COUNTY HIGHWAY RECORD, ROAD SECTION, AND NUMBER
1919—. 1 bundle.

County commissioners' resolutions and agreements covering construction cost of inter-county roads, showing state taking charge of improving certain roads, road section and number, estimates, preliminary surveys, plans, contracts, progress reports, detours, division of responsibility between county and state as to maintenance, cost borne by abutting property owners, purchase of road building materials and road maintenance machinery, and date of filing. Arranged numerically by road numbers. No index. Typed. 15 x 9 x 3. North storeroom.

9. EXPENSE RECORD OF LEROY FREE PIKE OR WESTFIELD FREE TURNPIKE
1882-1885. 4 vols.

Record of daily expense of repairing and improving roads, time book for men, and wages paid each day; also includes minutes of meetings of county commissioners pertaining to roads and the issuance of road bonds, showing date of meeting, names of those present, and business transacted. Condition of record poor. Arranged chronologically by dates of meetings. No index. Handwritten on printed forms. Average 100 pages. 7 x 12 x .5. North storeroom.

10. SEWER AND WATER DISTRICT RECORD, CHIPPEWA LAKE
1925. 1 vol. (1). 1926— in Special Assessments, entry 252.

Record of water contracts of Chippewa Lake, showing resolutions, cost of labor, samples of water test, name of district, names of property owners, description of property, footage, acreage, and assessments. Arranged alphabetically by names of districts and alphabetically thereunder by names of property owners. No index. Typed on printed forms. 140 pages. 18.5 x 12 x 1. Commissioners' office.

Institutions and Relief

11. BURIAL RECORD OF INDIGENT SOLDIERS
1888-1928. 3 vols. (1-3). 1928— in Commissioners' Journal, entry 1.

Report of burial commission to the county commissioners on the burial of indigent soldiers, sailors, and marines, showing name of decedent, rank, company regiment or vessel, town or township, date and cause of death, itemized statement of burial expenses, where buried, and date approved by county commissioners. Arranged alphabetically by names of decedents. Indexed alphabetically by names of soldiers, sailors, or marines. Handwritten. Average 280 pages. 10.5 x 8 x 1.5. North storeroom.

Financial Records

12. MONTHLY FINANCIAL STATEMENTS (Auditor)
1904—. 411 sheets.
Original monthly financial statements from the county auditor to the county commissioners, showing receipts from all sources to each fund, expenditures authorized by voucher or warrant against each fund, credit balance to each fund at beginning of report period, credit balance to each fund on date of statement, record of transfer of funds, date of filing and signatures of auditor and commissioners. Arranged chronologically by dates of statements. No index. Typed on printed forms. 16 x 10.5 391 sheets. 1904-1937, North storeroom; 20 sheets, 1938—, Commissioners' office.

13. CLASSIFICATION BLOTTER
1905-1908. 4 vols. Discontinued.
Classification of expenditures of county funds from which county commissioners make their annual report, showing name of fund, name of payee, order number, services rendered, amount and classification as to material, labor, fees, debt payment, interest, salaries, and sundries. Arranged alphabetically by names of funds. No index. Handwritten on printed forms. Average 40 pages. 17.5 x 13 x .5. North storeroom.

Claims

14. ANIMAL CLAIMS
1927—. 1 file box.
Claims presented to county commissioners by owners of livestock injured or killed by dogs, showing name of township, name and address of owner, type of livestock, grade, quality, and value,

whether injured or killed, amount and nature of injury, and net amount claimed, name and address of owner of dog (if known), oath and signature of affiant, signatures of witnesses, township trustees fees, dog warden's statement of investigation, and seal of notary. No systematic arrangement. No index. Handwritten on printed forms. 10 x 4.5 x 14.5. Auditor's office.

Miscellaneous

15. COMMISSIONERS ANNUAL INVENTORY OF COUNTY PROPERTY
1934—. 100 sheets.
Original lists from all county departments to the county commissioners of all county property in custody of each office, showing date of inventory, name of office, articles, quantity of each, notes, remarks, and signature of person preparing lists. Arranged chronologically by dates of inventory. No index. Handwritten and typed. Sizes vary. Commissioners' office.

16. REQUISITIONS
1932—. 2 file boxes
Requisitions for supplies from the various department heads, submitted to the county commissioners for approval, showing date filed, name of department, type and amount of supplies needed, and remarks. Arranged chronologically by dates filed. No index. Typed on printed forms. 10 x 14 x 25. Auditor's main office.

Aid for the Blind

17. BLIND RELIEF COMMISSION
1908-1927. 1 vol. (1).
Record of blind relief commission, 1908-1914, and of county commissioners on blind relief matters, 1914-1927, showing list of claims, name and address of claimant, date of action on claim, annual amount awarded, and date order issued to auditor; also includes minutes of blind relief commission's meetings, showing

date of meeting, resolutions for and adoption of individual grants, and request for the annual appropriation. Arranged chronologically by dates of meetings and chronologically thereunder by dates of claims. Indexed alphabetically by names of claimants. Handwritten on printed forms. 250 pages. 14 x 8 x 11. North storeroom.

18. BLIND RELIEF
1908-1936. 1 file box.
Original applications to county commissioners for relief of needy blind, showing date of filing, name and sex of applicant, length of residence in the state of Ohio, affidavits stating applicants by reason of loss of eyesight are unable to support themselves and have insufficient means for maintenance; also record of written evidence of blindness, showing date of record, name and sex of applicant, local address, supporting testimony of competent witnesses, and copy of medical certificate. Arranged alphabetically by names of applicants. No index. Handwritten on printed forms. 10 x 4.5 x 13.5. Auditor's office.

19. [CASE RECORDS]
1936— in Miscellaneous File, entry 213.
Case records of blind relief applicants, showing name of applicant, date of application, family history, examining physician's report on condition of eyes, action taken, grants made, rejections, withdrawals, and correspondence pertaining to case. Arranged alphabetically by names of applicants. No index. Handwritten on printed forms. 85 x 11.

20. AID TO THE BLIND, UNDER SOCIAL SECURITY ACT
1936—. 1 file box
Complete case history of applications for blind aid made out in the blind relief office, including physicians' certificates as to condition of applicant's eyes, showing name, address, age, and sex of applicant, action taken, grants, rejections, denials, withdrawals, and change of status. Arranged alphabetically by names of

applicants. No index. Handwritten on printed forms. 10 x 4.5 x 13.5. Aid to dependent children office. 2nd floor.

21. AID TO THE BLIND [Active Cases]
1936—. 7 folders.
Record of active cases, showing amount of grant, case history, physician's report, social data card, county issuance of warrant to auditor, county monthly statistical report, detailed report on medical care and hospitalization, verification of age, name and address of applicant, date of application, date approved, rejected, or deferred, name of examining physician, personal history of applicant, educational background, applicant's employment record, monthly budget, and income. Arranged alphabetically by names of applicants. No index. Typed on printed forms. 8.5 x 11. Aid to dependent children office., 2nd floor.

22. AID TO THE BLIND [Closed Cases]
1936—. 1 file box.
Record of closed cases, showing amount of grant, case history, physician's report, social data card, county issuance of warrant to auditor county monthly statistical report, detailed report on medical care and hospitalization, verification of age, name and address of applicant, date of application, date approved, rejected, or deferred, name of examining physician, personal history of applicant, education background, applicant's employment record, monthly budget, and income. Arranged alphabetically by names of applicants. No index. Typed on printed forms. 8.5 x 11. Aid to dependent children office., 2nd floor.

Relief Administration
(See also entry 1)

23. ACTIVE CASE RECORDS
1934—. 4 file boxes.
Complete record of active cases, showing name and address of client, case number, marital status, age, nativity, number of

dependents, complete family history, investigator's report on the application, and itemized record of aid furnished. Arranged alphabetically by names of clients. No index. Handwritten and typed, some on printed forms. 11.5 x 16 x 28. Relief office, basement.

24. CASE RECORDS, CLOSED
1934—. 4 file boxes.
Complete record of closed cases, showing name and address of client, case number, marital status, age, nativity, race, sex, number of dependents, investigator's report on the application, itemized record of aid furnished, and reason for refusal to grant aid. Arranged alphabetically by names of clients. No index. Handwritten and typed, some on printed files. 11.5 x 16 x 28. Relief office, basement.

25. CCC RECORDS
1934—. 3 file boxes
Case records of Civilian Conservation Corps enrollees including applications, showing date of application, name, age, and address of applicant, number and names of dependents, name of proposed allottee, medical certificate, investigator's report on application, and enrollment certificate. All records of each case in folder. Arranged alphabetically by names of applicants. No index. Typed on printed forms. 6 x 8.5 x 12. Relief office, basement.

26. WPA CERTIFICATIONS
1935—. 3 file boxes
Certification record of persons for Work Projects Administration projects in Medina County, showing name and address of person certified, age, nativity, sex, race, educational background, number of dependents, date of certification, certification number, identification number, and date of first work assignment (if any). Arranged alphabetically by names of persons certified and chronologically thereunder by dates of certifications. No index.

Handwritten on printed forms. 6 x 8.5 x 12. Relief office, basement.

27. [RELIEF ENCUMBRANCE REGISTER]
1936—. 2 vols.

Record of encumbrances and vouchers; encumbrances, showing date of entry, amounts for food, fuel, clothing, shelter, medical care, and public utilities; vouchers, showing date of voucher, amount of encumbrance vouchered for payment, administration expense, poor relief expense, and totals; also includes amounts paid for fuel, food, clothing, shelter, medical care, and public utilities. Arranged chronologically by dates entered. No index. Handwritten on printed forms. Average 300 pages. 14 x 16 x 2.5. Relief office, basement.

The office of county recorder, although not unknown as an early English institution for the registration of land titles, developed in colonial America, where, because of the mobility of the restless pioneers, changes in land titles were frequent and some system was needed to protect purchasers against previous encumbrances. Public land registers, established in most of the colonies during the colonial period and continued by the states following independence, served as a model of land registration for the territory of which the present state of Ohio was then a part. Thus the office county recorder was established by an act of the Northwest Territory, effective August 1, 1795. This act, adopted from the Pennsylvania Code, provided for the appointment by the governor of a recorder in each county which principal duty was the recording of deeds.[1]

When Ohio entered the Union in 1803, no constitutional provision was made for the continuance of the office, but the legislature during its first session passed an act providing for a recorder in each county to be appointed by the judge of the court of common pleas for a seven-year term.[2] The recorder continued to be an appointive officer until 1829, when, by an act of the legislature, the office became elective for a three-year term.[3] The tenure of the office remained at three years until the constitutional amendment of November 7, 1905, which provided for the election of all county officers in the even-numbered years.[4] The term of office was fixed at two years, and so continued until the amendment of 1933, which extended the tenure of the incumbent until January 1937, at which time the recorder, elected at the regular election in November 1936, began to serve a four-year term.[5]

---

1. Theodore Calvin Pease, comp., *The laws of the Northwest Territory, 1788-1800* (Illinois State Bar Association *Law Series,* Springfield, 1925, I), 197-199.
2. *Laws of Ohio,* I, 136.
3. *Ibid.,* XXVII, 65.
4. *Ohio Const. 1851* (Amendment, 1905), Art. XVII, secs. 1, 2; *Laws of Ohio,* XCVIII, 271.
5. *Laws of Ohio,* CXV, 191.

The first county recorder was directed by statute to record "all deeds, mortgages and conveyances of land and tenements," lying within his county, and also all instruments of writings required by law to be recorded.[6] In 1805 he was directed to record all plats and maps of newly laid-out villages.[7] In 1835 he was permitted, when authorized by the county commissioners, to transcribe from the records, other counties all deeds, mortgages, and other instruments of writing for the sale or conveyance of land, tenements, or hereditaments affecting land titles in his county.[8]

Since the establishment of the office many duties besides those of recording land titles have been added. The present practice of recording powers of attorney and its beginning in 1818.[9] Although the mechanics of Cincinnati were authorized to file mechanics' liens with the recorder as early as 1823, it was not until 1843 that the privilege was extended to the laborers of Hancock County. Successive acts in 1865, 1872, 1881, 1884, 1888, 1904, and 1923 added new duties to the office in the recording of soldiers' discharges,[11] copies of certificates of compliance authorizing insurance companies not incorporated under the laws of Ohio to transact business in the state, and certified copies of renewal as granted by such companies to their agents,[12] limited partnership agreements,[13] stallion keepers' liens,[14] oil and gas leases,[15] partition fence records,[16] and federal tax liens.[17]

---

6. Ibid., I, 137.
7. *Ibid.,* III, 213-215.
8. *Ibid.,* XXXIII, 8; XXXV, 10-11.
9. *Laws of Ohio,* XVI, 155-156.
10. *Ibid.,* XXI, 8-10; XLI, 66.
11. *Ibid.,* LXII, 59.
12. *Ibid.,* LXIX, 32, 148; XCVII, 405.
13. *Ibid.,* LXXVIII, 248.
14. *Ibid.,* LXXXI, 43.
15. *Ibid.,* LXXXV, 179.
16. *Ibid.,* XCVII, 140.
17. *Ibid.,* CX, 252.

The recording of chattel mortgages and conditional sales began in 1846. Such instruments were to be deposited with the township clerk where the mortgagor was a resident. In all townships, however, in which the recorder maintained his office such instruments were to be deposited with him.[18] Since 1906 chattel mortgages have been filed with the county recorder exclusively.[19] It is provided that in order to be valid against subsequent mortgages, the chattel mortgage must first be deposited with the county recorder of the county where the mortgagor resides at the time of its execution, and to retain its validity the mortgage must be renewed every three years.[20] In 1936 the legislature passed an act authorizing the recorder to destroy such instruments six years after the time of refiling has expired.[21]

An important extension of the method of recording land titles known as the "Torrens System," was provided by an act of the general assembly in 1896.[22] In 1897 this act was declared unconstitutional by the supreme court of Ohio as being contrary to section 16 of bill of rights of the state constitution.[23] The act of 1913, amended in 1913 and 1915, provides for the examination of land titles by the recorder and the issuance, if the title proved to be held in fee simple, of a certificate of title by the court of common pleas or probate court. The official certificate becomes the title of ownership and is indefeasible. However, in the event an interest is found in the land, after the issuance of the certificate, a claim is allowed to the legal claimant from a fund created for that purpose at the time of registration.[24] It was established in Medina in 1914, and is still being used.[25]

---

18. *Ibid.,* XLIV, 61.
19. G. C. sec. 8561.
20. G. C. sec. 8565.
21. *Laws of Ohio,* CXVI, 324.
22. *Ibid.,* XCII, 220.
23. *Ohio State Reports* (Cincinnati, 1852—), LVI, 575.
24. G. C. secs. 8572-34 - 8572-56; *Laws of Ohio,* CIII, 914-960; CVI, 24; CXV, 443.
25. Registered Lands, years covered, *see* entries 55-57.

The recorder, like other county officials, had been required in earlier years to keep records of the business of his office, but it was not until the middle of the nineteenth century that the legislature, looking forward to some uniformity in land registration, enacted measures prescribing the form and contents of such records. Since 1850 the recorder has been required to keep a record of deeds in which is recorded all deeds, power of attorney, and other instruments of writing for the unconditional sale of land, tenements, or hereditaments.[26] The same year saw the beginning of a record of mortgages in which was recorded all mortgages, powers of attorney, and other instruments of writing by which land, tenements, or hereditaments "shall or may be mortgaged" or otherwise conditionally sold; and a record of plats in which was to be recorded all plats and maps of towns lots and of the subdivisions thereof, and of other divisions of surveyed lands, in like regular succession according to the priority of their presentation.[27] Since 1851 the recorder has been required to keep a separate record of deeds and mortgages denominated respectfully as "Record of Deeds" and "Record of Mortgages."[28] Since 1865 the recorder has been required to keep a separate record of leases.[29] The present practice of keeping a daily register of deeds and a daily register of mortgages has been required by statute since 1896.[30] In Medina County the register was duly instituted in that year and has been continued to date.[31]

Although indexes had been prepared in earlier years, the present system of indexing had its beginning in 1851 and took practically its present form in 1896.[32]

----

26. *Laws of Ohio*, XLVIII, 64
27. *Ibid.,* XLVIII, 64
28. *Ibid.,* XLIX, 103.
29. *Ibid.,* LXII, 170.
30. *Ibid.,* XCII, 268.
31. *See* entries 32, 34.
32. *Laws of Ohio,* XLIX, 103; XCII, 268; CII, 288.

At present the recorder, at the beginning of each day's business, is required to make and maintain a general alphabetical index, direct and reverse, of all names of both parties of all instruments recorded by him. The indexes show the kind of instrument, the date, the range, the township and section, the survey number and the number of acres or the lot and sublot numbers and the part thereof, of each tract or lots of land described in any such instrument of writing; the name of each grantor is entered in the direct index under the appropriate letter and followed on the same line by the name of the grantee; the name of each grantee is entered in the reverse index under the appropriate letter and followed on the same line by the name of grantor.[33]

Since 1859, the county commissioners have been authorized to provide sectional indexes to the records of all real estate in the county, beginning with some designated year and continuing through a period of years as may be specified.[34]

The present duties of the recorder do not differ, in the main, from those prescribed in the middle of the 19th century. His bound records are open to the inspection of the public and are transferred to his successor.

The recorder in Medina County averages annually the recording of 1730 deeds, 60 mechanics' liens, 313 leases, 7 powers of attorney, 3938 chattel mortgages, and 978 real estate mortgages.[35] The office is self supporting, the total fees running over $6000 annually, while expenses average only $1000 annually.[36] All fees are paid into the county treasury and salaries and expenses are appropriated by the commissioners annually. The recorder is under a $2000 bond,[37] and the salary is $147.50 monthly.[38]

---

33. G. C. sec. 2764.
34. G. C. sec. 2766; *Laws of Ohio,* LXIV, 256; LXXVI, 49; CII, 289.
35. Register of Conveyances, *passim, see* entry 34.
36. *Ibid.*
37. Record of Official Bonds, 1940, *see* entry 325.
38. Pay Rolls, 1940, *see* entry 288.

Real PropertyTransfers

Deeds (See also entry 55)

28. DEED RECORD
1795—. 181 vols. (A-I, K-Z, AA, BB, 1-153).
Record of deeds, liens, and other instruments conveying title to
real estate, showing names of grantor and grantee, kind and date of
instrument, amount of consideration, description of property
transferred, lot and tract numbers, acreage, date filed, date
recorded, and instrument number, includes 1818—, easements for
highways and roads, and land contracts. Also contains: Plat Book,
1818-1860, entry 58; Record of Mortgages, 1795-1833, entry 43;
Lease Record, 1818-1864, entry 37; and Record of Power of
Attorney, 1818-1893, entry 67; two volumes 1795-1818,
transcribed from Portage and Trumbull County Records in 1895;
also includes Quitclaim Deeds, Sheriff's Deeds (Auditor's), and
Corporation Deeds (Old Chippewa Incorporated), Community
Club Company, and Briarwood Beach. These records were
transcribed from 1795-1818, from Trumbull and Portage Counties,
and transcribed from 1818-1874, from Medina County original
records. Arranged chronologically by dates recorded. 1818-1833
Mortgage Record, indexed alphabetically by names of mortgagors.
For separate indexes, see entries 30, 36. 1818-1883, handwritten;
1795-1818, 1883-1934, handwritten on printed forms; 1934—,
typed on printed forms. Average 600 pages. 18 x 12.5 x 3.
Recorder's vault.

29. ORIGINAL DEED RECORD
1818-1874, 22 vols. (3 labeled AB, E, V; 19 labeled 1-7,
1-7, 28-32).
Original deed records, liens, and other instruments conveying real
estate in Medina County, showing names of grantor and grantee,
kind and date of instrument, amount of consideration, description
of property transferred, date filed, instrument number, lot and
section numbers and acreage; also includes Record of Mortgage,

1818-1834; Land Contracts, Power of Attorney, Easements, 1818-1874, Mechanic's Lien Record, 1818-1874, also Quitclaim Deeds, Sheriff's Deeds, Auditor's and Corporation Deeds (Old Chippewa Incorporated, Community Club Company and Briarwood Beach). These records have been transcribed, see Deed Record, entry 28. Arranged chronologically by dates filed. For indexes, see entries 30, 36. Handwritten. Average 600 pages. 18 x 12.5 x 3. North storeroom.

30. GENERAL INDEX TO DEEDS [Direct and Reverse] 1795—. 13 vols. (1labeled 1-5; 12 labeled 1-12).
Index to Deed Record, entry 28, and Original Deed Record, entry 29, showing date of filing, names of grantor and grantee, volume and page numbers, date of record, name of township, tract, section, and lot numbers, and acreage. Five volumes, 1818-1897, were transcribed into one volume 1936-1937. Volume 7 indexes deeds, 1795-1818, transcribed from Trumbull and Portage Counties in 1895, and recorded in Deed Record, volumes 68 and 69. Arranged alphabetically by names of grantors and grantees and chronologically thereunder by dates filed. Handwritten on printed forms. Average 500 pages. 19 x 13 x 3.5. Recorder's vault.

31. DEED RECORD, REAL ESTATE DEVISED BY WILL
1904-1935. 3 vols. (1-3).
Real and personal property transfers (including delinquent) issued by the auditor through the authority of probate court on real estate devised by will and stamped original and signed by the probate judge, also quotation from will giving authority to devise it and that certain real estate was devised to date, showing date filed, name of deviser, description and location of property, and names of grantor and grantee. Arranged chronologically by dates filed. Indexed alphabetically by names of grantors and grantees. For separate index, see entry 36. Handwritten on printed forms. Average 250 pages. 15.5 x 12.5 x 2.5. Recorder's office.

32. DAILY REGISTER OF DEEDS
1896—. 8 vols. (1-8).

Daily register of deeds to be recorded, showing date of filing, names of grantor and grantee, instrument number, consideration, exact time received and filed, description and location of property, and acreage. Arranged chronologically by dates filed. Indexed alphabetically by names of grantors showing names of grantees. Handwritten on printed forms. Average 342 pages. 17 x 15 x 2. Recorder's office.

33. STATISTICAL RECORD [Register] OF DEEDS AND MORTGAGES
1867-1916 (5 vols. (1-5).

Register, showing names of grantor and grantee, date filed, numbers of deeds and mortgages, number of cancellations, amount released, and fee. Arranged chronologically by dates filed. No index. Handwritten on printed forms. Average 340 pages. 16 x 11 x 2.5. North storeroom.

34. REGISTER OF CONVEYANCES
1867—. 10 vols. (1-10)

Daily register of instruments filed for recording, showing date recorded, kind of instrument, names of grantor and grantee, amount of fee, and consecutive instrument number; also includes deeds to agricultural lands and town lots, mortgages on agricultural lands and town lots, cancellation of mortgages, leases on minerals, and miscellaneous instruments. 1867-1916, arranged chronologically by dates recorded; 1917—, arranged alphabetically by names of grantors. For separate index, see entry 36. Handwritten on printed forms. Average 340 pages. 1 x 11 x 2.5. 5 volumes, 1867-1916, North storeroom; 5 volumes, 1917—, Recorder's vault.

35. RECORDING FILE [Original Papers]
1865—. 24 file boxes. (Labeled by contained letters of alphabet).

Original papers, including deeds, mortgages, and leases, showing names of grantor and grantee and date of filing; mortgages, showing names of mortgagor and mortgagee and date of filing; leases, showing names of lessor and lessee and date of filing: also contains documents left for recording which were never called for. Arranged alphabetically by names of grantors. No index. Handwritten and typed, some on printed forms. 10 x 4.5 x 13.5. Recorder's storeroom.

36. SECTIONAL INDEX
1795—. 30 volumes (labeled by section numbers).
Subtitled by names of townships and corporations.

Sectional index to deeds and mortgages recorded in Deed Record, entry 28; Original Deed Record, entry 29; Deed Record, Real Estate Devised by Will, 1904-1935, entry 31; Register of Conveyances, 1867—, entry 34; Lease Record, 1865-1934, entry 37; Record of Mortgages, 1834—, entry 43; Torrens Lands, 1914—, entry 53; and Contracts and Miscellaneous Records, 1889-1934, entry 75, showing date of filing, to whom, from whom, volume and page numbers of record, township, section, and lot numbers, number of acres, consideration, and date of cancellation if referring to mortgages. Arranged numerically by section numbers and numerically thereunder by lot numbers. Handwritten on printed forms. Average 700 pages. 19 x 13.5 x 4. Recorder's office.

Leases (See also entries 28, 29, 34, 35, 55)

37. LEASE RECORD
1865—. 53 vols. (1-31, 33-54). 1818-1864 in Deed Record, entry 28.

Lease records, including farm, oil and gas leases, and assignments of leases, showing date of lease, names of parties, description of property, number of acres, consideration and agreements, signatures of parties witnessed by notary public, notice to state of Ohio by notary that lease was signed and sealed, and date recorded. Arranged chronologically by dates recorded. For index, 1865-1934, see entry 36; for 1934—, see entry 38. Handwritten on printed forms. Average 500 pages. 18 x 13 x 3. Recorder's vault.

38. GENERAL INDEX TO LEASES AND MISCELLANEOUS
1934—. 2 vols. (1, 2).
General index to Lease Record, entry 37 and Contracts and Miscellaneous Records, entry 75, showing kind of instrument, power of attorney, rights of way, release of mortgages, daily receipts of leases and miscellaneous, names of lessor and lessee, acreage, lot number, and volume and page numbers of record. Arranged alphabetically by names of lease holders. Handwritten on printed forms. 450 pages. 20 x 13 x 3. Recorder's office.

39. RECORD OF NINETY-NINE YEAR LEASES
1919-1928. 1 vol. (1).
Ninety-nine year leases to individual realtors of lots for residence purposes in township lots 13 and 16. These lots are large and are subdivided for cottages and tents: leases, showing date of entry, names of lessor and lessee, location of lot, and consideration. Arranged chronologically by dates entered. Indexed alphabetically by names of lessors and lessees. Handwritten on printed forms. 200 pages. 18 x 13 x 2.5. Recorder's office.

40. RECORD OF LAND CONTRACTS, MEDINA COUNTY
1920—. 1 vol. (1).
Leases to individuals on lots located at Chippewa Lake Park, showing names and addresses of lessors and lessees, location and description of lot, terms of lease, date filed, and consideration Arranged chronologically by dates filed. Indexed alphabetically by names of lessors and lessees. Handwritten on printed forms. 250 pages. 20 x 14 x 2. Recorder's office.

41. RECORD OF RIGHTS OF WAY CONTRACTS
1916—. 7 vols. (1-7)

Record of rights of way for oil and gas companies and pipe lines, showing names of grantor and grantee, date of filing, description and location of land, and terms of contract, including provisions for grantors to purchase gas or oil for their own use. Arranged chronologically by dates filed. Indexed alphabetically by names of grantors and grantees. Handwritten on printed forms. Average 400 pages. 20 x 14 x 2.5. Recorder's vault.

42. HIGHWAY EASEMENT RECORD
1929—. 1 vol. (1).

Easements for highway purposes and agreements for channel change, showing release of property to the state free of lien mortgage, name and address of grantor, description and location of property, value, date filed, and consideration. Arranged chronologically by dates filed. Indexed alphabetically by names of grantors. Typed. 400 pages. 18 x 13 x 3.5. Recorder's office.

For other easement records, see entries 28, 75.

Mortgages (See also entries 28, 29, 33-35, 55)

43. RECORD OF MORTGAGES
1834—. 104 vols. (1-104). 1795-1833 in Deed Record, entry 28.

Record of real estate mortgages, showing names of mortgagee and mortgagor, description of property, date filed, number of instrument, location of property, lot number, and amount of mortgage; the release in margin simply states that mortgage is satisfied and discharged, stamped by recorder with date, and signed by mortgagor. Arranged chronologically by dates filed. Indexed alphabetically by names of mortgagees showing names of mortgagors. For separate indexes, see entries 36, 44. 1834-1930, handwritten; 1930—, typed. Average 600 pages. 18.5 x 13 x 3. Recorder's vault.

44. GENERAL INDEX TO MORTGAGES
1834—. 9 vols. (1-9).

Index to Record of Mortgages, entry 43, showing names of mortgagor and mortgagee, date and amount of mortgage, if on printed, and volume and page numbers of record. Arranged alphabetically by names of mortgagees showing names of mortgagors. Handwritten on printed forms. Average 500 pages. 18 x 15 x 3. 6 volumes 1834-1930, Recorder's vault; 3 volumes, 1931—, Recorder's office.

45. RECORD OF CERTIFICATES OF DISCHARGE OF MORTGAGES
18912—. 4 vols. (1-4).

Record of certificates of release of mortgages, partial release of mortgages, assignment of mortgages, and court certificates of release of mortgages, showing date of release or assignment, conditions, names of grantor and grantee, certificate number, and date of filing. Arranged chronologically by dates filed. Indexed alphabetically by names of grantors showing names of grantees. 1891-1920, handwritten; 1921—, typed. Average 350 pages. 18 x 13 x 2.5. Recorder's vault.

46. RELEASES
1925—. 1 vol. (3).

Record of mortgage releases, showing instrument number, names of mortgagee and mortgagor, signature of mortgagee witnessed by recorder, and date of recording, also certain releases for sublots in Lafayette Township. Arranged chronologically by dates recorded. Indexed alphabetically by names of owners. Handwritten. 300 pages. 18.5 x 13 x 2.5. Recorder's vault.

47. PARTIAL RELEASES, GENERAL
1891—. 6 vols.

Releases granted by Lincoln Savings and Loan Company subdivision known as Gloria Glens and Chippewa Lake Community Company, showing names and addresses of grantors and grantees, description and location of property, conditions of release, and date recorded. Arranged chronologically by dates recorded. Indexed alphabetically by names of grantees showing names of grand tours. Handwritten. Average 500 pages. 18. 5 x 12 x 2.5. Recorder's vault.

Liens (See also entries 28, 29, 48, 55, 76)

48. INDEX TO LIENS AND NOTICES OF DISCHARGES
1929—. 1 vol.
Index record of liens and notices of discharge, showing file number, date of filing, court granting lien or discharge, name of surety, date of issue, description and location of property, and date of cancellation. Arranged alphabetically by names of sureties. Handwritten on printed forms. 400 pages. 21 x 17.5 x 3. Recorder's office.

49. [Personal] EXCISE AND FRANCHISE TAX LIENS
1932—. 1 vol.
Record of excise and franchise tax liens, showing recorder's file number of notice of lien, name of public utility or corporation, description of property, date and hour filed, amount of tax, penalty (if any), total, recorders file number, notice of payment of tax, date of discharge of lien, date tax paid, date and hour of filing notice of payment of tax, and discharge of lien, also includes Personal Tax Liens, 1931—. Arranged chronologically by dates filed and alphabetically thereunder by names of public utilities or corporations. No index. Handwritten on printed forms. 300 pages. 17 x 9 x 1.5. Recorder's office.

50. MECHANIC'S LIEN RECORD
1843—. 6 vols. (16).
Record of mechanic's liens filed and recorded, showing names of creditor and debtor, itemized account of labor and material furnished, for what construction or improvement, copy of

notarization of claim, and dates of filing and recording. Arranged chronologically by dates recorded. Indexed alphabetically by names of creditors and debtors. 1843-1934, handwritten; 1935—, typed on printed forms. Average 390 pages. (No location given).

51. RAILROAD LIEN RECORD
1890-1893. 1 vol. (1).
Record of liens against Pittsburgh, Allegheny, and Western Railroad Company by mechanics or contractors, showing name of railroad, statement made by holder of lien before notary public, proof that agent was authorized to make contract valid, amount of claim, statement of articles sold or amount due for articles used, and date of filing. Arranged chronologically by dates filed. Indexed alphabetically by names of contractors or mechanics. Handwritten. 270 pages. 26 x 11 x 2. Recorder's vault.

52. FEDERAL TAX LIENS
1923—. 1 vol. (1).
Record of federal tax liens, showing recorder's certificate number, name and address of taxpayer, location and description of property, date and hour of filing, amount of tax assessed, and date canceled. Arranged chronologically by dates filed. Indexed alphabetically by names of taxpayers. Handwritten on printed forms. 250 pages. 16 x 13 x 1. Recorder's office.

Registered Lands (See also entry 76)

53. TORRENS LANDS
1914—. 3 vols.
Original and transfer certificates of title to registered lands, showing date of filing, names of grantor and grantee, lot number, tract number, and description of property; also includes plats, showing location and area of real property. Prepared by county surveyor. Arranged chronologically by dates filed. For indexes, see entries 36, 54. Handwritten. Plats, printed black on white. Scales vary. Average 450 pages. 20 x 17 x 3. Recorder's vault.

54. INDEX OF OWNERS' LIENS AND LESSER ESTATES
1914—. 1 vol. (1).

Index to Torrens Lands, entry 53 and Registered Lands-Surveys, entry 56, showing name of property owner, certificate and document numbers, date of filing, volume and page numbers of record, description of land, number of acres, and date canceled. Arranged alphabetically by names of owners. Handwritten. 500 pages. 21 x 17.5 x 3. Recorder's vault.

55. REGISTER OF LANDS AND REGISTER OF TITLE
1914—. 1 vol. (1).

Record of registered lands, including contracts, deeds, warranty deeds, mortgages, leases, and mechanics' liens, showing kind of instrument, date of filing, names of grantor and grantee, consideration, and location and description of property. Arranged alphabetically by names of grantors. No index. Handwritten on printed forms. 600 pages. 20 x 13 x 3. Recorder's vault.

56. REGISTERED LANDS —SURVEYS
1914—. 1 VOL. (1).

Surveys of registered lands, showing plat, names of property owner and township, acreage, lot and tract numbers, foot frontage, names of streets or roads, certification and signature of county surveyor, and date filed. Arranged chronologically by dates filed. For index, see entry 54. Handwritten on printed forms. 500 pages. 24 x 30 x 4. Recorder's vault.

57. REGISTERED LANDS, RECEPTION BOOK
1914—. 1 vol. (1).

Reception book of registered lands, showing type of instrument, date and time filed, terms, document number, names of grantor and grantee, description and location of land, and certificate number. Arranged chronologically by dates filed. No index. Handwritten on printed forms. 500 pages. 24 x 18 x 5. Recorder's vault.

Plats and Maps (See also entries 28, 53)

58. PLAT BOOK
1860—. 5 vols. (15). 1818-1860 in Deed Record, entry 28.
Plat books of townships and villages, showing lot number, name of
owner, acreage, location of roads and streams, and date of entry.
Prepared by county engineer. Marked by township or village. In
back of volumes, 1834-1850 (1-4), are typed affidavits of need of
police protection and annexation petitions and proceedings. Page
one, volume two, contains index to plats, 1818-1860, entry 28.
Arranged chronologically by dates entered. No index. Handwritten
and typed. Scale, 1 inch equals 50-80 feet. Average 55 pages. 24
x 40 x 1. Recorder's vault.

59. [PLATS OF TOWNSHIPS]
1836-1870. 5 vols. (Dated).
Plats of township and municipalities, showing name of property
owner, acreage, locations of roads, streams, railroads, lots, and
sections. Arranged numerically by section numbers and also
arranged numerically by lot numbers. No index. Hand drawn and
handwritten. Average 40 pages. 24 x 18 x 1. Recorder's vault.

60. [PLATS]
1920. 1 vol.
Blueprints of townships and municipalities in Medina County
showing names and locations of townships and municipalities,
location of gas mains, rural mail routes, steam and electric
railroads, name of property owners, acreage, and section and lot
numbers; also contains plat copies from original deeds, showing
names of property owners, locations of crossroads and settlements,
names of townships and roads, section and lot numbers, and
acreage. Arranged alphabetically by names of townships and
municipalities. No index. 45 pages. 18 x 16 x 1.5. Recorder's vault.

61. ATLAS AND DIRECTORY OF MEDINA COUNTY
1874, 1879. 2 vols.

Maps of Medina County, showing townships, corporations with roads, streets, alleys, railroads, streams, section and range numbers, boundary lines of land tracts with area, and name and address of owner; corporations, showing boundary lines of corporations, lot lines with lot numbers, street names, location of public buildings, and a brief summary of industrial pursuits of each township or town. Drawn and prepared by Cyrus Wheelock, Medina County engineer. No systematic arrangement. No index. Scale, 2 2/3 inches equals 1 mile. Printed. Average 100 pages. 17 x 14 x 1. Recorder's vault.

62. PARTITION FENCE RECORD
1905-1907. 1 vol. (1). Discontinued.

Application for determination of line fence and what portion of said fence shall be repaired by each party, showing date of filing, names and addresses of parties, and determination and agreement signed by both parties. Arranged chronologically by dates filed. Indexed alphabetically direct by names of parties of the first part and reverse by names of parties of the second part. Handwritten. 480 pages. 18 x 13 x 3. Recorder's vault.

Personal Property Transfers
(See also entry 31)

63. CHATTEL MORTGAGES
1906—. 15 bdls., 37 file boxes (labeled by inclusive instrument numbers).

Chattel mortgages filed in Medina County, showing instrument number, date filed, mortgage number, names and addresses of mortgagee and mortgagor, description of property and amount of mortgage. Cancellation is shown by card acknowledging payment. This card replaces the original mortgage when it is removed from the file. Arranged numerically by instrument numbers and chronologically thereunder by days filed. For separate index, see entry 64. Typed on printed form. Bundles, 4.5 x 10 x 12. File box, 10 x 4.5, x 13. Recorder's office.

64. INDEX TO CHATTEL MORTGAGES
1876—. 17 vols. (1-17).

Index record of Chattel Mortgages, entry 63, showing name and addresses of grantor and grantee, mortgage number, date of instrument, date filed, consideration, date canceled and remarks. These volumes contain final records of all chattel mortgages except the mortgages themselves which are kept on file. Arranged alphabetically by names of grantors and chronologically thereunder by dates filed. Average 250 pages. 18 x 14 x 5. 6 volumes, 1876-1923, North storeroom. 11 volumes, 1924—, Recorder's office.

Corporations and Partnerships
(See also entry 61)

65. RECORD OF CORPORATIONS
1832—. 2 vols.

Record of articles of incorporation of business, religious organizations, and societies, showing date of special meeting for the purpose of becoming incorporated with record of officers present, purpose for which organized, name under which group desires to be organized, signatures of secretary and directors, date received, and date recorded. Arranged chronologically by dates recorded. Indexed alphabetically by names of corporations. Handwritten on printed forms. Average 425 pages. 16 x 14 x 2. Recorder's vault.

66. INDIVIDUAL PARTNERSHIP AND TRADERS' RECORDS
1884-1896. 1 vol.

Partnership and traders record, showing names of partners, name of partnership, business engaged in, location of business, and residences of owners; also includes Limited Partnership Agreements, 1884-1896, showing date, names of partners, addresses, conditions of agreement, witnesses, and notarizations. Arranged alphabetically by names of partnerships. No index. Handwritten on printed forms. 450 pages. 17.5 x 112 x 3 Recorder's office.

Grants of Authority
(See also entries 28, 29, 31, 38, 75)

67. RECORD OF POWER OF ATTORNEY
1893—. 1 vol. (1). 1818-1893 in Deed Record, entry 28. Copies of grants of authority to act for the grantor in the matter set forth in instrument, showing names of grantor and grantee, enumeration of duties to perform, date of instrument, name of grantor and witnesses, copy of notarization, date filed for record, and date recorded. Arranged chronologically by dates recorded. Indexed alphabetically. by names of grantors showing names of grantees. Handwritten on printed forms. 600 pages. 20 x 13 x 3. Recorder's vault.

68. INSURANCE CARDS
1934—. 1 file box.
Puppies of licenses issued by the State Department of Insurance to insurance agents and filed with the county recorder, showing name and address of company and home office, name and address of agent, date of license, and date filed; also includes record of compliance certifying the insurance company has complied with insurance regulations, 1936-1937, showing name of company, home office, kind of insurance, itemized financial statement of company, date of certificate, and date filed. Arranged alphabetically by names of insurance companies and chronologically thereunder by dates filed. No index. Handwritten on printed forms. 12 x 1 x 26. Recorder's office.

69. REGISTER OF INSURANCE AGENTS
1936—. 1 file box.
Register of agents permitted to operate for and by certain

companies, showing date registered and name and address of agent; also contains certificates of compliance with insurance regulations, showing name of company, home office, kind of insurance, itemized financial statement of company, date of certificate, and date filed. Arranged chronologically by dates registered and alphabetized thereunder by names of companies or agents. No index. Hyped. 11 x 16 x 24. Recorder's office.

Fiscal Accounts

70. RECORDER'S RECORDS OF FEES
1907—. 8 vols. (1-8).
Recorder's cash book and record of fees, showing consecutive number of instrument, subject and description of instrument, date of entry, name of payer, recording, filing, and cancellation fees, and total fees. Arranged chronologically by dates entered. No index. Handwritten on printed forms. Average 325 pages. 7 volumes, 1907-1934, Recorder's office; 1 volume, 1935—, Recorder's vault.

71. DAILY RECEIPTS OF LEASES AND MISCELLANEOUS
1920—. 6 vols. (1-6).
Receipts for money collected for recording of leases transfers, rights of way, agreements, bills of sale, mortgages, and chattel mortgages, showing date of receipt, time of recording, kind of instrument, by whom recorded and amount collected. Arranged chronologically by dates of receipts. No index. Handwritten. Average 400 pages. 14.5 x 17 x 3. 2 volumes, 1920-1930, North storeroom; 4 volumes, 1931—, Recorder's vault.

72. RECEIPTS
1914—. 23 vols. (labeled by contained receipt numbers).
Copies of receipts given by recorder for fees for filing documents, including mortgages, liens, and contracts, showing date of filing, name and address of party paying recording charge, receipt

number, description of document filed, and amount of fee paid.
Arranged numerically by receipt numbers. No index. Handwritten
on printed forms. Average 250 pages. 11.5 x 8 x 1.25. 17 volumes,
1914-1919, North storeroom; 6 volumes, 192—, Recorder's office.

Miscellaneous

73. SOLDIER'S AND SAILOR'S DISCHARGE
RECORD
1862—. 2 vols (1-2).
Copies of official discharges from the United States Army or Navy
of soldiers and sailors enlisted for the War of the Rebellion,
Spanish-American War, Philippine Insurrection, and World War,
with discharges of regular army enlistments, showing name of
soldier or sailor, rank, company, regiment or vessel, physical
description of soldier or sailor, date and place of discharge, reason
for discharge (honorable or dishonorable), service record, name of
commanding officer, and date of recording. Arranged
chronologically by dates recorded. Indexed alphabetically by
names of soldiers and sailors. Handwritten on printed forms.
Average 500 pages. 18 x 15.5 x 3. Recorder's vault.

74. DAY BOOK
1862-1904. 1 vol.
Complete list of Civil War Volunteers in Medina County, showing
name of volunteer, date of enlistment, and name of township; also
contains school levies, 1874-1904, showing levies upon joint
districts, name of township, valuations, name of township to which
levy is due, amount charged to each township, and totals;
distribution of laws and journals, 1864-1866, showing date entered,
name and date of journal, number of copies, names of townships
to which journals were sent, and signature of clerk. Civil War
volunteers and school levies arranged by names of township;
distribution of laws and journals Arranged chronologically by

dates entered. No index. Handwritten. 352 pages. 13.5 x 9 x 1.5.
North Storeroom.

75. CONTRACTS AND MISCELLANEOUS RECORDS
1889—. 6 vols. (1-6).

Record of miscellaneous instruments, powers of attorney, rights of
way, leases, easements, cancellation of contracts, land contracts,
and trust agreements, showing date of recording, Names and
addresses of principals, names of attorneys, subject, and facts of
litigation. Arranged chronologically by dates recorded. Indexed
alphabetically by subjects. For separate index, 1889-1934, see
entry 36; 1934—, see entry 38. 1889-1920, handwritten; 1920—,
typed on printed forms. Average 600 pages. 20 x 13 x 3.
Recorder's office

For other easement records, see entries 28, 42.

76. MISCELLANEOUS
1854—. 4 file boxes.

Miscellaneous group of land registration documents, Torrens,
1916—, showing kind of document, certificate of title, lease or
deed, showing names of grantor and grantee, date, time of
recording, location and description of property, and consideration
involved; Corporation Liens, 1935—, showing name of
corporation, place of business, amount of lien, amount assessed,
and date paid; State Insurance Certificate of Compliance, 1936—,
and Agent's Certificates of Application, 1935—, showing name of
company, kind of insurance, date of filing, statement of financial
standing, name and address of agent, name of company, and date
of filing application. No systematic arrangement. No index.
Handwritten and typed, some on printed forms. 17 x 11.5 x 25.
North storeroom.

The office of clerk of courts, an ancient English institution originating before the time of Edward I[1] was transplanted to America during the colonial period. The American Revolution made no radical change in the political heritage derived from England, and the office was continued by the states. The duties of the office were modified in the newer states, however, because of a separation of administrative and judicial functions, which under the English system had been combined.

The sections of the Ohio Constitution of 1802 creating the judicial system for the state provided for the appointment of a clerk of courts by the judges of the court of common pleas. He was to serve a seven-year term, but was subject to removal by the appointing power for a breach of good behavior.[2] The constitution of 1851 made the office of clerk elective with a three-year term.[3] A constitutional amendment in 1905 provided that the terms of all elected offices should be for an even number of years not exceeding four. In compliance with this amendment, the general assembly passed an act fixing the term of office of the clerk at two years.[4] The term remained at two years until 1936, when it was extended to four years.[5] The remuneration of the office was entirely by fees until 1906, when the legislature prescribed a definite salary based on the population of the county.[6]

The duties of the clerk of courts, like those of other county officers are prescribed by statute. And 1853, a code of civil procedure was adopted summarizing the earlier duties and forming the basis for the present ones which are in most respects similar to those prescribed during the earlier years of the office.

---

1. Sir Francis Pollock and Frederick William Maitland, *The History of English Law Before the Time of Edward I* (Cambridge, 1895), 1, 184.
2. *Ohio Const. 1802,* Art. III sec. 9.
3. *Ohio Const. 1851,* Art. IV, sec. 16.
4. *Laws of Ohio,* XCVIII, 273.
5. *Ibid.,* CXVI, pt. ii, 184.
6. *Ibid.,* XCVIII, 94, 117.

The clerk of courts was directed to issue all *writs* and orders for provisional remedies; endorse the date upon all papers filed in his office; keep the journal, record books, and papers appertaining to the court of common pleas and record its proceedings, keeping the appearance docket and the trial docket, as well as a printed duplicate of the trial docket, the journal, the record, and the execution docket.[7] The present practice of preparing an index, direct and reverse, to judgments began in 1868.[8] In 1871, the clerk was made official custodian of the law reports and books furnished by the state for the use of the court and bar, and was made liable in the event of their destruction.[9]

Some of the duties of the clerk, as defined by the civil code of 1853, are still effective, others have been added by subsequent legislation. Thus, for example, in 1858 the clerk was directed to receive notary commissions for record.[10] He was required, also, to receive for record special police commissions (1867), timber trademarks (1883), partnership agreements (1894), copies of judgments of federal courts (1893), marks of ownerships ['trademarks] (1911), motor vehicle bills of sale (1921), and certificates of judgments to operate as liens (1935).[11] Since January 1, 1938, he has issued certificates of title to motor vehicles.[12] On the other hand, many of the earlier duties of the clerk have been transferred to other departments of local government or have been abolished. The clerk issued marriage licenses and recorded ministers' licenses until 1852. Since that date the former has been issued and the latter recorded by the probate court,[13] to which court the records have been transferred.

7. *Ibid.,* LI, 107, 158-159; LXXVIII, 108; LXXIX, 115; LXXXVI, 174.
8. *Ibid.,* LXIII, 10; LXXV, 108; LXXVIII, 88; LXXXII, 33; LXXXVI, 26.
9/ *Ibid.,* LXVIII, 109.
10. *Laws of Ohio,* LV, 13; XCIII, 406.
11. *Ibid.,* LXIV, 60; LXXX, 195; XCI, 357; XCII, 25; XCIII, 285; CII, 513-514; CIX, 333; CXVI, 274.
12. G. C. sec. 6290-6.
13. *Laws of Ohio,* I, 31; XXXIX, 429; L, 84; *Ohio Const., 1851,* Art. IV, sec. 8.

More over, the clerk issued peddlers' licenses until the decade of the 1860s, since when they have been issued by the auditor.[14] These records were not found in the inventory. The clerk has been authorized to act as an agent of the state in the sale of hunting and trapping licenses to nonresidents of the state since 1904 and to residents since 1919.[15] He has been authorized also to serve as agent in the sale of fishing licenses to nonresidents since 1919 and to residents since 1925.[16] The practice of recording in the office of the clerk, the names of black or mulatto persons to be used as certificates of freedom was, of course, discontinued after the close of the War between the States in 1865.

In 1856, the clerk was directed by the legislature to preserve a list of births, marriages, and deaths as returned to his office by the assessors, and to transmit annually, on or before the first day of June, a copy of such statistics to the secretary of state. These lists are no longer preserved. From these county lists, the Secretary of State prepared tabular statements showing the vital statistics in each county. The clerk received 10 copies of the report, one of which he was required to preserve in his office.17. The clerk was relieved of the task of collecting and preserving vital statistics, when, in 1867, such powers and duties were vested in the probate judge.[18]

Clerk of courts was given other duties in addition to those of serving the court of common pleas and receiving documents for a record. Since 1850, he has been required to report each year to the county commissioners all finds assessed by the courts in criminal cases, together with the names of the parties to each case, and the amount of money he has paid to the county treasurer.[19]

---

14. *Laws of Ohio*, LIX, 67.
15. *Ibid.*, XCVIII, 474; CVIII pt. i, 595.
16. *Ibid.*, CVIII, 923; CXI, 276.
17. *Ibid.*, LIII, 73-75.
18. *Ibid.*, LXIV, 63-64
19. *Ibid.*, XLVIII, 66; LVIII, 69; LXXXVI, 239.

Duplicate copies of these reports have not been preserved in the clerk's office. Moreover, since 1867, he has been required to report annually to the secretary of state the number of crimes committed in the county, the number of pending cases, and the amount of fines collected.[20] An act of 1927, amending the act of 1867, directed the clerk to report on any matters which the secretary of state might require, and to forward a duplicate copy of his report on crime in the county to the state board of clemency (board of pardons and parole).[21] The state board of pardons and parole within the department of public welfare.[22]

The county clerk of courts, like the county prosecuting attorney, is one of the important persons in a judicial system. His significance and influence, however, were not recognized until recent years.

The clerk of courts in Medina County is bonded for $10,000[23] and receives a salary of $2,325 annually. He is assisted by four deputies, also bonded and who receive an annual aggregate compensation of $4,220.[24] The office is self supporting. Fees received during the year 1940 for services rendered to the public totaled $12,000,[25] far exceeding the cost of operation.

---

20. *Laws of Ohio*, LXIV, 17.
21. *Ibid.*, CXII, 203.
22. *Ibid.*, CIX, III, 124.
23. Record of Official Bonds, 1940, *see* entry 325.
24. Pay Rolls, 1940, *see* entry 288.
25. Cash Book, 1940, *see* entry 107.

Court Proceedings

77. GENERAL INDEX
1818-1932. 5 vols. (A-E)

General index to all civil cases tried before the supreme court and court of common pleas, and clerk of courts records, showing case number, names of plaintiff and defendant, volume and page numbers of docket of supreme court, 1834-1849, entry 130; Record, Supreme Court, 1820-1849, entry 131; Appearance and Execution Docket, entry 122; Common Pleas Journal, entry 125; Record, Common Pleas, entry 127; and Praecipe Docket, Medina county, 1903-1932, entry 79. This does not index any criminal records, other than references made to criminal records by case numbers. Arranged alphabetically by names of plaintiffs and defendants. Handwritten on printed forms. Average 550 pages. 16.5 x 10.5 x 3. Clerk of courts' record room.

78. INDEX TO PENDING SUITS, LIVING JUDGMENTS, AND EXECUTIONS
1879——. 6 vols. (1-6).

Index to Common Pleas Journal, 1879——, entry 125; Record, Common Pleas, 1879——, entry 127; Civil Cases, 1879——, entry 116; Praecipe Docket, Medina County, 1932——, entry 79; and Appearance and Execution Docket, 1818, entry 122, showing date of entry, names of plaintiffs and defendants, case number, judgment case numbers, and execution numbers. References made to criminal records by case numbers only. Arranged alphabetically by names of plaintiffs and chronologically thereunder by dates entered. No index. Handwritten on printed forms. Average 500 pages. 18 x 13 x 4. Clerk of courts' office.

79. PRAECIPE DOCKET, MEDINA COUNTY
1903——. 2 vols. (2, 3).

Clerk of court stocking on *praecipes* issued, showing names of plaintiffs and defendants, kind of action, kind of *writ*, date issued, and name of attorney. Arranged chronologically by dates issued.

For index 1903-1932, see entry 77; 1932—, entry 78. Handwritten on printed forms. Average 475 pages. 14 x 9.5 x 2. Clerk of courts' record room.

80. JUDGMENT DOCKET [Certificate of Judgment to Operate as a Lien].
1935—. 1 vol. (1).

Record of certificate of judgment to act as a lien, showing date of entry, name of court, case number, title of action, name of judgment creditors and debtors, amount of judgments and costs, date judgment or decree rendered, volume and page numbers of Common Pleas Journal, entry 125 and Appearance and Execution Docket, entry 122, and time satisfied and released. Arranged chronologically by dates rendered. Indexed alphabetically by names of judgment creditors and debtors. Typed on printed forms. 480 pages. 18.5 x 12 . 5 x 2.5. Clerk of courts' office.

81. JUDGMENT INDEX [Direct]
1818-1933. 4 vols. (1, 1-3). Title varies: Direct #1, 1877-1882, 1 vol. Discontinued.

Index record of judgments of the court of common pleas, showing court terms, date of judgment, names of judgment creditor and judgment debtor, terms of judgment or decree, case number, journal number, final record, nature of suit, amount of judgment or decree, date of execution, and when judgment satisfied. This serves as an index to Appearance and Execution Docket, entry 122 and Record, Common Pleas, entry 127, by showing case number. Arranged alphabetically by names of judgment creditors and chronologically thereunder by dates of judgments. No index. Handwritten on printed forms. Average 300 pages. 18.5 x 12 x 3.5. Clerk of courts' record room.

82 JUDGMENT INDEX [Reverse]
1818-1933. 4 vols. (1, 1-3). Title varies :Reverse #1, 1877-1882, 1 vol. Discontinued.

Index record of judgments of the court a common pleas, showing court term, date of judgment, names of judgment debtor and judgment creditor, term of judgment or decree, execution, and date when judgment satisfied. This serves as an index to Appearance and Execution Docket, entry 122; Common Pleas Journal, entry 125; and Record, Common Pleas, entry 127 by showing case number. Arranged alphabetically by names of judgment debtors and chronologically thereunder by dates of judgments. No index. Handwritten on printed forms. Average 300 pages. 18.5 x 12.5 x 3.5. Clerk of courts' record room.

83. WITNESS DOCKET, COMMON PLEAS COURT
1828—. 11 vols. (B; 1-10). 1818-1828 in Common Pleas Journal, entry 125.

Docket of witnesses subpoenaed in civil and criminal actions heard in common pleas court, showing date of entry, names of plaintiff and defendant, case number, date of trial, number of witnesses for plaintiff and defendant, number of certificates issued for fees, date subpoenaed, date witness reported, name of witness, date discharged, number of days served, mileage, total fee, and date certified to the auditor. Arranged chronologically by date entered. Indexed alphabetically by names of plaintiffs showing page numbers. 1828-1839, handwritten; 1840—, handwritten on printed forms. Average 425 pages.13 x 20 x 2.5. Clerk of courts' record room.

84. [ORIGINAL CASE PAPERS]
1818—. 23 cartons, 35 file drawers (dated)

Case papers filed in all cases before the Common Pleas Court, including transcripts from lower courts, affidavits, indictments, subpoenas, petitions, answers, recipes, sheriff's summonses, executions, and returns, paroles, bonds, bills of exceptions, dispositions, and cost bills. All papers of each case are filed together in a jacket, showing date case filed, date closed, case number, names of plaintiff and defendant, and volume and page numbers of Judges Calendar, Civil Cases, entry 115; Judges Calendar, Criminal Cases, entry 119; Criminal Appearance and

Execution Docket, entry 120; Appearance and Execution Docket, entry 122; Common Pleas Journal, entry 125; and Record, Common Pleas, entry 127. Also contains: Civil Cases, 1818-1875, entry 116; Criminal Cases, 1818-1882, entry 129; [Original Papers, District Court], 1851-1884, entry 128; [Original Papers, Circuit Court], 1884-1913, entry 143; Court of Appeals Record [Original Papers], 1913-1921, entry 148, and [Original Papers, Supreme Court], 1820-1849, entry 132. Arranged numerically by case numbers. For index the entry 122. Handwritten and typed, some on printed forms. Cartons, 10 x 15.5 x 23; file drawers, 12 x 15 x 26. 23 cartons, 35 file drawers, 1818-1921, North storeroom; 1922—, Clerk of courts' office.

Jury and Witness Records

85. JURY BOOK
1850—. 32 vols. (1-32).

Record of grand and petit juries venires; grand jury records, showing court terms, jury decisions, juror's signatures, date subpoenaed, name and address of juror, date reported, number of days served, mileage, total fee, and date certificate for fees issued; records, showing court-term, case, nature of case, trial date, jury decision, signatures of jurors, date subpoenaed, name and address of your, date reported, number of days served, mileage, total fee, and date certificate for fees issued. Arranged chronologically by court terms. Indexed alphabetically by names of jurors. Handwritten on printed forms. Average 240 pages. 15 x 10 x 1.25. Clerk of courts' record room.

86. ANNUAL JURY LISTS
1921—. 1 vol.

Lists of grand and petit jurors drawn for jury duty for each term of court, also special venires; jury lists, showing court term, date drawn, name and address of juror, name of township, city, or ward, and date subpoenaed; petit jury list, showing case and trial date. Arranged chronologically by court terms and alphabetically thereunder by name so jurors. No index. Handwritten on printed forms. 250 pages. 16 x 12 x 1.5. Clerk of courts' office.

87. GRAND JURY ENTRY BOOK
1901-1920. 25 vols. (dated).

Record of grand jury venires, showing court term, date subpoenaed, name of township, city, or ward, name and address of juror, date reported, number of days served, mileage, total fee, date certificate for fees issued, name of defendant, charge, and vote of jury. Arranged chronologically by dates reported. No index. Handwritten on printed forms. Average 75 pages. 12 x 8 x .5. North storeroom.

88. REPORT OF GRAND JURY
1919—. 15 file boxes.

Report of the grand jury to the common pleas court of all matter legitimately brought before them, including examination of witnesses covering cases, finding true bills or returning no bill, visiting the county jail and inspecting conditions and recommendation of changes or improvement (if any), and signed by foreman of the grand jury, showing date of report, number of witnesses examined, number of cases covered, number of bills presented, and cases considered by grand jury; also reports on visits to the county jail as to conditions of prisoners, their habits, diet, accommodations, treatment, discipline of prisoners, and whether rules presented by court have been observed and no laws violated. Arranged chronologically by dates of reports. No index. Handwritten on printed forms. 4.25 x 4.25. X 10. Clerk of courts' office.

Motor Vehicles

89. INDEX TO MOTOR VEHICLE BILLS OF SALE, AND SWORN STATEMENT OF OWNERSHIP
1921—. 6 vols.

Index record of motor vehicle bills of sale or sworn statements of ownership, showing consecutive instrument number, date of filing, date of transfer, names of grantor and grantee, name of manufacturer, factory and motor numbers, year, horsepower, make, type, model, oath of grantor, and date of filing; also if a car is a used vehicle, name of original purchaser, and names of subsequent owners. This serves as an index to Sworn Statements of Motor Vehicle Owners, 1921-1937, entry 90; Bills of Sale, and Sworn Statement of Ownership, 1921-1937, entry 91, and Certificate of Title, 1938—, entry 100. Arranged alphabetically by names of grantees and chronologically thereunder by dates filed. No index. Handwritten on printed forms. Average 800 pages. 217.5 x 14. 5 x 3.5. Clerk of courts' office.

90. SWORN STATEMENTS OF MOTOR VEHICLE OWNERS
1921-1937. 2 file boxes (1-4999).

Original statements of ownership of automobiles, showing name and address of owner, certificate number, name and description of car, date of filing, and signatures of grantor and grantee. Arranged numerically by certificate numbers. For index, see entry 89. Typed on printed forms. 11 x 16 x 25. Clerk of courts' record room.

91. BILLS OF SALE, AND SWORN STATEMENT OF OWNERSHIP
1937-1937. 1 carton.

Applications for certificates of title together with bills of sale, showing certificate of title number, name and address of car owner, name of grantor, make, model, type, engine number, Factory number, horsepower, and manufacturer's number of car, and date filed. Also includes Certificate of Title, 1931-1937, entry 100. Arranged numerically by certificate numbers. For index, see entry 89. Handwritten on printed forms. 8 x 10 x 20. South storeroom.

92. RECORD OF RECEIPTS
1925-1939. 28 vols. (4-31).

Duplicate receipts of clerk of courts in filing bills of sale in sworn statements of ownership in sales of Motor Vehicles, showing name of owner, make of car, engine and license numbers, horsepower, amount of fee, name of payee, and date and number of receipt. Arranged numerically by consecutive receipt numbers. No index. Handwritten on printed forms. Average 325 pages. 16 x 9.5 x 2. Clerk of courts' office.

Commissions

93. JUSTICE RECORDS
1818-1848, 1862-1903, 1925—. 5 vols. (1 unlabeled; 1-4). Records of commissions, oaths, and certificates of justices of the peace and mayors; commissions, showing name of township, name of justice, date of commission, and date recorded; oaths, showing name of state, county, city and township, name and address of justice, name of attorney, date of oath, and date recorded; justice of the peace oaths, 1818-1848, showing name of state, county, and city, name and address of justice, date of oath date recorded, and signature of clerk; mayor's certificate of election 1883-1904, showing names of mayor, village, county, and state, date term of office commenced, date of expiration, and date of resignation (if resigned). Mayor's oath, showing names of state, county, and city, name and address of mayor, date elected, date mayor took office, date sealed, date recorded, and signature of clerk of courts; statements of justice of the peace appointments, 1924-1928, showing names of state, county, and city, name and address of justice, date recorded, and signature of clerk. Arranged chronologically by dates recorded. Indexed alphabetically by names of justices or mayors. Handwritten on printed forms. Average 300 36 pages. 14 x 9 x 1.5. Clerk of courts' record room.

94. RECORD OF NOTARIES' COMMISSIONS
1858—. 7 vols. (1-7). Copies of notaries' commissions granted by governor of Ohio, showing name of notary, date and term of appointment, names of governor and secretary of state, copy of oath of office of notary,

date recorded, and date of expiration of commission. Arranged chronologically by dates recorded. Indexed alphabetically by names of notaries. Handwritten on printed forms. Average 300 pages. 14 x 9 x 1.5. Clerk of courts' record room.

95. RAILROAD POLICEMEN'S COMMISSIONS
1858—. 1 file box.

Original papers of railroad policemen's commissions issued by the governor to individuals appointed to act as policemen on railroad property, showing names of appointee and railroad company, date issued, signatures of governor and secretary of state, copy of oath of appointee and date recorded. Arranged chronologically by dates recorded. No index. Handwritten on printed forms. 9 x 14 x 24. Clerk of courts' office.

Licenses and Certifications

96. RECORD OF FISHER'S LICENSE
1919-1937. 2 vols. (1,2).

Record of fishing licenses, showing license number, date of issue, age, occupation, and name and address of licensee, and fee. Arranged chronologically by dates issued. Indexed alphabetically by names of licensees. Handwritten on printed forms. Average 200 pages. 16 x 11 x 2. Clerk of courts' office.

97. HUNTER'S LICENSE BOOK
1913-1937. 3 vols. (1-3).

Record of hunting licenses, showing name and address of applicant, resident or non-resident, license number, date of application, age and description of applicant, and amount of fee. Indexed alphabetically by names of applicants. Handwritten on printed forms. Average 150 pages. 16 x 11 x 1.5. Clerk of courts' office.

98. OPTOMETRIST'S RECORD
1922—. 1 vol.

Copies of certificates issued by Ohio State Board of Optometry to applicants passing the examination for optometrists, showing license number, name of licensee, date of issue, and names of president and secretary of the board; also includes a photograph of licenses. Arranged chronologically by dates issued. Indexed alphabetically by names of licenses. Handwritten on printed forms. 150 pages. 16.5 x 11 x 1.5. Clerk of courts' record room.

99. REGISTER OF REAL ESTATE BROKERS AND SALESMEN
1927—. 1 vol.

Register of licenses issued to brokers and salesmen to sell, trade, and buy real estate for clients, showing date of issue, name and address of broker or salesman, by whom employed, license number, and fee. Arranged chronologically by dates issued. Indexed alphabetically by names of brokers or salesmen. Handwritten on printed forms. 200 pages. 14 x 9.5 x 1.5. Clerk of courts' office.

100. CERTIFICATE OF TITLE
1938—. 18 file boxes. (1-42,000). 1931-1937 in Bills of Sale and Sworn Statement of Ownership, entry 91.

Duplicate certificates of title to motor vehicle, showing certificate number, date of entry, names of purchaser and vendor, if new or used vehicle, make, type, model, motor number, date purchased, and amount of lien and fee. Arranged chronologically by dates entered and numerically thereunder by certificate numbers. For separate index, see entry 89. Handwritten and typed, some on printed forms. 11 x12 x 27. Clerk of courts' office.

101. CERTIFICATE OF TITLE CASH BOOK
1938—. 1 vol.

Daily record of registration of certificates of title to Motor Vehicles, showing date filed, certificate number, names of purchaser and vendor, total fee, issuing fee, notation of lien fee, memorandum of certificate fee, cancellation of lien fee, certified copy fee, acknowledgment fee, and amount of fee to state and county. Arranged alphabetically by names of purchasers and chronologically thereunder by dates filed. No index. Handwritten on printed forms. 500 pages. 18 x 16 x 3. Clerk of courts' office.

Partnerships

102. CERTIFICATES OF REGISTRATION OF BOTTLE AND TRADE-MARKS.
1927—. 1 file box. Subtitled Mark of Ownership, Certificate of Ownership.

Certificates of registration and trade-marks, showing name and address of applicant, date and number of application, description of article or trade-mark, date of filing with secretary of state, sworn statement of ownership, signature of applicant, certification of notary public, stamp of common pleas court, and date of filing. Arranged chronologically by dates filed. No index. Typed on printed forms.4 x 4.5 x 9. Clerk of courts' record room.

103. CERTIFICATES OF CO-PARTNERSHIP
1928—. 2 file box.

Legal papers of co-partnership, showing names of co-partners, trade name, dates and articles of agreement, names of attorneys, signatures of partners, certification of notary public, certificate number and date filed. Arranged numerically by certificate numbers and also arrange chronologically by dates filed. No index. Typed on printed forms. 4 x 4.5 x 9. Clerk of courts' record room.

104. PARTNERSHIP AGREEMENTS
1894—. 1 vol. (1).

Certificates of ownership, showing date of filing, names and addresses of partners, name of firm, certificate number, nature of business, and signature of notary public. Arranged chronologically by dates filed. Indexed alphabetically by names of partners.

Handwritten on printed forms. 300 pages. 19 x 11.5 x 2. Clerk of courts' office.

Elections

105. POLL BOOKS AND TALLY SHEETS
1930—. 18 bdls. 45 vols.
Record of registered voters in each ward and precinct, showing name and full address of voters, certificate of qualifications, oaths of clerk and judge, name of absent or disabled voters, name of township, and columns for board of education or extra bond issues. Poll books, in the front of volume, showing name and address of elector and date of election; tally sheets, in the back of volume, showing names of candidate and office and total number of votes cast. Poll book arranged chronologically by dates of elections and alphabetically thereunder by names of electors. Tally sheets Arranged by offices and alphabetically thereunder by names of candidates. No index. Handwritten on printed forms. Bundles,18 x 11.5 x 9; volumes average 20 pages. 18 x 11.5 x ?. 18 bundles, 1930-1936, Board of election office basement; 45 volumes, 1939—, Clerk of courts' office.

Coroner's Inquest

106. [Coroner's] INQUESTS
1850—. 5 file boxes.
Record of coroner's inquest and post-mortems to clerk of courts to determine cause of death where violence is known or suspected, showing date and place of death, date filed, name of deceased, description of body, findings, names of witnesses and jurors if impaneled, and report of examination signed by the coroner; also authority for post-mortem examination of the body, signed by the prosecuting attorney, and a certificate signed by the coroner, for physician's fee for the post-mortem examination. Arranged chronologically by dates filed. No index. Handwritten on printed

forms. 10 x 11 x 26. 4 file drawers, 1850-1927, South storeroom; 1 file drawer, 1928——, Clerk of courts' office.

Financial Records

107. CASH BOOK
1850——. 19 vols. (One unlabeled; 1-18).
Record of cash and disbursements, show in case number, names of litigants, volume and page number of Appearance and Execution Docket, entry 122, amount due, amount received, date of payment, and name of payee arranged alphabetically by names of payees and chronologically thereunder by dates of payments. No index. Handwritten on printed forms. Average 450 pages. 17 x 11 x 2.5. 1 volume 1850-1907, South storeroom; 18 volumes 1908——, Clerk of courts' record room.

108. COST BILLS [Criminal Cases]
1818——. 12 cartons, 3 file drawers
Original cost bills in criminal cases including cost bills in criminal cases from Magistrates courts, showing case number, criminal docket volume and page numbers, court term, date of trial, name of defendant, date of filing, names of attorneys and clerk of courts, charge, detailed cost of clerk of courts' office, sheriff, miscellaneous and total costs. All papers to each case are kept in jackets. Arranged numerically by case numbers. No index. Handwritten and typed, some on printed forms. Cartons, 10 x 14.25 x 23; file drawers, 12 x 15 x 26. 12 cartons, 1818-1892, North storeroom; 3 file drawers, 1892——, Clerk of courts' office.

109. RECORD OF ACCRUED FEES
1870-1889, 1907——. 7 vols. (1-4, 1-3).
Amount of money due clerk for services rendered, showing case number, date of accrued, name of debtors, total amount, date of payment, and cost of transcripts, certificates, and sundries. Arranged chronologically by dates accrued. Indexed alphabetically

by names of debtors. Handwritten on printed forms. Average 350 pages. 14 x 9 x 2. Clerk of courts' office.

110. UNCLAIMED FEES AND COSTS
1883—. 2 vols. (A, B).
Record of unclaimed fees and costs, showing date of entry, name of payee, case number, reason payment is due, amount paid to treasurer, date paid, date certificate issued to owner for recovery, and number of certificates. Arranged chronologically by dates entered. Indexed alphabetically by names of payees. Handwritten on printed forms. Average 250 pages. 14 x 9 x 2. Clerk of courts' office.

111. RECEIPTS
1925—. 36 vols. (Labeled by contained receipt numbers).
Copies of receipts given by clerk of courts to attorneys or litigants in case, for fees, fines, and costs paid, showing date and number of receipt, names of litigants, date paid, case number, volume and page numbers of Appearance and Execution Docket, entry 122, and amount paid. Arranged numerically by receipt numbers. No index. Handwritten on printed forms. Average 150 pages. 16 x 9.5 x .5. 7 volumes, 1925-1929, Clerk of courts' office; 18 volumes, 1930-1937, North storeroom; 11 volumes, 1937—, Clerk of courts' record room.

Miscellaneous

112. JUDICIAL STATISTICS TO SECY [Secretary] OF STATE
1936—. 1 envelope.
Copies of annual judicial criminal statistics to Secretary of State, showing year, data report, date filed, number of criminal cases, criminal offense classification, list of other offenses (if any), number of defendants, sentence or disposition of case, and fines and costs; also includes judicial statistics other than criminal, showing year, date of report, number of divorce cases, reason for

which granted, disposition of children, total number of civil cases, total civil judgments in verdicts, foreclosure and equity cases, and total amount of costs, fines, and fees. Arranged chronologically by dates of reports. Typed on printed forms. Approximately 15 reports, 24 x 24 in envelope, 10 x 17. Clerk of courts' office.

113. ESTRAY RECORDS
1845-1921. 1 vol.

Record of reported estrays, showing date entered, detailed description of stray animals, time and place found, by whom found, and disposition of animal. Arranged chronologically by dates entered. No index. Handwritten. 300 pages. 13 x 8 x 1.5. Clerk of courts' office.

114. ALIMONY AND SUPPORT PAYMENTS
1938—. 1 vol. 1875-1938 in Appearance and Execution Docket, entry 122.

Record of alimony and support payments, showing title of case date of entry, common pleas case number, whether divorce or non-support case, name and address of person to whom payments are to be made, date payment received, from whom, amount, date paid out, to whom, amount, and cash book entry number. Arranged chronologically by dates entered. Indexed alphabetically by names of plaintiffs and defendants. Handwritten on printed forms. 800 pages. 18 x 12.5 x 6. Clerk of courts' office.

The court of common pleas, like many other county institutions, originated in England during the reign of Henry II.[1] Established in America during the colonial period, the office was continued by the states following the War of American Independence.

The Northwest Ordinance of 1787 established a government consisting of a governor, a secretary, and three judges all appointed by Congress. The judges were to form a court, known as the general court, which had common law jurisdiction and together with the governor were authorized to draw up a code of civil and criminal law. The territorial act of 1788, establishing the American colonial policy in the newer west in respect to the judiciary, contained sections authorizing the establishment in each county of a common pleas court to be composed of not less than three nor more than five members. These members appointed and commissioned by the territorial governor were given jurisdiction in all civil matters.[2] The same act established in each county a primary court called the court of general quarter session of the peace to be composed of no more than five nor less than three justices of the peace, appointed and commissioned by the governor.[3] This court, which had limited jurisdiction in criminal matters, was not re-established by the constitution of 1802 and the jurisdiction which had been exercised by this court was conferred upon the justices of the peace and the court of common pleas.[4]

When a constitution was drafted for Ohio in 1802, preparatory to the entrance of the state into the Union, provision was made for a continuation of the territorial court of common pleas.[5] The articles of the Ohio Constitution, regarding the judiciary, provided for a court of common pleas in each county to be composed of a president and associate judges.

---

1. George Burton Adams, *Constitutional History of England* (New York, 1921), 109, 134.
2. Pease, *op. cit.,* 7.
3. Pease, *op. cit.,* 4.
4. Pease, *op. cit.,* 5; *Laws of Ohio,* I, 40; II, 235.
5. *Ohio Const. 1802,* Art. III, sec. 1.

For each county[6] not more than three or less than two associate judges were to be appointed, with one president for each of three judicial districts into which the counties were grouped. The associate judges were not as a rule men who had a legal education.[7] The members of the court, appointed by joint ballot of both houses of the general assembly, were to hold court in three judicial districts into which the state was to be divided by legislative action. Their term of office was seven years "if so long they behave well."[8]

It was almost half a century before any significant changes were made in the structure of the court. The constitution of 1851 provided that judges of the common pleas courts were to be elected for a five-year term. For the purpose of their election the state was divided into nine districts composed of three or more counties. Each district, in turn, was to be subdivided into three parts, in each of which one common pleas judge was to be elected. The court of common pleas was to be held by one or more of these judges in each county in the district.[9] Power was given to the general assembly to increase or diminish the number of districts of the court of common pleas, the number of judges in any district and to change the districts of the subdivisions thereof, whenever two-thirds of the legislature concurred therein.[10] Provision was also made for the removal of judges by a concurrent resolution of two-thirds of the members elected to each house of the legislature.[11] An appellate court known as the district court was created and was to be composed of one supreme court judge and the several common pleas judges of the district.

---

6. At this time there were eight counties in the state.
7. Francis J. Amer, *The Development of the Judicial System in Ohio from 1787 to 1932* (Johns Hopkins University, Baltimore, 1932. *Institute of Law Bulletin No. 8*), 17.
8. *Ohio Const. 1802*, Art. III, sec. 8.
9. *Ohio Const., 1851*, Art. IV, secs. 3, 4.
10. *Ibid.*, Art. IV, sec. 15.
11. *Ibid.*, Art. IV, sec. 17.

This court was to be held in each county of the district at least once in each year or at least three annual sessions in not less than three places.[12] The district courts were not a success, and after many attempts at revision the circuit courts, staffed by a separate group of elected judges, were adopted by vote of the people in 1883, thus relieving the common pleas judge us of this appellate work.[13]

The juvenile court was created in 1904, with jurisdiction in special matters relating to minors and was to be held by a judge of the court of common pleas, court of insolvency, or probate court who should be designated by the judges to hold such court.[14]

At the opening of the 20th century sweeping changes in the organization of the courts were made. Constitutional amendments adopted in 1912 abolished the divisions and subdivisions of the common pleas provided by the constitution of 1851, and authorized the election of one or more common pleas judges in each county.[15] The chief justice of the supreme court was given authority to determine the disability or disqualification of any judge of the court of common pleas and also to assign any judge to hold court in any county.[16] Eleven years later the selection of a chief justice of the court of common pleas was authorized. Under an act of March 13, 1923, in counties having two or more common pleas judges, a chief justice was designated by vote of the judges. The justice so designated by his colleagues was to serve in such capacity until the expiration of his term, after which time the office was to be an elective one.[17]

9. *Ohio Const. 1851,* Art. IV, secs. 3, 4.
10. *Ibid.,* Art. IV, sec. 15.
11. *Ibid.,* Art. IV, sec. 17.
12. *Ibid.,* Art. IV, sec. 5, 6.
13. Amer. *op. cit.,* 31-33; *Laws of Ohio,* LXXXI, 168.
14. *Laws of Ohio,* XCVII, 562. See also pp. 171-174.
15. *Ohio Const. 1851,* Art. IV, sec. 3.
16. *Ibid.,* Art. IV, secs. 3, 6.
17. *Laws of Ohio,* CX, 52.

The elective section of the act was nullified in effect, in 1924, by the supreme court on the grounds that the creation of a new elective office was unconstitutional. Accordingly, in 1927, an amendment was passed eliminating the elective provision of the act.[18]

In recent years attempts have been made to improve the efficiency of the court by imposing stricter qualifications upon those who seek election to the bench. In 1917 an act was passed providing that a common pleas judge shall have been admitted to practice as an attorney at law for a period of six years preceding his election.[19] The salary of the office was also increased to $3,000 per year plus an amount based on the population of the county[20] – thus making the position financially attractive, especially as the term of office is six years.[21] In addition to the regular salaries, common pleas judges may be paid a per diem allowance and expenses when assigned to special duty by the chief justice of the supreme court in a district not their own. When dockets become crowded or judges are incapacitated or disqualified, such assignments may be made[22] in the more populous counties, judicial efficiency is promoted by assigning to certain common pleas judges specialized duties such as the hearing of domestic relations and juvenile court cases.

---

18. *State ex rel.,* v. *Powell, Ohio State Reports,* CIX, 383; *Laws of Ohio,* CXII, 5; G. C. sec. 1558.
19. *Laws of Ohio,* CVII, 164.
20. G. C. secs. 2251-2252.
21. G. C. sec. 1532.
22. *Ohio Const., 1851* (Amendment, 1912), Art. IV, sec. 3; G. C. secs.1469. 1687, 2253.

The jurisdiction of the court of common pleas has also been a product of a long period of historical development. The territorial law of 1788 which created the court provided that "the judges so appointed and commissioned . . . shall hold pleas of assizes, *scire, facias, replevins,* and hear and determine all manner of pleas, actions, suits, and causes of a civil nature, real, personal, and mixed, according to the constitution and laws of the territory."[23] Individually, each judge of the common pleas was given jurisdiction over contract actions not exceeding $5.24.[24] The probate court was established by an act adopted August 30, 1788, and two of the judges of the court of common pleas sat with this judge in ruling on contested points, definitive sentences, and final judgments. Under the laws of 1788 the common pleas had no criminal jurisdiction, and the quarter sessions of the peace had no civil jurisdiction. There was no provision for an appeal from one court to another except from the probate court to the general court of the territory.[25]

In 1795 the judicial system underwent the first general revision and this increased the duties of the court of common pleas. A single justice of the peace or judge of the common pleas was given jurisdiction to hear certain civil actions up to $12. Actions under $5 were exclusive with the judges or justices and there was no appeal from their judgment. Actions between $5 and $12 could be appealed to the court of common pleas. In 1799 this jurisdiction was raised to $20 and appeals could be taken to the common pleas if the judgment was over $2. If the judgment was for plaintiff, he could appeal only if the original demand was $4 more than the sum recovered.[26]

---

23. Salmon P. Chase, comp., *The Statutes of Ohio and of the Northwest Territory, 1788-1833* (Cincinnati, 1833), I, 94.
24. Pease, *op. cit.,* 8.
25. Chase, *op. cit.,* I, 96.
26. Chase, *op. cit.,* I, 143, 233, 307.

Appeal from the common pleas to the general court was provided for in 1795, and could not be taken unless the title to land was in question or when the amount and controversy exceeded $50.[27]

The constitution of 1802 gave the court of common pleas jurisdiction in such common law and chancery cases that should be directed by law. In addition it was given jurisdiction of all probate and testamentary matters, and the appointment and supervision of guardians.[28] Moreover, the court of common pleas and supreme court were assigned original cognizance of criminal cases as might be provided by law.[29] By statutory provision in 1804, appeals in civil cases might be made to the court of common pleas from the county commissioners, justices of the peace, and other inferior courts.[30]

An act of the first general assembly in 1803 provided for the organization of the courts and defined their jurisdiction. The court of common pleas was given original jurisdiction in all cases, both in law and in equity, when the matter in dispute exceeded the jurisdiction of the justice of peace; of all probate, testamentary, and guardianship matters; and of all criminal matters exceeding the jurisdiction of the justice of peace, except when the punishment of the crime was capital. It was allowed to review certain cases from the justices of peace and also to review the decisions of the county commissioners in highway matters. In addition, the court had the same power to issue remedial and other process, *writs* of error and *mandamus* excepted, as had the supreme court.[31] In 1804 the courts' jurisdiction in chancery cases was limited to cases involving less than $500[32] and in 1805 it was given appellate jurisdiction from the justices of peace in all cases regardless of the amount involved.[33]

----

27. Chase, *op. cit.,* I, 306.
28. *Ohio Const. 1802,* Art. III, secs. 3, 5.
29. *Ibid.,* Art. III, sec. 4.
30. Chase, *op. cit.,* I, 421, 425.
31. *Ibid.,* I, 355.
32. *Laws of Ohio,* II, 261.
33. *Ibid.,* III, 14.

In 1806 crimes wherein the punishment was capital could be tried in the common pleas court if the accused so elected.[34] In 1807 it was given jurisdiction in all chancery cases and concurrent jurisdiction with the supreme court in such cases involving over $500.[35] In 1810 all cases in which the common pleas had original jurisdiction were permitted to be appealed to the supreme court.[36] By this act right to appeal was established in Ohio in all civil cases. However, the business of the supreme court increased so rapidly, that in 1845, the right to appeal from a judgment of the common pleas court to the supreme court in actions at law, was abolished. Instead, new trials were allowed "when law and justice required it."[37] Even earlier, appeals to the common pleas from inferior courts had been limited.[38] The chancery act, adopted in 1824, then for general chancery powers on the court, [39] and in 1843, it was given concurrent jurisdiction with a supreme court in cases of divorce and alimony.[40]

The constitution of 1851 left the jurisdiction of the common pleas court to be fixed by law.[41] The jurisdiction conferred on this court by subsequent legislation was essentially the same as that exercised since 1810, with the exception of the jurisdiction which was transferred to the probate court, [42] and the addition, in 1853, of exclusive jurisdiction in divorce and alimony cases.[43]

---

34. *Ibid.,* IV, 57.
35. *Ibid.,* V, 117.
36. *Laws of Ohio,* VIII, 259.
37. *Ibid.,* XLIII, 80.
38. *Ibid.,* XXXVIII, 27.
39. *Ibid.,* XXII, 75.
40. *Ibid.,* XLI, 94.
41. *Ohio Const. 1851,* Art. IV, secs. 3, 4.
42. *Laws of Ohio,* L, 87. Records pertaining to probate matters were to be transferred to the probate court wherever it was possible to separate them from common pleas records. *Ibid.,* L, 88.
43. *Ibid.,* LI, 377

The court of common pleas was denied jurisdiction in cases of probate, testamentary, and guardianship matters, but final orders, judgments, and decrees of the probate court could be reviewed in common pleas on appeal or by writ of certificates.[44] In 1853 the court of common pleas was given original jurisdiction of all crimes and offenses except minor criminal cases, the exclusive jurisdiction of which was vested in the justice of peace or other minor courts.[45]

The creation of criminal, mayors', and police courts also made certain changes in the powers and duties of common pleas courts.[46] The right to appeal from common pleas to the district court was restored in all civil actions in which the common pleas had original jurisdiction, [47] but by an act of 1858 appeals were allowed to the immediate court only in non-jury cases. However, the same act provided for a second jury trial in common pleas as a matter of right in jury cases. This was granted upon demand made by either party at the close of the first trial on condition of his giving bond.[48] The abuse of this privilege led to its abolishment in 1875.[49] This period witnessed the reestablishment of superior courts in the state, which were given the same jurisdiction as the court of common pleas with certain exceptions.[50] At the same time the superior court was established at Cincinnati, the legislature abolished the criminal court and transferred its jurisdiction to the common pleas court.[51] The criminal jurisdiction of the probate court was transferred to the common pleas court in 1857.[52]

---

44. *Laws of Ohio,* L, 84; LI. 145.
45. G. C. sec. 13422-5; *Laws of Ohio,* LI, 474; LII, 73.
46. *Laws of Ohio,* L, 90, 240, 246, 251, 253.
47. *Ibid.,* L, 93.
48. *Ibid.,* LV, 81.
49. *Ibid.,* LXXII, 34.
50. *Laws of Ohio,* LII, 34; LIII, 38; LIV, 37.
51. *Ibid.,* LII, 107.
52. *Ibid.,* LIV, 97.

The limitation was placed on the right to appeal from probate court to common pleas in 1854.[53] This limitation was repealed, however, in 1856.[54]

For many years there were few changes in the powers of the court of common pleas except in the form of appeal to higher courts,[55] and such added powers as resulted from the decline in the number of superior courts.[56] In 1906 the probate court was given concurrent jurisdiction with common pleas in all counties in the trial of misdemeanors and all proceedings to prevent crimes.[57]

Since 1906 the court of common pleas has had jurisdiction in naturalization proceedings. In that year the federal statute was amended to limit jurisdiction in the granting of naturalization to the United States district courts and state courts having a clerk, a seal, jurisdiction in matters of law and equity in which the amount of controversy is unlimited.[58]

Constitutional amendments adopted in 1912 had little effect upon the jurisdiction of the court of common pleas, this power being determined by law.[59] In 1911, the juvenile courts were given jurisdiction of all misdemeanors against minors and certain other offenses.[60] Provision was also made for error proceedings from juvenile court to the court of common pleas.[61] The jurisdiction of the common pleas court of today is essentially the same as that of 1913. The few changes that have been made in the judicial system are found in the local, special courts, particularly in the rapid developing municipal courts.

_____

53. *Ibid.,* LII, 104.
54. *Ibid.,* LIII, 8.
55. *Ibid.,* LXXIV, 359; LXXXII, 230.
56. *Ibid.,* LXII, 58; LXXII, 89, 105; LXXXII, 85.
57. *Ibid.,* X CVIII, 49.
58. *United States Statutes at Large,* XXXIV, pt. i, 596.
59. *Ohio Const. 1851,* Art. IV, sec. 6.
60. *Ibid.,* CII, 425.
61. *Ibid.,* CIII, 875.

The common pleas court was never possessed extensive a point of powers. The constitution of 1802 authorized each court to appoint a clerk, [62] and in 1805 it was directed to appoint a county prosecuting attorney.[63] During the first three decades of Ohio history, the movement for the extension of the popular election of public officers deprived the court of common pleas of the privilege of appointing the court recorder (1829), the county surveyor (1831), and the county prosecuting attorney (1838).[64] The court continued to appoint a clerk of courts until 1851. In recent years however, as new functions have been added to the county government, the court has again been given a limited appointive power. Successive acts in 1886, 1891, 1913, 1914, and 1925, authorized the court to appoint a soldiers' relief commission, a jury commission, and assignment commissioner, a conservancy district board, and a probation officer.[65] In 1882, the court was empowered to appoint a board of county visitors but this power was transferred to the probate court in 1913.[66] Other appointments authorized are those of court interpreter and criminal bailiff (1911), [67] inspectors of meetings of corporation stockholders, trustees for county memorial buildings, boards of trustees for endowed libraries, and one member of the metropolitan housing authority in such counties as maintained these agencies.[68]

62. *Ohio Const., 1851,* Art. III, sec. 6.
63. *Laws of Ohio*, III, 47.
64. *Laws of Ohio*, XXVII, 65; XXIX, 399; Chase, *op. cit.*, III, 1935.
65. *Ibid.,* LXXXIII, 232; LXXXVIII, 200; CIII, 512; CIV, 13-64; CXI, 423.
66. *Ibid.,* LXXIX, 107; CIII, 173.
67. G. C. sec. 1541.
68. *Laws of Ohio,* LXXXIV, 115; XCV, 41; CVI, 4?5; CXV, pt. ii, 56.

The court may also appoint a court reporter (or reporters), [69] and may cooperate with the county commissioners for the establishment of county department of probation, in which case the court appoints certain probation officers and supervisors their work.[70] In case the sheriff is absent, disabled, or disqualified from serving the court warrant, the judge may appoint temporarily and official for this service.71. By and large, however, the patronage power of the court of common pleas is a negligible factor in county government. Since 1805, the court has been authorized to issue ferry licenses[72]and tavern keepers' licenses.[73] Both ferry and tavern licenses may now be issued by municipal corporations also in the latter by the state fire marshal.[74] From 1803 to 1852, this court also issued licenses to ministers to solemnize marriage ceremonies; this function has since been exercised by the probate court.[75]

The keeping of the records of the common pleas court presented no particular difficulties for many decades, However, with the increased number of issues presented to the court in recent years, the problem of judicial administration becomes greater. This problem was solved in part by the creation of the office of chief justice of the court of common pleas who has been given the duties of the court, classifying it, and distributing it among the judges. Besides the duties enumerated, the chief justice annually makes a report to the clerk of courts showing the work performed by the court and by each judge in the preceding calendar year. Moreover he reports such other data as the chief justice of the supreme court may require.[76]

---

69. G. C. secs. 1546-1554.
70. G. C. secs. 1554-1 to 1554-6/
71. G. C. sec. 2828.
72. *Laws of Ohio,* III, 96; G. C. secs. 5947, 5949.
73. *Laws of Ohio,* XXIX, 310.
74. G. C. secs 3642, 3672, 843-3.
75. *Laws of Ohio,* I, 31; L, 84.
76. G. C. sec. 1552.

Judges of the common pleas courts are also required to issue an annual order as to the exact time of sessions. The clerk of courts is required to make this information public and to send a copy to the secretary of state. The law sets certain requirements as to the sessions of the court and the power of the judge to call special sessions.77. The records of the court are deposited for safekeeping with the clerk of courts. The clerk is custodian also of all law's reports and books furnished by the state for the use of the court and the bar and is made liable in the event of their destruction.[78]

This court in Medina County is presided over by but one judge, whose salary is $3,890 annually, $890 of which is paid by the county.[79] During the year 1940, this court heard 305 civil cases, 46 criminal cases, [80] 40 petitions for naturalization, [81] and granted 91 divorces.[82] The clerk from the office of clerk of courts is usually in attendance, as well as a bailiff.

77. G. C. secs 1533-1539.
78. *Laws of Ohio,* LXVIII, 109.
79. Pay Rolls, 1940, *see* entry 288.
80. Judicial Statistics to Secy. [Secretary] of State, 1940, *see* entry 112.
81. *Ibid.*
82. *Ibid.*

Civil Cases

115. JUDGES CALENDAR, CIVIL CASES
1896-1899, 1910——. 8 vols.

Calendar of civil cases filed in common pleas court, showing names of prosecuting and defense attorneys, court term, names of plaintiff and defendant, case number, cause of action or charge, disposition, including judge's own memoranda, and volume letter or number and page number of Common Pleas Journal, entry 125, and Record, Common Pleas, entry 127. Arranged chronologically by court terms, thereunder by case numbers. No index. Handwritten. Average 1000 loose leaf pages. 9 x 15 x 7.5. 2 volumes, 1896-1899, South storeroom; 6 volumes, 1910——, Clerk of courts' record room.

116. CIVIL CASES
1876——. 48 file boxes (labeled by contained case numbers). 1818-1875 in Original Case Papers, entry 84.

Original records of civil cases brought to court, including common pleas court criminal cases, 1818-1893, divorce, recovery of money or property, transfer of funds, foreclosures, subpoenas, sheriff's summons, executions, and return of *writs*, journal entries, and court findings showing names of plaintiff and defendant, names of attorneys, date filed, court proceedings, and final disposition of case. All papers in each case are in individual folders, showing common pleas case number, names of plaintiff and defendant, date commenced, date disposed of, calendar volume and page numbers, journal volume and page numbers and names of attorneys for plaintiff and defendant; also contains Criminal Cases, 1818-1882, entry 129. Arranged numerically by case numbers. For separate indexes, see entries 77, 78, 1816-1916, handwritten on printed forms; 1917——, typed on printed forms. 18 x 26 x 52. Clerk of courts' office.

Naturalization

117, NATURALIZATION RECORD
1835-1862. 1 vol.

Record of naturalization of aliens, showing name of applicant, date of declaration, nativity, names of witnesses to residence in United States, copy of affidavit and oath of allegiance to the United States by applicant, final certificate, and date filed. Arranged chronologically by dates filed. Indexed alphabetically by names of applicants. Handwritten. 200 pages. 15 x 10.25 x 1. Clerk of courts' record room,

118. NATURALIZATION SERVICE PETITION AND RECORD
1902—. 13 vols. (1unlabeled; 9 labeled 1-5, 1-3, , 1; 3 A, B, C). Title varies: Naturalization Record, 1904-1906, 1 vol.

Petition of aliens to become naturalized citizens of United States on regular forms prescribed by United States Department of Commerce and Labor, Bureau of Investigation and Naturalization, with affidavit of citizens of United States affirm the petition of aliens; also Oaths of Allegiance by aliens upon receipt of final papers, showing name of alien, date of recording and naturalization, signature of officer receiving oath, and naturalization paper receipt number. Arranged chronologically by dates recorded and also arranged numerically by nationalization paper receipt numbers indexed alphabetically by names of aliens. Handwritten on printed forms. Average 100 pages. 16 x 10 x 2. 9 volumes, 1902-1903, 1907-1928, Clerk of courts' record room; 1 volume, 1904-1906, 3 volumes, 1929—, Clerk of courts' office.

Criminal Cases

119. JUDGES CALENDAR, ORIGINAL CASES
1875-1879, 1907—. 2 vols

Calendar of criminal cases filed in common pleas court, showing names of prosecuting and defense attorneys, court term, name of defendant, case number, cause of action or charge, disposition, including judges own memoranda, and volume and page numbers of Criminal Record, entry 128; also includes probation record, 1908—. Arranged chronologically by court terms and numerically thereunder by case numbers. No index. Handwritten. Average 1,000 loose leaf pages. 9 x 15 x 7. 1 volume 1875-1879, South storeroom; 1 volume 197—, Clerk of courts' record room.

120. CRIMINAL APPEARANCE AND EXECUTION DOCKET
1879—. 6 vols. (1-6). 1818-1879 in Appearance and Execution Docket, entry 122.

Docket of criminal cases, showing case number, court term, names of plaintiff, defendant, and attorneys, volume letter or number and page number of Common Pleas Journal entry 125, statement of court proceedings, charge, affidavits, warrants, recognizance bonds, pleadings, *demurrers*, and if jury trial, date jury sworn, jury viewing, charge, verdict, sentence (if guilty), warrant to convey, date of parole (if paroled), volume and page numbers of criminal record, entry 128, where complete case is recorded, volume and page number of Sheriff's Foreign Execution docket, 1879-1884, entry 219; Sheriff's Docket of Foreign Summons and Returns, 1879-1884, entry 220, and itemized cost bill; also contains: Prosecuting Attorney's Criminal Docket, 1909—, entry214; Prosecuting Attorney's Cash Book, 1908—, entry 218; and Probation Records, 1908—, entry 199. Arranged chronologically by court terms. Indexed alphabetically. by names of defendants. Handwritten on printed forms. Average 400 pages. 18 x 13 x 4. Clerk of courts' record room.

121. BILLS OF EXCEPTION, 1912— in Court of Appeals Record, entry 147 and Court of Appeals Record [Original Papers], entry 148, and 1922— in [Original Case Papers], entry 84.

Original bills of exception, showing date appealed to higher court, volume letter or number and page number of Appearance and Execution Docket, entry 122, type of case, date overruled or decision of court, date filed with clerk of courts, signatures of clerk and deputy, date of notice of filing, transmission to trial judge, objections to exceptions, date received, signature of trial judge, dates corrected, date of exceptions, date received by clerk and filed with court of appeals, volume letter or number and page numbers of Court of Appeals Record, entry 147, case number, names of defendants' witnesses, name of attorney, disposition of case, motions carried, certificate of correction, and signatures of courts stenographer and common pleas judge.

122. APPEARANCE AND EXECUTION DOCKET
1818—. 90 vols. (57 vols. labeled by contained letters of alphabet; 33 vols 1-33). Title varies: Execution Docket, 1818-1883, 21 vols.

Appearance docket of civil cases in common pleas court, show in court term, pace number, cause of action, names of plaintiff, defendant, and attorneys, whether case was settled out of court or came to trial, date of court proceedings, court orders, judgment and itemized cost bill, date judgment satisfied, and volume letter or number and page numbers of journal entry and complete record. Also contains: Criminal Appearance and Execution Docket, 1879—, entry 120; Alimony and Support Payments, 1875-1938, entry 115; Trial Docket, 1818-1839, 1842-1844, 1847-1884, 1913—, entry 123; Sheriff's Docket of Foreign Summons and Returns, 1818-1884, entry 220; and Sheriff's Foreign Execution Docket, 1818-1884, entry 219. This serves as an index to entry 84. Arranged chronologically by court terms. Indexed alphabetically by names of plaintiffs and defendants. For separate indexes, see entry 77, 78, 81, 82.1818-1912, Handwritten on printed forms;

1912—, typed. Average 425 pages. 18.5 x 13 x 3. Clerk of courts' record room.

123. TRIAL DOCKET
1885-1912. 2 vols. (1, 2). 1818-1839, 1842-1844, 1847-1884, 1913— in Appearance and Execution Docket, entry 122.

Trial docket showing names of attorneys, data filing, names of plaintiff and defendant, title of case, and judges memoranda. Arranged chronologically by dates filed. Indexed alphabetically by names of plaintiffs and defendants. Handwritten on printed forms. Average 100 pages. 16.5 x 11 x 1.25. 1 volume, 1885-1903, South storeroom; 1 volume, 1904-1912, Clerk of courts' record room.

124. MOTION DOCKET
1897—. 3 vols. (3-5).

Docket of motions presented in common pleas court, including approval of appointment of deputy sheriff, showing name of deputy sheriff, date appointed, and oath of office and signature of deputy; also contains jury commissioners' records, showing motion of jury commission to draw names for jurors, motions for meetings of grand and petit juries, lists of grand and petit jurors, court term, name and address of juror, name of township or city ward, date drawn, and date subpoenaed; petit jury, showing type of case, case number, and date of trial. Arranged chronologically by dates of appointment, court term, or trials. No index. Handwritten on printed forms. Average 80 pages. 16 x 11 x .25. 2 volumes, 1897-1937, Clerk of courts' record room. 1 volume, 1937—, Clerk of courts' office.

125. COMMON PLEAS JOURNAL
1818—. 37 vols. (A-Z; 1-11).

Journal entries of all cases filed and heard in common pleas court; civil cases, including divorce, showing court term, case number, names of plaintiff and defendant, title of case, court proceedings consisting of petitions, bills of particulars, affidavit of information, cross petitions, exceptions, *demurrers*, motions for new trials, court orders and decrees, judgments, and decisions; criminal cases, showing court term, case number, names of plaintiff and defendant, indictment, disposition of case, date of parole (if paroled), and if jury trial, name of jurors, verdict, reports of adult probationers to common pleas judge, and changing of names, 1816-1851. Also contains: Witness Docket, Common Pleas Court, 1818-1828, entry 83, and serves as a judgment docket, 1818-1934. Arranged chronologically by court terms. Indexed alphabetically by names of plaintiffs and defendants. For indexes, see entries 77, 78, 126. References to Criminal Cases made by case numbers only. Handwritten on printed forms average 525 pages. 15.5 x 10.5 x 3. Clerk of courts' record room.

126. INDEX TO JOURNAL
1818-1902. 2 vols. (1, 2).

Index to Common Pleas Journal, entry 125, showing names of plaintiff and defendant in civil cases, names of defendants in criminal cases, and volume letter or number and page number of journal where entry is found. Arranged alphabetically by names of plaintiffs and defendants. Handwritten on printed forms Average 300 pages. 16 x 11.5 x 2. Clerk of courts' record room.

127. RECORD, COMMON PLEAS
1818----. 88 vols (A-1, K-Z; 1-63).

Final record of all cases filed and heard in common pleas court including testamentary letters, guardianship, and record of wills, showing court terms, names of plaintiff and defendant, title of case, case number, date filed, copy of bill of particulars, affidavit of information of transcript from magistrates' courts, copies of petitions, cross petitions, answer of exceptions or *demurrers*, motion for new trial, jury verdict or court's findings, court orders, judgments, and decrees; also includes Criminal Record, 1818-1860, entry 128, testamentary letters, guardianship, and record of wills, 1818-1851 was transcribed into entry 161. Arranged chronologically by dates of court terms. Indexed alphabetically by names of plaintiffs and defendants. For separate indexes, see entries 77, 78. 1818-1913, handwritten on printed forms; 1914—, typed. Average 600 pages. 18 x 13 x 5. Clerk of courts' record room.

128. CRIMINAL RECORD
1861—. 12 vols. (1-11, 6). 1818-1860 in Record, Common Pleas, entry 127.

Complete record of all criminal cases heard in court of common pleas, showing date of trial, names of court and judge, case number, name of defendant, indictment by court, notice to sheriff to serve copy of indictment, sheriff's return, warrants, charges and pleas, together with a copy of the journal entry of the trial, sentence or fine, and copies (if any) to sheriff to transport prisoner to institution or punishment and date of parole (if paroled). Arranged chronologically by dates of trials. Indexed alphabetically by names of defendants. 1861-916, handwritten; 1916—, typed. Average 600 pages. 18.5 x 13 x 3.11 volumes, 1861-1940. Clerk of courts' record room, 1 volume, 1941—, Clerk of courts' office.

129. CRIMINAL CASES
1883—. 3 cartons, 3 file drawers. 1818-1882 in Civil Cases, entry 116.

Original criminal cases, showing date of trial, case number, name of court, names of defendant and attorneys, including indictments, sheriff's summons, executions, returns, recognizance, and transcript from Criminal Record, entry 128, copies of journal entries, verdict of trial, sentence (if any), record of paroled prisoners (if any), and cost bill. Arranged numerically by case numbers. No index, reference made to Criminal Record by case numbers only. Handwritten and typed. Carton, 10 x 15.5 x 23; file drawer, 12 x 15 x 26. 3 cartons, 1883-1920, North storeroom; 3 file drawers, 1921—, Clerk of courts' office.

The first constitution of Ohio provided for a supreme court consisting of three judges appointed by a joint ballot of the legislature for a seven-year term. This court was required to hold sessions at least once a year and each county.[1] The number of judges, according to constitutional provisions, might be increased to four after a period five years, in which case the judges were permitted to divide the state into two circuits. Accordingly, in 1808, the membership of the court was increased to four and the state was divided into the requisite number of circuits.[2] Two years later, in 1810, the membership of the court was reduced to three;[3] in 1824 it was again increased to four.[4]

By constitutional provision, this court was given original and appellate jurisdiction "both in common law and chancery," in such cases as should be provided by law.[5] Accordingly, by statutory provision of 1803, the supreme court was given original jurisdiction of all cases both in law and equity, where the title of land was in question or where the sum or matter in dispute exceeded the value of $1,000, and appellate jurisdiction from the court of common pleas "in all cases respecting the title of lands, or where the matter in controversy exceeded the value of one hundred dollars, and all cases were the proof of validity of wills or the right of the administration shall be in question."[6] During the first half century of Ohio history the legislature granted decrees of divorce. Although the constitution of 1802 did not prohibit the legislature from exercising such jurisdiction, the supreme court prohibited the practice in 1848.[7]

---

1. *Ohio Const. 1802,* Art. III, secs. 2, 8, 10.
2. *Laws of Ohio,* VI, 32.
3. *Ibid.,* VIII, 259.
4. *Ibid.,* XXII, 50.
5. *Ohio Const. 1802,* Art. III, sec. 2.
6. *Laws of Ohio,* I, 36, 37, 42.
7. *Bingham v. Miller,* Ohio Reports, XVII, 445.

The constitution of 1851, Article II, section 32, contained a prohibiting clause. Moreover, the court was given original cognizance in the trial of capital offenses.[8] All cases in which the title to land or freehold was in question were to be tried in the county where the land was situated. Furthermore, the court was given appellate jurisdiction from the court of common pleas, in all cases in which the court of common pleas had original jurisdiction.[9]

In 1831, the supreme court was directed to meet annually in the city of Columbus for the final adjudication of all such questions of law as may have been reserved in any county for decision. This session of the court, known as the court in bank, was required to have its decisions in each case reduced to writing, and transmitted to the clerk of the supreme court in each county in which such question was reserved. The clerk was directed to enter such decisions "on the journal of the said court" and such proceedings were to be taken as if such decisions had been made in the county.[10] Six years later, in 1837, an act was passed providing that the final judgments in the supreme court, held within any county within the state, could be reexamined and reversed or affirmed in the court in bank upon a *writ* of error.[11]

This judicial arrangement continued until the adoption of the constitution of 1851, which provided a judicial system modeled upon the federal system existing at the time. The supreme court, as established in 1851, became for the first time in Ohio history a reviewing court of last resort in the state. At the same time the jurisdiction of the supreme court was restricted. In 1853, the court of common pleas, rather than the supreme court, was given original cognizance of all crimes and offenses, except minor criminal cases, the exclusive jurisdiction of which was vested in the justices of the peace and other minor courts.[12]

---

8. *Laws of Ohio,* I, 36-37.
9. *Ibid.,* XIV, 310-354.
10. *Laws of Ohio.* XXIX, 93-94.
11. *Ibid.,* XXV, 60-62.
12. G. C. sec. 13422-5; *Laws of Ohio,* I, 474; LII, 72.

The supreme court between the years 1803 and 1843, had exclusive original cognizance in divorce and alimony cases, and from 1843 to 1853, had concurrent jurisdiction with the court of common pleas in such cases, but was denied such jurisdiction in 1853, when the latter court was granted exclusive jurisdiction in these cases.[13]

The opinions of the supreme court on circuit and the decisions of the court in bank, as transmitted to the clerk of the supreme court in each county, are in the offices of the respective clerks of courts.

---

13. *Laws of Ohio,* XLI, 94; LI, 377.

130. DOCKET OF SUPREME COURT
1824-1849. 3 vols. (B, C, D).

Docket of cases filed in supreme court, showing court term, names of litigants, title of case, date filed, names of attorneys, dates of issuing various *writs*, dates of court and final order, itemized cost bill, and volume and page numbers of supreme court record in which case is recorded; also includes sheriff's summonses, executions, and returns. Arranged chronologically by dates filed. For index, see entry 77. Handwritten. Average 250 pages. 13 x 18 x 1.5. Clerk of courts' record room.

131. RECORD, SUPREME COURT
1820-1849. 2 vols. (A, B).

Complete record of proceedings in cases filed and heard in supreme court, showing names of litigants, attorneys, and witnesses, date filed, resume of cases, from which court appealed, reasons for appeal, fees, and disposition of case. Arranged chronologically by dates filed. For index see entry 77. Handwritten. Average 400 pages. 16 x 10.5. x 2. Clerk of courts' record room.

132. [ORIGINAL PAPERS, SUPREME COURT]
1820-1849 in [ORIGINAL CASE PAPERS], entry 84.
Original papers of cases filed in supreme court and court of
common pleas, showing case numbers of common pleas and
supreme court cases, names of litigants and attorneys, volume and
page numbers of journal, and docket, arguments upon which appeal
to supreme court was made, objections, amendments, bills of
exceptions, disposition of case, and itemized cost bill. Papers for
each case in separate jacket, showing date of trial, title of case,
name of court, case number, common please appealed case
number, date of appeal, names of attorneys, and volume and page
numbers of journal and docket. North storeroom.

Until 1851, the judicial power of the state of Ohio in matters of both law and equity was vested in the supreme court, the court of common pleas, and the justices court.[1] During the first 50 years of Ohio history the supreme court served as a court of appeals, holding court in each county annually.[2] When a new constitution was adopted in 1851, the judicial system was extended by the creation of district courts composed of one supreme court justice and several common pleas judges in the district. These courts were assigned original jurisdiction in the same matter as the supreme court, and such appellate jurisdiction as might be provided by law.[3] Does by constitutional provision the courts were assigned original cognizance in *quo warranto, mandamus, habeas corpus*, and *procedando*.[4] In addition to this, in 1852, the legislature authorized the courts to issue *writs* of error, *certiorari, supersedeas, ne exeat* and all other *writs* not specially provided by statute, whenever such *writs* were necessary for the exercise of its jurisdiction. The same at the courts appellate jurisdiction from the court of common pleas in civil cases where in the ladder court had original jurisdiction.[5]

For the purposes of district courts the nine common pleas districts were apportioned into five judicial districts. A judge of the supreme court was designated to preside at the sessions of the district courts; in the event that no judge of the supreme court were present, as was often the case, the judge of the court of common pleas in whose subdivision court was being held was directed to preside.[6]

---

1. *Ohio Const. 1802,* Art. III sec. 1.
2. See p. [None given]
3. *Ohio Const. 1851,* Art. IV, secs. 5, 6.
4. *Ibid.,* Art. IV, sec. 2.
5. *Laws of Ohio,* L. 69.
6. *Ibid.*

The district courts failed to function properly. Evidence seems to indicate that the increasing number of cases coming before the supreme court made it difficult for the justices to attend the meetings of the district courts. Indeed, six years after the creation of the district courts, the supreme court dockets were overcrowded. In 1845 the legislature found it necessary to afford temporary relief by prohibiting appeals from the courts of common pleas to the supreme court.[7] Similar condition of overcrowding existed in the 1860s so that in 1865, the supreme court justices were relieved of the duty of attending the meetings of the district courts for that particular year.[8] The judicial system had become slow and cumbersome. The courts declined rapidly after 1865, and we're finally abolished.

Following the complete collapse of the district courts an amendment to the constitution, adopted in 1883, made provision for circuit courts. "The circuit courts," stated the amendment, "shall be the successors of the district courts, and all cases, judgments, records, and proceedings pending in said district courts, in the several counties, of any district, shall be transferred to the circuit courts." The district courts, however, were to continue in existence until the election and qualification of the judges of the circuit courts.[9] The circuit courts were assigned the same "original jurisdiction with the supreme court, and such appellate jurisdiction as might be provided by law." The composition of the courts and the number of circuits were left to the discretion of the legislature. Accordingly, in 1884, an act was passed dividing the state into seven circuits, and providing for the election of three judges in each circuit.[10]

---

7. *Ibid.,* XLIII, 80.
8. *Ibid.,* LXII, 72.
9. *Ohio Const. 1851,* Art. IV, sec. 6.
10. *Laws of Ohio,* LXXXI, 168.

The circuit courts, in addition to the jurisdiction conferred upon them by the constitution, [11] were authorized by the legislature to issue *writs* of *supersedas* in any case, and all other *writs* not specifically provided by statute when they were necessary for the exercise of their jurisdiction.[12] Moreover, the courts were authorized to make and publish, as they deemed expedient, rules of procedure in their respective circuits, not in conflict with the law or rules of the supreme court. The legislature directed that all cases taken to the circuit courts were to be entered on the docket in the order in which they were commenced, received, or filed, and "to be taken up and disposed of in the same order." However, cases in which persons seeking relief were imprisoned or were convicted of a felony; cases involving the validity of any tax levy or assessment; cases involving the constitutionality of a statute; and cases involving public right and proceedings *quo warranto, mandamus, procendendo,* or *habeas corpus,* could be taken up in advance of their assignment or order on the docket.[13]

The judicial system of Ohio was again slightly changed in 1912 when, by constitutional amendment the circuit courts were renamed courts of appeals. "The court of appeals shall continue the work of the respective circuit courts and all pending cases and proceedings in the circuit courts shall proceed to judgment and determine by the respective courts of appeals." The judges of the several circuit courts were designated as judges of the courts of appeals, and were directed to perform the duties thereof until the expiration of their terms of office. Vacancies caused by the expiration of the terms of office of the judges were to be filled by the electors of the respective appellate district. The term of office was fixed at six years.[14]

---

11. *Ohio Const. 1851,* Art. IV, sec. 6.
12. *Laws of Ohio,* LXXXI, 168.
13. *Ibid.*
14. *Ohio Const. 1851,* (amendment, 1912), Art. IV, sec. 6.

The jurisdiction of the court of appeals remained much the same as that of the district court in 1851. However, the court was assigned original cognizance in *writs* of prohibition and appellate jurisdiction in the trial of chancery cases.[15] Certain restrictions were imposed upon the court: "No judgement of a court of common pleas, a superior court or other court of record" shall be reversed except by "the concurrence of all the judges of the court of appeals."[16]

At present the court consists of three judges and each of the nine districts and through which the state is divided, each of whom shall have been admitted to practice as an attorney at law in the state for a period of six years immediately proceeding his election. The salary of court of appeals judges, fixed at $6,000 per year in 1913, was increased to $8,000 in 1920 and so continues.[17] The judges hold at least one session of court annually in each county in the district.[18]

Medina County was assigned to the sixth circuit court district when these courts were established[19] following the constitutional amendment of 1883.[20] It is now in the ninth district. As in all counties, the court holds at least one session in Medina each year. The record reveals an average of seven cases heard annually since 1931.[21]

15. *Ohio Const., 1851* (Amendment 1912) Art. IV, sec. 6.
16. *Ibid.*
17. *Laws of Ohio*, CIII, 418, CVIII, pt. ii. 1301.
18. G. C. sec. 1517.
19. *Laws of Ohio*, LXXXI, 168.
20. *Ohio Const., 1851*, Art. IV, sec. 1, 6.
21. Court of Appeals Appearance Docket, 1935-1941, *see* entry 144.

District Court

133. GENERAL INDEX–DISTRICT COURT
1852-1884. 1 vol.
General index to Execution Docket, entry 135; District Court Calendar, entry 134; District Court Journal, entry 136; and Record, District Court, entry 137, showing names of plaintiff and defendant and case, docket, record, and page numbers. Arranged alphabetically by names of plaintiffs and defendants. Handwritten. 400 pages. 18 x 12 x 2. Clerk of courts' record room.

134. DISTRICT COURT CALENDAR
1852-1884. 1 vol.
Docket of cases filed in district court, showing term of court, case number, date of filing, names of attorneys, plaintiff, and defendant, type of case and court orders. Arranged chronologically by dates filed. Indexed alphabetically by names of plaintiffs showing names of defendants. For separate index, see entry 133. Handwritten. 100 pages. 16 x 11 x 1. Clerk of courts' record room.

135. EXECUTION DOCKET
1852-1884. 2 vols. (1,2).
Execution docket of cases filed in district court, showing names of plaintiff and defendant, title of cases, case number, date appeal filed, dates of petitions and answers, dates *writs* issued, dates of filing notations of court orders and decisions in case, itemized cost bill, date costs paid and by whom, and volume and page numbers of journal, and record where case is recorded; also includes sheriff's summonses, executions, and returns. 1852-1867, Arranged alphabetically by names of defendants; 1868-1884, Arranged numerically by case numbers. 1852-1854, no index; 1868-1884, indexed alphabetically by names of plaintiffs showing names of defendants. For separate index, see entry 133. Handwritten on printed forms. Average 225 pages. 14 x 9 x 1/5/ Clerk of courts' office.

136. DISTRICT COURT JOURNAL
1852-1884. 1 vol. (1).
Journal entries of appealed cases, showing date of entry, time of convening and a journey each day, case number, names of plaintiff, defendant, and attorneys, resume of appealed lower court cases, reason for appeal, petition, answers, sheriff's returns, court orders and decisions, and cost bill. Arranged chronologically by dates entered. Indexed alphabetically by names of plaintiffs showing names of defendants. For separate index, see entry 133. Handwritten. 350 pages. 16 x 13 x 3. Clerk of courts' record room.

137. RECORD, DISTRICT COURT
1852-1884. 2 vols. (A, B).
Complete record of trials in district court, showing case number, court term, date of trial, resume of case appealed from lower court, reason for appeal, names of plaintiff, defendant, attorneys, and witnesses, evidence, and court decisions, and orders. Arranged alphabetically by names of plaintiffs showing names of defendants. For separate index, see entry 133. Handwritten. Average 500 pages. 18 x 14 x 4. Clerk of courts' record room.

138. [ORIGINAL PAPERS, DISTRICT COURT]
1851-1884 IN [ORIGINAL CASE PAPERS] entry 84.
Original papers of court and appealed cases, showing original and appealed case numbers, names of plaintiff, defendant, and attorneys, volume and page numbers of final record in journal entry of appealed cases, arguments upon which appeal is made, including objections, amendments, bills of exceptions, disposition of case, and itemized cost bill. Papers for each case in separate jacket or envelope, showing name of court, title of case, civil or criminal action, case number, date of hearing, and names of attorneys. North storeroom.

139. WITNESS BOOK
1851-1883. 1 vol. (1).

Record of witnesses subpoenaed in civil and criminal actions heard in district court, showing names of plaintiff and defendant, title of case, case number, date of entry, date of trial, number of witnesses for plaintiff and defendant, number of certificates issued for fees, date subpoenaed, date witness reported, name of witness, date discharge, number of days, mileage, total fee, and date certified to the auditor. Arranged chronologically by dates entered. Indexed alphabetically by title of case. Handwritten. 425 pages. 13 x 20 x 2.25. Clerk of courts' record room.

Circuit Court

140. APPEARANCE DOCKET
1884-1912. 2 vols. (1, 2).

Docket of cases filed for appearance and circuit court, showing common please case number, circuit court case number, names of plaintiff and defendant, title of appealed case, date original papers filed, dates of petitions, and motions together with decisions, journal entries, costs, and cash book entries; also includes sheriff's summonses, executions, and returns. Arranged numerically by case numbers. Indexed alphabetically by names of plaintiffs showing names of defendants. Handwritten on printed forms. Average 300 pages. 16.5 x 11.5 x 2. Clerk of courts' record room.

141. JOURNAL MEDINA CIRCUIT COURT
1885-1912. 2 vols. (1, 2).

Journal of cases and proceedings of circuit court, showing court term, case number, names of plaintiff and defendant, copy of appeal, copies of petitions, *writs*, *mandamus* issued, court orders, decrees, internal entries. Arranged chronologically by court terms. Indexed alphabetically. by names of plaintiffs showing names of defendants. Handwritten. Average 428 pages. 18.5 x 13 x 2.5. Clerk of courts' record room.

142. RECORD OF MEDINA CIRCUIT COURT
1885-1912. 3 vols. (1-3).

Complete record of cases tried before circuit court of Medina County, showing names of plaintiff, defendant, and attorneys, case number, title of case, date of entry, and final disposition. Arranged chronologically by dates entered. Indexed alphabetically. by names of plaintiffs showing names of defendants. Handwritten average 450 pages. 18.5 x 13 x 2.5. Clerk of courts' record room.

143. [ORIGINAL PAPERS, CIRCUIT COURT]
1884-1913 in [ORIGINAL CASE PAPERS], entry 84.

Original papers of court and appealed cases, showing original and appealed case numbers, names of plaintiff, defendant, and attorneys, volume and page numbers of final record in journal entry of appealed cases, arguments upon which appeal is made, including objections, amendments, bills of exception, disposition of case, and itemized cost bill. Papers for each case in separate jacket, showing name of court, title of case, whether civil or criminal action, case number, date of hearing, and names of attorneys. North storeroom.

Court of Appeals

144. COURT OF APPEALS APPEARANCE DOCKET
1912—. 1 vol. (1).

Docket of cases filed in court of appeals, showing names of plaintiff, defendant, and attorneys, case number, title of case, date case was filed, days of filing *writs* and exceptions, and dates of court decrees and mandates; also include sheriff's summonses, executions, and returns in Court of Appeals Trial Docket, 1933—, entry 145. Arranged chronologically by dates cases filed. Indexed alphabetically by names of plaintiffs. Handwritten on printed forms. 300 pages. 16 x 11.5 x 2. Clerk of courts' office.

145. COURT OF APPEALS TRIAL DOCKET
1913-1932. 1 vol. (1). 1933— in Court of Appeals Appearance Docket, entry 144.

Docket of cases filed in court of appeals, showing names of plaintiff and defendant, case number, names of attorneys, volume and page number of Court of Appeals Journal, entry 146, title of case, date case was filed, dates of filing *writs* and exceptions, dates of court decrees, and mandates. Arranged chronologically by dates filed. Indexed alphabetically by names of plaintiffs showing names of defendants. Handwritten on printed files. $185 pages. 16 x 11.5 x 1.5. Clerk of courts' office.

146. COURT OF APPEALS JOURNAL
1912—. 1 vol. (1).

Record of cases appealed from the court of common pleas, showing term, case number, date of entry, names of plaintiff and defendants, copy of appeals, copies of petitions, *writs*, *mandamus* issued, court orders, decrees, and journal entries. Arranged chronologically by dates entered. Indexed alphabetically by names of plaintiffs showing names of defendants. No index. Handwritten on printed forms. 300 pages. 18 x 12 x 2.5. Clerk of courts' office.

147. COURT OF APPEALS RECORD
1912—. 3 vols. (1-3).

Record of court of appeals cases, showing date of entry, date of filing, case number, names of plaintiff and defendant, bills of exception, statement of facts of case, action of court, motions for appointment of receivership, order of sale, land appraised, description and location of property, confirmation of sale, directions and disposition of money, approval of court, petitions, causes of action, applications for exemption, answers, *demurrers*, records of *praecipe*, summons, and journal entry. Arranged chronologically by dates entered. Indexed alphabetically by names of plaintiffs showing names of defendants. Handwritten and typed, some on printed forms. Average 450 pages. 18 x 13 x 2. Clerk of courts' office

148. COURT OF APPEALS RECORD [ORIGINAL PAPERS]

1922—. 200 bdls. 8 file drawers. 1913-1921 in [ORIGINAL CASE PAPERS], entry 84.

Original papers issued in cases filed on appeal from lower courts in court of appeals, including affidavits on appeal, appeal bonds, petitions, amended petitions, answers, *demurrers, writs*, sheriff's Returns on *writs*, depositions, and journal entries, showing names of plaintiff and defendant, nature of case, case number, docket number, date issued, itemized cost bill, and bills of exception. Each case in an individual folder, showing court of appeals case, number, court of common pleas case number, plaintiff against defendant, volume and page numbers of journal, volume and page numbers of record, date filed, names of clerk, deputy, and plaintiff's attorney. Arranged numerically by case numbers. No index. Typed on printed forms. Bundles, 15 x 10 x .5. file drawers, 11 x 16 x 24. Clerk of courts' office.

The probate court, established by an act of the Northwest Territory on August 30, 1788, consisted of a probate judge with jurisdiction in probate, testamentary, and guardianship matters, and two judges of the court of common pleas, who sat with him and ruled on contested points, definitive sentences, and final judgments.[1]

The judicial system established under the first constitution of Ohio in 1802 did not provide for a probate court but vested the court of common pleas with such powers as had been exercised by the court in the territorial period. The constitution of 1851 re-created the probate court and gave its original jurisdiction in "probate and testamentary matters, the appointment of administrators and guardians, the settlement of accounts of executors, administrators and guardians, and such jurisdiction in *habeas corpus* . . . and for the sale of land by executors, administrators and guardians, and such other jurisdiction . . . as may be provided by law."[2] An amendment to the constitution, adopted in 1912, authorized the common pleas judge, when petitioned by 10 percent of the qualified voters in counties having a population less than 60,000 to submit to the voters at any general election the question of combining the probate court and the court of common pleas.[3]

One of the primary functions of the court since its inception has been the settlement of estates. The civil code adopted in 1853 gave the court original jurisdiction in taking proof of wills, in granting letters testimony, and in settling accounts of executors and administrators.[4] Until 1854 the court had jurisdiction in enforcing the payment of debts and legacies of deceased persons. While the court retains the original jurisdiction regarding estates, new duties have been added in recent years.

---

1. Pease, *op. cit.*, 9.
2. *Ohio Const., 1851*, Art. IV, secs. 7, 8.
3. *Ibid.*, Art. IV, sec. 7.
4. *Laws of Ohio,* LI, 167.

With the development of inheritance tax laws in 1919 as a new means of taxation the probate court has been required to determine and assess the tax after the county auditor has appraised the descendant's estate.[5]

By constitutional provision the probate court has original jurisdiction in granting marriage licenses.[6] The court also issues licenses to ministers to solemnize marriages.[7] The former provision was modified by an act adopted in 1931, which requires a lapse of at least five days between the time of application and that of the issuance of marriage licenses. However, power to suspend the operation of the act is vested in the probate judge.[8]

The jurisdiction of the court extends to the state's unfortunates. By the probate code of 1853, re-enacted in 1854, exclusive jurisdiction was granted to the court to make inquests respecting lunatics, insane persons, idiots, deaf and dumb persons, subject by law to guardianships.[9] In 1856, the court was authorized to commit mentally incompetent persons to state institutions maintained for the care of such persons.[10] Two years later the court was given power to appoint and remove guardians over minors.[11] The act, of 1859, authorized the court to render adoption decrees.[12] In 1904, the court was given jurisdiction in trial cases involving neglected, dependent, and delinquent children, [13] and in Medina County the probate judge assumed this duty in that year.[14]

---

5. *Ibid.,* CVIII, pt. i, 561
6. *Ohio Const., 1851* Art. IV, sec. 8.
7. *Laws of Ohio*, L, 84.
8. *Ibid.,* CXIV, 93.
9. *Laws of Ohio,* LI, 167; LII, 103.
10. *Ibid.,* LIII, 81-86.
11. *Ibid.,* LV, 54.
12. *Ibid.,* LVI, 82; LXVII, 14.
13. *Ibid.,* XCVII, 561.
14. *See* entry 154.

Since the middle of the 19th century the probate judge has been required to keep a record of vital statistics. In 1867, the duty of keeping a permanent record of births and deaths, which, in 1856, had been conferred upon the clerk of courts, was transferred to the probate judge.[15] When, in 1908, a bureau of vital statistics under the direction of the secretary of state was created, the probate judge was relieved temporarily of this task.[16] In 1921, the act of 1908, was amended so as to require the local registrars to transmit to the district health commissioner, who was directed to serve as the state deputy registrar of vital statistics, all certificates of births and deaths received during the preceding month, and a copy of all such certificates to the probate court. Although the general code still requires the probate judge to keep a permanent record of births and death and an index to such records, [17] neither has been kept in Medina County since 1908.

Jurisdiction and naturalization proceedings were exercised by the probate court until 1906, when an amendment to the federal statute vested exclusive jurisdiction in naturalization matters in the United States district courts and all state courts of record having a seal, a clerk, and jurisdiction in actions at law and equity in which the amount in controversy was unlimited.[18] The general code still requires the probate judge to keep a naturalization record and an index to the records, [19] but jurisdiction was transferred to the court of common pleas. No naturalization records have been kept since 1905.

---

15. *Laws of Ohio.* LXIV, 63-64.
16. *Ibid.,* XCIX, 296-307.
17. G. C. sec. 10501-15.
18. *United States Statutes at Large,* XXXIV, pt. i, 596. See also *State of Ohio* v. *George G. Metzger and Albert L. Irish,* 10 n. p., n. s., 97 *et seq.*
19. G. C. secs. 10501-15, 10501-16.

During the early years of its existence the court was given limited criminal jurisdiction in cases in which the sentence did not impose capital punishment or punishment by imprisonment. By the code of civil procedure adopted in 1853, the judgments and final decrees of the probate court could be reviewed by the court of common pleas on error.[20] In 1857, the criminal jurisdiction of the probate court was transferred to the court of common pleas,[21] but later acts remained it in certain counties only. Thus, in 1858, the probate court of certain counties, exclusive of Medina, were granted jurisdiction in all crimes in which the sentence did not impose capital punishment or imprisonment in a penitentiary.[22] This act was repealed, in 1878, and the probate courts of certain counties were granted concurrent jurisdiction with the court of common pleas in all misdemeanors and proceedings to prevent crime.[23] Such jurisdiction, however, was not granted to Medina County until 1885.[24] The probate court continued to exercise such jurisdiction, until 1931, when the last vestige of criminal jurisdiction disappeared with the adoption of the probate code.[25]

Miscellaneous duties, remotely related to probate and testamentary matters, have been added by legislative action. Since 1888, the court has been required to file a certified list of all unknown depositors as furnished by institutions or persons engaged in lending money for profit.[26] In 1896, the probate court was given concurrent jurisdiction with the court of common pleas in the matter of changing the names of persons who desired it,[27] a matter in which the court of common pleas had exclusive cognizance from 1842 to 1896.[28]

20. *Laws of Ohio,* LI, 145.
21. *Ibid.,* LIV, 97.
22. *Ibid.,* LV, 186
23. *Ibid.,* LXXV, 960
24. *Ibid.,* LXXXII, 168.
25. *Ibid.,* CXIV, 475.
26. *Ibid.,* LXXV, 65; G. C. sec. 99864.
27. *Laws of Ohio,* XCII, 28.
28. *Ibid.,* XL, 28-29.

Since 1896, the probate court has been required to record certificates of doctors and surgeons, and since 1916, the certificates of registered nurses which authorize them to practice their professions in the state.[29] Since 1913, the court has been vested with the power to grant injunctions, [30] and since 1915, has had concurrent jurisdiction with the court of common pleas in condemnation proceedings for roads.[31]

In like manner the appointive powers of the probate judge have been expanded. In addition to the authority to appoint administrators and guardians he was authorized by the act of 1891 to appoint the members of the county board of elections; however this appointive power was abrogated by the act of 1892.[32] Then, too, from 1908 to 1913 the probate judge was authorized to appoint a county blind relief commission[33] comprised of three members each of whom served a three-year term.[34] Since 1906 he has had authority to appoint members of the board of county visitors.[35]

The probate judge, like other county officials, has been required by statute to keep a record of the business of his office. The present system of records, originating for the most part in 1853 and continued by the probate code of 1931, includes an administrative docket, a guardians' docket, a marriage record, a record of bonds, a naturalization record, a criminal record for cases initiated prior to 1931, and a permanent record of births and deaths.[36]

29. *Ibid.,* XCII, 46; XCIX, 499; CVI, 193.
30. *Ibid.,* CIII, 427.
31. *Ibid.,* CVI, 583.
32. *Ibid.,* LXXXVIII, 449; LXXXIX, 455.
33. *See* page [None given].
34. *Laws of Ohio,* XCIX, 56; CIII, 60.
35. *Ibid.,* XCVIII, 28, 29; CIII, 173-174.
36. *Ibid.,* LI, 167; LII, 103; LXXV, 9; CXIV, 324.

The probate judge has the care and custody of the files, papers, books, and records belonging to the probate office and is ex-officio clerk of the court. The probate code, adopted in 1931, directed the probate judge to preserve for future reference and examination all pleadings, accounts, vouchers, and other papers in each estate, trust, assignment, guardianship, or other proceedings, such papers to be properly jacketed and tied together; he is required also to make proper entries and indexes omitted by his predecessor. Certificates of marriages, reports of births, and similar papers not a part of a case or proceeding are to be arranged and preserved separately in the order of dates in which they are filed.[37]

At present the probate judge is elected for a four-year term.[38] In recent years there has been an attempt to raise the qualifications of those seeking election to the office. Accordingly, an amendment to the probate code in 1935, restricted eligibility to the office to a practicing attorney or to be a person who *"shall have previously served as probate judge immediately prior to his election."*[39]

The probate judge in Medina County receives an annual salary of $3240[40] and his bond is set at $5000.[41] His office staff consists of two clerks and two deputies, who receive an aggregate salary of $3960, and are bonded at $1000 each.[42] The probation officer receives an annual salary of $1500[43] and is bonded for $1000.[44]

---

37. *Ibid.,* CXIV, 321-322.
38. *Ibid.,* CXIV, 320.
39. CXIV, 481.
40. Pay rolls, 1940, *see* entry 288.
41. Record of Official Bonds, 1940, *see* entry 325.
42. *Ibid.*
43. Pay rolls, 1940, *see* entry 288.
44. Record of Official Bonds, 1940, *see* entry 325.

A brief examination of the records of the probate court of Medina County will serve to show the general nature of its work. From 1936 to 1941, 639 wills were probated, 1226 estates administered, 1453 guardians appointed, and 75 children placed in adoptive homes.[45] Fifty-five persons were declared mentally ill.[46] Inheritance taxes were paid upon 1031 estates, five names were changed, and 72 estates were released from administration because they involved less than $300.[47] Vital statistics were also kept in probate court from 1867[48] to 1908. During these years, 15,375 births and 8250 deaths were recorded.[48] Since 1936, 11 doctors were issued certificates,[49] 20 nurses were registered, and five limited practitioners were issued certificates.[50]

---

45. Judges Calendar, Civil Cases, 1940, *see* entry 115.
46. Judges Calendar, Civil Cases, 1936-1941, *see* entry 115.
47. *Ibid.*
48. *Ibid.*
49. *Ibid.*
50. *Ibid.*

Civil Cases

149. PROBATE COURT CALENDAR
1837-1900, 1933—. 12 vols. (1, 2; A; 9 dated). Title varies: Court Calendar, 1837-1880, 2 vols.; Administrator's and Executor's Docket, 1881-1900, 1 vol.; Court Docket, 1891-1895, 2 vols.; Probate Docket, 1894-1897, 1 vol.

Daily calendar of matters regarding estates, showing case number, date of entry, date set for hearing, date administrator appointed or executor approved, dates bond ordered and estate inventories filed and approved, determination of heirship, waivers of next of kin, applications to transfer real estate to corporate stock, and all court matters pertaining to wills and estates; also includes appointments of guardians, adoptions, commitment for insanity or epilepsy, liquor law violations, and other criminal matters assigned to probate court, 1852-1931; determination of inheritance tax, 1919—; and Appearance Docket, Juvenile Court 1904-1936, entry 194. Arranged chronologically by dates entered. No index. Handwritten on printed forms. Average 112 pages. 17 x 12 x .25. 2 volumes, 1837-1868, 1881-1900, North storeroom; 4 volumes 1869-1880, 1891-1897, South storeroom; 6 volumes, 1933—, Probate court vault.

150. CIVIL DOCKET
1852—. 24 vols. (A-W, Y).

Docket of all proceedings of civil cases before the probate court, including guardianship, adoption, mentally ill, feeble-minded, and epileptic cases; settlement of claims; personal injury claims; trusteeships; determination of heirship; request for bank records; change of names; construction of wills; itemized cost bills; sheriff's summonses, returns, and executions of court orders, showing case number, title of case, date of entry, and volume letter or number and page number of Probate Journal, entry 154; also includes appointments of board of county visitors, 1913—; Appearance Docket, Juvenile Court, 1904-1936, entry 194; Administration Docket, 1852-1932, entry 151; and Cost Bill Record, 1933—, entry 171. Serves as an index to entry 161, by case numbers. Arranged chronologically by dates entered. Indexed alphabetically by names of cases or estates. Handwritten and typed, some on printed forms. Average 600 pages. 16 x 11.5 x 4. Probate court vault.

151. ADMINISTRATION DOCKET
1820-1851, 1933—. (1, 1, 2, 2; X, Z).

Docket of administration of estates, showing date of entry, case number, name of case, date of decedent's death, name and address of executor or administrator, name of attorney, date of probation of will, appointment of administrator or approval of executor, construction of will, determination of heirship, schedule of debts, inventory of property, transfer of real estate, election of surviving spouse, sale of personal property and real estate, first, second, and final accounts, distribution of property, inheritance tax determination, and itemized cost bill; also includes sheriff's summons and returns and Appearance Docket, Juvenile Court, 1904-1936, entry 194. Arranged chronologically by dates entered. Indexed alphabetically by names of cases or estates. Handwritten and typed, some on printed forms. Average 600 pages. 16 x 11.5 x 4. Probate court vault.

152. GUARDIAN DOCKET
1882-1899. 1 vol.

Docket, showing date of entry, guardian's application filed, petition filed, file box number of Original Probate Documents [and case papers], entry 160, name and age of ward, statement of property (real and personal), annual rents, bond filed, volume and page numbers of Record of Bonds [Administrators, Executors], entry 165; letter issued, volume and page numbers of Probate Journal, entry 154; volume and page numbers of Record of Guardians' Applications, Bonds, and Letters, entry 164; sureties, inventory of estates filed, estate personal amount, real property amount, volume and page numbers of Final Record of Land Sales [Probate Court], entry 158, first account due, file, notice published, account for hearing, exceptions filed, amount found due, second account due, third account due, fourth account due, and so on as to number of accounts. Arranged chronologically by dates entered. Indexed alphabetically by names of wards. Handwritten on printed forms. 350 pages. 18 x 12 x 2.5. Probate court vault.

Criminal Cases

153. CRIMINAL DOCKET
1852—. 2 vols. (A, B).

Docket of liquor law and traffic violations 1852-1931 and all other criminal cases assigned to probate court in Medina County, showing date of entry, case number, date of hearing, names of attorneys, name of defendant, charges, findings of the court, disposition of the case, sheriff's summons and return of *writs*, and volume and page number of Criminal Record, entry 157, and Miscellaneous Record, entry 155, where complete case is recorded; also includes Appearance docket, Juvenile Court, 1904-1936, entry 194. Arranged chronologically by dates entered. Indexed alphabetically by names of defendants. Handwritten on printed forms. Average 500 pages. 16.5 x 11 x 2. Probate court vault.

General Court Proceedings

154. PROBATE JOURNAL
1852—. 37 vols. (A-Z; A1-A7; 8-11).

Journal entries of all estates and cases filed in probate court, including liquor law violations and traffic cases, and any other criminal cases assigned to probate court, 1852-1931; juvenile cases, 1852-1904; lunacy records, 1852-1890; record of appointment for board of county visitors, 1913—; and appointments of guardians, trustees, assignees, and all other matters coming before probate court, show in case number, date of entry, name of estate, appointment of administrator, approval of executor, orders for bond, order to file accounts, petition to admit will to probate, petitions to sell real estate, orders to take inventory and appraise property, orders to sell property, inheritance tax determination, and all matters relative to estates and wills; also includes Juvenile Court Journal, 1904-1936, entry 195. Arranged numerically by case numbers. Indexed alphabetically by names of defendants, awards, estates, or principals. Handwritten and typed. Average 600 pages. 18 x 12.5 x 3 Probate court vault.

155. MISCELLANEOUS RECORD
1839-1851, 1873—. 21 vols. (labeled by contained letters of alphabet).

Complete record of probate court cases, including estate matters, showing case number, date of entry, name of estate, description of property, names of heirs, name and compensation of administrator, executor, or trustee, division of property, claims against estates, bonds, petitions to sell property, appointment of guardian, commitments of epileptic and mental cases, and adoptions; also includes violations of traffic and liquor laws, 1852-1931, juvenile court cases, 1852—, and all other cases heard in probate court. Arranged chronologically by dates entered. No index. 1839-1851, 1873-1911, handwritten: 1912, typed. Average 600 pages. 20 x 14 x 5. 19 volumes, 1839-1851, 1873-1937, 1940—, Probate court vault; 2 volumes, 1938—, South storeroom.

156. ADOPTION RECORDS
1922—. 1 vol. (1).

Record of original papers issued in adoption proceedings, showing case number, name and address of applicant, names and addresses of child and child's parents, age of child, report of investigation of application, description and location of child's property (if any), case number, and journal entry approving the application. Arranged numerically by case numbers. Indexed alphabetically by family names. Typed. 500 pages. 18 x 12 x 3. Probate court vault.

157. CRIMINAL RECORD
1852-1859, 1898-1923. 3 vols. (A; 1, 2).

Record of liquor law violations, traffic violations, and other criminal cases assigned to probate court in Medina County, showing name of defendant, case number, date of entry, offense, warrant to arrest, sheriff's summons, execution, and return of *writs* transcriptions from magistrates' courts, bond, plea of accused, record of trial, journal entries, court's decision and orders, sentence or probation, and order to sheriff to transport the accused; also includes juvenile cases. Arranged numerically by case numbers. Indexed alphabetically by names of defendants. Handwritten on printed forms. Average 260 pages. 16.5 x 11 x 2 Probate court vault.

158. FINAL RECORD OF LAND SALES [Probate Court]
1852—. 30 vols. (26 labeled by contained letters of alphabet; 14).

Record of sales of real estate by administrator, executor, or guardian, showing date of application for authority to sell, names of litigants and estates, copies of order of appraisal and sale, copies of sheriff's return of *writs*, and copies of notices of sale. Arranged chronologically by dates of applications. Indexed alphabetically by names of estates. 1852-1912, handwritten; 1912——, typed. Average 575 pages. 18 x 13 x 3. Probate court vault.

159. APPLICATION FOR ADOPTION OF CHILD
1922——. 1 file box

Original applications of persons desiring to adopt children, showing name, age, address, and occupation of applicant, financial status, complete family history, result of physical examination, whether experienced in child rearing, and type of child wanted. Arranged alphabetically by name of applicants. No index. Handwritten on printed forms. 12 x 16 x 26. Probate court office.

Original Documents

160. ORIGINAL PROBATE DOCUMENTS [And Case Papers]
1818——. 146 file drawers, 3 file cabinets. (labeled by contained case numbers).

Original probate documents, including all original estate papers, original papers concerning wills, appointments of administrators, notices of filing claims, inventories, petitions to sell personal property and real estate, to remove executor or administrator, waivers of next of kin, transcripts, court orders, decrees, determination of heirship, and determination of inheritance tax, showing case number, date of document, names of principals, volume and page numbers of Probate Journal, entry 154, itemized cost bills, guardians appointed, adoptions, ministers' licenses, names changed, commitments of mental, epileptic, other incompetence, and all other probate court cases; also includes testamentary letters, guardianships, and record of wills transcribed from record, common pleas, 1818-1851, entry 127; [Juvenile Court Cases], 1904——, entry 197, and Cost Bill record, 1911-1932, entry

172. All papers of each case filed in envelopes and labeled by case numbers and name of estate or principals. Arranged numerically by case numbers. No index. Handwritten and typed, some on printed forms. File drawers, 12 x 15 x 19; file cabinets, ?7 x 15 x 32, 78 file drawers, 2 file cabinets, 1818-1905, South storeroom; 6? File drawers, 1906—, Probate court vault.

Estates and Guardianships

Wills

161. WILL RECORD
1818—. 28 vols. (A, A-Z; 1).
Record of wills probated by the court, showing names of testator and witnesses, date of will, date filed for probate, names of heirs, disposition of estate (personal and real), name of executor or administrator, copy of journal entry approving probation of will, and estate number; also testimony of witnesses concerning sanity of testator, and a statement that all just debts will be paid. 1818-1851, transcribed from entry 127. Arranged alphabetically by names of testators and chronologically thereunder by dates of wills. 1818-1851, no index; entry 150 serves as an index by case numbers, 1852—. 1818-1911, handwritten and typed, some on printed forms; 1912—, typed. Average 500 pages. 17 x 12 x 3 Probate court vault.
    For original papers, see entry 160.

162. WILLS [Deposited]
1883—. 1 file box
Original wills filed and held by the court for safekeeping, showing name of person making will, date of filing, names of heirs, disposition of estate (real and personal property), name of executor or administrator, statement from probate judge as to the legality of the will, names of witnesses, and notarization (if any). 1883-1886, arranged chronologically by dates filed; 1887—, arranged alphabetically by names of testators and chronologically

thereunder by dates. 1883-1886, no index; for index, 1887—, see entry 163. Handwritten on printed forms. 5.5 x 11 x 7. Probate court vault.

163. INDEX AND [Record] RECEIPTS FOR WILLS DEPOSITED
1887—. 1 vol.

Index record of wills received by probate court for deposit, showing date received, name and address of testator, receipt number, and remarks; this serves as an index to Wills [Deposited], entry 162 by showing names of testators. Arranged alphabetically by names of testators and chronologically thereunder by dates received. Handwritten on printed forms. 50 pages. 14 x 8.5 x 1. Probate court vault.

Applications, Appointments, Bonds, and Letters (See also entries 149, 154, 160)

164. RECORD OF GUARDIANS' APPLICATIONS, BONDS, AND LETTERS
1852—. 12 vols. (A-L).

Record of papers issued in guardianships concerning appointments of guardians for minors, incompetents or confined persons, showing case number, date entered, name of guardian, appointment of guardian by the probate judge, notice of hearing, sheriff's return, affidavit of service, name, age, and address of ward, description and amount of property, sworn statement, signature of notary public, names of attorneys, waiver of notice, amount of bond of guardian, and signature and approval of probate judge; also contains Trustees' Bonds and Letters, 1852-1884, entry 166. Arranged chronologically by dates entered. Indexed alphabetically by names of wards. Handwritten on printed forms. Average 500 pages. 18 x 15 x 34. Probate court vault.

165. RECORDS OF BONDS [Administrators, Executors]
1818-1832. 1 vol. (1). 1861-1917,1933— in Record of
Assignments, entry 175.

Record of bonds as posted by administrators, executors, or
guardians to probate court to insure proper performance regarding
sales of real estate and for the purpose of liquidation of debts of
estates, showing name of administrator, executor, or guardian,
name of estate, date entered, amount of bond, names of sureties,
case title, date of filing, and case number. Arranged
chronologically by dates filed. Indexed alphabetically by names of
states or wards. Handwritten on printed forms. 300 pages. 16.5 x
10.5 x 1. Probate court vault.

166. TRUSTEES' BONDS AND LETTERS
1885—. 1 vol. (1). 1852-1884 in Records of Guardians'
Applications, Bonds, and Letters, entry 164.

Record of appointments, bonds, and letters of trustees of estate
funds, showing what trusteeship, name of principal, case number,
date of application, copy of application for appointment as trustee,
copy of journal entry ordering appointment, and bond; copy of
bond, showing names of appointee and sureties, kind of surety,
copy of journal entry of appointment of trustee, and signature of
probate judge. Arranged chronologically by dates of applications.
Indexed alphabetically by names of principals. Handwritten on
printed forms. 160 pages. 16 x 10 x 1.5. Probate court vault.

Inventories and Appraisements (See also entries 151, 154)

167. RECORD OF INVENTORY AND
APPRAISEMENTS
1839—. 49 vols. (26 dated and lettered A-Z; 1 dated and
numbered 27; 2 numbered 28-49). Subtitled With Widow
or Without Widow.

Record of inventories and appraisements of estates, showing
appointment of appraisers, order to appraise, case number, name of
estate, oath of appraiser, return of order with appraised valuation

of property, amount of money, accounts, real estate, certificate of true inventory by appraisers, affidavit of administrator or executor, waiver of notice of filing, consent or approval, order to file inventory, volume letter and page numbers of Probate Journal, entry 154; also contains Inventory and Sales Bills, 1860-1912, entry 169. Arranged numerically by case numbers. Indexed alphabetically by names of estates. Handwritten and typed. Average 600 pages. 18 x 13 x 3.5. Probate court vault.

168. GUARDIANS' INVENTORIES
1879—. 1 vol. (A).

Record of settlement of accounts by guardians and record of guardians' inventories of wards, showing name of incompetent or minor, address, report of personal and real property, description of property, value, and recapitulations of all debts and liabilities, date account was due, date notice was issued, date account was filed, case number, and what account, guardian's oath, and signature of court. Arranged numerically by case numbers. Indexed alphabetically by names of incompetents or minors. Handwritten on printed forms. 530 pages. 18.5 x 13 x 3. Probate court vault.

169. INVENTORY AND SALES BILLS
1839-1859, 1913—. 6 vols. (A, B, C, C; 1, 2). Title varies: Probate Record, 1839-1848, 1 vol.; Probate Court, 1852-1854, 1 vol. 1860-1912 in Record of Inventory and Appraisements, entry 167.

Record of inventories of estates of deceased persons and wards, showing case number, name of estate, name of state, name of decedent or ward, name of administrator, executor, or guardian, date inventory ordered, names of appraisers, itemized appraisement list, date filed, date sale was ordered, copy of order, date of sale, itemized account of sale of chattels, and date sale account was filed. The apparent duplication in dates 1852 - 1854, was due to the fact that an extensive inventory of drugs, surgical instruments, and chemicals, was listed in a separate volume, labeled A. Arranged numerically by case numbers. Indexed alphabetically by names of estates. Handwritten. Average 200 pages. 17.5 x 12 x 3. 3 volumes, 1839-1859, North storeroom; 3 volumes, 1913—, Probate court vault.

Schedule of Debts (See also entry 151)

170.SCHEDULE OF DEBTS RECORD
1932—. 2 vols. (A, B).
Schedule of claims, debts, and liabilities filed in probate court Medina County, showing name of estate, case number, name of deceased, itemized list of names of persons to whom estate is indebted, date of hearing, and approval of debts. Arranged numerically by case numbers. Indexed alphabetically by names of estates. Typed. Average 600 pages. 18 x 12 x 3. Probate court vault.

Cost Bills (See also entry 160)

171.COST BILL RECORD
1892-1911. 22 vols. Discontinued. 1911-1932, in Original Probate Documents [and Case Papers], entry 160; and 1933— in Civil Docket, entry 150. Subtitled Miscellaneous, 1892-1911, 2 vols; Probate of Wills, 1892-1911, 2 vols. Inventory and Appraisement, 1892-1911, 3 vols.; Inquest of Lunacy, 1892-1911, 2 vols.; Sale of Personal Property, 892-1911, 2 vols.; Sale of Real Estate, 1892-1912, 2 vols.; Guardian, 1892-1911, 2 vols.; Appointment of Administrator, 1892-1911, 3 vols.; Election of Widow, 1892-1911, 2 vols.; Accounts, 1892-1911, 2 vols. 1912— in Record of Accounts, entry 172.
Record of final costs and fees charged and settlement of estates for the following items: for probating, inventorying, filing, recording, petitions, applications, the account of final distribution of estate, including fees for sheriffs, notaries, printers, and witnesses, showing names of court and county, case number, date entered, name of estate, name of item or subject for which fee is charged,

amount of fees, amount collected in dollars and cents, date fees paid, and total amount of fees collected. Arranged chronologically by dates entered. Indexed alphabetically by names of items or subjects. Handwritten on printed forms. Average 300 pages. 14 x 9 x 1.5. 10 volumes, 1892+1898, North storeroom; 12 volumes, 1899-1911, South storeroom.

Settlements and Accounts

172. RECORD OF ACCOUNTS
1847—. 51 vols.

Complete record of accounts in connection with the settlement of estates, showing date of filing, name of decedent, assignor, or ward, case number, name and title of person filing account, itemized copy of account filed, and date approved by court; includes Cost Bill Record, 1912—, entry 171. Arranged numerically by case numbers. Indexed alphabetically by names of decedents. Handwritten and typed, some on printed forms. Average 600 pages. 18.5 x 12 x 3. Probate court vault.

Inheritance Tax (See also entries 149, 151, 160)

173. INHERITANCE TAX RECORD
1894-1895, 1919—. 3 vols. (1, 1, 2). Law repealed 1895, reinstated and revised 1919.

Record of estates subject to inheritance tax assessments, showing name of decedent, names of heirs and devisees, name of administrator, executor or trustee, kind of inheritance, value of estate, legal exemption, net value for taxation, date certificate issued to county auditor, costs assessed, amount of tax due, and date paid. Arranged chronologically by dates of certifications to auditor. Indexed alphabetically by names of decedents. 1894-1895, handwritten; 1919—, typed on printed forms. Average 263 pages. 16 4 14 x 2.5. 1 volume, 1894-1895, South storeroom; 2 volumes, 1919—, Probate court vault.

174. INHERITANCE TAX RECORD
1919——. 1 vol. (1).

Inheritance tax record, showing case number, Administration Docket, volume and page numbers, entry 151, name of decedent, date of death, post office address, administration of execution, value as fixed by judge (real and personal), estimated value of personal property, estimated value of real property, total value, value of auditor's appraisal (real and personal), total indebtedness, total cost of administration, total value auditor's appraisal, net value of estate, names and addresses of heirs-at-law, names and addresses of legatees and devisees, and total amount. Arranged chronologically by dates entered. Indexed alphabetically by names of decedents. Handwritten on printed forms. 240 pages. 18 x 12 x 3. Probate court vault.

Assignments

175. RECORD OF ASSIGNMENTS
1861——. 5 vols. (A-E).

Complete record of proceedings in assignments by insolvent debtors, showing date of assignment, date filed, names of assignor and assignee, copies of deed of assignment, order to appraise assets, appointment of appraiser, inventory and appraisement, schedule of claims against assignor, orders of sale, sale bill, and assignor's account on settlement, case number, and copy of cost bill. Also contains Records of Bonds [Administrators, Executors], 1861-1917, 1933——, entry 165. Arranged numerically by case numbers and also arranged chronologically by dates filed. Indexed alphabetically by names of assignors showing names of assignees. Handwritten. Average 600 pages. 16 x 12 x 3. Probate court vault.

Dependents
(See also entries 149, 150, 155, 160).

176. LUNACY RECORD
1891—. 4 vols. (A-D). 1852-1890 in Probate Journal,
    entry 154.
Record of proceedings on lunacy affidavits, showing case number,
name of patient, date of filing charges, name of person filing
affidavits, copies of warrant to arrest, medical certificate filed by
physician making examination of alleged lunatic, proceedings at
inquest hearing, application for admission to state institution,
warrant to convey to institution, sheriff's returns on *writs* with cost
bill, and record of discharge from institution or death of patient.
Arranged numerically by case numbers. Indexed alphabetically by
names of patients. Handwritten and typed. Average 460 pages. 13.5
x 12.5 x 2.5. Probate court vault.

Naturalization

177. NATURALIZATION RECORDS [First Papers]
1860-1895. 2 vols. (1 unlabeled; 2).
Record copies of declarations of aliens to become naturalized
citizens of the United States, showing date of filing, name of alien,
nativity, date and place of entry into the United States, date
recorded, age, residence, and occupation of alien, and certificate
number. Arranged numerically by naturalization certificate
numbers. Indexed alphabetically by names of aliens. Handwritten
on printed forms. Average 200 pages. 10 x 8 x 1. Probate court
vault.

178. NATURALIZATION RECORDS [Final Papers]
1836-1902. 7 vols. (2 unlabeled; A-C; 2, 3). Subtitled
    Minors, 1866-1885; Minors–Aliens, 1860-1844
Record of naturalization, showing date of first papers, name and
address of alien, nativity, names of witnesses to residence in the
United States, copy of affidavit and oath of allegiance to the

United States by applicant, date filed, and consecutive certificate number. One volume covers declaration and naturalization of minors only. Arranged numerically by naturalization certificate numbers and also arranged chronologically by dates filed. 1836-1859, no index; 1860-1902, indexed alphabetically by names of aliens. Handwritten on printed forms. Average 250 pages. 14 x 10 x 2.5. Probate court vault.

Vital Statistics

Births and Deaths

179. RECORD OF BIRTHS
1867-1908. 4 vols. (1 unlabeled; 1-3). Title varies: Record of Births and Deaths, 1867-1882, 1 vol.

Record of birth, showing certificate number of birth, name of child, date and place of birth, sex and race of child, name and occupation of father, maiden name of mother, and residence of parents; last half of volume contains a Record of Deaths, 1867-1882, see entry 180. Arranged numerically by certificate numbers. Indexed alphabetically by family names of children. Handwritten on printed forms. Average 200 pages. 18 x 12 x 2.5. Probate court vault.

180. RECORD OF DEATHS
1882-1908. 2 vols. (1, 2). 1867-1882 in Record of Births, entry 179.

Record of death, showing date reported, certificate number, name of decedent, date and place of death, marital status, age, occupation, date and place of birth, names of next of kin, color, cause of death, late residence, and name a person reporting death. Arranged numerically by certificate numbers. Indexed alphabetically by names of decedents. Handwritten on printed forms. Average 200 pages. 18 x 12 x 2.5. Probate court vault.

181. STATEMENT OF BIRTHS, STATEMENT OF DEATHS
1872-1909. 547 vols. 1909——, records kept by township and village clerks.
Statements of births and deaths in each township as originally reported by the township trustees; statement of births, showing statistical number, name of child, names of parents, address, place of birth, father's occupation, mother's maiden name, sex, color, and weight of child; statement of deaths, shows statistical number, name and address of deceased, age, sex, color, marital status, occupation, cause and date of death, place and date of birth, and names of next of kin. Arranged numerically by statistical numbers. Indexed alphabetically by names of decedents or children. Handwritten on printed forms. Average 20 pages. 9 x 12 .25. 14 volumes, 1872-1890, Probate court vault; 533 volumes, 1891-1909, North storeroom.

Marriages (See also entry 192)

182. MARRIAGE RECORDS
1818——. 17 vols. (A-Q).
Record of marriages performed, showing date of application, names of applicants, ages, occupations, addresses, names of parents, places of birth, license number, and clerk's certification of license; includes Minister's License Record, 1818-1851, entry 185, and Marriage Licenses Affidavits, 1880——, entry 183. 1818-1851 was transferred from common pleas court at the establishment of probate court in 1852. Arranged numerically by license numbers. For index, 1818-1869, see entry 184; 1870——, indexed alphabetically by names of males showing names of females. 1818-1859, handwritten; 1859——, handwritten on printed forms. Average 450 pages. 15 x 10 x 3.5. Probate court vault.

183. MARRIAGE LICENSE AFFIDAVITS
1833-1880. 6 vols. (A-E, E). 1880— in Marriage Records,
entry 182.
Affidavits by applicants for marriage licenses declaring themselves
to be of legal age, to have no wife or husband living, and not first
cousins or nearer of kin, showing names of applicants, ages,
occupation, address, names of parents, dates and places of birth,
date and consecutive license number, and name of probate judge.
Arranged numerically by license numbers. For index, 1833-1869,
see entry 184; 1880— indexed alphabetically by names of males
showing names of females. Handwritten on printed forms. Average
350 pages. 9 x 13 x 2.5. Probate court vault.

184. GENERAL INDEX TO MARRIAGE RECORDS
1818-1869. 2vols. (1, 2). Discontinued.
Index to Marriage Records, entry 182 and Marriage License
Affidavits, entry 183, 1833-1869, showing names of applicants,
license date, volume and page numbers of Marriage Records and
Marriage License Affidavits. Arranged alphabetically by names of
males showing names of females. Handwritten on printed forms.
Average 200 pages. 18 x 14 x 2.5. Probate court vault.

Licenses, Certificates, and Permits
(See also entry 16)

185. MINISTER'S LICENSE RECORDS
1881—. 1 vol. (1). 1818-1880 in Marriage Records, entry
182.
Record copies of licenses issued to ordained ministers to solemnize
marriages, showing the date issued, license number, name of
minister, church denomination, date recorded, and name of probate
judge. Arranged numerically by license numbers and
chronologically thereunder by dates issued. Indexed alphabetically
by names of ministers. Handwritten on printed forms. 213 pages.
16 x 11 x 2. Probate court vault.

186. PHYSICIAN'S RECORD
1896—. 1 vol. (1).
Record of physicians' certifications, showing date and number of certificate, name of physician, record of examination, evidence of doctor's degree, and recognition of right to practice medicine; also includes register of nurses and limited practitioners, 1916—, showing name, address, educational background, hospital training, and if limited practitioner. Arranged numerically by certificate numbers. Indexed alphabetically by names of doctors, nurses, or limited practitioners. Handwritten on printed forms. 200 pages. 16 x16 x2. Probate court vault.

Financial Records

187. RECORD OF ACCRUED FEES
1868-1890, 1907—. 15 vols. (A-L; 1-3).
Record of fees in administration, guardianship, and criminal cases appearing before court, showing date accrued, case number, in what matter, to whom charged, total fee, civil cases due from county, and juvenile cases, transcript and copies, sundries, and date of payment. Arranged numerically by case numbers. No index. Handwritten on printed forms. Average 353 pages. 18 x 12 x 3. 12 volumes, 1868-1891, North storeroom; 1 volume, 1907-1922, South storeroom; 2 volumes 1923—, Probate court vault.

188. CASHBOOK
1898—. 10 vols. (1, 1, 2, 4-10).
Record of cash receipts and disbursements, showing date received, from whom received, title of case, volume and page numbers of dockets, and Probate Journal, entry 154 in which case is recorded, amount received, to whom paid, date paid, signature of payee, amount paid, and judge's fee; also includes Juvenile Cashbook, 1937—, entry 198. Arranged chronologically by dates of receipts. No index. Handwritten on printed forms. Average 15 pages. 12 x 18 x 2. 3 volumes, 1898-1912, South storeroom; 4 volumes, 1915-1930, South storeroom; 3 volumes, 1931—, Probate court vault.

189. RECEIPTS
1921—. 7 vols.

Carbon copies of receipts for money paid (fees) to court, including receipts for marriage licenses, costs of settling estates, and occasional fines, costs of guardianship, land sales, copies of wills, petitions for adoption, money received on accounts, application for transfer of real estate, court costs, and final settlement of estates, showing receipt number, date of receipt, name of payer, and amount and for what purpose. Arranged by consecutive receipt numbers. No index. Handwritten. Average 500 pages. 16 x 8 x 2.5. 3 volumes, 1921-1930, South storeroom; 4 volumes, 1931—, Probate court vault.

190. RECORD OF UNCLAIMED DEPOSITS
1913—. 1 vol.

Record of unclaimed deposits as reported by bank officials to probate court, showing date of report, name of bank official making the report, name of depositor, amount credited to account, and date of last credit or debit to account. Arranged chronologically by dates of reports. No index. Handwritten on printed forms. 150 pages. 14 x 9.5 x 1.5. Probate court vault.

191. CHECKS
1933—. 1 cardboard box.

Canceled checks issued by probate court for witness, appraiser, and notary fees, showing date of issue, check number, name of payee, for what purpose and amount. Arranged numerically by check numbers and also arranged chronologically by dates issued. No index. Handwritten on printed forms. 3 x 8 x 10. Probate court vault.

Miscellaneous

192. ANNUAL RECORD OF STATISTICS
1903—. 35 reports.
Duplicate copies of annual statistical report of the probate-juvenile judge of Medina County to the secretary of state, showing date of report, number of marriage licenses issued, estates administered, estates less than $500 without administrator, estates released from administrator, letters of administrators issued, wills admitted to probate, testamentary letters issued, epileptic and mental cases committed to institutions, and number of juveniles committed to correctional institutions. Arranged chronologically by dates of reports. No index. Handwritten and typed, some on printed forms. 16 x 12 x 24. Probate court office.

193. REPORTS OF BOARD OF COUNTY VISITORS
1913—. 1 vol.
Reports filed by the board of county visitors with the probate court, showing date of report, description of visits to the various charitable and correctional institutions of the county, changes recommended, notice of hearings, copies to serve, appointment and certificate to state board, oath of office, and annual report. Arranged chronologically by dates of reports. No index. Typed. 13 x 8 x 2.5. Probate court vault.

The juvenile court, though of uncertain origin, has been generally recognized as an American contribution to the administration of social justice. The establishment of such courts was the logical outcome of the practical philosophy of enlightened public men that child offenders against the law, our conventional social standards, should not be treated as criminals, but as unfortunates needing the help, supervision, and protection of the state.[1] Although the first separate court in the United States for the trial of juvenile offenders was established in 1899 in Chicago, Cook County, Illinois, by an act of the legislature of that state, the juvenile court was an institution of gradual growth. The Illinois experiment gave impetus to the children's movement in the middle west.[2]

The Ohio legislature was not slow in meeting the advantage of the Illinois experiment, and accordingly, in 1902, an act was passed creating the juvenile court in Cuyahoga County. $380,000 and insolvency court were authorized, under an extension of the jurisdiction of this court to establish children's courts. The stipulations of this act excluded Medina County. It gave the court jurisdiction of the trial of cases involving delinquent and neglected children define the terms of "delinquent, dependent, and neglected"; authorized the appointment of a probation officer, and made it his duty to investigate the facts of cases coming before the court, and to take charge of this offender before and after trial. The clerk of the juvenile court was directed to keep a journal in which were to be recorded the minutes of the case.[3]

Two years after the establishment of the Cuyahoga County juvenile court, the assembly provided by statute for the establishment of juvenile courts in the rural counties of the state, which, because of the population requirement, were unable to create the newer agencies under the provisions of the act of 1902.

---

1. Miriam Van Waters, *Youth in Conflict* (New York, 1925), 147, 159, 161.
2. Edwin H. Sutherland, *Principles of Criminology* (Chicago, 1934). 270-272.
3.*Laws of Ohio*, XCV, 785.

Under the act of 1904, the judges of the court of common pleas, probate court, and where established, the insolvency courts, wherein three or more judges held court concurrently, were authorized to appoint one of their members its "juvenile judge."The court was given original jurisdiction in all cases involving neglected, dependent, and delinquent children under the age of 16 years; and all children who had been scheduled in the past for trial in a justice of the peace or police court were in the future to be tried before a juvenile judge. As under the act of 1902, the judge was authorized to appoint a probation officer, and the clerk of courts was directed to keep a journal of the minutes of each case.[4] In 1908, the court was given jurisdiction in cases involving minors under 17 years of age, and such children as were brought before the juvenile judge were to become wards of the court until they had attained the age of 21 years. The county commissioners were authorized to provide by lease or purchase a "detention home" where neglected or dependent children might be detained pending the final disposition of their cases. The clerk of courts was directed to keep not only a journal, but also an appearance docket containing all orders, judgments, and findings of the court. The age jurisdiction of the court was increased to 18 in 1913.[5]

   While provisions were being made for the establishment of juvenile courts, the legislature gave the court jurisdiction in cases involving adults charged with committing crimes against children or contributing to the delinquency of dependent children. It was made a misdemeanor to contribute to the delinquency of a child under 17 years of age.[6] Two years later, the "lack of parental care" was defined and it was made a misdemeanor to fail to support a minor, or to cause him to engage in begging.[7] In 1913, proper parental care was defined by statute.[8]

---

4. *Ibid.,* XCVII, 561.
5. Ibid., CIII, 869.
6. *Laws of Ohio,* XCVIII, 314.
7. *Ibid.,* XCIX, 193.
8. *Ibid.,* CIII, 870.

Marked progress has been made in the medical treatment of juveniles. While the act of 1913 authorized the juvenile judge to submit any child sentenced to an institution for correction to a mental test, the act of 1929 authorized him to submit any child coming before the court to a mental and physical test to be made by physician or psychiatrist. [9] To facilitate the scientific handling of children, the county commissioners were authorized, in the same year, to lease or construct a separate building to be known as the "juvenile court" which should be appropriately constructed, arranged, furnished, and maintained for the convenient and effective transaction of the business of the court, including adequate facilities to be used as laboratories, dispensaries, or clinics for the scientific use of specialists attached to the court.[10]

It has been one of the guiding principles of the court to make its "custody and discipline" of the children approximate as nearly as possible that which should be given by their parents. In the cases involving neglected or dependent children not sentenced to state institutions, it has been the policy of judges to assign children to private homes, and make arrangements for their adoption. Many other functions were gradually taken over by the juvenile court, such as administering mothers' pensions,[11] now known as aid to dependent children.

The juvenile court of Cuyahoga County is the only independent juvenile court in the state. There are seven other juvenile courts in Ohio attached to courts of domestic relations. Juvenile court has been held in Medina County since 1904.[12] The probate judge now presides over the court under the provision of the act, April 29, 1937, which repealed the 1904 statute.[13]

9. *Ibid.,* CIII, 872, CXIII, 471.
10. *Ibid.,* CXIII, 470.
11. *Ibid.,* CIII, 877.
12. *Ibid.,* XCVII, 561.

As in most agricultural counties few juveniles are brought to court, although the number is sufficient to justify the court's functioning. About 10 cases are heard annually, and the majority of the offenders are either put on probation in a home which is (illegible) adapted to the offence and offender or is returned to their own home where they are kept under observation by the probation officer.[14]

(Illegible) here as elsewhere (illegible) to juvenile delinquency, an average of some divorces being granted annually.[15]

---

13. G. C. sec. 1639-7.
14. *Laws of Ohio*, XCVII, 561.
15. Judicial Statistics to the Secretary of State, *passim, see* entry 112.

General Court Proceedings

194. APPEARANCE DOCKET, JUVENILE COURT
1937—, 1 vol. (1). 1904-1936 in Civil Docket entry 180; Probate Court Calendar, entry 149; Administration Docket, entry 151; and Criminal Docket, entry 153.
Journal entries of juvenile cases, showing date of entry, case number, title of case, findings or pleadings, court orders, disposition of case, and signature of judge and clerk of the juvenile court. Arranged chronologically by dates entered. Indexed alphabetically by titles of cases. Typed on printed forms. 600 pages. 18 x13 x 3.5 Probate court office.

195. JUVENILE COURT JOURNAL
1937—. 1vol. (1). 1904-1936 in Probate Journal, entry 154.
Journal entries of juvenile cases, showing date of entry, case number, title of case, findings or pleadings, court orders, disposition of case, and signature of judge and clerk of the juvenile court. Arranged chronologically by dates entered. Indexed

alphabetically by titles of cases. Typed on printed forms. 600 pages. 18 x 13 x 3.5. Probate court office.

196. JUVENILE RECORD
1911-1919. 1 vol. Discontinued.
Record of cases filed in juvenile court, showing case number name, address, age, sex, and race of juvenile, names of school and teacher, names, address, nativity, and occupations of parents, name of guardian or next friend, date filed, name of person filing affidavit of delinquency, and date of filing or issuing all *writs* with brief notation of each step in proceedings of case. Arranged alphabetically by names of juveniles and numerically thereunder by case number. No index. Handwritten on printed forms. 325 pages. 16.5 x 11 x 2.5. Probate court vault.

197. [JUVENILE COURT CASES]
1904— in Criminal Probate Documents [and Case Papers], entry 160.
Original papers filed in juvenile court cases, including *writs* issued, finances, transcripts, affidavits, and court orders, showing case number, date of filing, names of juvenile and other principals, and volume and page numbers of Probate Journal. 1904-1936, entry 154 and Juvenile Court Journal, 1937—, entry 195.

Financial Records

198. JUVENILE CASHBOOK
1937— in Cashbook, entry 188.
Cash record, showing date received, from whom, amount, to whom paid, and purpose. These entries have been entered in back of Cashbook, number 10.

Probation of convicted offenders was legalized in Ohio by the laws of 1908, which permitted courts of common pleas to place on probation such offenders as in the judge's opinion were not likely to again become involved in criminal conduct.[1] In 1925, probation was extended by an act which enabled the judge of common pleas to establish a county department of probation to consist of a chief probation officer and other helpers as the judge might deem necessary. It is required that appointees have the qualifications prescribed by the state department of public welfare and be subject to civil service regulations.[2] According to the judge of the probate court, who serves as the juvenile judge, a department for juveniles under 18 years of age was established in Medina County on January 2, 1923, under the jurisdiction of the juvenile court, although probation had been carried on prior to this date. The work is carried on by a chief probation officer and his deputy, who are paid annual aggregate salaries of $2520.[3] Probation acts as a deterrent to crime, not only because of the supervision and instruction provided by the staff, but because, according to law, a lapse into delinquency would lead to the arrest of the probationer. Between 1937 and 1940, 10 out of a total of 17 official delinquency cases were placed on probation.[4] Probationary care has become one of the most important treatments for young delinquents, and it is the intention of the probation department that no young people of Medina County be sent to reform schools, if it is possible for them to be helped by probation. The department itself does not deal with paroled cases, this activity being under the jurisdiction of the institution from which the offender has been conditionally released. The responsibility for the care of neglected children has also been placed in the hands of the probation officer.

---

1. *Laws of Ohio,* CIXI, 512; CVI, 534; CVIII, pt. ii, 1114l; CIX, 152, 281; CXIV, 212; (illegible) sec. 3007.
2. Common Pleas Journal, LXVII, 100, *see* entry 237.
3. General Appropriation Ledger, 1923, *see* entry 150.
4. Civil Docket, 1937-1940, *see* entry 277.

Prior to 1923, probation was carried on by the common pleas court and, in 1931, a regular adult probation department was also set up for this court.[5] However, the limited number of cases here caused the abandonment of the department, in 1933,[6] although some probationary matters are still handled by the common pleas judge. Approximately 90 percent of Medina's probation cases have been successful which means that almost all of the offenders who have been placed on probation cause no further trouble.[7] This figure including both official cases and those who were merely warned after their first offense, no public record being made of the latter type.

---

5. Common Pleas Journal, 1931, *see* entry 150.
6. *Ibid.,* 1933.
7. Civil Docket, *passim, see* entry 150.

199. PROBATION RECORDS
1923—. 1 file box.

Record of reports of offenders placed on probation by county court made to the probation officer, showing name of probationer, type of offense, date placed on probation, term and conditions of probation, record of reports made by probationer, age, church affiliations, home conditions, and school record of probationer, and comments by the probation officer; also includes probation records from common pleas court, 1931-1933. Arranged alphabetically by names of probationers. No index. Handwritten on printed forms. 11 x 16 x 24. Probation office.

200. REGISTERS AND CASE RECORDS
1923—. 2 file boxes.

Record of children placed in private homes, showing name of ward, date committed, from what township entered, date child becomes ward of county, complete family history, school record, where placed, amount paid for board, and name and address of boarding parent. Arranged alphabetically by name of wards. No index. Typed on printed forms. 12 x 16 x 2.5. Probation office.

201. CASE RECORDS [Dependent, Neglected, Crippled Cases]

1923—. 2 file drawers. Subtitled Open; Closed.

Case records of the dependent, neglected, and crippled children in Medina County, showing name of county, date referred, case number, name and address of child, sex, verified birth date, county and state of birth, race, nativity, religious affiliation, name of school attended, grade completed in school or reason for not being in school, and other information, including whereabouts of child when referred, status of child's own parents, history of case, by whom reported, place of care pending hearing, and date and method of disposition of case; also includes identifying date of parents showing names and addresses of father and mother, age, county and state of birth, religious affiliation, name of school and grade completed, nativity, and marital status. All papers of each case are kept together in folders. Arranged alphabetically by names of children. No index. Handwritten. 16 x 12 x 26. Probation office.

202. CARD RECORDS [Delinquency]

1938—. 2 file drawers. Subtitled Open; Closed.

Case record of delinquent children in Medina County, showing name of county, date referred, case number, name and address of delinquent, sex, verified birthday, county and state of birth, race, name of school, great completed, if in school at present time, and other information, including whereabouts of child when referred, status of child's own appearance, history of delinquency, by whom and reason referred, place of care, pending hearing or final disposition of case (dismissed, committed, or referred to), and costs and finds; also includes identifying data of parents, showing names and address of mother and father, age, religious affiliation, name of school and grade completed, and county of state of birth. All papers of each case are kept in individual folders. Arranged alphabetically by names of delinquents. No index. Hand written and printed cards. 12 x 16 x 27. Probation office.

203. DEPENDENCY REPORTS
1923—, 72 reports. (Dated).

Copies of quarterly statistical reports to the Ohio State Board of charities relative to minor children, showing date of report, number of children placed in suitable boarding homes, charitable and correctional institutions, and on probation. Arranged chronologically by dates of reports. Typed. 8.5 x 13. Probation office.

204. DAY BOOKS
1934—. 3 vols.

Record of names and errands of people who call in the office daily, showing date registered, name of caller, and reason for call. Arranged chronologically by dates registered. No index. Handwritten on printed forms. Average 185 pages. 6 x 4.5 x .5. Probation office.

205. CORRESPONDENCE
1929—. 2 file boxes.

Correspondence concerning various divisions of probate court, including juvenile cases and child welfare, showing name of division, date of correspondence, name of correspondent, and subjects discussed. Arranged alphabetically by names of divisions and chronologically thereunder by dates of correspondence. No index. Handwritten. 17 x 27 x 52. Probation office.

206. RECEIPTS AND EXPENDITURES
1923—. 1 file box.

Probation officer's record of all receipts and expenditures for children made wards of the court; receipts, showing date of receipt, name of payer, receipt number, and fund to which credited; expenditures, showing date of payment, name of payee, and for what purpose. Arranged chronologically by dates of receipts or payments. No index. Handwritten on printed forms. 12 x 16 x. 26. Probation office.

Aid to dependent children, although provided for by the Ohio legislature, in 1913, in the form of mothers' pensions, assumed a new significance, when in April 1936, the Ohio legislature accepted the provisions of the Federal Social Security Act. With the acceptance of the act, the sections of the general code[1] relative to mothers' pensions were repealed.

The administration of the act in the state I delegated to the department of public welfare, through the division of charities. In the administration of the act, the department was authorized to prescribe forms, certificates, reports, records, and accounts to be kept by the local departments.

The administration of the act and the counties is delegated to the juvenile judge or to the judge of the court of domestic relations, accepting and counties in which by charter or by law the powers were vested in or imposed upon "a county department, board, commission, or officer other than the juvenile judge." In Medina County the probate judge assumes this duty. The judge serving in the capacity of county administrator, is directed to utilize the services of the employees of the court exercising juvenile jurisdiction. In the performance of his duties the judge is authorized to compel the attendance of witnesses and the production of books, and may institute contempt proceedings against persons refusing to testify. Except for this, powers conferred upon a judge are administrative powers only.

Those entitled to aid under the act include, among others, a child residing in the state less than 16 years of age who has been deprived of parental support or care by reason of death, continued absence of a parent, or mental or physical incapacity of a parent. However, a child more than 16 but less than 18 years of age may receive aid at the discretion of the county administration.

---

1. G. C. secs. 1683-2, 1683-10.

Application for aid is made to the juvenile court by the parent or a relative with whom the child must be living. Before aid is granted, a careful examination of the home is made by the employees of the juvenile court. If the child is found to be eligible, the court may grant such amount as is deemed proper. The amount of aid payable to any child is determined on the basis of actual needs "and shall be sufficient to provide support and care requisite for health and decency." In the event aid is granted, the home of such a child must be visited four times during each year. Each month the county auditor issues warrants upon the county treasurer for the payment of the warrants certified by the court. The decisions of the juvenile judge are subject to abrogation or modification by the department of public welfare. Any person attempting to receive aid on behalf of any child not entitled to such aid is deemed guilty of a misdemeanor and upon conviction may be punished by fine or imprisonment, or both.

The agencies are financed by federal, state, and local funds. The county commissioners are required to include in the annual tax budget an amount not less than that computed to yield a levy of fifteen one-hundredths of one mill on each dollar of the general tax list of the county. If the commissioners fail to comply with the provisions of the act relative to appropriations, the state department of public welfare is directed to request the attorney general to institute *mandamus* proceedings against them.[2]

In Medina County, the division of aid to dependent children is administered by the probate judge, who appoints a secretary and a case worker to investigate the dependency cases. The county provides 25 percent of their salaries, the remainder being paid by state and federal appropriations. The agency investigated 150 cases in the period from 1936 through 1940, extending aid to an average of 84 children a month, the average monthly amount of aid afforded each being approximately $13.

---

2. G. C. sec. 1359-31 – 1359-45; *Laws of Ohio*, CXVI, pt. ii, 188-195.

207. CARD INDEX

1936—. 1 file drawer

Simplified reference file, showing name and address of applicant, date of application, date case opened, approval, denial, or withdrawl of application, and reason for action taken; register of grants, showing name and address of applicant, number of children covered by budget, monthly amount of grant (if any), case number, and names and addresses of father and mother (if living). This serves as an index to Application for Aid, entry 208; Case Records [Pending], entry 209; and Case Records [Closed], entry 210. Arranged alphabetically by names of applicants and chronologically thereunder by dates of applications. Typed on printed forms. 11 x 13 x 22. Aid to dependent children office.

208. APPLICATION FOR AID

1936—. 2 file drawers

Record of application and verifications of births, deaths, disabilities, marriages, divorces, and social history of cases receiving aid, showing name of applicant, date of application, residence, age, sex, race, names, and ages of children, signed affidavit in cases of desertion, complete family history, and report of financial status. Arranged alphabetically by names of applicants and chronologically thereunder by dates of applications. For index, see entry 207. Typed on printed forms. 11.5 x 13 x 22. Aid to dependent children office.

209. CASE RECORDS [Pending]

1936—. 1 file drawer

Cases that have been investigated, history compiled, and waiting action, showing name of applicant, date of application, notes and correspondence, health record, and confidential school report. Arranged alphabetically by names of applicants and chronologically thereunder by dates of applications. For index, see entry 207. Typed on printed forms. 11.5 x 13 x 22. Arranged alphabetically by names of applicants and chronologically thereunder by dates of applications.

210. CASE RECORDS [Closed]
1936. 1 file drawer

Record of cases closed by reason of death of dependent or crippled children, children reaching the maximum age, admitted to institutions, or relative able to support, including application, investigation, record of case, correspondence, health record, and minor service (meaning no financial aid given), showing date of application, name of applicant, reason for rejection or denial, and remarks. When case is marked closed, the folder is moved into closed file. All papers of each case filed in separate folders. Arranged alphabetically by names of applicants and chronologically thereunder by dates of applications. For index, see entry 207. Typed on printed forms. 11.5 x 13 x 22. Aid to dependent children office.

211. REPORTS UNDER SOCIAL SECURITY ACT.
1936——. 1file drawer

Statistical and financial reports from the aid to dependent children of Medina County to state office of the division of public assistance, showing statistical reports of active and inactive cases, quarterly estimates of fund needed, and payment list of changes in grants. Arranged alphabetically by subjects. No index. Typed on printed forms. 11.5 x 13 x22. Auditor's office.

212. MILEAGE REPORTS
1936——. 1 file drawer

Report of field worker's total mileage covered in conducting investigations, showing name and address of worker, date filed, district, distance covered daily, and total mileage. Arranged alphabetically by names of workers and chronologically thereunder by dates filed. No index. Typed on printed forms. 11.5 x 13 x 22. Aid to dependent children office.

213. MISCELLANEOUS FILE

1935—. 1 file drawer

Case histories of families receiving aid for dependent children, showing date of filing, name and address of applicant, name and age of each dependent child, verifications of birth, father's ability, institutional confinement, or death, and correspondence. Also contains [Case Records], 1936—, entry 19. Arranged chronologically by dates filed. No index. Handwritten on printed forms. 11 x 16 x 24. Aid to dependent children office.

Jury commissioners were first authorized for Hamilton and Cuyahoga Counties in 1881.[1] In 18 90, provision was made for the appointment of jury commissioners in counties having a city of the first class or of the first grade, second class.[2]

In 1891, the judges of the court of common pleas in counties having a city with a population of not less than 33, 000 nor more than 50,000 were authorized to appoint for residents of the county to serve as a jury commission for a term of one year. The limitations of these acts excludes Medina County. It was the duty of this commission to determine the qualifications and fitness of persons to be selected as jurors.[3] three years later, in 18 94, the provisions of the act were extended to all other counties in the state except Cuyahoga, Franklin, Hamilton, Lucas, Montgomery, and Mahoning.[4] In 1902, the statute was amended to include all counties.[5] In 1913, the number of jury commissioners in each county was reduced to two.[6]

The jury code, which became effective August 2, 1931, provided for a jury commission of the same number and same qualifications previously specified, to hold office at the pleasure of the court, and to meet and select prospective jurors, both grand and petit, for the ensuing year from a list provided by the board of elections.[7] At the beginning of each jury year the commissioners are required to make up a new and complete jury list, known as the annual jury list, arranged alphabetically by precincts, districts, and townships, recording the name, occupation, business address, and residents of each prospective juror, and to prepare an index to this list.

---

1. *Laws of Ohio,* LXXVII, 95.
2. *Ibid.,* LXXXVII, 327.
3. *Ibid.,* LXXXVIII, 200.
4. *Ibid.,* XCI, 176.
5. *Ibid.,* XCVI, 3.
6. *Ibid.*, CIII, 513; CVI, 106.
7. *Ibid.,* CXIV, 193-213.

A duplicate list is certified by the commissioners and filed in the office of the clerk of the court of common pleas.[8]

The jury commissioners select prospective jurors for civil and criminal cases as well as for the grand jury. It selects jurors for the probate court, juvenile court, and other minor courts.

Medina County appointed its first jury commission on May 19, 1894. There are, as elsewhere, two commissioners, who are appointed annually and receive a yearly salary of $25.[9] The annual jury list is of 38 names made according to the uniform method prescribed in the jury code of 1932. Each person listed is investigated by the commissioners regarding his fitness to serve before he is summoned.[10]

Jury commissioners keep no separate records; for records of minutes of jury commissioners, 1891—,see Common Pleas Journal, entry 125; for annual Jury List, 1931—, see entry 86.

---

8. *Ibid.,* CXIV, 205.
9. Common Pleas Journal, 1940, *see* entry 125.
10. *Laws of Ohio*, CXIV, 193.

GRAND JURY

The grand jury, sometimes called the palladium of English liberty, has as its function the preliminary examination of persons charged with a capital or other infamous crime. The right, guaranteed by the federal constitution, to an examination by a grand jury, is recognized in the provisions of the Ohio Constitutions of 1802 and 1851 and in the amendments of 1912.[1]

---

1. *Ohio Const. 1851*, Art. I, sec. 10.

Under the present system, which does not differ in detail from that inaugurated in the early days of the state's history, the grand jury is composed of fifteen members, resident electors of the county having "the qualifications of jurors."[2] It is the duty of the grand jury "to inquire of and present all offenses committed in the county in and for which it was empaneled and sworn."[3] The proceedings of the grand jury are secret and each juror is required to take an oath to preserve such secrecy. Moreover, no grand juror may be required to reveal the way he or other grand jurors voted.[4]

The grand jurors are aided in their investigations by the county prosecuting attorney, who, since 1869, has been authorized by statute to present evidence before this body and compel the attendance of witnesses against whom he may institute contempt proceedings if they refuse to testify. The prosecuting attorney must leave the room before the jurors begin the expression of their views or before a poll is taken. The courts have decreed however, that the mere presence of the prosecuting attorney in the room during the deliberation is "not sufficient to sustain a plea in the statement."[5] Since 1902, if the official court stenographer of the county may take shorthand notes of the testimony and furnish a transcript to the prosecuting attorney at his request. This reporter, like the prosecuting attorney and his assistant, is required to retire from the jury room before the grand jury begins its deliberations.[6]

At least 12 of the 15 jurors must concur in finding an indictment.[7] Indictments found by the grand jury are presented by the foreman to the court and are filed with the clerk of courts.[8]

---

2. G. C. sec. 13436-2.
3. G. C. sec. 13436-5.
4. G. C. sec. 13436-16.
5. *See State of Ohio* v. *William Stichtenoth*, 8 n. p., 297-339
6. G. C. sec. 13436-8.
7. G. C. sec. 13436-17.
8. G. C. sec. 13436-21.

No grand juror or officer of the court is permitted to disclose that a person has been indicted before such an indictment is filed and the case docketed.[9] Any incarcerated person charged with an indictable offense who has not been indicted during the term of court at which he is held to answer is discharged.[10]

Since 1869 it has been the duty of the grand jury to visit the county jail once at each term of court at which they may be in attendance, examine its state and condition and inquire into the discipline and treatment of prisoners, and return a written report to the court.[11]

The majority of contemporary opinion holds that the grand jury, although still defended as a safeguard against oppressive prosecution, seems to be of little usefulness in the administration of modern criminal justice. It is argued that the grand jury not only delays the prosecution of criminal offenses but makes it impossible to place responsibility for neglect of duty, and is, in many instances a rubber stamp for the opinions of the county prosecuting attorney.

The grand jury meets in Medina County three times annually or for each term of court, although special sessions may be called at the request of the county prosecutor. The sessions are short, the indictments few, three terms or sessions in 1941 yielded but 66 indictments and 33 no bills.[12] Of these 66 indictments, only six were for the more serious offenses. Grand jurors receive $3 a day.

The grand jury keeps no permanent records; for clerk of courts' record, see Jury Book, entry 85; Annual Jury List, entry 86; Grand Jury Entry Roster, entry (illegible); Report of Grand Jury, entry 8-; Motion Docket, entry 1-; and Term Report from Clerk of Courts, entry (illegible).

---

9. G. C. sec. 13436-15.
10. G. C. sec. 13436-13.
11. G. C. sec. 13436-20.
12. Common Pleas Journal, 1941, *see* entry 125.

PETIT JURY

The petit jury, like the grand jury, had its origin in England during the reign of Henry II.[1] The right of trial by jury, guaranteed by the federal constitution, was included in each of the Ohio constitutions. At any trial, in any court, for the violation of a statute of the state of Ohio, or any ordinance of any municipality, except in cases where the penalty involved does not exceed a fine of $50 dollars, the accused are entitled to a trial by jury.[2]

Except in the method of selecting prospective jurors, the petit jury has remained unchanged for over 134 years. At each session of the court the jury commissioners[3] selects not less than 50 nor more than 75 names for jury service. A venire is issued to the county sheriff for the persons whose names are so drawn to appear on the day fixed for the trial.[4] From the persons so summoned a jury of 12 is impaneled. The county prosecuting attorney and the defense counsel may, in capital cases, peremptorily challenge six of the jurors. In other cases, four peremptory challenges are allowed.[5] Other challenges, alternately made, may be made for reasons prescribed by statute.[6]

When the case is submitted, the jury may decide the question before it in court, or retire to deliberate. Upon retiring, the jury members must be kept together at a convenient place by an officer of the court until they agree upon a verdict or are discharged by the court. The court may permit them to separate at night.[7]

---

1. Adams, *op. cit.,* 116.
2. G. C. sec. 13443.
3. Annual Jury Lists, *see* entry 86.
4. G. C. sec. 13443-1.
5. G. C. secs. 13443-4, 13443-6.
6. G. C. sec. 13443-8
7. G. C. sec. 11420-3.

If the jurors disagree as to testimony, or desire to be further instructed on the law in the case, they may request the officer in charge to conduct them to the court for additional information.[8] In civil actions a jury renders a written verdict upon the concurrence of three-fourths or more of its members. This verdict is signed by each juror concurring therein.[9]

Under the criminal code, adopted in 1929, the accused may waive his right to a jury trial in favor of a trial by a judge Under the criminal code adopted in 1929 the accused may waive his right to a jury trial in favor of a trial by a judge. This procedure, although criticized by some, is considered by others to be a logical step in the administration of criminal justice in a modern state.

In Medina, as in most counties, petit juries are being waived in favor of the trial judge. Frm January 16, 1939 to December 19, 1940, there were only 30 jury trials. [10] Petit juries serve for a term of court or until they are discharged of further duty.

The petit jury keeps on separate records; for clerk of courts' records see Jury Book, entry 85; Annual Jury List, entry 86; Term Report from Clerk of Courts, entry 346; and Motion Docket, entry 123.

The office of county prosecuting attorney, unlike those of the sheriff and the coroner, is one of the relatively newer agencies in the administration of criminal justice. Established in America by the English during the colonial period, it offers a striking difference in the development of American criminal procedure as contrasted with English procedure where criminal prosecutions were usually instituted by private persons. As developed in recent years, the office of the prosecuting attorney has become one of the state's most important agencies in its defense against modern crime.

The acts of the Northwest Territory placed the responsibility for criminal prosecutions upon the attorney general, who, in turn, appointed and commissioned persons to prosecute cases in their respective counties.[1]

While the acts of the Northwest Territory outlined the local institutions for the newer states, the constitution of Ohio contained no provisions for a prosecutor, leaving the creation of the office to the discretion of the legislature. In 1803, during the first session of the legislature, an act was passed authorizing the supreme court to appoint in each county an attorney to prosecute cases in behalf of the state.[2] Two years later, the appointing power was vested in the court of common pleas.[3] The office remained an appointive one until 1833 when the electorate of the county was directed to choose a prosecuting attorney in each county for a two-year term.[4] The act of 1852 left the office elective and the term unchanged, but in 1881 the term of office was set at three years, and in 1906 it was reduced to two years, and in 1936 increased to four years.[5]

1. Chase, *op. cit.,* I, 287, 348.
3. *Laws of Ohio,* I, 50.
3. *Ibid.,* III, 47.
4. *Ibid.,* XXXI, 13-14; Chase, *op. cit.,* III, 1935.
5. *Laws of Ohio,* LXXVIII, 260; XCVIII, 271-272; CXVI, pt. ii, 184.

Under the present system the prosecuting attorney is elected for a four-year term.[6] He is required to give a bond of not less than $1,000 conditioned for the faithful performance of the duties of his office. If the office becomes vacant, the court of common pleas is authorized to appoint a successor.[7]

The county prosecuting attorney is authorized to appoint clerks, assistants, and stenographers and to fix their salaries subject to the approval of the county commissioners. Since 1911, he has been authorized to appoint a secret service agent or officer whose duty it is to aid him in the collection of evidence to be used in the trial of criminal cases and in matters of a criminal nature. The compensation of such an officer is determined by the court of common pleas.[8]

Most important among the duties of the prosecuting attorney are those connected with criminal prosecution. Differing little from those of the early days of the office, these duties include the prosecution on behalf of the state of all complaints, suits, and controversies in which the state is a party, and such other suits, matters, and controversies as he is directed by law to prosecute within or without his county, in the probate court, court of common pleas, and court of appeals. In conjunction with the attorney general, he prosecutes cases in the supreme court which originated in his county.[9]

In felony cases, when a complaint is made to the prosecuting attorney, he is required to examine the evidence and determine if it is sufficient for prosecution. If he decides in the affirmative, he prepares the evidence for presentation to the grand jury.[10] If this body returns an indictment the prosecutor prepares to present the evidence in trial court.

---

6. G. C. sec. 2909.
7. G. C. secs. 2911, 2912.
8. G. C. secs. 2914, 2915-1.
9. G. C. sec. 2916
10. See p. [None given].

The court of common pleas may appoint an attorney to assist the prosecuting attorney in criminal cases.[11] In the case of conviction, the prosecutor causes execution to be issued for the fines or costs and pays into the county treasury all moneys so received.[12] Without reference to the grand jury, the prosecuting attorney may initiate prosecutions in misdemeanor cases in the court of common please by information.[13] After prosecution is inaugurated, he may eliminate the case without trial by means of the *nolle prosequi* without leave of the court on good cause shown, his requests are usually granted.[14] After prosecution has begun, it remains with the prosecuting attorney whether the case shall be pressed and steps taken that will lead to conviction.

Besides prosecution in criminal cases, the prosecuting attorney also acts in civil matters. He may bring suit in the name of the state when he is convinced that public money is being misapplied or is being illegally withheld or withdrawn from the county treasury. Moreover, he may bring suit against persons violating the obligations of contracts of which the county is a party, or when county property is being used or occupied illegally.[15]

In addition to these, other duties have been prescribed by statute. On the request of the judge having jurisdiction over juvenile cases, he must prosecute adults for committing crimes against children.[16] Furthermore, when directed by the court of common pleas, he must prosecute persons for keeping a house of prostitution.[17] At the instance of the secretary of state, he must prosecute any officer who refuses to furnish gratuitously statistical information for the use of that office.[18]

---

11. G. C. sec. 2918.
12. G. C. sec. 2916.
13. G. C. sec. 13437-34.
14. G. C. sec. 13437-32.
15. G. C. sec. 2921.
16. G. C. sec. 1639-42.
17. G. C. secs. 6212-5, 6212-7.
18. G. C. sec. 174.

The prosecuting attorney has also served in an advisory capacity since 1906.[19] He acts as an adviser to all county boards and officials and to township officers who may require his opinion in writing on matters connected with their official duties.[20] In addition to this, he prepares official bonds for all county officers.[21]

The prosecuting attorney is required to make a report annually to the county commissioners stating the number of criminal prosecutions completed, the name or names of the party or parties to each, and the amount collected in fines and costs, and the amount forfeited.[22] Moreover, on the demand of the attorney general he must make an annual report on forms provided by the state on all criminal actions prosecuted by indictments in his county.[23]

In the period between January 9, 1939 and December 23, 1940, the Medina County prosecutor tried eight offenders, of whom six were convicted. During the same period, 15 cases were suspended, five entries of *nolle prosequi* were made, and 62 defendants pleaded guilty.[24] This record indicates a fairly busy department. The civil cases were concerned mostly with foreclosure actions for taxes, of which there were 25 cases.[25] The prosecutor requires but one assistant and keeps his work well (illegible), although his services as legal advisor are in considerable demand. His salary is $152.50 monthly,[26] and his bond is $2500.[27]

---

19. *Laws of Ohio*, XCVIII, 160, 161.
20. *Ibid.*, XCVIII, 160, 161; G. C. sec. 2917.
21. G. C. sec. 2920.
22. *Laws of Ohio*, LVIII, 69; G. C. sec. 2926.
23. G. C. sec. 2925; *Laws of Ohio*, XC, 225.
24. Criminal Appearance and Execution Docket, 1939-1940, *see* entry 128.
25. Appearance and Execution Docket, 1939-1940, *see* entry 122.
26. Pay Rolls, 1940, *see* entry 258.
27. Record of Official Bonds, 1940, *see* entry 385.
NOTE: These footnote page numbers are very lightly printed.

214.   PROSECUTING   ATTORNEY'S   CRIMINAL
DOCKET
1887-1908. 2 vols. (1, 2). 1909— in Criminal Appearance
and Execution Docket, entry 128.
Record of prosecutor's criminal cases, showing date of case, case
number, name of defendant, name of state, names of attorneys,
case charged, names of witnesses, cost bill, and disposition of case.
Arranged numerically by case numbers. Indexed alphabetically by
names of defendants. Handwritten on printed forms. Average 7(?)
Pages. 16 x 11 x 1. County commissioners, South storeroom.

215. FORFEITED RECOGNIZANCE BOND RECORD
1887-1905. 1 vol. (1).
Prosecutor's record of forfeited recognizance bonds, showing case
number, names of litigants, date recognizance bond posted, name
of person posting bond, amount, date forfeited, and signature of
prosecutor. Arranged numerically by case numbers. No index.
Handwritten on printed forms. 137 pages. 15 x 10 x 1.County
commissioners, South storeroom.

216.   PROSECUTING   ATTORNEY'S   ANNUAL
REPORT TO COUNTY COMMISSIONERS
1925—. 1 file box.
Annual report of prosecuting attorney to county commissioners,
showing itemized list of expenses in connection with prosecution
of cases in Medina County courts, date of report, type of case,
mileage, date of trip, to what place, regarding what matter, total
monthly and annual amount, and certified statement of prosecuting
attorney. Fines and fees are paid by parties, of court cases directly
to clerk of courts office since prosecutor's office is located outside
the courthouse. Arranged chronologically by years. Typed and
handwritten on printed forms. 10 x 4.5 x 14.5 Auditor's office.

217. MISCELLANEOUS RECORDS
1939—. 1 file box.

Miscellaneous file containing papers pertaining to criminal cases and pending suits, showing briefs, transcripts of testimony, date filed, name of plaintiff, schedule of pending suits due to be heard in the various courts, term of court, and names of witnesses in criminal cases, also opinions and rulings of prosecuting attorney on matters of contracts and agreements of township trustees, and opinions to boards of education. Arranged by subjects. No index. Handwritten on printed files. 16 x 10 x 25. Prosecutor's office, 36 Public Square, Medina, Ohio.

218. PROSECUTING ATTORNEY'S CASHBOOK
1880-1907. 2 vols. 1908— in Criminal Appearance and Execution Docket, entry 129.

Prosecutor's record of cash handled, showing date and total amount received, (illegible) to quit, offense, date and amount of disbursement, amount paid treasurer, name of payer, and percentage of fees. Arranged chronologically by dates entered. Indexed alphabetically by names of payers. Handwritten on printed forms. Average 170 pages. 16 x 11 x 2. 1.County commissioners, South storeroom.

The office of coroner, next to that of sheriff the oldest county office in America, had its inception in England during the latter part of the twelfth century when the coroner kept a record of the activities in the county, especially in regard to the administration of criminal justice. At the end of the thirteenth century it was his duty to make inquests whenever there was a sudden death in the shire, and the results were recorded in the coroners rolls and presented to the justices when they made their eyre.[1]

This office, transplanted to America during the colonial period, was continued by the states, and was adopted by the territory of which the state of Ohio was then a part. An ordinance of the Northwest Territory published in 1788 authorized the governor to appoint a coroner in each county within the Territory. This act, together with a supplementary act of 1795 adopted from the Massachusetts code, fixed the power and duties of the coroner. He was empowered to do any act which, by previous legislation had been delegated to the sheriff; and was given the ancient duty of English coroners in holding preliminary investigations over the bodies of all persons found within his county, who were believed to have died by violence or casualty.[2]

The Ohio Constitution of 1802 continued the historic office, making it elective for a two-year term.[3] A statute of 1805 defined the duties and authority of the coroner which, in the main were comparable with those prescribed in the territorial code, except that he was denied the privilege of concurrent jurisdiction with the sheriff.[4] The act further provided that the coroner should receive his remuneration from fees; and that if the office of sheriff were to become vacant, the coroner was to execute temporarily the duties of the sheriff.[5]

---

1. Pollock and Maitland, *op. cit.,* I, 519, 571; II, 641.
2. Pease, *op. cit.,* 24-25, 272-75.
3. *Ohio Const. 1802,* Art. VI, sec. 1.
4. *Laws of Ohio,* III, 156-161.
5. *Ibid.,* III, 158-161.

The latter provision remained active until its abrogation in 1887.[6]

The constitution of 1851 and the constitutional amendments of 1912 left the duties of the coroner unchanged and it was not until recent years when he became an aid in the scientific detection of crime that laws have been passed which materially affected his office. By the legislative act of 1921, the coroner was made official custodian of the morgue in counties where a morgue is maintained. The same act provided that only licensed physicians were eligible to the office in counties having a population of 100,000 or more,[7] and in 1937 such restriction was extended to all counties.[8]

The coroner is required to draw up and subscribe his findings of facts in inquests and autopsies and to report them to the clerk of courts. This record contains a detailed description of the body over which the inquest has been held and a statement of the coroner's findings as to the cause of death.[9] He is required also to return to the judge of the probate court an inventory of articles of property found on or about the body and to preserve such property until the proper distribution may be made.[10] All records are open to public inspection.[11] In 1936, the tenure of office of the coroner was extended from two to four years.[12]

6. *Ibid.,* LXXXIV, 208-210.
7. *Ibid.,* CIX, 543-544.
8. *Ibid.,* CXVII, 43.
9. G. C. secs. 2856, 2857.
10. G. C. sec. 2859
11. G. C. sec. 2856-2
12. G. C. sec. 2823.

In Medina County, the absence of any large agglomeration of urban population made to reduce the work of the coroner to a minimum. There were 12 cases requiring coroners' investigation in 1939 and 15 in 1940, but criminal prosecution resulted from only one of these.[13] The salary of the coroner is made up from annual appropriations of $150 authorized by the commissioners, minus any income from fees.[14] In the years 1931 to 1940, the fees ranged from a low of $2 in 1938 to a high of $22.95 in 1939.[15]

The coroner keeps no permanent records, for record of inquests, see entry 108; bonds, see entry 325; coroners' statement, see entry four.

13. [Coroner's] Inquests, 1936-1940, see entry 108.
14. Pay Rolls, 1940, see entry 288.
15. Annual Reports, 1938-1939, see entry 323.

The office of sheriff antedates the Norman Conquest. This official was enjoying great power and importance centuries ago, and was probably brought into the English system after a model which existed in the Roman law. The name comes from the Saxon "shire-reeve" softened to "shireve" "shyrife," and finally to "sheriff." In ancient times he received his commission directly from the king and specifically represented the sovereign. Originally, the sheriff in England was a judicial as well as a ministerial officer. He once held court in the shire and exercised no inconsiderable jurisdiction. By the time of Lord Coke (1560-1634), the functions of the English sheriff had become standardized under three general heads: (1) to serve process by which a suit was begun: (2) to execute the decrees of the court: (3) to act as conservator of peace within the county.[1]

The office appeared in America in modified form among the earliest colonial institutions, being created in Virginia in 1634, and in Massachusetts in 1654. This ancient office was continued by the states created after independence.[2] The office assumed a new significance in the latter part of the eighteenth century when a flood of colonists swept across the ineffective Allegheny barrier to establish homes in the Northwest Territory organized by Congress in 1787. In the remote West the pioneers, far removed fro the orderly legal processes and courts of the East, were subjected to the machinations of the lawless element prevalent in every new community.

In 1792 the governor and judges of the territory adopted an act providing for the appointment by the governor of a sheriff in each county and defining his duties.[3]

---

1. Adams, *op. cit.*, 17-19; William A. Morris, "The Office of Sheriff in the Anglo-Saxon Period," *English Historical Review*, XXI (1916), 29-40; Raymond Moley, "The Sheriff and the Coroner" (New York, 1926. *The Missouri Crime Survey*, pt. ii), 59, 60.
2. For a comparative study of the sheriff in England and the Chesapeake colonies, see Cyrus Harreld Karraker, *The Seventeenth-Century Sheriff* . . . (Chapel Hill, 1930).
3. Pease, *op. cit.*, 8.

This pioneer law clearly established three of the four major duties of the sheriff as they remain today namely: attendance upon the court; execution of writs, warrants, and the like; and policing and the arrest of criminals.

When Ohio entered the Union as a state in 1803, the office of sheriff was continued by constitutional provision, and was made elective for a two-year term.[4] Since that time relatively few changes have been made in the structural organization of the office. When a new county was erected, the associate judges appointed a day on which the qualified voters met at the temporary seat of justice and elected a sheriff who served until the next general election.[5] Although the constitution of 1851 did not specifically provide for this office, it did declare that no person should be eligible to the office for more than four in any period of six years.[6] No county officer was to have a longer term than three years[7] but the matter of removal from office was left to legislative action.[8] The limitation upon the consecutive terms which a sheriff might serve remained in force until 1933, when it was repealed by an amendment authorizing any county to adopt a charter form of government. The term of office remained at two years until 1936 when it was extended to four years.[9] The sheriff received his remuneration from fees until 1875. From 1875 to 1906 he received a definite salary based upon the population of the county according to the last federal census preceding his election, plus a percentage of the fees collected.[10]

---

4. *Ohio Const. 1802*, Art. VI, sec. 1.
5. A. E. Gwynne, *A Practical Treatise on the Law of Sheriff and Coroner with Forms and References to the Statutes of Ohio, Indiana, and Kentucky*. (Cincinnati, 1849), 3.
6. *Ohio Const. 1851*. Art. X, sec. 3.
7. *Ibid.,* Art. X, sec. 2
8. *Ibid.,* Art. X, sec. 6.
9. *Laws of Ohio,* CXVI, pt. ii, 184.
10. *Ibid.,* III, 49-51; XXXIII, 85; LXXII, 126.
11. *Ibid.,* XCVIII, 89.
12. *Ibid.,* XXIX, 410.

Since 1906 the compensation has been derived entirely from a salary determined on a population basis.[11] In 1831, due to the increasing complexity of the duties of the office, the sheriff was authorized to appoint, with the consent of the court of common pleas, one or more deputies. These men, like their superior, were required to give bond for the faithful performance of the duties of their office, and the sheriff was made responsible for their neglect of duty or misconduct in office.[12]

The present organization of the office may be briefly summarized: The sheriff is elected for a four-year term,[13] can hold no other elective office at the same time, and may not practice law while in office.[14] He is required to give bond, the cost of which is paid by the county commissioners[15] who are also required to provide an office for the sheriff at the county seat, equipment, supplies, and other essentials of the office.[16] The commissioners also appropriate funds for the expenses incurred by the sheriff and carrying out the various duties of his office.[17] The sheriff may appoint a deputy or deputies but all appointees must be endorsed by the local judge of the common pleas court, be electors of the county, and no deputy may be a justice of peace or mayor.[18] Deputies are also forbidden to practice law while in office.[19] The sheriff fixes the salaries of the deputies, subject to the budget limitations of the county commissioners,[20] and shares with his deputies certain civil and criminal liabilities.[21]

---

11. *Ibid.,* XCVIII, 95.
12. *Ibid.,* XXIX, 410.
13. G. C. sec. 2823.
14. G. C. secs. 11, 1706, 2565, 2783, 2910.
15. G. C. sec. 2824.
16. G. C. sec. 2832.
17. G. C. sec. 2997.
18. G. C. sec. 1706, 2830.
19. G. C. sec. 1706.
20. G. C. sec. 2981.
21. Willis A. Estrich, ed., *Ohio Jurisprudence* (Rochester, 1938), XXXVI, 660-672, 699-701.

The salary of the sheriff, based on a graded scale according to population is set at a maximum of $6000 a year.[22] The office may be vacated by failure to give proper bond, nonacceptance, or death.[23] Vacancies in the office are filled by the county commissioners.[24]

The sheriff may be removed for various financial defalcations,[25] for willfully refusing or neglecting his duty in criminal cases,[26] for malfeasance in office,[27] or for permitting the lynching of a person in his custody.[28] In the latter case the governor conducts the hearing and may remove the sheriff. If for some reason the sheriff is unable to serve a court order the judge of the common pleas court is authorized to make a temporary appointment for the post.[29] The retiring sheriff is required to deliver to his successor all moneys, papers, books, and the like, as well as the custody of all the prisoners.[30]

Aside from his power to appoint deputies, the sheriff has other special powers which are largely the products of historical development. From earliest years the sheriff has been empowered to call to his aid such persons as he deemed necessary to perform his lawful duty in the apprehension of criminals.[31] Thus the *posse comitatus* was at his disposal as it is today.[32]

---

22. G. C. secs. 2994, 2996, 2997; *Ohio Jurisprudence* (Rochester, 1938, XXXVI, (illegible), 698-701.
23. G. C. secs. 2827, 12196.
24. G. C. sec. 2828.
25. G. C. secs. 3036, 3049.
26. G. C. secs. 12850, 12851.
27. *Ohio Const. 1851* (Amendment, 1912), Art. II, sec. 38.
28. *Laws of Ohio*, CI, 109.
29. G. C. sec. 2828.
30. G. C. secs. 2842, 2843.
31. *Laws of Ohio*, III, 156-158; XXIX, 112, 113.
32. G. C. sec. 2833.

The specific duties of the sheriff were and are prescribed by statute and may be classified under four main divisions: (1) attendance upon the courts; (2) execution of summonses, warrants, processes, and other writs; (3) control and responsibility in the care of the jail and courthouse; (4) policing the county and the arrest of criminals.

The territorial law of 1792 required the sheriff to attend upon the court of common pleas and the court of appeals during their sessions,[33] and this requirement has been carried over into the laws of Ohio;[34] the present duties of the sheriff in this respect are survivals from the provisions of this act. He is required to attend the county court of common pleas,[35] the appellate court,[36] and the probate court if required by the judge of that division.[37] The sheriff may adjourn the court of common pleas from day to day upon failure of the judge to appear at regularly scheduled sessions.[38]

The duty of the sheriff to execute all warrants, writs, and processes directed to him by the proper and lawful authority has also been operative since the territorial period.[39] At present he executes every summons, order, or other process, and makes return thereof as required by law.[40] He executes processes from the probate, juvenile, common pleas, and appellate courts. Although the jury commission has supplanted the clerk of courts in the matter of selecting names of prospective jurors from the jury wheel, the sheriff's duties in this respect remain much as they were in the earlier years of his office.

---

33. Pease, *op. cit.* 8.
34. *Laws of Ohio*, III, 156-158; XXIX, 112; LXXXII, 26.
35. G. C. sec. 2833.
36. G. C. secs. 1530, 2833.
37. G. C. sec. 2833.
38. G. C. sec. 2855.
39. Pease, *op. cit.*, 8; *Laws of Ohio* III, 156-158; XXIX, 112; LXXXII, 26
40. G. C. sec. 2834.

He also executes warrants issued by the governor of the state,[41] and serves writs and subpoenas issued by various state officers and boards.[42] In other words, the sheriff serves all the papers which concern the county as a unit of government and some for the state as well.

As early as 1805 the sheriff was made official custodian of the county jail.[43] Although the early statutes direct to the county commissioners to provide dungeons for the incarceration of prisoners, the act of 1847 directed at the sheriff to exercise reasonable care for the preservation of the life, health, and Welfare of those committed to his care. He was and is authorized to transport prisoners to other counties for safekeeping.[44] Under the direction and control of the county commissioners the sheriff is also given charge of the courthouse.[45]

The sheriff has had extensive and important police powers since 1792 when the territorial act authorized him to keep and preserve the peace, and suppress a phrase, routes, riots, unlawful assemblies, and insurrections; to apprehend and confine in jail all felons and traders; and to return persons who, having committed a crime in his county, had taken refuge in another.[46] During the legislative session of 1805 the general assembly passed an act defining the duties of the sheriff which were in all respects similar to the provisions inherited from the territorial code.[47]

---

41. G. C. sec. 118.
42. G. C. secs. 285, 346, 2709, *et al.*
43. *Laws of Ohio*, III, 157.
44. *Ibid.*, III, 157; XXIX, 112, 113; XCIII, 131. For general provisions as to jail duties, see G. C. secs. 3157-3176, *passim.*
45. G. C. sec. 2833.
46. Pease, *op. cit.*, 8.
47. *Laws of Ohio*, III, 156-158.

In the same year the sheriff was designated as the county's executioner, and was bound to carry out sentences of death by hanging when imposed by the courts upon those convicted of murder.[48] Public executions, the general rule during the earlier years, we're abolished in 1844.[49] In 1886 the sheriff's duties in this respect were delegated to the warden of the Ohio Penitentiary.[50]

An act of 1831, repealing the act of 1805 redefined the duties of the sheriff as a conservator of the peace in his county,[51] and his present duties in this respect are survivals from the provisions of this act.[52] Although the sheriff is still regarded as the chief peace officer in the county, many of his earlier duties in this respect have been abolished by the development of other agencies of law enforcement, notably the state highway patrol. On the other hand, the powers of the sheriff to suppress a phrase, riots, and unlawful assemblies become especially important in times of strikes or threatened riots. On a properly issued warrant he may arrest any person charged with the probability of doing injury to another person or the property of another.[53] Moreover, since 1921 the sheriff has forwarded to the bureau of criminal identification all fingerprints of persons arrested for a felony,[54] and since 1913 has been authorized to arrest any person violating his parole.[55]

The present police powers of the sheriff are quite comprehensive his jurisdiction is coextensive with the county, including all municipalities and townships, and he is the chief law enforcement officer of the county. In municipalities the sheriff and mayor stand on an equality to cast the burden of action upon the other.[56]

---

48. Chase, *op. cit.*, I, 442.
49. *Laws of Ohio*, XLII, 71.
50. *Ibid.*, LXXXIII, 145.
51. *Ibid.*, XXIX, 112, 113.
52. *Ibid.*, LXXXII, 26.
53. G. C. sec. 13428-1.
54. *Laws of Ohio*, CIX, 584; CX 5.
55. *Ibid.*, CIII, 404.
56. Estrich, *op. cit.*, XXVI, 645. For the most important police powers see G. C. secs 2833, 3345, 4112, 12811.

The sheriff has possessed and still possesses many powers and duties which are miscellaneous in nature. As in England the sheriff, during the earlier years of his office, was required to notify the electors of his county of the time and place of holding elections. He was enjoined to furnish ballot boxes at the expense of the county, hold special elections when so directed by the governor, and deliver the poll books to the secretary of state.[57] Since 1891 these duties have been taken over by the board of elections.[58] The sheriff also has many heterogeneous powers and duties regarding elections,[59] executive orders of the secretary of agriculture,[60] fish and game laws,[61] probation officers,[62] military census,[63] traffic rules and regulations,[64] funds and deposits in court,[65] shanty boats,[66] and executive orders of the governor.[67]

The multiplicate duties of the sheriff have made it necessary to require many records of the business of the office to be kept. The sheriff has been required to keep a foreign execution docket since 1838,[68] a cash book since 1842,[69] and a jail register since 1843.[70] These records for Medina County are extant only for 1865, 1869, and 1858 to date respectively.[71] Indexes, direct and reverse, to the foreign execution docket were prescribed by the legislature in 1925.[72]

---

57. *Laws of Ohio*, II, 88-90; III, 331, 332.
58. *Ibid.*
59. G. C. secs. 4785-124, 4829.
60. G. C. sec. 1110.
61. G. C. secs. 1434, 1441, 1444, 1451.
62. G. C. sec.1639-19.
63. G. C. sec. 5188-5.
64. G. C. sec. 7251-1.
65. G. C. sec. 11900.
66. G. C. sec. 13403-1.
67. G. C. sec. 118
68. *Laws of Ohio*, XXVI, 18; LVII, 6; LXXXIV, 208, 209.
69. *Ibid.*, XL, 25; LXV, 115; LXXXIV, 208; LXXXVI, 239.
70. *Ibid.*, XLI, 74.
71. Sheriff's Foreign Execution Docket, *passim, see* entry 219; Sheriff's cash book, *passim, see* entry 225; Jail Register, *passim, see* entry 283.
72. *Laws of Ohio,* CXI, 31.

Since 1843, he has been required annually to transmit the jail register, in certified copies to the clerk of courts, the county auditor, and the secretary of state.[73] Since 1850 he has been required, about the first Monday of September in each year, to submit to the county commissioners a certified statement of all fines and costs collected during the year, and the amount of fees collected and paid to the clerk of court of common pleas .[74]

Thus, the modern sheriff keeps the following records: (1) a cash book, which is a record of all monies received from all sources; (2) a foreign summons docket which is a record of all summonses from counties other than his own; (3) a foreign execution docket which is a record of executions from counties other than his own; (4) a service record which includes all probate and divorce papers served; (5) an execution register which records all executions handled; (6) an accrued fee record which lists fees received; (7) a commission register which records the commissions of all special deputies; (8) a jail register which records all prisoners brought in, the charge, how long detained, and when released.[75] By statute the sheriff is also required to make an annual financial report to the county commissioners.[76]

---

73. *Ibid.,* XLI, 74.
74. G. C. sec. 2844; *Laws of Ohio,* XLVIII, 66.
75. G. C. secs. 2837, 2839, 2979, 3045, 3046.
76. G. C. sec. 2844.

The sheriff of Medina County is bonded for $5000,[77] and receive a salary of $1975 annually.[78] He has one deputy and one clerk, and is provided with cars equipped with radio sets. The present jail, built in 1852,[79] contains cells for six men and two women and is administered by the sheriff with the assistance of a matron. It has housed during the past 10 years an average of 275 persons annually.[80]

In 1940, 25 traffic accidents were investigated and 23 sales on foreclosure are conducted.[81] Fees received by sheriff's office were $1968.81.[82]

---

77. Record of Official Bonds, 1940, *see* entry 385.
78. Pay Rolls, 1940, *see* entry 238.
79. Commissioners' Journal, II [1851-1852], 8, 9, 30.
80. Jail Register, 1931-1941, *see* entry 223.
81. Miscellaneous Report, 1940, *see* entry 232.
82. Receipts Journal, 1940, *see* entry 282.

Court Orders

219. SHERIFF'S FOREIGN EXECUTION DOCKET
1885—. 4 vols. (1-4). 1818-1884 in Appearance and Execution Docket, entry 122; 1879-1884 in Criminal Appearance and Execution Docket, entry 120.

Docket of court orders from outside Medina County, carrying judgments into force within Medina County, showing name of plaintiff and defendant in civil cases, name of defendant in criminal cases, names of state, county, and court of origin, foreign court cases, docket and page numbers of record, date and time (of day) judgment received in Medina County, number of days in which returnable, amount of judgment, interest rate and date, plaintiffs and defendants original cost, sheriff's return of Rick with date, property appraisal, sheriff sale (if any), fees of clerk, sheriff, printer, and appraiser, total judgment, interest and costs, and amount made on execution with signature of sheriff. Arranged chronologically by dates *writs* received. Indexed alphabetically by names of plaintiffs and defendants. Handwritten on printed forms. Average 500 pages. 16 x 12 x 4. 1 volume 1885-1913, North storeroom; 3 volumes, 1913— Sheriff's office.

220. SHERIFF'S DOCKET OF FOREIGN SUMMONS AND RETURNS
1885—. 8 vols. (1-8). 1818-1884 in Appearance and Execution Docket, entry 122; 1879-1884 in Criminal Appearance and Execution Docket, entry 120.

Docket of summonses issued by courts outside of Medina County, to be served to residents of Medina County, showing names of state, county, and court, foreign court's case number, names of plaintiff and defendant (in civil cases), defendant (in criminal cases), and attorneys, date summons issued, received, served, and returned, copy of return endorsed on *writ,* sheriff's fees, amount received with *writ,* fees deposited to pay sheriff, and volume and page numbers of Sheriff's Cash Book, entry 285 and signatures of clerk of courts and sheriff. Arranged chronologically by dates *writs* received. Indexed alphabetically by names of plaintiffs and defendants. Handwritten on printed forms. Average 500 pages. 16.5 x 18.5 x 4. 4 volumes, 1885-1931, North storeroom; 4 volumes, 1932—, Sheriff's office.

221. SHERIFF'S EXECUTION DOCKET
1870-1929. 3 vols. (one unlabeled; 2, 3).

Docket of sheriff's executions of court orders of Medina County, showing date of entry execution number, case number, docket and page numbers of record, date issued, date returnable, names of plaintiff and defendant (in civil cases), defendant (in criminal cases), amount of judgment, rate and date of interest, plaintiff's and defendant's costs, fees of sheriff, printer, and appraiser, total amount of judgment and costs with sheriff's sign statement of date and time (of day) *writ* received, levies (if any) upon goods and chattels, and date and amount of payment by defendant if judgment is fully satisfied. Arranged chronologically by dates entered. Indexed alphabetically by names of plaintiffs and defendants.

Handwritten on printed forms. Average 400 pages. 16 x 12 x 3.5. North storeroom.

222. RECORD OF SUMMONS AND RETURNS
1870-1912. 5 vols. (1-5).

Record of summonses issued to sheriff of Medina County by Medina County courts, and of his return, showing case number, name of person subpoenaed, name of plaintiff, name of court, date petition filed in clerk's office, date return of summons due, signature of clerk of courts, volume and page numbers of courts docket, names of plaintiffs attorneys, and sheriff's signed statement of date and time (if any), *writ* received, served, and returned. Arranged chronologically by dates *writs* received. Indexed alphabetically by names of plaintiffs and defendants. Handwritten on printed forms. Average 400 pages. 16 x 12 x 3.5. North storeroom.

Jail Records
(See also entries (illegible), 231, 232)

223. JAIL REGISTER
1858-1881, 1919—. 3 vols. (2 unlabeled; 3).

Register of commitments to county jail, showing commitment number, name of prisoner, nativity, age, offense charged, date of commitment, date of discharge, by whose authority committed, number of days in jail number of days in solitary confinement, and sheriff's fees; also includes arrests of parole violators. Arranged chronologically by dates committed. No index. Handwritten. Average 240 pages. 18 x 13 x 2.5. 1 volume, 1858-1881, North storeroom; 2 volumes,. 1919—, Sheriff's office.

224. CRIMINAL CASES [Record of Fingerprints]
1937—. 1 file box.

Henry system of fingerprint recording, showing name of person fingerprinted, charge, description and detailed account of fingerprints, and case history; also includes photograph of

criminal, identification number, aliases, date of crime, and place
where crime was committed. The Henry system is used, due to its
giving the entire set of prints of both hands. It was named for Sir
E. H. Henry of England and was made for the use of Scotland
Yard. Arranged numerically by identification numbers. No index.
Hand written on printed forms.5 x 8 x 18. Sheriff's office.

Financial Records

225. SHERIFF'S CASHBOOK
1869-1886, 1898-1913, 1921—. 10 vols. (1, 1-3), 3-8).
Sheriff's record of cash receipts and disbursements, showing date
of entry, date received, case number, names of litigants, nature of
suit, amount, manner of payment, cost to plaintiff and defendant,
clerk's fees, and date of payment, also description of channels
attached to satisfy judgment. Arranged chronologically by dates
entered. No index. Handwritten on printed forms. Average 300
pages. 16 x 13 x 2. Sheriff's office.

226. RECORD OF ACCRUED FEES
1907—. 3 vols. (1-3).
Sheriff's record of accrued fees, showing date accrued, case
number, in what matter, to whom charged, total fee and civil and
criminal cases, also amount due from county, foreign *writs*, probate
and juvenile cases, minutes, and date of amount. Arranged
chronologically by dates accrued. No index. Handwritten on
printed forms. Average 160 pages. 6 x 12 x 1.5. Sheriff's office.

227. RECEIPTS
1929—. 5 vols.
Duplicate copies of receipts to payer by the sheriff for settlement
of judgment, executions, foreclosures, serving of summons orders
of both county and foreign courts, showing court case number, date
of payment, names of litigants, name of payer, consecutive receipt
number, and signature of sheriff or deputy. Arranged
chronologically by years and also arranged numerically by

consecutive receipt numbers. No index. Handwritten on printed forms. Average 600 pages. 15.5 x 9 x 1.5. 4 volumes, 1929-1938, North storeroom; 1 volume 1939——. Sheriff's office.

Miscellaneous

228. RECORD OF IMPOUNDED DOGS
1918-1923. 1 vol.

Copies of reports of sheriff to county commissioners of all dogs seized, showing date of report, name of owner, keeper, or harborer (if known), sex, breed, color, address where dog was kept, date of seizure, date disposed of, whether sold, redeemed, or destroyed, amount of fees and costs collected, (illegible). Arranged chronologically by dates of reports. No index. Handwritten. 150 pages. 15 x 10 x 1.5. North storeroom.

229. REPORT TO COMMISSIONERS OF FINES AND FEES
1907——. 4 vols. (1-4)

Copies of sheriff's reports to county commissioners of fines and fees collected, showing date of report, name of payer, in what matter, amount of fine and cost, total collected, and date received by clerk of courts. Arranged chronologically by dates of reports. No index. Handwritten. Average 160 pages. 18 x 13 x 1.5. 1 volume, 1907-1910, North storeroom; 3 volumes 1911——, Sheriff's office.

230. UNCLAIMED MONEYS
1913——. 1 vol (1).

Sheriff's record of unclaimed moneys, showing date of entry, name of person whom money belongs, date and amount paid into treasury, case number, volume and page numbers of cashbook and docket entries, date of entry, date certificate issued to owner for recovery (if any), and signature of receiver of certificate. Arranged chronologically by date centered. No index. Handwritten on printed forms. 200 pages. 8 x 14 x 1.5. Sheriff's office.

231. [MONTHLY EXPENSE ACCOUNT]
1941—. 6 vols. (1-6).
Copies of requisitions accompanying sheriff's itemized statements
for expenses, showing date of entry, monthly travel expenses,
monthly statement of number of meals served to county prisoners,
supplies for jail, repairs to jail, medical and dental care of
prisoners, printing, servants subpoenas to grand and petit jury
members, repairs to automobiles used by sheriff's office and radio
receiving sets, and miscellaneous expenses of county sheriff's
office. Arranged chronologically by date entered. No index.
Handwritten on printed forms. Average 100 pages. 14 x 9 x .5.
Sheriff's office.

232. MISCELLANEOUS REPORT
1933—. Approx. 800 sheets.
Sheriff's miscellaneous reports, including grand and petit larceny,
theft, burglary, suicides, accidental death, traffic accidents, and
correspondence, showing date of report, names of parties involved,
amount of fees collected, number of sales on foreclosures, and
number of prisoners committed and released from jail annually.
Arranged chronologically by years and alphabetically thereunder
by subjects. No index. Typed. 8 x 10. Sheriff's office.

The county dog warden, appointed by the county commissioners, has as his duty the enforcement of the provisions of the general code relative to licensing dogs, impounding and destruction of unlicensed dogs, and payment of compensation for damages to livestock inflicted by dogs. This officer, like other county officials is required to give bond conditioned for the faithful performance of the duties of his office. This bond, in the sum of not less than $500 nor more than $2000, is filed with the county's auditor. His compensation and tenure, like that of his deputies, is determined by the county commissioners.[1]

The warden is required to make a record of all dogs owned, or harbored in the county; to patrol the county; to seize and impound dogs more than three months of age found not wearing a valid registration tag. The latter provisions do not apply, however, do dogs kept in a regularly licensed kennel. Moreover, he is required to make weekly written reports to the commissioners of all dogs seized, impounded, redeemed, and destroyed. Then, too, he is required to report all claims for damages to livestock inflicted by dogs.

The dog warden and his deputies have, in the performance of their legal duties, the same police powers as are conferred by statute upon sheriffs and police. They may summon the assistance of bystanders in performing their duties, serve *writs* and other legal processes issued by any court in the county with reference to enforcing the provisions of the law relating to dogs.[2]

---

1. G. C. sec. 5652-7.
2. G. C. sec. 5652-7.

In Medina County the duties of dog warden were made under the jurisdiction of the sheriff, from 1917 to 1927, as provided by statute.[3] In 1927, an act authorized the commissioners to appoint a county dog warden responsible to them, under which act the Medina County dog warden was appointed in August 1927.[4] During the year 1940, 730 dogs were seized. Five were redeemed, 25 were sold, and the remainder were destroyed. Since 4454 licenses were issued that year[5] for dogs and 48 kennels, the office is self sustaining, the appropriation for 1940 being $3600.[6] The dog warden is under $1000 bond and is paid $125 monthly.[7]

---

3. *Laws of Ohio,* CVII, 535.
4. Commissioners' Journal, XV [1926-1930], 2208.
5. Annual Financial Report, 1940, *see* entry 324.
6. Commissioners' Journal, XVII, [1936-1940), 509.
7. Record of Officials' Bonds, 1940, *see* entry 325; Pay Rolls, 1940, *see* entry 288.

Dog Warden

233. POUND KEEPER'S RECORD
1927—. 14 vols.
Record of dogs seized by dog warden, showing number of seizure, description of dog, owner's name and address, keepers or harborers name and address, date impounded, they disposed of, and manner of disposition semicolon also gives itemized cost bill for dogs seizure, serving or posting notice, housing and feeding, and sale or destruction of dog, with date of payment of cost, or sale of dog, showing purchaser's name, address, amount received, and pound keepers signature. Arranged numerically by seizure numbers. No index. Hand written on printed forms. Average 200 pages. 15 x 10 x 1.5. 10 volumes, 1927-1938, County commissioners, North storeroom; 4 volumes, 1938—, Dog Pound Office, State Route #162, R. D. #5, Medina, Ohio.

The first Ohio Constitution, adopted in 1802, did not provide for the office of county auditor and it was not until 1820 that the general assembly by joint resolution appointed an auditor in each county for a one-year term.[1] In 1821 the office became elective and the term was fixed at one year.[2] In 1831 the term was set at two years, in 1877 at three years, in 1906 reduced to two years, and in 1919 extended to four years.[3]

The county auditor is required to take oath and give bond for faithful performances of the duties of his office; to preserve all copies of entries, surveys, extracts, and other documents transmitted to his office from the state auditor; and to transfer to his successor all books, records, maps, and other papers pertaining to his office.[4] With the approval of the county commissioners he is authorized to appoint deputies, for whose official acts he and his sureties are held liable; since 1869 the record of these appointments has been required to be filled with the county treasurer.[5] If the office of county auditor falls vacant, the county commissioners are authorized to appoint a successor.[6]

The first auditor in each county was required to list all lands in his county subject to taxation. From this list and one submitted to him by the county commissioners and one from the state auditor the county auditor was directed to make a tax duplicate to be kept in a book for that purpose, and to give a copy of the list to the tax collector.[7]

---

1. *Laws of Ohio,* XVIII, 70.
2. *Ibid.,* XIX, 116.
3. *Ibid.,* XXX, 280; LXXIV, 381; XCVIII, 271; CVIII, pt. ii, 1294.
4. *Ibid.,* XIX, 116; LXVII, 103; G. C. sec. 2559, 2582.
5. *Laws of Ohio,* LV, 20; LXVI, 35; G. C. sec. 2563.
6. G. C. secs. 2579, 2580, 2990, 2996.
7. *Laws of Ohio,* XVIII, 79.

The auditor was also directed to compile from the treasurer's duplicate a list of lands on which taxes were delinquent, and of such lands were sold for taxes to grant a deed to the purchaser.[8]

Subsequent legislation expanded and itemized the duties of the auditor regarding taxation; with modifications to meet modern requirements these duties have been continued much as they were during the earlier years of the office. During the 1840s the office of county assessor was abolished and provision was made for township assessors who study it was to list all taxable property and make a return to the auditor.[9] Since 1874 the auditor is required by statute to keep a book in which he lists additions to and deductions from the amount of tax assessment.[10] In 1915 he was made chief assessing officer of the county.[11]

The county auditor has been a member and served as a secretary of the county budget commission since its beginning in 1911, his duties include keeping fall and accurate records of the proceedings of that body. For the purpose of adjusting the tax rates and fixing the amount to be levied each year, the commissioners are governed by the amount of taxable property as shown on the auditor's tax list for the current year. He submits to the commissioners the annual tax budget given him by each taxing authority of each subdivision, together with it an estimate of any state levy prepared by the state auditor, and other information as the budget commission may request or the state tax commission require.[12]

Tax settlements had been made annually until 1858 when the auditor was required to make semiannual settlements with the treasurer to ascertain the amount of taxes with which the treasurer is to stand charged.[13]

---

8. *Ibid.,* XVIII, 82; XIX, 115.
9. *Ibid.,* XXXIX, 22-25
10. *Ibid.,* LXXI, 30.
11. Ibid., CVI, 246.
12. G. C. sec. 5625-19; *Laws of Ohio,* CXII, 402.
13. G. C. sec. 2596; *Laws of Ohio,* LVI, 132; LXXVII, 226.

Since 1904 liquor, cigarette, and inheritance taxes have been constituted separate funds. All other taxes are credited to the general fund.[14]

Since 1831 the county auditor has kept an account current with the county treasurer showing the payments of monies into the treasury, listing the date, by whom paid, and on what fund. On receiving the treasurer's daily statement the auditor enters on his account current the amount shown as a charge to the treasurer.[15] Another important function of the county auditor is the approval before payment of bills and other claims against the county. Since 1831 he has been authorized to issue, on presentation of the proper voucher, all warrants on the county treasurer for moneys payable from the county treasury; and to preserve all warrants, showing the number, date of issue, I'm out for which drawn, in whose favor, and from which fund.[16] County money due the state is paid on warrant of the state auditor. Since 1904, a bill or voucher for payment from any fund controlled by the county commissioners or board of county infirmary directors is filed with the county auditor and entered in a book for that purpose at least five days before its approval for payment by the commissioners, and when approved the data is entered opposite the claim.[17]

Besides approving bills and claims against the county, the auditor in 1835 was given to duty of certifying all moneys, except collections on the tax duplicate, into the county treasury, specifying by whom paid and the fund to which such payment is credited. Such moneys he charges to the treasury, keeping a duplicate copy of the statement in his office. Since 1835 all costs collected in penitentiary cases which have been or are to be paid to the state have been certified into the treasury as belonging to the state.[18]

---

14. *Laws of Ohio,* XCVII, 457
15. *Ibid.,* XXIX, 280-291; LXVII, 103.
16. G. C. sec. 2570; *Laws of Ohio,* XXIX, 280-291; LXVII, 103.
17. *Laws of Ohio,* XCVII, 25; CVIII, pt. i, 272.
18. *Laws of Ohio,* XXXIII, 44; LXVII, 103.

In 1902 the legislature provided for a system of uniform accounting and auditing of all public offices, and for the annual examination of their finances, under the direction of a bureau of inspection in the office of the state auditor.[19] Since 1904 the county auditor has been required to report to the commissioners on the state of county finances; on the first business day of each month he prepares in duplicate a statement of the county finances for the preceding month, compares it with the treasurer's balance, and submits it to the commissioners who post one copy of it in the auditor's office for thirty days for public inspection.[20]

During the development of the office additional duties in great diversity have been delegated to the county auditor. Since 1833, he has been authorized to discharge prisoners jailed for nonpayment of any fine or amercement due the county when in his opinion payment is not collectible.[21] In 1838 an act was passed making him county superintendent of schools. He was relieved of his duty in 1848 when a county superintendent of schools was authorized in each county.[22] Since 1846, he has served as the sealer of weights and measures, is responsible for the preservation of the copies of the original standards delivered to his office, and enforces in the county all state laws regulating weights and measures.[23] In 1861, he was authorized to report to the state auditor statistics concerning the death, dumb, blind, insane, and idiots in the county, with the names and addresses of their parents or guardians.[24] Eight years later, in 1869, he was authorized to report to the same officer statistics concerning livestock in the county as returned to his office by assessors, and an abstract of the funded indebtedness of the county, and of each township, city, village, and school district.[25] Since 1827, he has been authorized to issue

19. *Ibid.*, XCV, 511-515.
20. *Ibid.*, XCVII, 457.
21. G. C. sec. 2576; *Laws of Ohio*, XXXI, 18; LXVII, 103.
22. See pages [None given].
23. G. C. sec. 2615; *Laws of Ohio*, XLIV, 55; LVIII, 78; CI, 234.
24. *Laws of Ohio*, LVIII, 40.
25. G. C. sec. 2604.

Licenses to traveling public shows and exhibitions, although municipal authorities may impose an additional license.[26] In 1862, he was authorized to issue peddlers' licenses to persons who filed a statement of stock in trade in conformity with the law requiring the listing of such stock for taxation, and since 1917, he has issued dog licenses.[27] The auditor has issued licenses to wholesale and retail dealers in cigarettes since 1892,[28] in brewers' wort and malt since 1933,[29] and issued cosmetic licenses from August 1, 1933 to Jun3 30, 1936.[30]

Since 1850, the auditor has been official custodian of the reports submitted to the commissioners by the prosecuting attorney, the clerk of courts, the sheriff, and the treasurer; these reports are required to be recorded by the auditor and books kept specifically for the purpose.[31] The auditor is a member of the county board of revision established in 1825, secretary of the budget commission, and serves as a trustee and the secretary of the board of trustees of the sinking fund established in 1919.

In Medina County, the work of the auditor's office is carried on by a staff of five in addition to the auditor himself. The total appraised value of property in the county has shown some increase in recent years, being given as $34,434,780 in 1935, and as $35,401,500 in 1940.[32] In the same period the tax rate has increased, having been set at 3.41 mills in 1935, 3.43 in 1936, and at 3.55 in 1940.[33] The bonded indebtedness of the county has decreased in these years from $269,307 in 1938 to $213,000 in 1940.[34]

---

26. Chase, *op. cit.*, III, 1582; *Laws of Ohio,* XXIX, 446; G. C. secs. 6374, 6375.
27. *Laws of Ohio*, LIX, 67; LXXXIX, 96; CVII, 534.
28. G. C. sec. 5894-5
29. G. C. sec. 5545-5.
30. *Laws of Ohio,* CXV, 649; CXV, pt. ii, 83; CXVI, pt. ii, 323.
31. G. C. sec. 2504; R. S. sec. 826; *Laws of Ohio,* XLVIII, 66.
32. Auditor's Annual Financial Report, 1935-1940, *see* entry 324.
33. *Ibid.*
34. *Ibid.*

Property Transfers

234. TRANSFER RECORD
1818—. 19 vols. (Dated)
Record of real estate transfers, showing date filed, date of entry, names of grantor and grantee, and township, tract, section, and lot numbers, description of land, number of acres, valuation of land and buildings, total value, and remarks; also contains real estate transfers by Auditor's Deeds, 1904—, entry 235. Arranged alphabetically by names of townships and chronologically thereunder by dates entered. No index. Handwritten on printed forms. Average 300 pages. 16 x 12 x 3. Auditor's main office.

235. AUDITOR'S DEEDS
1843-1903. 1 vol. 1904— in Transfer Record, entry 234.
Record of Deeds for land sold by county auditor in forfeited sale for delinquent taxes, showing names of taxing district and original owner, date of sale, names of purchaser and township, range and section numbers, acreage, description of tract, quantity sold, amount of sale, to whom deed was made, date of deed, and signature of county auditor. Arranged chronologically by dates of deeds. No index. Handwritten. 300 pages. 13 x 8.5 x 2. North storeroom.

236. [Memoranda of] PROPERTY TRANSFERS
1927—. 4 file boxes.
Memoranda slips made up by county surveyors office by checking original property transfer with county plats, and turned over to auditor for transfer on real estate duplicate, showing date of transfer, names of township and village, section, tract, and lot numbers, acreage, description of property, and names of grantor and grantee. Arranged alphabetically by names of grantors and chronologically thereunder by dates of transfers. No index. Handwritten not printed forms. 9 x 7 x 15. Auditor's main office.

237. CERTIFICATE OF TRANSFER OF OWNERSHIP OF DOGS
1929. 1 vol.
Copies of certificates of transfer of ownership of dogs, showing date of certificate, names of vendor and vendee, license number, and age, sex, color, and breed of dog. Arranged chronologically by dates of certificates. Indexed alphabetically by names of vendees. Handwritten on printed forms. 200 pages. 8 x 10 x 2. Auditor's main office.

Maps and Plats

238. [AUDITOR'S MAPS AND PLATS]
1923—. 24 vols.
Photostatic copies of the county engineer's real estate plats current in 1923, to be used by the auditor as field sheets in making reappraisals upon additions or complaints concerning regular appraisals, showing all real property lying in the 17 townships and in the municipalities of the county. No systematic arrangement. No index. Black on white. Average 30 pages. 14 x 11 x 3. Auditor's main office.

Taxes

Real Property

239. TAX RATES
1927—. 10 rate sheets.
Tax rates determined from the valuations set by the assessors, appraisers, and the district board of revision, showing state and county levies, general, state, road and bridge, county road and bridge funds, and library and sinking fund levies, showing date of entry, and rates for each of the 54 taxing districts in county; also contains the resume of various levies by districts for indebtedness, showing date passed by vote or levied, year levy begins, and number of years to run. Arranged chronologically by dates entered.

No index. Handwritten on printed forms. 20 x 14. Auditor's main office.

240. LEVIES
1929—. 1 file box.
Records of levies for roads, including county levies against townships and the county for inter-county highways and state roads; levies against townships, showing name of township, name and number of road, principal, interest, and date payments end; levies against county, showing year due, name and number of road, principal and interest due each year listed, and date filed. Arranged chronologically by dates filed. No index. Handwritten and typed, some on printed forms. 10 x 4.5 x 14.5. Auditor's main office.

241. APPRAISEMENTS
1834, 1840, 1846, 1925, 1931, 1937. 142 vols. (4 unlabled; 144 dated and sublabeled by taxing districts).
Assessor's record of taxable real estate (made every six years) 1834, 1840, 1846, showing names of township and taxpayer, description of land, number of acres, valuation of land and buildings, at total value; agricultural lands, 1925, 1931, 1937, showing name and address of owner, name of taxing district, description of land (pasture and timber), number of acres, valuation fixed by assessor, board of revision, or state tax commission, and total valuation of land, deduction for roads, and final valuation for taxation; suburban and business properties 1925, 1931, 1937, showing year of appraisement, name and address of property owner, ward, block, street, and lot numbers, additions, acreage, type of street, depth and frontage of lot, valuations fixed by assessor, board of revision, and state tax commission, size, construction, age and condition of buildings, total value of land, total value of buildings, and grand total of valuation. Arranged alphabetically by names of townships or taxing districts and alphabetically thereunder by names of taxpayers. No index. 1834, 1840, 1846, handwritten; 1925, 1931, 1937, typed. Average 150

pages. 11 x 7.5 x 1. 105 volumes, 1834, 1840, 1846, 1925, 1931, North storeroom; 43 volumes, 1937, Auditor's main office.

242. DECENNIAL APPRAISEMENT
1900, 1910. 62 vols.

Appraisement of the county's real estate for 1900 and 1910. The 1900 edition contains plats of properties and lists of names of property owners in the same volume for each township and municipality, and 1910 edition contains plats and list of names of property owners for each township or municipality in separate volumes; list of property owners in each edition showing name and address of property owner, tract, section, and lot numbers, part of lot, classification and number of acres in arable, meadow, and uncultivated or woodlands, value of land, value of buildings, total value, and value as equalized by county board or state board; also contains list of properties of each township or municipality exempt from taxation, showing kind of property, lot number, location, number of acres, and value of lands and buildings; plats of properties in each edition, showing section and lot numbers, name of owner, acreage, and dimensions by chains; 1910 edition also contains the appraiser's account and oath, showing number of days and dates he worked, total amount earned, and receipt of payment by county auditor. Of the 1900 edition, 19 volumes list names of property owners on left hand page and plats are on right hand page; 1910 edition, 19 volumes contain plats only and 24 volumes contain lists only. Plats arranged numerically by lot numbers; lists arranged alphabetically by townships or municipalities. Plats indexed by section and lot numbers. No index for lists. Plats hand drawn; scale, 8 chains equal one inch. Average 30 pages. 17 x 17 x .5. 19 volumes, 1900; 19 volumes, 1910, Auditor's main office; 24 volumes, 1910, North storeroom.

243. FOREST LANDS
1926—. 1 file box.

Sworn statements by owners of timber, showing date of filing, name of owner, location of land, number of feet of timber removed, and its value for each year ending March 31. Filed with the county auditor prior to May 1, yearly. Arranged chronologically by dates filed. No index. Handwritten on printed forms. 10 x 4.5 x 14.5. Auditor's main office.

244. RECAPITULATION OF TAXES
1900-1919, 1920-1924, 1928-1934. 28 vols. (Dated).

Summary of taxes assessed for the year, showing name of township, amount of general road and special tax, and total amount of taxes. Arranged alphabetically by names of townships. No index. Handwritten on printed forms. Average 150 pages 14 x 11 x 1. 15 volumes, 1900-1919, South storeroom; 5 volumes, 1920-1924, North storeroom; 8 volumes, 1923-1934, Auditor's main office.

Tax Duplicates and Abstracts

245. AUDITOR'S RECORD OF TAXES [Tax Duplicate]
1818—. 184 vols. Title varies: Record Duplicate, 1818-1872, 83 vols.

Records from 1818-1919, contain tax list of real property, showing name of owner, section, tract, and lot numbers, description, acreage, value of lands, value of buildings, value as equalized by board of revision, value as equalized by tax commission, delinquent tax, road, dog, total tax due, penalty, and transfers. Records from 1920-1929, contain tax duplicate, showing tax duplicate number, owner's name, description of property, lot number, number of acres, value as equalized by tax commission, delinquent tax for preceding year, specials, actual tax due, penalty, volume and page numbers of transfer records, and name of party to whom property has been transferred; also has special pages headed Personal Tax Duplicate, 1837-1931, entries 256, 257, showing owner's name and address, value as established by board of revision, changes made by tax commission, total value, delinquent, special tax, penalty, and total amount due. Records from 1930—, contain tax duplicate, showing owner's name section, tract and lot numbers, description, acreage, value of lands and buildings, value as equalized by tax commission and by board of revision, kind of instrument, date of transfer, and to whom transferred; also contains Ditch Duplicate, 1924—, entry 246. Arranged by names of taxing districts and alphabetically thereunder by names of taxpayers. No index. 1818-1908, handwritten; 1909—, typed. 60 volumes average 100 pages. 12 x 8 x 1.5. 23 volumes average 350 pages. 16 x 12 x 1.5; 41 volumes average 350 pages. 15 x 13 x 3.5; 60 volumes average 300 pages. 18 x 16 x 5. Auditor's main office.

246. DITCH DUPLICATE
1885-1923. 5 vols. (1-5). 1924— in Auditor's Record of Taxes [Tax Duplicate], entry 245.

Duplicate of assessments on ditch improvement, showing name of landowner, lot number, acreage, and tax due. Arranged alphabetically by name of landowner. No index. Handwritten on printed forms. Average 79 pages. 16 x 11.5 x 1.5. North storeroom.

247. [ASSESSMENT CERTIFICATES]
1932—. File boxes.

Auditor's assessment certificates, showing name of owner, value of real and personal property, tax rate, name of township, amount, and total assessments. Arranged alphabetically by names of townships. No index. Handwritten and typed, some on printed forms. 10 x 4.5 x 14. Auditor's main office.

248. ROADS
1919—. 2 file boxes. 1 subtitled Current; 1 Paid Out

Road assessment records, showing name of township and section road numbers, property assessment and rate, number of miles, name of property owner, lot numbers, description of property, amount of assessment, and date paid. When the assessments are fully paid the records are moved from the current file and placed in the paid out file. Arranged by names of townships and chronologically thereunder by date filed. No index. Handwritten and typed, some on printed forms. 10 x 4.5 x 14. Auditor's main office.

249. ROAD LIST
1903, 1904. 14 vols. (Labeled by names of townships).
Record of road tax paid in cash or worked out, showing names of landowner and township, section and lot numbers, description, number of acres, value of buildings, total value, amount of road tax, and date of payment. Arranged by names of townships and alphabetically thereunder by names of landowners. No index. Handwritten on printed forms. Average 30 pages. 10 x 15 x .5. North storeroom.

250. EXEMPTED REAL AND PERSONAL PROPERTY
1932—. 1 vol.
Record of property exempt from taxation, showing name of property owner, location and description of property, names of municipalities, townships, state, and county, and names and value of churches, hospitals, charitable institutions, and cemeteries. Arranged by names of townships and alphabetically thereunder by names of property owners. Now index. Typed on printed forms. 75 pages. 14 x 18 x 1. Auditor's main office.

251. EXEMPT PROPERTY APPLICATIONS
1927—. 1 file box.
Original applications of real property owners qualifying by law of state for tax exemption, including schools, churches, cemeteries, charitable institutions, armories, and public buildings, showing date of application, name of taxing district and property owner, and location and description of property with county auditor's findings. Arranged alphabetically by names of taxing districts and alphabetically thereunder by names of property owners. No index. Handwritten on printed forms. 18 x 4.5 x 14. Auditor's main office.

Special assessments

252. SPECIAL ASSESSMENTS
1926—. 9 vols.
Auditor's record of special assessments levied on real estate for public improvements, including highways, streets, and sewers, showing names of improvement, taxing district, and owner, description of property, number of acres or feet frontage, value, amount of assessment, amount of each annual installment, years and amount delinquent, and penalty; also includes Sewer and Water District Record, Chippewa Lake, 1926—, entry 10. Arranged alphabetically by names of taxing districts and alphabetically thereunder by names of owners. No index. Typed on printed forms. Average 150 pages. 17.5 x 18 x 2. 2 volumes, 1926-1930, North storeroom; 7 volumes, 1931—, Auditor's main office

Personal Property

253. PERSONAL PROPERTY TAX RETURNS
1929–. 205 bdls., 7 file boxes (Dated).
Returns of personal property for taxation by individuals, showing name of taxing district, year, name and address of owner, itemized list of chattels, and value of each item; also agricultural statistics by farmers, total value of chattels, and credits as listed by owner, value as revised by auditor, county board of equalization, and state tax commission. Arranged alphabetically by names of taxing districts. And alphabetically thereunder by names of individuals or corporations. No index. Handwritten on printed forms. Bundles, 14 x 8 x 3; file boxes, 17 x 12 x 24. Auditor's main office.

254. TIME EXTENSION PERMITS
1932—. 1 file box.
Permits for time extension for making personal tax returns, showing date and number of application, name of applicant, extension of time asked, rate, reason for request, affidavit of truth of statements by applicant, auditor's approval date, and signature

of auditor. Arranged numerically by application numbers. No index. Handwritten on printed forms. 10 x 4.5 x 14.5. Auditor's main office.

255. ASSESSORS' RETURNS
1906-1931. 62 vols. (Dated).

Personal property tax returns, showing year, names of taxing district and property owner, address, description of property, amount of assessment, and total return paid. Arranged alphabetically by names of taxing districts. No index. Handwritten on printed forms. Average 600 pages. 13 x 8 x 4. North storeroom.

256. AUDITOR'S PERSONAL DUPLICATE – CLASSIFIED
1932—. 1 vol. Initiated in 1932.

Auditor's duplicate of classified (intangible) personal taxes showing assessment certificate number, name of taxing district, name and address of taxpayer, amount of productive and nonproductive investments, credits, moneys, and other tangibles, total tax for year, advance payment, tax due, date paid, and amount of unpaid taxes for year. Arranged chronologically by years, alphabetically thereunder by names of taxing districts, and alphabetically thereunder by names of taxpayers. No index. Handwritten on printed forms. Average 650 pages. 17.5 x 13 x 3. Auditor's main office.

257. AUDITOR'S PERSONAL DUPLICATE – GENERAL
1932—. 1 vol. Initiated in 1932

Auditor's duplicate of general (tangible) personal taxes, showing taxing district, rate, assessment certificate number, number of taxing district, name and address of taxpayer, final assessment, total tax for year, tax due, and remarks. Arranged alphabetically by names of taxing districts, and alphabetically thereunder by names of taxpayers. No index. Handwritten on printed forms. 650 pages. 18 x 15 x 5. Auditor's main office.

258. ABSTRACT OF PROPERTY [Personal]
1932-1936. 5 vols. (Dated). 1987-1931in Auditor's Record
of Taxes [Tax Duplicate], entry 245.

Auditor's abstract of personal property in the several townships of
Medina County, including horses, cattle, merchants' capital,
money at interest, milk, distilleries, and tanneries, showing date of
entry, name of township, name and address of owner, location,
description, and value of property. Arranged alphabetically by
names of townships and chronologically thereunder by dates
entered. Handwritten. Average 150 pages. 8 x 6.5 x 1. Auditor's
main office.

259. ABSTRACT OF PERSONAL PROPERTY
1906-1931. 1 file box. 1932— in Record of Abstracts and
Settlements, entry 278.

Auditor's abstract of personal property, showing name of
township, value of tangible property outside and inside cities and
incorporated villages, county, township, school, and delinquent
tax, total of classified tax duplicate, and signature of auditor.
Copies of abstracts forwarded to tax commission by September 1,
of each year. Arranged alphabetically by names of townships and
chronologically thereunder by dates entered. No index.
Handwritten on printed forms. 12 x 12 x 30. Auditor's main office.

260. CERTIFICATE OF ADVANCED PAYMENT
1932—. 4 file boxes.

Copies of certificates of advanced payment of amount assessed
against personal property for year and half year, showing name and
address of taxpayer, assessment for whole and half year, amount of
assessment, and date paid. Arranged alphabetically by name of
taxpayers. No index. Typed on printed forms. 11 x 16 x 24.
Auditor's main office.

Delinquent

261. DELINQUENT TAXES
1898—. 26 vols. 6 subtitled Real and Personal; 4 Personal; 16 Real.

Recorded delinquent taxes, real and personal, 1898-1930, showing names of taxing district and property owner, year, real estate valuation, delinquent amounts, kind of personal tax, penalties carried forward, and amounts; delinquent taxes, personal, 1931—, showing name of property owner, total tax, date paid, monthly collection, and unpaid June collection carried forward; delinquent taxes, real estate, 1931—, showing lot number, name of property owner, real estate valuation, delinquent amounts, date of payment, and amount carried forward. Arranged alphabetically by names of taxing districts. No index. 1898-1930 handwritten on printed forms.; 1931—, typed. Average 400 pages. 16.5 x 15 x 3. Auditor's main office.

262. DELINQUENT LAND SALES [Notice of Sheriff's Sales]
1824-1922. 2 vols.

Record of delinquent land sales listing real property (by townships) offered for sale by sheriff, showing notice of date of sale, name of property owner, location of property, acreage, buildings, accumulated taxes, penalty, total amount, listing and name of purchaser, and sworn statements by auditor and treasurer. After two years, property is redeemed or auditor's deed is issued to purchaser. Arranged chronologically by years, alphabetically thereunder by names of townships and alphabetically thereunder by names of property owners. No index. Handwritten on printed forms. Average 300 pages. 14.5 x 9.5 x 2. 1 volume, 1824-1850, Auditor's main office; 1 volume 1851-1922, North storeroom.

263. RECORD OF UNCLAIMED FORECLOSURE ON FORFEITED LAND SALE MONEYS PAID INTO THE COUNTY TREASURY

1939—. 1 vol. Initiated in 1939.

Record of moneys in foreclosures and forfeited land sales that exceed the amount owed for delinquent taxes paid into the treasury until landowner recovers same, showing date of entry, name of township or municipality, to whom money belongs, date of entry, amount paid into treasury, pay-in order number, duplicate where tax items may be found, date certificate issued to owner for recovery, and signature of owner for money recovered. Arranged by townships or municipalities and chronologically thereunder by dates entered. No index. Typed on printed forms. 300 pages. 15 x 9 x 3.5. Auditor's main office.

264. RETURNED CERTIFICATE OF FORFEITED LAND SALES.

1939—. 1 file box. Initiated in 1939.

Returned auditor's certificate of sale of forfeited lands for nonpayment of taxes, showing date of certificate, date and amount of sale, name of taxing district, name of purchaser, amount of assessment, penalties, and interest, name of taxpayer, description of property sold, what part sold, value of property, total taxes, including assessment, penalties, and interest, and oath and signature of county auditor. Arranged chronologically by dates of certificates. No index. Typed on printed forms. 1 x 4.5. x 14.5. Auditor's main office.

265. FORFEITED LANDS

1939—. 1 vol. Initiated in 1939

Duplicate list of all forfeited lands and lots through auditor's sale for delinquent taxes, showing date of entry, names of owner and township or municipality, number of lot or survey, description of land or lot, acreage or foot frontage, value, total amount of taxes, including assessments, penalties and interest due, stamp of date of auditor's sale, and signatures of members of county board of revision. Original list filed with auditor of state. Arranged chronologically by dates entered. No index. Handwritten on printed forms. 500 pages. 18 x 14 x 4. Auditor's main office.

266. CERTIFICATE OF REDEMPTION
1926-1932. 1 vol. Discontinued.

Auditor's duplicate copy of certificate of redemption, showing date issued, certificate number, date certified delinquent, names of taxing district and landowner, lot number, amount of delinquent tax, penalty, interest, auditor's fee, total due, and date paid. Arranged chronologically by the issued. No index. Handwritten on printed forms. 400 pages. 7.5 x 15 x 2. Auditor's main office.

Complaints and Adjustments

267. ADDITIONS AND DEDUCTIONS
1874-1908, 1930—. 2 vols. 1 bdl.

Auditor's duplicate additions to or deductions from tax duplicate, showing name of taxing district, year, name of owner, range, township, section and lot numbers, description of tract, value of real estate, personal property, amount added or deducted, and reason for revision. Arranged chronologically by years and alphabetically thereunder by names of owners. No index. Handwritten on printed forms. Volumes average 150 pages. 17 x 11 x 1.5. bundles, 12 x 15 x 1.5. 1 volume, 1874-1908, North storeroom; 1 volume, 1 bundle 1930—, Auditor's main office.

268. AUDITOR'S ADDITIONAL TAX COLLECTIONS
1929—. 3 vols. (Labeled by contained order numbers).

Carbon copies of orders to treasurer to collect certain delinquent taxes, due to taxpayers failure to list property or same being listed too late or incorrectly, showing order number, names of taxpayer, and township, amount, and date paid. Arranged numerically by order numbers. No index. Handwritten on printed forms. Average 125 pages. 14 x 10 x 1. Auditor's main office.

269. [Complaints of] ADDITIONS AND DEDUCTIONS
1931—. 2 file boxes.

Record of complaints as to assessments on real property, showing
names of complainant, county, taxing district, and township,
address, amount considered excessive on both land and buildings,
number of acres, assessed value, decrease or increase asked, date
of purchase, from whom, improvements (if any), detailed
description of house, buildings, and land, signature and oath of
complainant, date of hearing, notice of complainant, and notation
of deduction (if allowed) or disposition of complaint. Arranged by
names of township and alphabetically thereunder by names of
complainants. No index. Handwritten on printed forms.
Approximately 175 documents in file box. 10 x 4.5 x 14.5.
Auditor's main office.

Inheritance

270. DETERMINATION OF INHERITANCE TAX
1923—. 4 file boxes (1 labeled Paid; 3 Unpaid).

Affidavits from probate judge to county auditor, showing name of
estate, case number, date of establishment of gross and net value
of estate, legatees and their ages, relationship to decedent, value of
estate to each legatee, amount of exemption, balance subject to
inheritance tax, amount of inheritance tax, date of accrual, names
of persons by whom tax must be paid in township or corporation
in which state is located, certification and signature of probate
judge, and date of settlement. Arranged chronologically by dates
of settlements and alphabetically thereunder by names of estates.
No index. Typed on printed forms. 10 x 4.5 x 14.5. Auditor's main
office.

271. ESTATES IN PROCESS OF SETTLEMENT
1927—. 1 file box.

Preliminary statement from probate court to auditor in matters of
inheritance tax, showing amount subject and not subject to tax,
name of decedent, date of death, residence and place of death,

name of administrator or executor, case number, description and value of property, and copy of notarization. Arranged numerically by case numbers. No index. Typed on printed forms. 10 x 4.5 x 14.5. Auditor's main office.

272. INHERITANCE TAX CHARGE
1923—. 1 vol.
County auditor's statement to county treasurer of inheritance tax due for collection on estates, showing case number, date of issue, name of estate, amount of inheritance tax as certified to auditor by probate judge, by whom payable, name and post office address of heir, date of accrual of tax, amount fixed by court, discount or interest, total amount paid, date of payment, name of township or corporation, and signatures of county auditor and deputy. Arranged chronologically by dates paid. Indexed alphabetically by names of estates. Handwritten on printed forms. 200 pages. 11 x 10 x 2.5. Auditor's main office.

Utility

273. PUBLIC UTILITIES VALUATION
1927—. 1 file box, 7 bdls.
Public utilities, including general, personal, and real property certificates of valuation distributed by tax commission of Ohio, showing names of railroads, electric power lines, gas lines, and taxing district, and valuation of land, buildings, and equipment; utilities are grouped under each township or taxing district, showing amount of tax for each district on all utilities operating therein, and date tax return filed. Arranged chronologically by dates tax returns filed. No index. Handwritten on printed forms. File box, 10 x 4.5 x 14.5; bundles, 6 x 10 x 1. Auditor's main office.

Excise

274. AUDITOR'S LIQUOR TAX DUPLICATE
1883-1916, 1929-1930. 5 vols. (1-5).

Duplicate of liquor tax, 1883-1918, showing names of township, village, and taxpayer, lot numbers, description of property, name of owner, total amount of assessment, and penalty; volume five contains the record of Illegal Liquor Traffic Penalties, 1929-1930, entry 275. Arranged chronologically by dates filed. No index. Typed on printed forms. 10 x 4.5 x 14.5. Auditor's main office.

275. ILLEGAL LIQUOR TRAFFIC PENALTIES
1929-1930. 1 file box.

Record of assessments or penalties against persons or firms for violation of the Liquor Prohibition Law, showing date of filing, name and address of person or firm selling illegal liquor, location and value of property, where sold, and amount of 20 percent penalty due. Record of penalties in volume five, Auditor's Liquor Tax Duplicate, 1929-1930, entry 274. Arranged chronologically by dates filed. No index. Typed on printed forms. 10 x 4.5 x 14.5. Auditor's main office.

276. CIGARETTE TAX ASSESSMENTS
1930—. 1 vol.

Record of cigarette tax assessments, showing receipt number, names of licensee and township, location of business, description of property, amount assessed, date of payment, and remarks. Arranged by names of townships. No index. Handwritten on printed forms. 50 pages. 17 x 11.5 x 1. Auditor's main office.

Fiscal Accounts

Budgets and Appropriations

277. GENERAL APPROPRIATION LEDGER
1929—. 14 vols. (Dated).
Auditor's record of appropriations to each fund or department by
county commissioners and expenditures from each fund, showing
name of fund or department, date and amount credited or debited
to each, name of payee or vendor, for what, warrant number and
amount, appropriation or authorization, and unencumbered
balance; also includes distribution of license fees, 1938—.
Arranged alphabetically by names of funds or departments. No
index. Handwritten on printed forms. Average 350 pages. 10.5 x 15
x 3. Auditor's main office.

Settlements

278. RECORD OF ABSTRACTS AND SETTLEMENTS
1890-1910, 1925—. 2 vols.
Auditor's abstracts of tax duplicates and annual and semiannual
settlements with the state auditor and county treasurer of receipts
from all sources, including:
    a.   Abstract of the duplicate of real and public utility
    properties, showing rate of taxation for township,
    city, and school districts, and totals.
    b.   Annual settlements with the state auditor, showing
    dates of settlement, total values of public utilities,
    state, county, and township taxers, special
    assessments, delinquents, and totals.
    c.   Annual settlements with county showing total tax
    for state, county, township, city or village, school
    districts, county special assessments, township
    roads, and township special assessments, and
    totals of each.

d. Abstracts of the duplicate of general and classified personal property tax and annual settlement with state and county, 1932—, showing names of state, township, and city or village, and distribution of state, township, local school, city or village, and miscellaneous taxes.

e. Settlements with the county, showing total undivided personal taxes with distribution to various county funds.

f. Semiannual detailed statement of receipts on account of inheritance tax collected, showing case number, name of decedent and payer, amount collected, and portions due local taxing district and state; also contains detailed statement of estates not subject to inheritance tax, showing case number, name of decedent, and expense and fees (if any) of auditor, probate judge, witnesses, and sheriff; also includes Abstract of Personal Property, 1932—, entry 259. Arranged by dates of settlements. No index. Handwritten and typed, some are printed forms. Average 160 pages. 24 x 15 x 2. Auditor's main office.

279. AUDITOR'S SCHOOL SETTLEMENT RECORD 1842—. 9 vols.

Record of semiannual settlements of the township school clerks with the county auditor, on right hand page, showing date of entry, names of township and school district, source of receipts, and disbursements, balance at close of last semiannual statement, date of settlement, advances made to districts, income from different funds and other sources, and total, warrant numbers and amounts of disbursements, deductions and clerk's balance, amount of outstanding warrants, an amount in depository as certified by depository official; auditor semiannual report, on the left hand page, showing auditors receipts for this particular school district from all sources, date of receipt, special deductions, advance draft, and net amount for distribution to districts. Arranged by dates entered, alphabetically thereunder by names of townships and municipal school districts, and chronologically thereunder by dates of settlement. No index. 1842-1921, handwritten; 1921— typed. Average 290 pages. 19 x 12.5 x 3. 7 volumes, 1842-1921, North storeroom; 2 volumes, 1922—, Auditor's main office.

General Accounts

280. AUDITOR'S LEDGER
1927—. 1 vol.
Auditor's final account of surplus revenues, showing date of entry, amount of surplus funds, name of fund or account, how and where invested, and balance in depository institutions, including county, township, and school accounts. Arranged alphabetically by names of funds or accounts and chronologically thereunder by dates entered. No index. Handwritten. 350 pages. 11.5 x 13.5 x 2.5. Auditor's main office.

281. AUDITOR'S RECORD OF FEES
1907—. 5 vols. (1-5)
Daily record of money's received by auditor from fees, fines, licenses, and miscellaneous sources, showing date of entry, name of payer, extension, and amount transferred to treasurer at end of month; also contains report of amount of Fees and Salaries, 1907-1928, entry 300. Arranged chronologically by dates entered. No index. Handwritten on printed forms. Average 200 pages. 16 x 11.5 x 1.5. 2 volumes, 1907-1925, South storeroom; 1 volume, 1926-1931, North storeroom; 2 volumes, 1932—, Auditor's main office.

282. RECEIPTS JOURNAL
1925—. 1 vol.
Record of receipts from all fees, fines, licenses, county home, unclaimed money, deposits on interest, gas tax, auto tags, and miscellaneous, showing name of account, date of receipt, name of payer, purpose, bill and receipt number, amount received,

memorandum, accounts receivable, debit, credit, and balance. Arranged by dates of receipts. No index. Handwritten on printed forms. 225 pages. 1.5 x 15 x 2.5. Auditor's main office.

283. EXPENDITURES AND RECEIPTS FROM MEDINA COUNTY INFIRMARY
1908—. 3 vols. (1-3).

Classification of expenditures and receipts of Medina County infirmary; expenditures, including salaries, groceries, stock, feed, machinery, nursing, and medical supplies, showing date of entry, name of payee, and amount; receipts from farm produce, stock, and friends, showing date received from whom, for what purpose, and amount. Arranged chronologically by dates entered. No index. Handwritten on printed forms. Average 200 pages. 17 x 15 x 2. 1 volume, 1908-1923, North storeroom; 1 volume 1924-1937, Auditor's main office.; 1 volume, 1938, Infirmary office.

284. AUDITOR'S DOCKET OF BILLS FILED
1904—. 3 vols. (1-3).

County auditors record of infirmary bills, showing name of creditor, purpose, date of filing, date and amount paid, and number of warrant; also includes expense accounts of county visitors, 1913—. Arranged numerically by warrant numbers. No index. Handwritten on printed forms. Average 138 pages. 18 x 13 x 2. 2 volumes, 1904-1924, South storeroom; 1 volume, 1925—, Auditor's main office.

285. [DISTRIBUTION OF MOTOR VEHICLE LICENSE FEES]
1925—. 3 vols.

Record of distribution of motor vehicle license fees to subdivisions of county by auditor, showing date of distribution, number of vehicles registered in each subdivision, amount, total, and distribution of fees to each subdivision. Arranged chronologically by dates of distributions and alphabetically thereunder by subdivisions. No index. Handwritten on printed forms. Average

175 pages. 12 x 11.5 x 2. Auditor's main office.

286. SCHOOL FUNDS
1930—. 1 file box.

Depository orders for school and township funds, showing name of township and county, date of filing, amount of bond, and certification to auditor to pay this bank all moneys belonging to township issuing order. Arranged alphabetically by names of townships and chronologically thereunder by date filed. No index. Typed on printed forms. 10 x 4.5 x 14.5. Auditor's main office.

287. AUDITOR'S MISCELLANEOUS ACCOUNTS
1899-1905. 1 vol.

Record of real estate assessor's services in the various townships and corporations, showing names of township or corporation and assessor, date of appointment, date and number of days worked, amount earned each day, total amount earned, and total paid. Arranged alphabetically by names of townships and alphabetically thereunder by names of assessors. No index. Handwritten. 415 pages. 16 x 12 x 2.5. North storeroom.

288. PAY ROLLS
1932—. 1 file box.

Record of pay rolls for county employees, showing date filed, name of employee, classification, amount, and deductions. Arranged chronologically by date filed. No index. Handwritten on printed forms. 10 x 4.5 x 14.5. Auditor's main office.

289. INDEBTEDNESS OF SCHOOL DISTRICTS, TOWNSHIPS, AND VILLAGES
1932—. 1 file box.

Annual school district reports to county auditor from (village and township) clerks of board of education, showing date filed, outstanding indebtedness in bonds and notes, and signature of clerk. Arranged by dates filed. No index. Handwritten on printed forms. 10 x 4.5 x 14.5. Auditor's main office.

290. DAILY STATEMENT OF COUNTY TREASURER TO THE COUNTY AUDITOR
1873—. 4 vols. 24 bdls.

Certified daily settlement from county treasurer to county auditor, showing balance in treasury and depositories for each previous day, date of issue, daily receipts, pay-in orders, general taxes, distributor's taxes, amount deposited in and checked from depositories, and total; also contains disbursements, general and court warrants, amount checked from depositories, amount deposited, balance, certification, and signature of treasurer. Arranged chronologically by dates issued. No index. Handwritten and typed, some on printed forms. Volumes average 500 pages. 16 x 10 x 2.5; 24 bundles, 14 x 8.5 x 30. 4 volumes, 1873-1902, North storeroom; 2 bundles, 1902-1919, Treasurer's office; 22 bundles, 1919—. Auditor's main office.

291. DEPOSITORIES' MONTHLY STATEMENTS
1934—. 1 file box.

Depositories' monthly statements to county auditor, showing date filed, name of bank, date of deposit, interest credited for past month, balance now on deposit to the credit of the county, amount on hand, deposits, withdrawals (if any), and daily balance. Arranged chronologically by dates filed. No index. Handwritten on printed forms. 10.5 x 4.5 x 14.5. Auditor's main office.

Special Accounts

292. RECORD OF GRANTS [Soldiers' Relief]
1888—. 2 vols.

Record of indigent soldiers, sailors, and marines eligible for relief, showing names of township and applicant, age, occupation, address, physical condition, name of company, regiment, or ship, length of service, number of dependents, and date and amount of relief awarded. The act of 1919, included grants to indigent veterans of the World War or to indigent parents, wives, widows, or minor children of such veterans, showing date of grant.

Arranged alphabetically by names of townships and
chronologically thereunder by dates granted. No index.
Handwritten on printed forms. Average 275 pages. 15.5 x 10.5 x 2.
Auditor's main office.

293. SOLDIERS' RELIEF COMMISSION REPORT TO COUNTY AUDITOR
1902—. 1 file box.

Monthly report of soldiers' relief commission to county auditor,
showing names of clients to whom relief has been awarded, date
filed, date of report, name and address of person applying for
relief, monthly allowance, date and amount granted, and approval
of auditor or deputy auditor. Arranged chronologically by dates of
reports. No index. Typed on printed forms. 10 x 4.5 x 14.5.
Auditor's main office.

294. BLIND RELIEF RECORD
1925-1936. 1 vol. (1).

Auditor's record of payments for blind relief made quarterly,
showing name and address of relief client, date of payment,
warrant number, and amount. Arranged chronologically by dates
paid and alphabetically thereunder by names of relief clients. No
index. Handwritten on printed forms. 250 pages. 17 x 9 x 2.
Auditor's main office.

295. AID TO THE BLIND
1936—. 1 file box (Dated).

Original claims for reimbursements to Department of Welfare
Division of Public Assistance, Columbus, Ohio, and signed by
county commissioners, certified grants as aid to the blind have
been made for month and year, and authorizing county auditor to
issue warrants on county treasury to cover same; also includes
auditors certification warrants have been issued, showing case
number, name of recipient, amount of warrant, warrant number,
amount of reimbursement (by state), amount not to be reimbursed,
and totals for each. Original copy sent to Columbus, Ohio,

duplicate retained in auditor's office, triplicate copy returned to local aid for the blind office. Arranged alphabetically by names of recipients and chronologically thereunder by months. No index. Typed on printed forms. 10 x 5 x 14. Auditor's main office.

296. RECORD OF DISBURSEMENTS FOR MOTHERS' PENSIONS
1915-1936. 1 vol. (1). Discontinued. Superseded by Aid to Dependent Children. 1913-1914 in Auditor's Journal of Warrants Issued and Payments into the Treasury, entry 306.

Auditor's record of payments from mothers' pension fund, showing name and address of payee, monthly award, date authorized, warrant number, and date paid. Arranged chronologically by dates paid. Indexed alphabetically by names of payees. Handwritten on printed forms. 200 pages. 16 x 11 x 1. Auditor's main office.

297. TUITION BILLS FOR DEPENDENT CHILDREN
1932—. 1 file box.

Correspondence to and from officials of school boards in adjoining counties and county school superintendents statement of public charge pupils attending school in the county, showing name of pupil, grade, age, attendance record, tuition rate, semester, address prior to coming to this county, and name of organization supporting child. Arranged chronologically by semesters and alphabetically thereunder by names of pupils. No index. Handwritten and typed. 10 x 4.5 x 14.5. Auditor's main office.

298. ANIMAL CLAIM RECORD
1879—. 3 vols. (1-3).

Record of claims filed for compensation for animals killed or injured by dogs, showing date filed with township trustees, name and address of claimant, number of animals killed and injured, affidavit on claim, testimony of supporting witnesses, date filed with county commissioners, amount of claim, amount of witness fees and mileage, total amount of claim, and date claim was approved by commissioners. Arranged alphabetically by names of claimants and chronologically thereunder by dates filed. Handwritten on printed forms. Average 150 pages. 15 x 11 x 1. 1 volume 1879-1905, South storeroom; 1 volume, 1906-1918, North storeroom; 1 volume, 1919—. Auditor's main office.

299. BOARD OF EDUCATION – FINANCIAL STATEMENTS
1928—. 1 file box.

Annual financial report of board of education for each school district, showing name of township or school district, date filed, detailed account of receipts from revenue, non-revenue, and other districts, total, and grand total, also salaries of teachers, operation of school plant, and maintenance. Arranged alphabetically by names of townships and chronologically thereunder by dates filed. No index. Typed on printed forms. 10 x 4.5 x 14.5. Auditor's main office.

300. REPORT OF AMOUNT OF FEES AND SALARIES
1928—. 1 file box. 1907-1928 in Auditor's Record of Fees, entry 281.

Auditor's record of fees received by and salaries due to county officials of Medina County for fiscal year, showing date of report, name of office, by whom paid, to whom paid, salaries of officers, assistants, deputies, and clerks, and total amount of fees. Arranged chronologically by dates of reports. No index. Handwritten on printed forms. 10 x 4.5 x 14.5. Auditor's main office.

301. WORKMEN'S COMPENSATION
1926—. 1 bdl., 1 file box. Records 1921-1926 destroyed.

Reports from incorporated town or township clerks, covering total amount of pay rolls, and total amount paid each employee as provided for under workmen's compensation law, showing date of report, names of county and taxing district, regular, township, and relief pay rolls, corporations, and school districts. Arranged chronologically by dates of reports. No index. Handwritten on printed forms. 10 x 4.5 x 14.5. Auditor's main office.

Bills and Claims

302. UNPAID BILLS
1933—. 1 file box, 2 folders.
Unpaid vouchers for bills which have been approved by county commissioners for supplies, materials, and contracts for county, showing date and number of voucher, name and address of creditor, amount claimed and approved, and for what purpose. Arranged numerically by voucher numbers. No index. Handwritten on printed forms. File box, 10 x 4.5 x 14.5. folders, 6 x 10 x 1. Auditor's main office.

Vouchers, Orders, and Warrants

303. PAID VOUCHERS [And Bills Paid]
1919—. 45 cartons; 39 file boxes (Dated).
Vouchers issued by authority of county commissioners for payment from county funds for bills and claims, showing date and number of voucher, name of payee, for what purpose, amount, date paid, and approval of auditor; also contains bills approved for payment by county commissioners, each voucher folded with the bill or bills it paid. Arranged numerically by voucher numbers. No index. Handwritten on printed forms. Cartons, 24 x 11 x 5; file boxes 10 x 4.5 x 14.5. 45 cartons, 1919-1938, North storeroom; 39 file boxes, 1939—, Auditor's main office.

304. MONTHLY PAY-INS
1932—. 1 file box.
Record of monthly pay-in orders issued to treasurer by auditor for transfer of accounts, showing date of order, amount of fees collected, name of department, auditors warrant to pay amount into county treasury as required by law, and signature of official or deputy. Arranged alphabetically by names of departments. No

index. Typed on printed forms. 10 x 4.5 x 14.5. Auditor's main office.

305. ORDERS REDEEMED
1894-1900. 1 vol.

Record of quarterly orders redeemed by treasurer including county, bridge, infirmary, dog, institute, special ditch, municipal, and indigent soldier funds, unclaimed cost, and recapitulation, showing date and number of order, to whom drawn, amount, and name of fund. Arranged numerically by order numbers. No index. Handwritten. 318 pages. 18 x 13 x 2. North storeroom.

306. JOURNAL OF WARRANTS ISSUED AND PAYMENTS INTO THE TREASURY
1904—. 19 vols. (1-9); (1-10).

Auditor's journal of warrants issued and payments into treasury divided into two parts; first part, journal of warrants issued, showing warrant number, date issued, for what purpose, name of payee, amount of warrant (credited treasurer), and distribution of amount from various county funds; second part, payments, showing date of payment, by whom paid, for what purpose, pay-in order number, amount of pay-in order (debited treasurer), date of entry, and distribution of amount to various county funds; also contains Record of Disbursements for Mothers' Pensions, 1913-1914, entry 296. Arranged by dates entered and number, thereunder by warrant numbers or pay-in order numbers. No index. Handwritten on printed forms. Average 500 pages. 18 x 16 x 5. 3 volumes, 1904-1914, North storeroom; 16 volumes, 1915—. Auditor's main office.

307. COURT WARRANTS ISSUED
1904—. 1 vol. (1).

Record of court warrants issued for jury and witness fees, showing date of warrant, name of payee, and warrant number for common pleas court petit jury, grand jury, also grand jury witnesses, and witnesses in criminal cases; probate court jury, criminal witnesses, and witnesses in lunacy and epilepsy cases; also for witnesses in minor courts, coroner's witnesses, and jurors. Arranged by dates of warrants and numerically thereunder by consecutive warrant numbers. No index. Handwritten on printed forms. 320 pages. 17 x 12.5 x 2.5. Auditor's main office.

308. COURT WARRANTS
1938—. 1 file box.
Common pleas and probate court warrants issued for grand and petit jury service and witness fees, showing amount of payee, date issued, amount of fee, for what service, days served, mileage, and date of payment, also detachable stub, showing auditor's warrant number, date and signature of county auditor, and amount submitted to be charged to general fund. Arranged by dates of payments. No index. Handwritten on printed forms. 18 x 4.5 x 14. Auditor's main office.

309. CANCELED WARRANTS
1905—. 30 cartons, 14 file boxes.
Auditor's on printed warrants on treasury for payment of bills and claims authorized by commissioners or other county officers by vouchers, showing date and number of warrant, name of payee, amount, for what purpose, what fund, and date on printed. Arranged by warrant numbers. No index. Typed on printed forms. Cartons, 11 x 5 x 24; file boxes, 14 x 4.5 x 14.5. 30 cartons, 1905-1930, North storeroom; 1 file box, 1931—, Auditor's main office.

310. REPORTS
1930—. (illegible) file boxes, 5 bdls.
Carbon copies of general warrants issued on county treasury, showing warrant number, date issued, amount of warrant, what fund, auditor's approval, for what purpose, and signature of payer. Arranged by warrant numbers. No index. Typed on printed forms. (illegible) file boxes, 12 x 15 x 25; bundles 18 x 8 x 4. 2 file boxes, 1930-1939, North storeroom; 5 bundles, 1936—, Auditor's main office.

311. [Bonds] (illegible)
1933—. 1 vol.

Record of warrants issued in payment of interest on outstanding bonds, for expenditures for materials, labor, and other road improvements, showing date of issue, for what purpose, name of payee, warrant number, amount credited to treasurer, and amount debited each fund. Arranged numerically by warrant numbers. No index. Handwritten on printed forms. Average 188 pages. (illegible) x 13 x 1.5. South storeroom.

312. (illegible) FOR (illegible) ISSUED
1931—. 1 file box.

Bonds given to county auditor to indemnify county in cases (illegible) a duplicate warrant has been issued to the rightful owner of a lost or stolen warrant should original warrant be redeemed, showing date filed, signatures of payee and two sureties, amount of bond, date and place of signing, and indemnifying clause should original warrant be collected. Arranged chronologically by dates filed. No index. Handwritten on printed forms. 18 x 4.5 x 14.5. Auditor's main office.

Licenses and Permits

313. CIGARETTE RECEIPTS
1913—. 10 vols. 4 bdls.

Record of cigarette licenses issued, showing name of township, receipt number, name and address of person, firm, or corporation licensed, date license issued, and amount of tax. Arranged alphabetically by names of townships and chronologically thereunder by dates licenses issued. No index. Handwritten on printed forms. Volumes average 130 pages. 14 x (illegible) x 1; bundles 10 x 4.5 x 14.5. Auditor's main office.

314. CIGARETTE LICENSE [Applications]
1938—. 1 file box.

Applications for cigarette dealer's license, showing name and address of applicant, location of business, date of issue, and name of township or village. Arranged alphabetically by names of townships and chronologically thereunder by dates issued. No index. Handwritten on printed forms. 10 x 4.5 x 14.5. Auditor's main office.

315. CIGARETTE DEALER'S LICENSES
1932—. 1 vol. 10 bdls. (Dated).

Carbon copies of cigarette licenses issued to dealers, showing license number, date issued, years within which license is effective, name of dealer, location of business, conditions under which license may be revoked, date license effective, and signature of county auditor. Arranged numerically by license numbers and chronologically thereunder by dates issued. No index. Typed on printed forms. Volumes 200 pages. 10 x 16 x 2.5; bundles (illegible) x 11 x .25. Auditor's main office.

316. RETAIL BREWER'S WORT OR MALT DEALER'S (illegible)
1933—. 8 bdls.

Duplicate licenses to sell wort or malt, showing date license issued, date of expiration, names of state and county, year license is effective, seal of the state of Ohio, name of licensee, location of business, conditions under which license is to be revoked, date license becomes effective, amount of license fee, and signatures of auditor and deputy. Arranged by years and thereunder by dates issued. No index. Handwritten on printed forms. 8.5 x 11 x .25. Auditor's main office.

317. BREWER'S WORT OR MALT LICENSE APPLICATIONS
1933—. 2 bdls.

Applications for wort or malt licenses, showing name and address of applicant, business address, wholesale or retail, and date license issued; also contains affidavit, showing signature or name of firm or corporation, official title of applicant, signature and seal of notary, application number, date filed, and signatures of auditor and deputy. Arranged by application numbers. No index. Handwritten on printed forms. 8.5 x 3.5 x .25. Auditor's main office.

318. APPLICATION FOR LICENSE TO SELL TANGIBLE PERSONAL PROPERTY AT RETAIL
1934—. 25 vols.

Original applications for vendor's licenses under sales tax law, showing date of application, name and business address of applicant, kind of business, date license issued, and consecutive license numbers. Arranged by license numbers. No index. Handwritten on printed forms. Average 100 pages. 8.5 x 11 x 2. Auditor's main office.

319. VENDOR'S LICENSE
1934—. 28 vols.

Duplicate copies of licenses issued to vendors, showing date issued, license number, date and address of vendor, place and kind of business, code number, and penal citation for law violation. Arranged by license numbers. No index. Handwritten on printed forms. Average 100 pages. 12 x 6.5 x 2. Auditor's main office.

320. DOG TAGS [Licenses]
1929—. 10 file boxes (labeled by contained letters of alphabet).

Applications for dog registrations, showing name and address of owner, license number, and treasurer's receipt for tags sold. Arranged by names of owners. No index. Handwritten on printed forms. 5 x 7 x 12. Auditor's main office.

321. AUDITOR'S CERTIFICATES, TREASURER'S RECEIPTS, AND CLERK OF COURTS APPLICATIONS
1818-1852. 1 bdl., 150 sheets.

Record of clerk of courts application and auditor's certificates for peddler's, auctioneer's, and tavern licenses and receipts of assessors' bonds; peddler's, auctioneer's, and tavern licenses, showing date of issue, name and address of licensee, kind and number of license, and fees; assessors' bonds, showing date and amount of bond, name of bondsmen, date filed, and approval of bond. Arranged by date issued or date filed. No index. Handwritten. Bundles, 8 x 2.5 x 1.5; sheets, 3 x 8. South storeroom.

Enumerations and Statistics

322. ENUMERATION OF SCHOOLS
1921—. 2 bdls. 1 file box.

Annual enumeration returns of number of youths between 5 and 18 years, showing name of township, name, address, and age of child, and total number of youths. Arranged alphabetically by names of townships. Handwritten on printed files. Bundles, 14 x 18 x 4; file box, 10 x 4.5 x 14.5. 2 bundles, 1921-1928, North storeroom; 1 file box, 1929—, Auditor's main office.

323. ANNUAL REPORTS
1913—. 1 bdl., 1 file box.

Copies of Auditor's annual financial statements to county commissioners, showing date of statement and itemized account of cash receipts from all sources credited to county funds; also itemized general account of expenditures, showing debt of each fund and balance or deficit of each fund. Arranged chronologically by dates of statements. No index. Typed. Bundles, 14 x 6 x 3.; file box, 10 b 4.5 x 14.5. 1 bundle, 1913-1924, North storeroom; 1 file box, 1925—, Auditor's main office.

324. ANNUAL FINANCIAL REPORT
1928—. 14 vols.

Annual report of general county statistics, from county auditor to auditor of state, showing date of report, financial summary for each fund administered by auditor, expenditures and receipts of each agency of county government, and signature of county auditor. Arranged chronologically by years. No index. Typed. 12 x 8 x .5. Auditor's main office.

Bonds

325. RECORD OF OFFICIALS' BONDS
1886—. 2 vols.

Record of bonds of treasurer, coroner, and sheriff, and their deputies, reports and copies of road commissioners' bonds, and bonds for members of board of revision, showing name of official, title, oath of office, names of sureties, amount of bond, date filed, and prosecuting attorney's certificate of approval. Arranged chronologically by dates filed. No index. Handwritten on printed forms. Average 370 pages. 19 x 12 x 2.5. 1 volume, 1886-1906, South storeroom; 1 volume, 1907—, Auditor's main office.

326. BONDS FOR TAX OFFICERS
1886—. 2 vols.

Auditor's copy of bonds for members of board of revision, assessors and assessors' assistants, showing date and amount of bond, name an address of officer, signatures of tax officer and sureties, and signature of approval by county auditor. Arranged chronologically by dates of bonds and alphabetically thereunder by names of bonded persons. Handwritten on printed forms. 144 pages. 16 x 11 x 2. South storeroom.

327. RECORD OF BONDS
1918—. 1 file box.

Surety bonds of school clerks and treasurers of townships and villages, showing name of clerk or treasurer, names of sureties, amount of bond, date of filing, and signatures of president and clerk of board of education. Arranged chronologically by dates filed. No index. Handwritten on printed forms. 10 x 4.5 x 14.5. Auditor's main office.

328. BOND REGISTER
1872—. 5 vols. (1-5).

Register of bonds authorized and issued by commissioners for highways, county buildings, poor relief, and for what purpose issued, names of commissioners and auditor authorizing issue of bond, amount and date of issue, date of sale, to whom sold, number of bond, denomination, rate of interest, maturity dates, record of redemption, and interest payments. Arranged by dates issued. No index. Handwritten on printed forms. Average 125 pages. 16 x 11 x 1.5. 1 volume, 1872-1904, North storeroom; 1 volume, 1904-1907, South storeroom, 3 volumes, 1908—, Auditor's main office.

329. RESOLUTIONS FOR BOND ISSUE
1922—. 2 file boxes.

Original resolutions for bonds authorized and issued by county commissioners for highways, county buildings, poor relief, and refunding purposes, showing for what purpose issued, names of commissioners and auditor authorizing issue, date and amount of issue, number of bond, denomination, rate of interest, maturity dates, schedule of redemption, and interest payments, arranged chronologically by dates issued. No index. Handwritten and typed, some on printed forms. 10 x 4.5 x 14.5. Auditor's main office.

330. CANCELED BONDS
1928-1929. 1 vol.

Coupon receipt for paid out bonds issued and sold to provide funds for city and township improvements authorized by county commissioners, showing date issued, amount of bond, rate of interest, bond number, and date redeemed. Arranged chronologically by dates issued and numerically thereunder by bond numbers. No index. Typed on printed forms. 700 pages. 12 x 18 x 6. Auditor's main office.

Weights and Measures

331. RECORD OF SEALER OF WEIGHTS AND MEASURES
1915—. 1 bdl., 1 file box.

Record of sealer of weights and measures, showing date of inspection, name and address of firm, individual, or corporation, kind of business, types of weighing and measuring devices tested, kind of commodities weighed or re-measured, number found correct and incorrect, and whether under or over; also contains record of orders issued to owners of weighing and measuring devices. Arranged by dates of inspections. No index. Handwritten on printed forms. 10 x 4.5 x 14.5. Auditor's main office.

Miscellaneous

332. APPOINTMENTS OF AUDITOR'S DEPUTIES
1923—. 1 file box.

Record of appointments of auditor's deputies, showing date of appointment, name of clerk or deputy, monthly salary of each, and signature of county official making appointment. Arranged chronologically by dates of appointments. No index. Typed on printed forms. 10 x 4.5 x 14.5. Auditor's main office.

333. BRIDGE ESTIMATE RECORD
1916-1931. 2 vols. (1, 2).

Record of estimated cost of improvements, showing date entered, names of township and bridge or culvert, date contract awarded, estimated cost, name of contractor, date of payment, and balance due. Arranged by dates entered. Indexed alphabetically by names of townships. Handwritten on printed forms. 190 pages. 17 x 11 x 1.5. South storeroom.

334. CRIPPLED AND DEPENDENT CHILDREN
1927—. 1 file box.

Certified copy of probate judge's record of dependent and

delinquent children appearing before the court, showing date of
hearing, name, age, birthplace, sex, and race of child, names of
parents, complete family history, financial disposition of case, and
signature of juvenile judge. Arranged alphabetically by names of
children and chronologically thereunder by dates of hearings. No
index. Handwritten. 10 x 4.5 x 14.5. Auditor's main office.

335. INVOICES
1882-1885, 1932—. 1 vol.

Invoices for material, labor, and truck hire for road improvement
including receipts in connection with the county home, showing
date of invoice, itemized statement of charges, and date filed.
Arranged chronologically by dates of invoices. No index. Hand
written on printed forms. 400 pages. 19 x 12 x 6. North storeroom.

336. UNCLAIMED COSTS
1900—. 1 file box.

Record of unclaimed costs and fees paid into county treasury by
county officials showing date paid, names of payer and payee, case
number, amount, warrant number, date warrant was issued by
auditor for recovery as required by law after one year, and date
filed. Arranged chronologically by dates filed. No index. Typed on
printed forms. 10 x 4.5 x 14.5. Auditor's main office.

337. CORRESPONDENCE
1918—. 10 file boxes.

Incoming and outgoing correspondence relative to all activities of
county auditor, showing date of correspondence, name of
correspondent, and subject discussed; includes county
commissioners' correspondence, 1922—. Auditor acts as clerk to
commissioners. Arranged chronologically by dates of
correspondence. No index. Handwritten and typed. 12 x 12 x 30.
Auditor's main office.

338. TRANSFER OF SCHOOL DISTRICTS
1872—. 1 file box.
Original papers, including petitions, plats, resolutions and court transfers regarding transfer of land of various school districts from one district to another, establishing or changing special school district; petitions, showing date of petition, signatures of petitioners, reason for transfer, names of school district and township, name of township into which school district is transferred, approval of county school board, and date filed; plats showing districts to be transferred, boundary lines of new districts established, and names of real estate owners in the new district set up; resolutions, showing data resolution, name of school district, and signature of county auditor; court transfers, showing date of transfer, reason, and approval of court. Arranged chronologically by dates filed. No index. Handwritten on printed forms. 10 x 4.5 x 14.5. Auditor's main office.

339. TOWNSHIP, SCHOOL, AND VILLAGE OFFICERS
1930—. 1 file box.
Records from township clerks to county auditor certifying the names of township and village school officers, showing name and address of officer, commencement and expiration of term, political party affiliation, name of office, signature of clerk, and date filed. Arranged chronologically by dates filed. No index. Handwritten on printed forms. 10 x 4.5 x 14.5. Auditor's main office.

340. APPRAISERS [Recommendations For]
1931—. 1 file box.
Letters of recommendations from mayors of villages and other persons suggesting names of persons who might be qualified as appraisers, including letters recommending industrial and utility experts, showing date of correspondence, qualifications of person recommended, signature of correspondent, and date filed. Arranged chronologically by dates filed. No index. Handwritten and typed. 10 x 4.5 x 14.5. Auditor's main office.

341. ESTATE BANK RELEASES
1931—. 1 file box.

Certificates of release issued by probate court to bank holding money belonging to an estate, authorizing bank to pay funds in account to the order of the administrator of the estate, showing date of release, name of decedent, description of funds or Securities deposited, and to whom transfer of authority is made. Arranged chronologically by dates released. No index. Handwritten on printed forms. 10 x 4.5 x 14.5. Auditor's main office.

342. MILITIA ENROLLMENT
1864-1865. 2 vols.

Record of males between 18 and 44 years for militia enrollment, showing name of township or village, names and addresses of enrollees, exemptions (if any), reason for exemption, assessment against individual, and if paid. Arranged alphabetically by names of townships or villages and alphabetically thereunder by names of enrollees. No index. Handwritten. Average 200 pages. 12 x 8 x 1. Auditor's main office.

343. RESIDENT OHIO STOCKHOLDERS
1932—. 1 file box.

Auditor's record of stockholders of corporations and companies in each taxing district, showing name and address of stockholders, type of stock (common or preferred), number of shares held by each stockholder, and amount of dividends paid. Arranged alphabetically by names of taxing districts, and alphabetically thereunder by names of stockholders. No index. Typed on printed forms. 3 x 9 x 32. Auditor's main office.

344. RECORD OF TEACHERS' EXAMINATION
1930-1934. 1 file box.

Original reports to county auditor from the clerk of the board of examiners on teachers' examinations held, showing date of filing, place and date of examination, number of applicants, grades of each applicant, number denied certificates, total number of certificates issued by examiners, total cost of examinations, total amount of fees collected, and signatures of clerk of board of school examiners and superintendent of county schools. Arranged chronologically by dates filed. No index. Typed on printed forms. 10 x 4.5 x 14.5. Auditor's main office.

345. P[robate] J[udge's] REPORTS OF ESTATES
1929-1931. 1 file box.
Statement from probate judge to county auditor of aggregate value of property other than real, showing names of estate and administrator or executor, case number, summary of personal goods, moneys, securities, and accounts. Arranged numerically by case numbers. No index. Handwritten on printed forms. 10 x 4.5 x 14.5. Auditor's main office.

346. TERM REPORT FROM CLERK OF COURTS
1931—. 1 file box.
Certified term report from clerk of courts of grand and petit jurors to common pleas court, showing date of report, names and addresses of grand and petit jurors, date served, total number of days, amount paid for attendance, names of excused, and reasons. Arranged chronologically by dates of reports. No index. Handwritten on printed forms. 10 x 4.5 x 14.5. Auditor's main office.

347. JUSTICES' REPORTS
1924—. 1 file box.
Reports of fines imposed by justices of the peace in various townships, showing name of township, date of report, name of person fined, amount of fine, costs, date paid, in what manner case disposed of, date of county treasurer's receipt, date statement filed with county auditor, and sworn statement by each justice of the peace as to the correctness of his report. Arranged alphabetically by name of townships, and chronologically thereunder by dates of reports. No index. Handwritten on printed forms. 10 x 4.5 x 14.5. Auditor's main office.

348. LAW LIBRARY REPORTS
1936—. 1 file box.

Annual report of Medina County Law Library Association to county auditor, showing date of report, amount received from county auditor and clerk of courts, total receipts, and balance; also contains itemized list of disbursements for law books and publications, balance, and signature of secretary of association. Arranged chronologically by years. No index. Typed. 10 x 4.5 x 14.5. Auditor's main office.

349. STATE EXAMINATIONS
1918—. 2 file boxes.

Return reports from auditor of state and bureau of inspection and supervision of public offices of regular examinations of all county offices, showing date of examination, name of examiners, receipts, expenditures, and balances in itemized report of each department; also contains bank deposits, balances on hand in treasury, and local examination of township, including offices of justice of the peace and township trustees. Arranged chronologically by years. No index. Typed on printed forms. 6 x 10 x 14.5. Auditor's main office.

350. ANNUAL REPORT OF DOG LICENSE FEES
1931—. 1 file box.

Copies of reports of dog license fees to state auditor, showing date of report, amount paid out for killed and injured sheep and other domestic animals, amount paid for witness fees, dog warden, and other purposes, balance on hand at beginning of fiscal year, receipts during year, total, amount transferred to other accounts, and balance on hand. Arranged chronologically by dates of reports. No index. Handwritten on printed forms. 10 x 4.5 x 14.5. Auditor's main office.

351. [MISCELLANEOUS PAPERS]
1927—. 1 file box.

Miscellaneous papers including affidavits of persons who cannot pay fines for violation of liquor laws, 1927-1934, showing date filed, name and address of person, and date and amount of fine; assignments of credits by road construction and supply companies, showing name of contractor, name of firm, and report and date of assignment; clerk of courts reports of fees due and injunction grants unpaid, showing names and addresses of plaintiff and defendant, nature of injunction, whether temporary or permanent, and by whom issued; resolutions of metropolitan park board showing minutes of meetings; complaints on capital stock assessments, showing names of stockholder and firm, amount of stock, valuation, and complaint; copy of prosecuting attorney's expense statement, showing number of cases prosecuted, amount of fines and fees assessed, total amount of fines and fees collected, and amount allowed for aid in prosecuting state cases. Arranged chronologically by dates filed. No index. Typed on printed forms. 10 x 4.5 x 14.5. Auditor's main office.

The office of county treasurer was established by an act of the Northwest Territory in 1792 and continued by the state of Ohio.[1] Although the constitution of 1802 made no provision for the office of county treasurer, it was created by the legislative act of 1803.[2] The treasurer, appointed by the associate judges in 1803 and by the county commissioners in 1804, was required to take an oath and give bond for the faithful performance of the duties of his office, and was subject to removal by the appointing power.[3] The treasurer remained an appointed official until 1827 when the office became an elective one by popular vote in the county.[4] Although it did not specifically create the office, the constitution of 1851 stated that no person should hold the office of treasurer for more than four years in any six. This provision was repealed in 1933 by an amendment authorizing any county to adopt a charter form of government.[5] Interpreting the constitutional provision, the legislature fixed the term of office at two years in 1859.[6] The term of office continued at two years until 1936 when it was extended to four years.[7] Until 1906 the county treasurer received his remuneration from fees; since that date his salary has been determined by law according to the population of the county.[8]

The duties of the treasurer were defined by statute in the earlier period and specified in detail by the acts of 1827 and 1831 repealing previous acts. The provisions of the latter act, although subject to amendment and repeal, furnished the basis for subsequent legislation and laid the foundation for the present duties of the treasurer, which do not differ greatly from those prescribed by earlier statutes.

---

1. Pease, *op. cit.,* 68.
2. *Laws of Ohio,* I, 97.
3. *Ibid.,* I, 97; II, 154.
4. *Ibid.,* XXV, 25-32.
5. *Ohio Const. 1851,* Art. X, sec. 3 (Amendment, 1933).
6. *Laws of Ohio,* LVI, 105.
7. *Ibid.,* CXVI, pt. ii, 184.
8. *Ibid.,* XCVIII, 89.

In 1803 the treasurer was given his present duty by giving public notice of the tax duplicate. On receiving from the county auditor a duplicate of the taxes assessed upon the property of the county, the treasurer prepares and post notices in three places in each township including the place in which elections are held; and inserts the notice for six consecutive weeks in the newspaper having the greatest circulation in the county.[9] He receives money in payment of taxes levied for the county, for the state, and for other purposes, and gives the payer a receipt.[10] In the earlier years of the office the treasurer was required to give announcement of the time he would be in the respective townships of the county and in his office at the seat of justice to receive tax collections. Since 1858, the treasurer has been authorized to prescribe the time for semiannual payment of taxes or assessments levied upon real estate or upon delinquent real estate taxes or assignments.[11] Moreover, since 1908, the commissioners have been authorized to extend the time for pain taxes to not more than 30 days after the time fixed by law.[12]

After each semiannual collection of taxes, the treasurer is required to report to the auditor, showing the amount of taxes received in each taxing district in the county since the last settlement. Since 1904, the semiannual settlements have been made under the heads of liquor, cigarette, inheritance, delinquent, personal, road, and general taxes. The treasurer keeps his accounts in books which enable him to compile such reports.[13]

After the taxes are collected and immediately after each settlement with the county auditor, the county treasurer, up on the presentation of the proper warrants from the auditor, pays to the township treasurer, city or village treasurer, the treasurer of the school district, or treasurer of any "legally constituted board

---

9. *Ibid.,* I, 98; XXIX, 291; LII, 124.
10. G. C. sec. 2650; *Laws of Ohio,* XXIX, 292; LXXVI, 70; LXXXV, 327.
11. *Laws of Ohio,* LV, 62; LVI, 101.
12. *Ibid.,* XCIX, 435; CXIV, 730; CXV, pt. ii, 226.
13. G. C. sec. 2643; *Laws of Ohio,* XXIX, 296; XCVII, 458.

authorized by law to receive the funds or proceeds of any special tax levy," or other officer delegated with authority to receive such funds, all money n the treasury belonging to such boards and subdivisions.[14] In addition, after the treasurer has made each settlement with the county auditor, he is required to pay to the state treasurer, on warrant from the state auditor, "the full amount of all sums" found by the latter to belong to the state.[15]

Another function of the County Treasurer, which had its inception in the earlier years of the office, is the collection of delinquent taxes. It was and is his duty to assess a penalty on the tax duplicate for nonpayment of taxes–which penalty when collected, is paid to the treasurer's fund. If the treasurer is unable to collect the delinquent taxes, he is authorized to apply to the clerk of the court of common pleas who serves notice to show cause by taxes were not paid. The court may enter a rule against the delinquent taxpayer for the payment and costs and enforce it by attachment.[16]

During the last decade provision has been made for the installment payment of delinquent taxes without interest or penalty. In 1931 it was provided that delinquent taxes, assessments, and penalties charged on the tax duplicate against any entry of real estate might be paid in installments during five consecutive semiannual taxpaying periods, "whether such real estate had been certified as delinquent or not."[17] The Whittemore Ace, passed as an emergency measure in 1933, provided for the collection in installments, without interest or penalty, of delinquent real estate assessments. Anyone electing to pay such delinquent real property taxes and assessments in installments pursuant to this act may, at any installments period, pay the entire unpaid balance, in which event no interest shall be charged or collected on the amount so paid. In 1934 the benefits of the act were extended to include

---

14. G. C. sec. 2689; *Laws of Ohio*, LVI, 101.
15. *Laws of Ohio,* LVI, 101; CXIV, 732.
16. G. C. sec. 2660; *Laws of Ohio*, LVI, 175; XCIX, 435.
17. G. C. sec. 2672; *Laws of Ohio*, CXIV, 827.

Delinquent personal and classified taxes.[18] With slight alterations the law was reenacted in 1935 and again in 1936.[19] An act was passed providing for the settlement of taxes delinquent prior to 1936 without interest or penalty in one payment or in 10 annual installments in February 1937 and reenacted in February 1938.[20]

The county treasurer has charge of the funds collected by taxes, and also of other funds belonging to the county. Although earlier acts made provision for storage vaults in the county treasury for county deposits, the commissioners have been authorized, since 1894, to receive sealed bids for the deposits of county funds; and the banks or trust companies offering the highest rates of interest are selected as the county depositories.[21]

The treasurer is required to keep an account current with the county auditor–a practice which originated in 1831. Each day the treasurer makes a statement to the county auditor for the previous day's business, showing the amount of taxes received on auditor's drafts, the amount received from other sources, together with the amount of money deposited in the depository, the total amount paid out by check and buy cash, and the balance in the treasury.[22]

The treasurer, as well as the sheriff, prosecuting attorney, and clerk of courts, has been required since 1850, to report annually to the county commissioners.[23] Since 1874, the county auditor and county commissioners have been required to make a thorough examination of all books, vouchers, accounts, moneys, bonds, sureties, and other property in the treasury at least every six months.[24] Besides being under the supervision of the county commissioners and county auditor, the treasurer is subject to the supervision of the state auditor. In 1902 an act was passed

18. *Laws of Ohio,* CXV, 101-164; CXV, pt. ii, 230, 332.
19. *Ibid.,* CXVI, 199, 468; CXVI, pt. ii, 14-21.
20. *Ibid.,* CXVIII, 32, 832.
21. *Laws of Ohio,* XCI, 403; CII, 59; CXV, pt. ii, 215.
22. G. C. sec. 2642; *Laws of Ohio,* XCVII, 457.
23. G. C. sec. 2504.
24. G. C. sec. 2699; R. S. 1129; *Laws of Ohio,* LXXI, 137.

providing for a uniform system of accounting and auditing for all
public offices in the state, under the direction of a bureau of
inspection in the office of the state auditor, and for the annual
examination of the finances of all public offices.[25]

The treasurer is a member of the budget commission and
the county board of revision, and serves as a trustee of the sinking
fund.[26] Since the early days of the office the treasurer has been the
official custodian of the bonds furnished to the state by the county
auditor, county commissioners, and other officials. Since 1869, he
has been required to record and preserve a record of the deputies
appointed and removed by the county auditor.[27]

Like other county officials, the treasurer is required at the
expiration of his term to turn over to his successor all books,
papers, moneys, and records appertaining to his office.[28]

In Medina County there are four on the treasurer's staff
including a deputy treasurer. The treasurer's salary is $201
monthly and his official bond is fixed at $25,000.[29] Taxes may be
paid either at the courthouse or at certain banks with the
arrangements having been made by the treasurer.[30] Until the advent
of the Parrett-Whittemore bill, taxes were paid semiannually, but
since the passing of this act, the treasurer accepts monthly
payments, a practice which has resulted in a noticeable decrease in
delinquent taxes. Medina's treasurer makes use of all banks in the
county as depositories for public funds.[31]

25. G. C. sec. 2641; *Laws of Ohio,* CXIV, 728; XCV, 511-515.
26. G. C. secs. 5629-19, 2976-18, 5580.
27. G. C. sec. 2563; *Laws of Ohio,* LXVI, 35.
28. G. C. sec. 2639.
29. Pay Rolls, 1940, *see* entry 288; Record of Officials' Bonds, 1940, *see* entry 325.
30. Treasurer's Cash Book, 1940, *see* entry 379.
31. *Ibid.*

Taxes

Real Property

352. TREASURER'S TAX DUPLICATE
1822—. 962 vols. (Labeled by names of corporations or townships, dated).

Duplicates of taxes assessed on real estate, 1822—, and on personal property, 1822-1931, showing year, name of township or municipality, names of property owners and taxing district, lot or tract number, description, number of acres, total valuation of property, special taxes due, delinquencies and penalties due, date paid, and remarks. Arranged alphabetically by names of taxing districts and alphabetically thereunder by names of taxpayers. No index. Handwritten on printed forms. Average 150 pages. 16 x 11 x 1. 285 volumes, 1822-1919, South storeroom; 530 volumes, 1920-1935, North storeroom; 147 volumes, 1936—, Treasurer's office.

353. DITCH DUPLICATE
1897-1923. 4 vols. (1-4). 1924— in Treasurer's Road Duplicate, entry 354.

Duplicates of tax assessments for improvement of various ditches in the county, showing name of taxing district, amount of tax assessed, names of abutting property owners and township, location and name of ditch, lot number, acreage, taxes due, amount, and date paid. Arranged alphabetically by names of taxing districts and alphabetically thereunder by names of property owners. No index. Handwritten on printed forms. Average 179 pages. 16 x 11.5 x 1.5. North storeroom.

354. TREASURER'S ROAD DUPLICATE
1917—. 25 vols. (Dated).

Duplicates of special assessments for road improvements in the various townships, showing name of taxing district, names of owners of abutting property, range, section and lot numbers, description of tract, valuation of land and buildings, date and amount of assessment, amount of annual payment, delinquency, and total due. Also contains Ditch Duplicate, 1924—, entry 353. Arranged alphabetically by names of taxing districts and alphabetically thereunder by names of taxpayers. No index. Handwritten and typed some on credit forms. Average 500 pages. 12 x 15 x 4. Treasurer's office.

355. TREASURER'S DUPLICATE OF TAX ASSESSMENTS
1928-1932. 1 bundle.
Duplicates of road and sewer assessments, showing name and address of property owner, location and description of property, location and name of sewer and road, special assessment, amount due, date due, and date paid. Arranged by years and alphabetically thereunder by names of sewers or roads. No index. Typed. 14 x 7 x 4. South storeroom.

356. TREASURER'S RECEIPTS.
1910—. 532 vols. (Dated). Subtitled by townships.
Record of receipts for money received for real estate and personal property taxes, showing receipt stub number, date of receipt, name of taxpayer, township, lot number or number of acres, rate, valuation, assessments, special road tax, total amount due and paid, and amount of unpaid taxes. Arranged by receipt numbers. No index. Handwritten on printed forms. 459 volumes average 600 pages. 7 x 15 x 1.5; 73 volumes average 300 pages. 14 x 17.5 x 1.5; 459 volumes, 1910-1932, North storeroom; 35 volumes, 1933-1935, Treasurer's vault; 38 volumes, 1936—, Treasurer's office.

357. REAL ESTATE TAX RECEIPT [Stubs]
1932—. 3 cartons, 3 file boxes.
Receipts for taxes paid on real estate, showing receipt number, name and address of taxpayer, name and number of taxing district, township, municipality, date of receipt, and amount paid. Arranged by townships, municipalities, or taxing districts, and alphabetically

thereunder by names of taxpayers. No index. Handwritten on printed forms. Cartons, 12 x 14 x 15; file boxes 10 x 12 x 24. 3 cartons, 1932-1937, North storeroom; 3 file boxes, 1938——, Treasurer's office.

Special Assessments

358. SPECIAL ASSESSMENTS
1934——. 8 vols. (Dated).
Special assessments for public improvements, including street paving, sidewalks, and sewers, showing name of improvement, name of taxing district, and property owner, township, section, and the lot numbers, acreage, property value, amount of assessment, semiannual payments, delinquencies, and total due. Arranged alphabetically by names of taxing districts and alphabetically thereunder by names of property owners. No index. Handwritten on printed forms. Average 250 pages. 17.5 x 18.5 x 2. Treasurer's vault.

Personal Property

359. TREASURER'S GENERAL PERSONAL PROPERTY TAX DUPLICATE
1932——. 10 vols. (Dated).
General personal property tax duplicate, showing name and address of taxpayer, final assessment, total amount of tax, amount of advanced payment, tax due, unpaid tax for year, and remarks. The record of tangible personal property is taken from original personal property returns. Arranged alphabetically by names of taxpayers. No index. Typed on printed forms. Average 200 pages. 16 x 18 x 1. Treasurer's office.

360. TREASURER'S CLASSIFIED PERSONAL TAX DUPLICATE
1932—. 10 vols. (Dated).
Classified personal property tax duplicate, showing name of taxing district, assessment certificate number, name and address of taxpayer, value of unproductive investments, tax assessed, moneys and other intangibles and tax assessed, total tax assessed, amount of advance payments, balance due, and taxes unpaid. Arranged alphabetically by names of taxing districts and alphabetically thereunder by names of taxpayers. No index. Handwritten on printed forms. Average 200 pages. 16.5 x 19 x 1. Treasurer's office.

361. PERSONAL [Property Tax Receipts]
1934—. 5 file boxes. (1, 5, 6, 9, 10).
Receipts for personal property taxes, showing receipt number, date of receipt, amount of tax, by whom paid, and name of taxpayer. Arranged chronologically by dates of receipts. No index. Handwritten on printed forms. 10 x 4.5 x 14.5. Treasurer's vault.

362. RECORD OF TAX COLLECTIONS
1904—. 9 vols. 56 bdls.
Record of tax collections, including a state and public utility, special assessment, and delinquent and personal taxes, showing date of payment, name of taxpayer, receipt number, road, interest, special, and all other taxes, total, and total for district; also includes general and classified personal tax 1932—. Arranged by subjects. No index. Handwritten on printed forms. Volumes average 400 pages. 17 x 13 x 2. Bundles average 14 x 11 x 1. 9 volumes, 52 bundles, 1904-1931, North storeroom; 4 bundles, 1939, Treasurer's vault.

363. CASHIER'S MEMO[randa] SLIPS [Personal Taxes]
1935—. 1 box, 45 bdls.
Classified and general personal property tax, showing name of taxing district, listed value of property, tax rate, total tax, advance

payment, balance due, and name of county treasurer. Arranged alphabetically by names of taxing districts. No index. Handwritten on printed forms. Box, 27 x 30 x 16; bundles, 8.5 x 4 x 4.5. 1 box, 1935-1939, North storeroom; 45 bundles, 1939——, Treasurer's vault.

Delinquent

364. TREASURER'S DELINQUENT PERSONAL PROPERTY TAX RECORD
1904——. 6 vols. (1 unlabeled; 1, 1, 2, 2, 3). Title varies: Treasurer's Delinquent Personal Tax Duplicate, 1904-1931, 5 vols.

Duplicate of delinquent personal taxes, showing name of taxing district, name and address of taxpayer, property valuation, amount unpaid, penalties, total amount due, and date of payment. Since 1932, pages are subdivided, classified delinquent personal property tax and general delinquent personal property tax, each showing above information. Arranged by names of taxing districts and alphabetically thereunder by names of taxpayers. No index. Handwritten and typed, someone printed forms. 5 volumes average 200 pages. 17 x 13 x 2; 1 volume 650 pages. 15 x 12 x 5.5. 5 volumes, 1904-1931, North storeroom; 1 volume, 1932——, Treasurer's office.

365. TRIENNIAL CERTIFICATES
1932——. 2 vols.

Treasurer's triennial tax certificates for delinquent taxes on tracts of land, showing name of taxing district, date of certificate, name of property owner, township, and municipality, section and lot numbers, acreage, description, taxes and penalties due, and certification to prosecuting attorney of unpaid taxes. Arranged by names of townships, municipalities, or taxing districts, and alphabetically thereunder by names of delinquent taxpayers. No index. Handwritten on printed forms. Average 200 pages. 18 x 14 x 1. Treasurer's vault.

366. TREASURER'S RECORD OF UNDERTAKING
[Whittemore Plan]
1933—. 2 vols.

Undertaking to pay full principal amount of delinquent real property taxes and assessments less penalties in partial payments, showing name and address of taxpayer, name of taxing district, amount of delinquent assessments charged less penalties, and date and amount of payment. Arranged alphabetically by names of taxing districts and alphabetically thereunder by names of taxpayers. No index. Handwritten on printed forms. Average 400 pages. 17.5 x 16 x 3. Treasurer's vault.

Adjustments

367. [INJUNCTIONS GRANTED RELATIVE TO COUNTY ASSESSMENTS]
1934—. 1 file box.

Injunctions granted to taxpayers restraining treasurer from collecting alleged excessive assessments declared excessive after hearing in common pleas court, showing name of taxpayer, dates of hearing and filing, amount declared excessive, assessment certificate number, and term of injunction addressed to county treasurer and signed by common pleas judge. Arranged chronologically by dates filed. No index. Handwritten on printed forms. 10 x 4.5 x 14.5. Treasurer's vault.

368. ADDITIONS AND DEDUCTIONS
1934—. 1 file box (11).

Certificates of additions to and deductions from the tax duplicate, showing date of filing, name of taxing district, year, name of taxpayer, range, township, section and lot numbers, description of track, value of real and personal property, amount added or deducted, and reason. Arranged by dates filed. No index. Handwritten on printed forms. 10 x 4.5 x 14.5. Treasurer's vault.

Inheritance

369. TREASURER'S DUPLICATE OF INHERITANCE TAX CHARGE
1923—. 1 vol., 1 file drawer

Duplicate copy of inheritance tax charge for collection by treasurer, showing the state's inheritance tax number, Medina County's probate court case number on real estate papers, auditor's certification that the probate judge has fixed the amount of inheritance tax, date certified, name of decedent, name and address of executor, administrator, trustee, or legatee by whom payable, date of tax accrual, amount fixed by court, interest, total amount paid, name of township or corporation, and signature of county auditor. Arranged chronologically by dates certified. No index. Handwritten on printed forms. Volume 300 pages. 12 x 11.5 x 3.5.; file drawer, 18 x 6 x 24. 1 volume, 1823-1938, North storeroom; 1 file drawer, 1939—, Treasurer's office.

370. INHERITANCE TAX RECEIPTS
1923—. 1 box, 1 vol.

Receipts of collateral inheritance tax payments, showing consecutive receipt number, date of receipt, amount of tax, name of taxpayer, name of decedent, penalties, and amounts. 1923-1936, no systematic arrangement; 1936—, arranged chronologically by date of receipts and also arranged numerically by consecutive receipt numbers. No index. Handwritten on printed files. Box, 11 x 4 x 14; Volume 40 pages. 18 x 9.25 x .5. 1 box, 1923-1936, North storeroom; 1 volume, 1936—, Treasurer's office.

Excise

371. TREASURER'S LIQUOR TRAFFIC TAX DUPLICATE
1906-1919. 1 vol.

Liquor tax duplicate, showing year, name of licensee, location of business, name of owner of real estate, description of real estate,

amount delinquent date commencing business, amount assessed
and due at June settlement, amount to be accounted for after June
settlement, and date payment made. Arranged by years and
alphabetically thereunder by names of licensees. No index.
Handwritten on credit forms. 40 pages. 17 x 15.5 x .5. Treasurer's
vault.

372. INVENTORY AND SALES RECORD [Sales Tax Receipts]
1935—. 1 vol.

Daily inventory and sales record of vendors' tax receipts, showing
number on hand, number received and sold, and number sold at
each denomination; also record of sales, showing date of entry,
name of vendor, license number, number of each denomination
sold, total amount of sales less vendor's discount, and total
collected. Arranged by dates entered. No index. Handwritten on
printed forms. 200 pages. 17.5 x 15 x 1. Treasurer's vault.

373. LIST OF VENDORS LICENSED TO ENGAGE IN THE MAKING OF RETAIL SALES IN MEDINA COUNTY
1935—. 4 file boxes.

Record of licenses issued to vendors, showing name and address
of licensee, date license issued, license number, code number,
amount of fee, kind and term of license, business address, and
occupation. Arranged alphabetically by names of licenses. No
index. Typed. 4 x 5.5 x 12.5. Treasurer's office.

374. COSMETIC TAX RECEIPTS
1934-1935. 1 bundle.

Record and duplicate receipts of cosmetic taxes; record, showing
name and address of licensee, kind of business, date of license, and
license fee; name and address of licensee, date of receipt, amount
of fee. Arranged by dates of receipts. No index. Handwritten on
printed forms. 12.5x 4.5 x 11. Treasurer's vault.

375. BREWERS' WORT OR MALT DEALERS' LICENSE FEE [Receipt Stubs]
1933—. 2 vols.

Receipt stubs for brewers' wort or malt dealers' licenses, showing receipt number, amount of fee, date of receipt, and name and address of brewer or dealer. Arranged by dates of receipts and also arranged numerically by receipt numbers. No index. Handwritten on printed forms. Average 200 pages. 14 x 4.5 x 1. 1 volume, 1933-1937, North storeroom; 1 volume, 1938—, Treasurer's office.

376. RECEIPT [Stubs] FOR CIGARETTE DEALERS' LICENSE TAX
1930—. 1 box, 1 vol.

Receipt stubs for cigarette dealers' license tax, showing receipt number, date of receipt, amount of tax, and name and address of dealer. Arranged by dates of receipts. No index. Handwritten on printed forms. 200 pages. 14 x 4.5 x 1. Box, 12 x 12 x 10. 1 box, 1930-1937, North storeroom, 1 volume, 1938—, Treasurer's office.

Fiscal Accounts

General Accounts

377. TREASURER'S ACCOUNTS
1873-1902. 4 vols. Discontinued.

Record of annual examination of treasurer's accounts by county auditor, showing date of entry, itemized accounted treasurer from all sources, itemized account of payments on auditor's order crediting treasure, and balance. Arranged chronologically by dates entered. No index. Handwritten on credit forms. Average 300 pages. 14 x 9 x 2.25. North storeroom.

378. RECEIPTS AND EXPENDITURES
1900-1909. 1 vol. (2).

Record of receipts, including pay-in orders, amounts from depositories, general taxes, cigarette tax, and inheritance tax funds, showing date of entry, total receipts, balance in treasury, total disbursements, general warrants, court warrants, deposits, drafts, balance and depository, and total balance in treasury and depository; also includes expenditures, showing debit to each fund, date of entry, for what amount, and monthly balance to each fund, including road, bonds, indigent soldiers, blind relief, mother's pension, in general funds. Arranged by names of funds and thereunder by dates entered. No index. Handwritten on printed forms. 360 pages. 17 x 12 x 2.25. North storeroom.

379. TREASURER'S CASH BOOK
1898——. 3 vols. (1, 2, 1). Title varies: Treasurer's Daily
Cash Balance, 1898-1907, 2 vols.

Treasurer's daily record of moneys, including disbursements, general and court warrants, showing date of entry, balance and treasury and it depositories from previous day, total daily receipts, pay-in orders, general tax, various Distributors taxes, amounts check from depositories, amount deposited, and totals. Arranged by dates entered. No index. Typed on printed forms. Average 1,000 pages. 14 x 9 x 7. 2 volumes, 1898-1907, North storeroom; 1 volume, 1907——, Treasurer's vault.

380. TREASURER'S LEDGER
1904——. 5 vols. 1 bundle. (1 unlabeled; 1-4).

Treasurer's record of moneys in county treasury and all county depositories, showing date and amount deposited, name of bank, name and amount of account credited with deposits; also includes records of funds withdrawn, showing date and amount withdrawn, and names of bank and fund. Arranged by dates entered. No index. Handwritten on printed forms. Volumes average 475 pages. 13 x 18 x 3; bundles, 13 x 18 x 6. 4 volumes, 1904-1927, North storeroom; 1 volume, 1 bundle, 1928——, Treasurer's office.

Special Accounts

381. TREASURER'S SETTLEMENT OF SCHOOL FUNDS – ACCOUNTS
1839-1922. 8 vols.

Record of school accounts, showing date of entry, amount of money received from county treasurer from various funds with exception of deduction for election expenses, apportionment of township tax for Medina County including tuition, salary, expense, school fund, sale of bonds, miscellaneous receipts, and a circus license from June 20 to July 3, 1839, signature of treasurer, auditor's warrant number, and final amount of settlement. 1839-1916, arranged by dates entered; 1916-1922, arranged numerically by warrant numbers. No index. Handwritten on printed forms. Average 300 pages. 16 x 12 x 2.5. North storeroom.

Warrants and Orders

382. TREASURER'S JOURNAL OF WARRANTS REDEEMED AND RECEIPTS INTO TREASURY
1904—. 18 vols. (1-9); 1-9). Title varies: Treasurer's Journal of Warrants Redeemed and Payments into Treasury, 1928-1940, 8 vols.

Journal of warrants into treasury is divided into two parts: first part, treasurer's journal of warrants redeemed by county treasury, showing date of payment, name of payee, purpose for which drawn, warrant number, amount, and the account debited to cover payment; second part, treasurer's journal of receipts into county treasury, showing date of receipt, receipt number, amount and distribution to accounts for credit. Arranged dates entered and thereunder by receipt or auditors warrant numbers. No index. Handwritten on printed forms. Average 600 pages. (500 pages for warrants, 100 pages for receipts). 18 x 16 x 4.5. 15 volumes, 1904-1937, North storeroom; 3 volumes, 1937—, Treasurer's office.

383. TREASURER'S COURT WARRANTS
1904—. 1 vol.

Record of court warrants, showing date of entry, number and amount of warrant, name of payee, purpose, including paying petit and grand jurors, grand jury witnesses, criminal case witnesses, lunacy, coroner's court witnesses, and minor court witness fees. Arranged by dates entered and thereunder by warrant numbers. No index. Handwritten on printed forms. 18 x 13 x 2.5. 320 pages. Treasurer's office.

384. ORDERS REDEEMED
1894-1904. 2 vols.

Record of warrants on treasury as presented for payment, showing date of issue, warrant number, date paid, name of payee, purpose for which drawn, credit column, amount, and date of distribution; also contains quarterly recapitulation signed by both treasurer and auditor. Arranged by dates issued. No index. Handwritten on printed forms. Average 300 pages. 18 x 16 x 2. North storeroom.

385. PAY-IN'S
1934—. 1 file box (12).

Original payments into treasury, showing date of payment, name of payee, purpose, pay-in order number, debit to treasurer, and credit to what fund. Arranged by dates of payments. No index. Hand written on printed forms. 10 x 4.5 x 14.5. Treasurer's vault.

386. PURCHASE ORDERS
1934—. 1 file box (7).

Treasurer's purchase orders from county commissioners, showing date and order number, description of article, quality, quantity, and total amount. Arranged by dates ordered. No index. Handwritten on printed forms. 10 x 4.5 x 14.5. Treasurer's vault.

Bonds

387. RECORD OF OFFICIALS' BONDS
1884—. 3 vols. (1-3).
Record of bonds filed by elected county officials, showing date of bond, name of official, office held, amount of bond, date filed, names of sureties, and oath of office sworn before probate judge. Bonds are approved by three county commissioners: also contains Treasurer's Inspection Certificates, 1885-1905, showing condition of all accounts, name of fund or account, name of depository, amount due, amount paid out, and balance of each account or fund. Arranged by names of officials. Indexed by names of offices. Handwritten on printed forms. Average 370 pages. 19 x 12 x 2.5. 2 volumes, 1884-1912, North storeroom; 1 volume, 1913—, Treasurer's office.

388. TOWNSHIP CLERK'S AND TREASURER'S OFFICIAL BOND RECORD
1923—. 1 vol. 1 file box.
Original bond and copies of bonds of township clerks and township treasurer has filed with county treasurer, showing date filed, name of elected township clerk or treasurer, names and signatures of sureties, amount of bond, term of office, signatures of township trustees, oath of office, and date of election. Arranged by dates filed. No index. Handwritten on printed forms. Volume 300 pages. 18 x 12 x3; file box, 10 x 4.5 x 14.5. Treasurer's office.

389. TREASURER'S RECORD OF COUNTY BONDS
1898—. 2 vols. (1, 2).
Treasurer's record of sales of county bonds, showing number and amount of bond, date of sale, when and where payable, name and address of purchaser, by whom payable, and rate of interest. Arranged by dates of sales and thereunder by bond numbers. Indexed alphabetically by names of purchasers. Handwritten on printed forms. Average 200 pages. 16 x 11 x 1.5. Treasurer's vault.

Miscellaneous

390. INSPECTION RECORD
1902—. 2vols. (1, 2).
Copies of state examinations filed with the county auditor, showing date of examination, balance to credit of each fund, total receipts into treasury of each fund account, total disbursements of each fund, grand total disbursements, total overpayments, total balance, auditor's attest report, names of examiners, amount of money in county depositories, and date filed. Arranged by dates filed. No index. Handwritten. Average 79 pages. 18 x 10.5 x 1. North storeroom.

391. SEMIANNUAL STATEMENT OF TREASURER
1894-1925. 2 vols.
Copy of semiannual statement of treasurer to county commissioners, showing date of statement, receipts into various funds, amount transferred from one fund to another, balance on hand at beginning of period, amount of orders redeemed, amount of treasurer's fees, amount paid to state treasurer, total disbursements, amount of overdrafts, and balance of each fund. Arranged by dates of statements. No index. Handwritten and typed, some are printed forms. Average 250 pages. 15 x 17 x 3. Treasurer's office.

392. CANCELED CHECKS
1934—. 1 file box (4).
Canceled checks, showing date of check, name of payee and payer, amount drawn, date paid, endorsement of payee, and date filed. Arranged chronologically by dates filed. No index. Handwritten on printed forms. 10 x 4.5 x 14.5. Treasurer's vault.

The budget commission functions under an act of 1911, which authorized the establishment of such an agency in each county, to be composed of the county auditor, mayor of the largest municipality, and the prosecuting attorney.[1] In 1915, the state legislature passed another law by which the state treasurer replaced the mayor, and it is under this law that the Medina commission operates.[2] It was not until after the World War, when county expenditures steadily increased, that the importance of improved methods of finance were forcibly brought to the attention of the legislature. This need was met in 1923 by enlarging the powers and minutely prescribing the duties of the budget commission. As in 1915, the county auditor, county treasurer, and county prosecuting attorney were made ex-official members of the commission.[3] Under the present law, past in 1927, the commission, consisting as before of the county auditor, county treasurer, and county prosecuting attorney, receives and examines the annual budget of the county, municipal, township, and school authorities, with an estimate of the amount to be raised for state purposes in each subdivision.[4] If the total amount exceeds the sum authorized to be raised, the commission adjusts the amount to be raised and may change and raise the estimates. The commission may reduce all items in the budget, but is prohibited from increasing the total of any budget or any item.

The adjusted budget is certified to the taxing authority in each subdivision. If the work of the commission is satisfactory, each taxing authority by ordinance or resolution of authorizes the necessary tax levies and certifies them to the county auditor. On the other hand, the taxing authority in any subdivision may appeal, through its fiscal officer, from the decision of the budget commission to the State Tax Commission of Ohio, which is

---

1. *Laws of Ohio,* CII, 271.
2. *Ibid.,* CVI, 180.
3. *Ibid.,* CX, 469. Under the provisions of this act elective commissioners might be substituted for the ex-officio members, at the option of the electors of the county.
4. *Ibid.,* CXII, 399.

empowered to adjust the estimates of revenues and balance in fixing the tax rates.[5]

The county auditor, as secretary to the commission, is required to keep a full and accurate record of the proceedings of the commission.

---

5. G. C. secs. 5625-23, 5625-28.

393. RECORD
1927—. 2 vols.

Record of minutes of meetings of budget commission, showing date of meeting total valuation of real and personal property for each taxing district, commission's budget for each fund for each district, tax rate, and all other business pertaining to the commission. Arranged chronologically by dates of meetings. No index. Handwritten. Average 370 pages. 14 x 9 x 2. Auditor's main office.

The county board of revision, the object of which was to correct some of the defects and inequalities of tax assessments, was established by the legislature in 1923. The first board of revision, or equalization as it was sometimes called, was composed of the county commissioners, county auditor, and the assessor. The board was authorized to meet at the seat of justice on the first Monday in June annually "to hear and determine the complaint of any owner of property listed and valued by the assessor . . . and shall correct any list or valuation made by the assessor, either by adding to or deducting from his valuation."[1] The act of 1831, repealing the act of 1825, left the duties and personnel of the board unchanged.[2]

In 1859, the legislature made provision for two county boards of equalization. One board, composed to the county auditor and the county commissioners, was directed to meet annually for the purpose of equalizing real and personal property, and moneys and credits in the county. The other board, composed of the county auditor, county surveyor, and the county commissioners, was authorized to meet sexennially for the same purposes.[3]

The act of 1863, amending the act of 1859, left the personnel and duties of the annual county board unchanged. The second county board, although continuing without alteration in composition or duties, was directed to meet decennially, rather than sexennially.[4] The legislative act of 1868, amending the act of 1863, left the membership of the annual and special boards, as well as their duties, practically unchanged.[5]

The annual and special Boards of Equalization work abolished, when, in 1913, the State Tax Commission of Ohio was given the task of supervising the assessment of real and personal property in the state.[6]

---

1. *Laws of Ohio,* XXIII, 64.
2. *Ibid.,* XXIX, 278.
3. *Ibid.,* LVI, 193-194.
4. *Ibid.,* LX, 57, 59.
5. *Ibid.,* LXV, 168-170.
6. *See* page [None given].

Under this arrangement each county constituted a district. In each district containing less than 60,000 inhabitants, by which stipulation Medina County was included, there was to be appointed by the governor one state tax commissioner. In all other districts there were appointed, in the same manner, two deputy tax commissioners. In each district, there was appointed a district board of complaints. This board, appointed by the state tax commission with the consent of the governor, took over the duties and powers formally vested in the boards of equalization. The county auditor, made secretary to the board of complaints, was required to be present at each meeting in person or by deputy, and keep an accurate record of their proceedings in a book for that purpose.[7] Moreover, the board was directed to take full minutes of all evidence given before it and might have such evidence taken in shorthand and extended into typewritten form. The auditor was required to preserve in his office separate records of all minutes and documentary evidence offered in each complaint.[8]

This arrangement, after being in operation for two years, was abrogated by legislature in 1915. In that year the county auditor, under the supervision of the Tax Commission of Ohio, became the chief assessing officer in the county. The county treasurer, county prosecuting attorney, probate judge, and president of the county commissioners were to serve as a board for the purpose of appointing three members to constitute a board of revision. Again the county auditor was made secretary of the board and was directed to keep a record of their proceedings and to preserve in his office a separate record of all minutes and documentary evidence offered in each complaint.[9]

Under the present system, inaugurated in 1917, the county treasurer, auditor, and president of the county commissioners constitute a board of revision.

---

7. *Laws of Ohio,* CIII, 791.
8. *Ibid.,* CIII, 794.
9. *Laws of Ohio,* CVI, 254-258.

This board organizes annually on the second Monday in June by electing a chairman for the ensuing year. The county auditor serves as secretary to the board.[10] The county board of revision may, with the consent and approval of the tax commission of Ohio, employ experts, clerks, and other employees.[11]

The duties of the board, not differing in detail from those prescribed in 1825, include the hearing of all complaints relating to valuation or assessments of the real and personal property as it appears upon the tax duplicate of the "then current year." The board is authorized to investigate all complaints and may increase or decrease any valuation or correct any assessment complaint of, or may order a reassessment of the original assessing official.[12] No valuation is increased without giving notice to the person in whose name the property affected is listed.[13] The board of revision, in all respects, is governor by the law relating to the valuation of real property and makes no change of any valuation "except in accordance with such law."[14]

On the second Monday in June, annually, the county auditor lays before the board of revision the statements and returns of assessments of any personal property for the current year, and the board proceeds to review the returns. On the first Monday in July, annually, the auditor lays before the board the returns of assessments of any real property for the current year. The board of revision reviews the assessments and certifies its action to the county auditor, who corrects the tax list and duplicate according to the additions deductions ordered by the board. The auditor is prohibited by statute from making up his tax list and duplicate until the board has completed its work and has returned to him all the returns laid before it with the revisions.[15]

---

10. G. C. sec. 5580.
11. G. C. sec. 5587.
12. G. C. sec. 5597.
13. G. C. sec. 5599.
14. G. C. sec. 5596.
15. G. C. sec. 5605.

But in the event the tax duplicate has been delivered to the county treasurer, the auditor is required to certify such corrections to him and enter such corrections in the tax duplicate.[16]

In its investigations the board may examine, under oath, persons as to their or others' real property. In the event witnesses fail to appear or refuse to testify, the board by its chairman is authorized to make a complaint in writing to the probate judge, who, by statute, is directed to institute proceedings against them.[17] The decisions of the board are subject to appeal to the Tax Commission of Ohio, within 30 days after a decision is served.[18]

The secretary of the board is required to keep "an active record of the proceedings of the board in a book to be kept for that purpose."[19] The county auditor, as in 1913, is required to preserve in his office separate records of all minutes and documentary evidence offered in each complaint.[20] The records of the board are open to the inspection of the pubic.[21]

Medina County's board of revision was organized in 1917. There have been no appeals from the state commission since the appraisement of 1937.[22] In 1940, the board investigated 15 complaints.[23]

---

16. G. C. sec. 5602.
17. G. C. sec. 5596.
18. G. C. sec. 5610
19. G. C. sec. 5592.
20. G. C. sec. 5603.
21. G. C. sec. 5591.
22. Board of Revision [Minutes], 1937-1941, *see* entry 394.
23. *Ibid.*

394. BOARD OF REVISION[Minutes]
1908—. 3 vols. (1-3).
Record of minutes of meetings of board of revision with record of complaints filed on property values for taxation by owners, showing date of meeting, names of complainant and taxing district, nature of complaint, and revision of assessments recommended. Arranged chronologically by dates of meetings. No index. Handwritten. Average. 315 pages. 18 x 13 x 2. 2 volumes, 1908–1925, North storeroom; 1 volume, 1936—, Auditor's main office.

Additions and Deductions

395. COMPLAINTS, ADDITIONS, AND DEDUCTIONS
1931—. 2 file boxes.
Original complaints as to assessments of real property, showing name of complainant, names of township and taxing district, description of property and buildings, assessed value, amount believed to be in excess, and amount of addition or deduction allowed. Arranged alphabetically by names of townships and alphabetically thereunder by names of complainants. No index. Handwritten on printed forms. 10 x 4.5 x 14.5. Auditor's main office.

The board of trustees of the sinking fund, composed of the prosecuting attorney, auditor, and treasurer, was organized in 1919, in Medina County and in each county owing a bonded debt. The county prosecuting attorney serves as president of the board and the auditor as secretary. It is the duty of the trustees to provide for the payment of all bonds issued by the county and the interest maturing thereon.[1]

From 1919 all bonds issued by the county were required to be recorded in the office of the trustees of the sinking fund, and to bear a stamp containing the words "Recorded in the office of the sinking fund trustees" and be signed by the secretary before they became valid in the hands of any purchaser. In 1921 the act was amended to allow such recording and authenticating to be performed by the county treasurer and in 1935 such provisions were abrogated by the legislature.[2]

On or before the first Monday in May of each year, the trustees certify to the county commissioners the rate of tax necessary to provide a sinking fund for the payment at maturity of bonds heretofore issued by the county and for the payment of interest on the bonded indebtedness. The amount certified by the trustees is set forth without diminution in the annual budget of the commissioners.[3] Then, after each semiannual settlement of taxes and assessments, the county auditor reports to the trustees the amount of money in the treasury of the county charged to the credit of the sinking fund. Money is drawn from the county treasury for investment or disbursements by the insurance of a voucher signed by all the members of the board and directed to issuance of a voucher signed by all the members of the board and directed to the county auditor.

---

1. G. C. secs. 2976
2. G. C. secs. 2976-18, 2976-19.
3. *Laws of Ohio,* CIX, 16; CXVI, 442.

The trustees are directed, by statute, to invest all moneys subject to their control in United States bonds, Ohio bonds, or bonds of a municipal corporation, school district, township, or county in the state.

The board members are required to keep a "full and complete record of their transactions, a complete record of the funded debt of the county specifying the dates, purposes, amounts, numbers, maturities, and rates and maturities of interest and installments thereof, and where payable, and an account exhibiting the amount held in the sinking fund for the payment thereof."[4]

The meetings of the trustees are open to the public. All questions relating to the purchase or sale of securities or the payment of bonds or interest are decided by a yea and nay vote, which is recorded in their journal.

---

4. G. C. sec. 2976-26.

396.   JOURNAL, SINKING FUND TRUSTEES, MEDINA COUNTY

1919—. 1 vol. (1).

Proceedings of board of trustees of the county sinking fund, showing date of meeting, names of members present, resolutions approved, bond issues, and interest amounts. Arranged by dates of meetings. Indexed alphabetically by subjects. Typed on printed forms. 288 pages. 15 x 11 x 2. Auditor's main office.

The responsibility for supervising and conducting elections in the county is delegated to state deputy supervisors of elections, the county board of elections. This board, created by the legislature in 1891 and consisting of four qualified voters in the county, is appointed for a four-year term by the secretary of state, who, by virtue of his office, is the chief election official of the state.[1] On the first day of March in the even-numbered years, the secretary of state now appoints two board members; one of whom is from the political party which cast the highest number of votes in the state for the office of governor at the last preceding state election, and the other from the political party which cast the next highest vote at such election.[2] The board members may be removed by the secretary of state for the neglect of duty, malfeasance, misfeasance in office: for willful violation of the election laws; or for other good and sufficient causes.[3] The compensation of the members is determined on the basis of population of the county and is paid by the county.[4] Similarly the expenses of the county board are paid from the county treasury, "in pursuance of appropriations by the county commissioners," in the same manner as other expenses are paid.[5]

The persons so appointed by the secretary, meeting five days after their appointment, select one of their members as a chairman and a resident elector of the county who is not a member of the board as clerk.[6]

---

1. *Laws of Ohio,* LXXXVIII, 449.
2. G. C. sec. 4785-8. For the method of appointment when the term of each of the four members of the board expires on the same date see G. C. sec. 4785-8a.
3. G. C. sec. 4785-11.
4. G. C. sec. 4785-18.
5. G. C. sec. 4785-20.
6. G. C. sec. 4785-10.

The board is vested with the authority to establish, define, and provide election precincts; fix places of registration; provide for the purchase, preservation, and maintenance of voting booths; ballot boxes, books, maps, flags, blanks, cards of instruction, and other equipment used in registration and to issue rules, regulations, and instructions consistent with the law or contrary to the rules and regulations as established by the chief election official.[7]

Besides providing places of voting and equipment, the board is authorized to appoint clerks and other officers of elections. On or before the first day of September before each November election the board by majority vote is authorized, after careful examination and investigation as to the qualifications, to appoint for each precinct six "competent persons, four as judges and two as clerks, who shall constitute the election officers of such precinct." Not more than two of the judges and one of the clerks, states the law, "shall be members of the same political party." Precinct election officers, appointed for a one-year term, may be removed by the board for neglected duty, malfeasance, or misconduct in office.[8]

The county board of elections is authorized to receive and examine nominating petitions and to certify to their sufficiency and validity. They receive the election returns, canvas the returns, then make abstracts therefrom and transmit them to the property authorities. They issue certificates of elections on forms prescribed by the secretary of state and report annually to the same official, on forms prescribed by him, the number of voters registered, the elections held, votes cast, appropriations received, expenditures made, and such other information as the secretary of state may require. Moreover, the board prepares and submits to the proper authorities a budget estimating the cost of elections for the ensuing year.[9]

---

8. G. C. sec. 4785-25.
9. G. C. sec. 4785-13.

Finally the board is empowered to investigate irregularities, nonperformance of duty, or violation of election laws by election officials. For the purpose of conducting investigations they may administer oaths, issue subpoenas, summon witnesses, and compel the presentation of books, papers, and records in connection with any investigation and report the facts to the prosecuting attorney.[10]

The secretary of state, in 1930, ruled that the members of the various boards of elections were to be considered as state officers. This ruling had reference to appointments made under section 4785-8a of the General Code.[11]

In Medina County the board supervises elections in 47 precincts in which at last registration there were 17,000 voters.[12] A clerk and a part-time assistant clerk are employed by the board. The board members receive $33 monthly, but the total appropriations for the board vary from year to year with the number and importance of the elections to be held. In the last few years the sums spent have ranged from $8742 in 1940 to $4934 in 1941. The appropriation for 1942 was $6434.[13]

10. G. C. sec. 4785-13.
11. *See* George C. Trautwein, ed., *Supplement to Page's Annotated General Code 1926-1935* (Cincinnati, 1935). Note on p. 688.
12. Poll Books and Tally Sheet, 1940, *see* entry 395 (?).
13. Appropriation Ledger, 1942, *see* entry 277.

Minutes

397. MINUTE BOOKS
1901—. 5 vols.
Minutes of monthly meetings of the Medina County board of elections showing number of members present, date of meeting, record of all businesses and financial transactions, resolutions adopted, and result of vote. Arranged chronologically by dates of meetings. No index. Handwritten and typed. Average 400 pages. 14 x 9 x 2. Board of elections office.

Elections

398. POLL BOOKS AND TALLY SHEETS
1936—. 370 vols. (Dated).

Record of registered voters in each ward and precinct, showing name and full address of voter, certificate of qualifications. Oaths of clerks and judge, names of absent or disabled voters, name of township, and columns for board of education or bond issues. Poll books, in the front of volume, showing name and address of elector and date of election; tally sheets, in the back of volume, showing names of candidates and office and total number of votes cast. Poll books, no systematic arrangement; tally sheets, arranged by names of offices and issues. No index. Handwritten on printed forms. Average 22 pages. 17.5 x 10.5 x .25. Board of elections office.

399. CERTIFIED ABSTRACT OF VOTES.
1928—. 2 vols. (1, 2). Title varies: Abstract book, 1936—. 1 vol.

Record of results of local elections, showing date of election, names of candidates for national, state, county, and local office, name of issue, number of votes cast for each, and name of township, municipality, or precinct with certification of board of elections. Copies of certified abstract sent to secretary of state. Arranged by dates of elections. No index. Handwritten on printed forms. Average 20 pages. 18 x 16.5 x .5. Board of elections office.

400. CERTIFIED ABSTRACT OF VOTES
1928—. 1 file box.

Summary of votes cast in each township, municipality, or precinct in Medina County, showing date of election, votes cast for national, state, county, township, and municipal candidates, total votes cast for each issue, certification by the board of elections, and signatures of board members. Arranged alphabetically by names of townships and alphabetically thereunder by names of municipalities. No index. Handwritten on printed forms. 24 x 3.25 x 24. Board of elections office.

401. ABSTRACTS OF ELECTIONS
1818-1887. 1 vol.
Record transcribed in 1887 from original election returns, showing name of township, record number, date of election, names of state, national, and county candidates, total number of votes cast for each, official summaries, and signature of clerk of board of elections making the transcription. The original election returns from which this record is transcribed in two file boxes in south storeroom. Arranged chronologically by dates of election. No index. Handwritten on printed forms. 160 pages. 22 x 17 x 2. Engineer's storeroom.

402. ELECTION RETURNS
1818-1887. 2 file boxes.
Original election returns for general elections in Medina County for national, state, and local elections, showing name of candidate, number of votes cast for each in each township, and signature of clerks and counting officials. No systematic arrangement. No index. Handwritten. 12 x 12 x 14. Engineer's storeroom.

Miscellaneous

403. POLL LIST
1941—. 47 vols. (Dated) Initiated in 1941.
Poll list of Medina County, showing signature, name, and address of each voter, ward number, and precinct letter. Arranged alphabetically by names of voters. No index. Handwritten on printed forms. Average 50 pages. 15 x 10 x .5. Board of elections office.

404. SUMMARY STATEMENT AND REPORT OF ACCOUNTING FOR BALLOTS
1936—. 18 rolls. (Labeled by general or primary election; dated).

Summary statement and report of ballots cast in each voting district, showing names of candidates for national, state, county, township, city, or village officer, precinct letter, ward number, questions and issues before voters, total number of votes cast for each candidate and issues, and certification of votes by clerk and county officials of each voting district. Arranged numerically by ward numbers and alphabetically thereunder by precinct letters. No index. Handwritten on printed forms. Approximately 11 sheets, 19 x 22 in roll, 19 x 4. 8 rolls, 1938-1940, North storeroom; 2 rolls, 1941—, Board of elections office.

405. [RECORD OF APPOINTMENT AND PAY ROLL OF JUDGES AND CLERKS, MEDINA COUNTY, OHIO
1936—. 2 vols.

Record of appointment and pay roll of judges and clerks of elections, showing names of township, municipality, and election appointments, names and addresses of clerks or judges, service, date of election, mileage, and total amount due. Arranged by dates of elections. No index. Handwritten on printed forms. Average 200 pages. 17 x 12 x 1. Board of elections office.

406. MISCELLANEOUS RECORDS
1936—. 5 file boxes.

Miscellaneous correspondence referring to election supplies, printing of ballots, advertising, oaths of election officials, and acceptance of appointments, showing date of correspondence, to whom, from whom, and subject discussed. Arranged alphabetically by subjects. No index. Handwritten and typed some on printed forms. 9 x 30 x 38. Board of elections office.

The county board of education, a modern administrative and supervisory agency developed during the last two decades, supplanted the smaller educational units, which, established during the early period of Ohio history, became inefficient and unable to meet the modern requirements as demanded by rural communities.

During the earlier period of Ohio history, educational administration, because of the newness of the state, the sparseness of the population, and the undeveloped means of transportation was, by necessity, local in character. For fourteen years after the accession of Ohio to statehood, though the constitution stated that means of education should be encouraged by the general assembly, no legislation was enacted for public schools.[1] It was not until 1817 that the legislature authorized six or more people to form associations to build school houses and to be incorporated for educational purposes.[2]

The first permanent law for the organization of schools in Ohio was passed in 1821. Under the provision of this act, the electors of the township were authorized to vote on the proposition of dividing the townships into school districts. If the proposal carried, there were to be elected three school commissioners, who, in turn, were authorized to select a clerk and a collector who should act as a treasurer. They were instructed also, to levy taxes for the support of schools and to hire teachers.[3]

As education began to advance in the early years of the nineteenth century, some kind of state control was needed. Accordingly, in 1837, the office of the state superintendent of schools was established.[4] A year later an act was passed making the county auditor also the county superintendent of schools; and in each township the clerk became superintendent of the smaller unit. The county superintendent was made responsible to the state superintendent in all educational affairs. In the same year each

---

1. *Ohio Const. 1802,* Art, VIII, secs. 3, 25, 27.
2. *Laws of Ohio,* XV, 107.
3. *Ibid.,* XIX, 52.
4. *Ibid.,* XXXV, 82.

incorporated city, town, or borough not regulated by a charter was made a separate school district. The voters in each division were authorized to elect three directors.[5] The effectiveness of this organization, however, was destroyed in 1840, when the legislature abolished the office of state superintendent and the secretary of state took over his functions of tabulating and transmitting school statistics.[6] Seven years later, 25 counties, exclusive of Medina, were allowed to have county superintendents,[7] and in 1848 the provisions of the previous act were extended to Medina and all other counties in the state.[8]

Although marked changes were made in the curricula of the schools, the history of education in Ohio from 1850 to the early part of the 20th century was largely one of the gradual transference of power from districts to townships, and from townships to county in the interest of a better system of education. It was not, however, until within the last three decades that the county became a unit for educational administration.[9]

Although the county superintendent was known as early as 1838, the first permanent law for the establishment of a county board of education was enacted in 1914. Under this act the school districts were classified, and provision was made for a county school district, exclusive of the territory embraced in any city or village having a population of 3000 or more desiring exemption. The county district was to be under the supervision of five board members elected by the presidents of the village and rural school boards. The members were to hold office for one, two, three, four, and five years respectively, and each year thereafter one member was to be selected to serve for a five-year term.[10]

_____

5. *Ibid.*, XXXVI, 21.
6. *Ibid.*, XXXVIII, 130.
7. *Ibid.*, XLV, 32.
8. *Ibid.*, XLVI, 86.
9. *Ibid.*, LXX, 195, 242; XCVII, 354.
10. *Ibid.*, CIV, 133.

The county board of education was authorized to change school district lines; provide transportation for children living more than two miles from a schoolhouse; appoint a county superintendent; and certify annually to the county auditor the number of teachers and superintendents employed, their salaries, and the amount apportioned to each school district for the payment of the salaries of the county and district superintendents. The county superintendent, acting as secretary of the board, was required to keep in a book provided for that purpose a full record of the proceedings of the board properly indexed. Each motion, together with the name of the person making it and the vote thereon, was to be entered in the record.[11]

The county was divided into administrative divisions containing one or more villages or rural school districts. Each district was to be under the supervision of a district superintendent, who was required to visit the schools in his charge, direct and assist teachers in the performance of their duties, and classify and control promotion of pupils. He was required also to report annually to the county superintendent on matters under his charge, and to assemble teachers for the purpose of conferring on curricular matters, discipline, and school management.[12]

Significant changes were made by the act of 1921, under which the board members became elective by popular vote. They were authorized to appoint one or more assistant county superintendents for a term of three years. The board was authorized also to publish, with the advice and consent of the county superintendent, a minimum course of study to serve as a guide to the local board members. The same act abolished the office of district superintendent.[13]

---

11. *Ibid.,* CIV, 133; CVIII, pt. i, 704.
12. *Ibid.,* CIV, 133-145.
13. G. C. secs. 4728-1, 4729; *Laws of Ohio,* CIX, 242.

The county organization has placed the rural schools on a plane of equality with the city schools. The consolidation of the smaller units has eliminated the small, ill-equipped schools, and provides under one roof facilities and instruction suited to the needs of the rural children under the supervision of educational specialists.

Medina County's board was organized in 1914 after the passage of the authorizing legislation. Its centralized direction of educational activities has consolidated all one-room grade schools and most of the old elementary schools into 18 modern grade schools, 13 high schools, and one junior high school. These are administered in 18 districts by a personnel of one county superintendent, four assistant superintendents, 14 principals, and 183 teachers. The annual salaries of the superintendents range from $1500 to $4200, while the principals and teachers receive annual aggregate salaries of $32, 516 and $185,996, respectively.[14] About 4200 pupils attend the schools, and 3269 of them receive free transportation, each of the 18 districts financing its own bus service.

The tax rate for county schools in recent years has ranged from 5.5 to 13.6 mills.[15] The city of Wadsworth and the village of Medina are the only communities having separate school systems, all the others being under the jurisdiction of the county board.

Unless otherwise specified all records are located in the superintendent's office, in Old Eagles Building corner of West Friendship and North Elmwood Streets, Medina, Ohio.

---

14. Annual Statistical Report, 1941, see entry 410.
15. Ibid.

Minutes

407. RECORD OF PROCEEDINGS
1914——. 1 vol. (1). 1882-1914 in School Examiners' Record, entry 411.

Record of minutes of meetings, regular and special, of county board of education, showing date of meeting, order of business, name of person making each motion, and copies of all resolutions passed; also itemized list of bills and claims allowed, showing date of bill, name of creditor, supplies rendered, amount of bill, and payment voucher number. Arranged chronologically by dates of meetings. No index. Typed. 300 pages. 16 x 12 x 2.25.

Pupils

408. [ANNUAL REPORT-SCHOOL ATTENDANCE DEPARTMENT]
1924——. 1 file box.

Copies of annual reports to state department of education, from school attendance department of Medina County, showing date of filing, name of school district, and year; summary of attendance, showing total number of pupils in county, number absent because of illness, absent because of illness in the family, and quarantine. Arranged chronologically by dates filed. No index. Handwritten on printed forms. 10 x 4.5 x 13.5.

409. PUPILS PERMANENT RECORD
1926——. 6 file boxes (1-6).

Record of pupils, showing name of school, name of pupil, individual advancement record, and date pupil left school or graduated. Arranged alphabetically by names of schools and thereunder by names of pupils. No index. Handwritten on printed forms. 10 x 14 x 24.

Statistics

410. ANNUAL STATISTICAL REPORT
1929—. 1 file box.

Copies of county superintendent's annual reports to state department of education on school statistics, showing date of filing, number of schools, consolidated schools, school rooms, high schools, principals, teachers, pupils, elementary and high school pupils in county, number of school weeks, and total of each. Arranged chronologically by dates filed. No index. Handwritten on printed forms. 10 x 4.5 x 13.5.

411. SCHOOL EXAMINERS RECORD
1882-1935. 1 vol.

Complete record of number of applicants, showing date of entry, name, residence, age, subjects taken and grades in each, failures, and certificates granted; also includes Record of Proceedings, 1882-1914, entry 407. Arranged chronologically by dates entered. Indexed alphabetically by names of applicants. Handwritten on printed forms. 450 pages. 18 x 12 x 2.5. County commissioners, North storeroom.

Financial Records

412. [CERTIFIED ANNUAL FINANCIAL REPORT OF BOARD OF EDUCATION, MEDINA COUNTY]
1932. 1 file box.

Copies of county superintendent's annual financial reports to state department of education, showing date of filing, cash receipts from all sources for school purposes, total amount of tuition fund, contingent fund, and to state aid; itemized account of expenditures, showing total for teaching, supervision, transportation of pupils, janitors, and other expenses. Arranged chronologically by dates filed. No index. Handwritten on printed files. 11 x 16 x 24.

Miscellaneous

413. MISCELLANEOUS SUBJECTS

1922—. 4 file drawers, 13 file boxes, 1 box. (4 file drawers, 18 file boxes, unlabeled; 1 box labeled by contained letters of alphabet).

Record of miscellaneous subjects, including teachers' applications and credentials, teachers' lists, music record of students, and school activities, including rules, names of judges, and blanks on oratory debate, spelling contests, scholarship contests, fair exhibit rules and field and track day, salaries of teachers, drivers, janitors, clerks and board members, individual progress reports, record of working permits issued to students, principals' annual reports, daily attendance report and graduation reports, showing name of school, name of subject, and information related to the various subjects or reports. Arranged alphabetically by names of schools and alphabetically thereunder by subjects. No index. Handwritten on printed forms. File drawers, 12 x 12 x 26; file boxes, 5 x 11 x 17; box, 23 x 22 x 17. 4 file drawers, 18 file boxes, 1 box, 1922—.

The general health district, or county health department, is one of the recent developments in county health administration. An act of the legislature in 1919 provided that townships and municipalities in each county, exclusive of any city with 25,000 population, should constitute a general health district; cities with 25,000 or more population a municipal health district; and municipalities of not less than 10,000 nor more then 25,000 population, and maintaining a board of health meeting the qualifications of the legislative act, were authorized after examination by the state health department to continue operation as separate health districts.[1]

An amendment in December 1919 made each city a health district; the townships and villages in each county were combined into a general health district; and a city and general health district might combine for administrative purposes.[2] The mayor of each municipality not constituting a city health district, and the chairman of the trustees of each township, are authorized to meet at the seat of justice and by selecting a chairman and a secretary organize a district advisory council which selects and appoints a district board of health composed the five members, one of whom must be a physician, who serves without compensation.[3]

Within 30 days after their appointment the members of the district board of health – the county board of health – organize by appointing one of their members president and the other president *pro tempore*. The board is authorized to appoint as district health commissioner a licensed physician who serves as secretary to the board. This official is designated deputy state registrar of vital statistics and is required to report monthly to the state registrar of vital statistics.[4]

-----

1. *Laws of Ohio*, CVIII, pt. i, 238.
2. *Ibid.*, CVIII, pt. ii, 1085.
3. Ibid.,
4. G. C. Sec. 1261-32; *Laws of Ohio*, CVIII, pt. i, 238-242.

On recommendation of the district health commissioner the board appoints a full-time public health nurse, a clerk, and such additional public health nurses, physicians, and others as may be necessary for the proper conduct of its work. The board studies the prevalence of disease, especially communicable diseases, provides treatment for venereal diseases, and is authorized to make any and all regulations it deems necessary for the prevention or restriction of disease, and the prevention, abolition, or suppression of nuisances. It provides for inspection of public charitable, benevolent, correctional, and penal institutions; and may provide inspection for dairies, stores, restaurants, hotels, and other places where food is manufactured, handled, stored, sold, or offered for sale. The board is authorized to carry on necessary laboratory tests by establishing a laboratory or contracting with existing laboratories, and all state institutions supported in the whole or in part by public funds must furnish such laboratory service to a county board of health under the terms agreed upon.[5]

The health department is financed by public taxation. The district board of health annually estimates in itemized form the amount needed for the fiscal year, and these estimates are certified to the county auditor and submitted by him to the county budget commissioners who may reduce any item but cannot increase any item or the aggregate of all items. The total amount fixed by the budget commissioners is apportioned by the county health department on the basis of taxable valuations in the townships and the municipalities composing the district.[6]

In Medina County the board of health carries on its work with a health commissioner, two county nurses, two clerks, and two sanitarians, all under the supervision of the state health department. Laboratory tests of water and milk, for typhoid, diphtheria, syphilis, undulant fever, and Bangs disease are made for the district at Ohio State University. Rabies treatment serum

---

5. *Laws of Ohio,* CVIII, pt. ii, 1088, 1089.
6. *Ibid.,* CVIII pt. ii, 1091.

is available at the local office at all times, and the state health department provides free treatment of syphilis when application is properly made through the local office. The annual budget of the board amounted in 1940, to $9340 of which the state department contributed $3000.[7]

Since Medina County maintains no sanitarium, it sends its indigent patients to the Edwin Shaw Sanatorium, Akron, Ohio; the Ohio State Hospital for Tuberculosis, Mt. Vernon, Ohio; the Avalon Sanatorium, Mt. Vernon, Ohio; and the Oak Ridge Sanatorium, Green Springs, Ohio. The county pays the maintenance costs of all indigent patients sent to these institutions. In 1940, the commissioners appropriated for this purpose $8400, supporting nine patients at one or another of these institutions.[8]

---

7. General Appropriation Ledger, 1940, *see* entry 277.
8. Commissioners' Journal, XVII [1936-1940], 509.

Minutes

414. MINUTES OF MEETINGS
1919—. 1 vol.
Minutes of meetings of Medina County board of health, showing date and place of meeting, resolutions brought before the board, and signatures of president and secretary. Arranged by dates of meetings. No index. Typed. 650 pages. 18 x 12 x 3. Board of health office.

415. ORTHOPEDIC AND TUBERCULAR CASES
1919—. 1 file box.
Card record of orthopedic and tubercular cases, showing date filed, name and address of patient, sex, color, age, case number, case history, name of family physician, date of onset, diagnosis, treatment, date of discharge, and condition of patient at time of discharge. Arranged alphabetically by names of patients and chronologically thereunder by dates filed. No index. Handwritten on printed forms. 5 x 8 x 14.

Immunization

416. VACCINATION [By School And Grade]
1919—. 2vols.

Record of vaccinations given school children by the health department, showing name of school, name and address of child, age, and grade. Arranged alphabetically by names of schools and numerically thereunder by grades. No index. Handwritten and typed, some on printed forms. Average 150 pages. 10 x 11 x 1. Board of health office.

Communicable Diseases

417. COMMUNICABLE DISEASES
1919—. 2 vols.

Record of required reportable communicable diseases, showing date reported, name of district, name and address of patient, age, sex, color, race, physicians signature, date of quarantine, and date quarantine lifted. Arranged alphabetically by names of districts and alphabetically thereunder by names of patients. No index. Handwritten on printed forms. Average 200 pages. 14 x 20 x 1. Board of health office.

Inspections

418. PHYSICAL EXAMINATION OF SCHOOL CHILDREN
1919—. 3 file boxes.

Record of physical examinations of school children, showing name, address, age, name of school, grade, and condition of health. Arranged alphabetically by names of schools and numerically thereunder by grades. No index. Handwritten. 15.5 x 7 x 19. Board of health office.

Vital Statistics

419. CERTIFICATES OF BIRTHS AND DEATHS
1930—. 1 file box.

Copies of birth certificates (in back of file box) and death certificates (in front of file box); birth certificates, showing registration and district numbers, full name of child, sex, color, legitimacy, single or multiple birth, mother's name and age, father's name and age, occupation, name of attending physician, date, and place of child's birth; death certificates, showing place of death, registration district number, if death occurred in hospital, name, sex, and color of decedent, marital status, date of death, date of birth, age, parents' names and addresses, cause of death, and name of attending physician. Arranged alphabetically by names of children or names of decedents. No index. Handwritten on printed forms. 9.5 x 10.5 x 29. Board of health office.

420. BIRTH RECORDS
1909—. 4 file drawers

Card record of birth, showing name of child, place of birth, sex, color, legitimacy, parents names, ages, and birthplaces, date of birth, physicians name and address, and registrar's name. Arranged alphabetically by names of children. No index. Typed. 5.5x x13.5 x 24. Board of health office.

421. DEATH RECORDS
1909—. 2 file drawers

Card record of deaths, showing name and address of decedent, district and registration numbers, sex, color, and marital status of the seated, dates of birth and death, age, cause of death, and names of physician and registrar. Arranged alphabetically by names of decedents. No index. Typed. 5.5 x 13.5 x 24. Board of health office.

Miscellaneous

422. [Miscellaneous] FILE
1919——. 6 file boxes. (Dated).
Original papers including agreements between board of health and county commissioners to provide for payment by the latter for hospitalization and care for tubercular cases and crippled children, x-rays, bills paid and unpaid, budgets, correspondence, general publications, clinic reports of crippled children, financial reports, monthly tuberculosis reports, maternity hospital reports, retirement fund reports, venereal disease reports, reports of death from communicable diseases, dog warden's reports of persons bitten by dogs, septic tank permits, sewage disposal, water test, vaccination, and immunization; disease reports, showing month, date of report, suspected disease, date of onset, name of patient, age, color, attending physician, date of quarantine, outcome of case, and date quarantine lifted; chart cards showing entire record of each individual case; correspondence, showing date of correspondence, to whom, from home, and signature of correspondent. Arranged alphabetically by subjects and alphabetically thereunder by names of patients. No index. Handwritten on printed forms. 12 x 12 x 26. Board of health office.

TUBERCULOSIS HOSPITAL

Medina County has no tuberculosis hospital. Their patients are sent to Edwin Shaw Sanatorium, Akron, Ohio, Molly Stark Sanatorium, Canton, Ohio, and Oak Ridge Sanatorium, Sandusky, Ohio.

By the provisions of the legislative act of 1816, the county commissioners were authorized to build a "poor house," and to appoint annually seven persons to constitute a board of directors. This board, a corporate body, was authorized to make such rules and regulations as were necessary for the management of the institution, and to appoint a superintendent, who might receive duly persons who had the required order from the township trustees. He was directed to keep a book listing the name and age of every person admitted, together with the date of admission.[1] The board of directors, or a committee of that body, was required to visit the "poor house" monthly to examine the condition of the paupers and to make a report on such matters as the food, clothing, and treatment of the inmates. Moreover, they were required to inspect the books and accounts of the superintendent. The board was required to report annually to the county commissioners the "state of the institution" with a full and correct account of all their proceedings, contracts, and disbursements; and the expenses of establishing and supporting the institution were to be paid on the order of the county commissioners out of the money in the treasury not otherwise appropriated.[2]

By the legislative act of 1831, the membership of the board was reduced to three. This board, like its predecessor, was authorized to appoint a superintendent. It was his duty, upon the order of the board, to discharge from the poor house any person who had been admitted because of illness when he had sufficiently recovered.[3] The directors were further authorized to remove paupers to their legal place of residence,[4] and any paper rejected by the board of directors could be turned over to the township overseers to be cared for by contracting with the lowest bidder.[5]

---

1. *Laws of Ohio,* XIV, 447.
2. *Ibid.,* XIV, 499.
3. *Ibid.,* XXIX, 319.
4. *Ibid.*
5. *Ibid.,* XXIX, 321-322.

In 1850 the name county poorhouse was changed to that of county infirmary. Fifteen years later, in 1865, the board of infirmary directors, consisting of three resident electors, was made elective by the voters of the county for a three-year term. The board was still authorized to appoint a superintendent, and was still required to make inspection visits, and to report its findings to the county commissioners.[7]

Although reports had been required of the infirmary management in previous years, it was not until the decade of the seventies that the legislature enacted measures looking to really systematic management of this ancient institution. Accordingly, in 1872, an act was passed which required each infirmary director, as well as the superintendent, to give bond conditioned for the faithful performance of the duties of his office.[8] Under this act the directors were required to report semiannually to the county commissioners the condition of the infirmary, the number of inmates, and such other information as the county commissioners believed proper. Furthermore, the board of directors was required to file a full account "of all moneys received and paid out" together with the vouchers. . . from whence received, to whom and for what paid out with the county commissioners, who, after examination, entered the report in the minutes of their proceedings. This report, as well as the vouchers, was to be filed in the auditor's office, and must be "safely preserved" by that officer.[9]

The county infirmary served also as a place for the confinement of children, the mentally ill, and persons afflicted with epilepsy. Although the state assumed responsibility for the mentally ill in the early years of the nineteenth century, it was not until 1898 that it was made unlawful to confine the adult insane and epileptics in the county home.[10]

------

7. *Ibid.*, LXII, 24-25.
8. *Ibid.*, LXIX, 120-121.
9. *Laws of Ohio*, LXIX, 121-122.
10. *Ibid.*, XCIII, 274.

Previously, in 1884, the legislature had prohibited the housing in the county infirmary of children who ere eligible to the county children's home or to some other charitable institution, unless separate from adults.[11] Exceptions were made, however, in the case of insane, idiotic, and epileptic children.[12] The latter provision is still effective in Ohio.[13.]

By an act of May 31, 1911, effective January 1, 1913, the board of infirmary directors was abolished and powers formerly exercised by this body were transferred to county commissioners and infirmary superintendent.[14] The superintendent is still required to keep a record of inmates, as prescribed by statute, and to report annually to the county commissioners. This report, the acceptance of which is evidence by an entry in the minutes of the commissioners' journal, is filed with the county auditor and by him preserved.[15] In 1919 the name county infirmary was changed to that of county home.[16]

The county commissioners still make provision for the establishment and maintenance of the county home, appoint a superintendent, and make regular inspection visits. Since December 1, 1932, the superintendent has been appointed from a list of names of persons eligible under civil service regulations,[17] and is authorized to appoint a matron and other employees.[18] Since 1882, the commissioners have been authorized to appoint an infirmary physician, who, like the superintendent, is required by statute to report to the county commissioners.

---

11. *Ibid.*, LXXXI, 92.
12. *Ibid.*, CIII, 850.
13. G. C. sec. 3089.
14. *Laws of Ohio,* CII, 433.
15. G. C. sec. 2535.
16. *Laws of Ohio,* CVIII, pt. i, 68.
17. Ohio Attorney General, *Opinions*, III, 2021.
18. G. C. sec. 2522.

This report, made quarterly, includes such information as the nature and extent of medical services rendered, to whom, and the character of the disease treated.[19]

Although there is some relation between the old age pension system and the county home, the newer form of aid is merely supplementary to the institution. As always, the county home cares for those whose condition is such that cannot be satisfactorily cared for except in an institution.[20] The contract for the Medina County infirmary was let in 1854 by the county commissioners[21] under authority of the act of 1816.[22] Before this time, the commissioners allowed necessary funds to various township trustees for care of the needy, who were usually placed in the homes of relatives.

The Medina Home has given refuge to an annual average of about 95 persons the past quarter century, these persons ranging in age from babyhood to the nineties. While a few of the inmates pay a part of the cost of their care, by far greater number do not. In 1940 the commissioners appropriated $18,000 for the maintenance of the home.[23] The nine resident members of the staff received an aggregate salary of $4860.[24]

A nonresident physician is employed by the commissioners to care for any illness which might arise. The county home has its own hospital, treating all cases except those requiring special attention, the latter being sent to Lodi Hospital in Lodi, Ohio, at the expense of the county. Religious services are provided once a month by the Medina County Ministerial Association.

---

19. G. C. sec. 2546; *Laws of Ohio*, LXXIII, 233; LXXIX, 90; CII, 436; VIII, pt. i, 269.

20. *The Reorganization of County Government in Ohio; Report of the Governor's Commission on County Government* (n. p., n. d.). Submitted to the Governor December, 1934.

21. Commissioners' Record, II (1851-1854), 37.

22. *Laws of Ohio*, XIV, 447.

23. Commissioners' Journal, XVII, (1934-1940), 509.

24. Receipts and Expenditures 1940, *see* entry 378.

Minutes

423. MINUTES OF MEETINGS
1880-1887. 1 vol.

Minutes of meetings of board of infirmary directors, showing dates of meetings, admission of inmates, all resolutions before the board, county farm activities, and expenses, including purchase of farm machinery, stock and horses, sale of farm products, reports of home and farm conditions, semiannual and annual financial reports, and signatures of directors. Arranged chronologically by dates of meetings. No index. Handwritten. 100 pages. 6 x 7 x 1. Superintendent's office.

For other records, see entry 3. Commissioner's Office.

Case Records

424. RECORD OF INMATES
1854—. 1 vol.

Record of inmates of county home, showing date received, name of inmate, address of prior residence, date and place of birth, occupation, age, race, sex, and complete family history, reason for discharge, and remarks. Arranged alphabetically by names of inmates. No index. Handwritten on printed forms. Average 16 x 12 x 2.5. Superintendent's office.

425. CASE RECORDS
1854—. 4 file boxes.

Complete case history of each inmate, showing name of inmate, age, former address, names of relatives, education, and former occupation; also admittance date and physical condition. Arranged alphabetically by names inmates. No index. Handwritten on printed forms. 12 x 18 x 26. Superintendent's office.

426. DAILY LEDGER
1854-1896. 3 Vols.

Daily register of activities, of inmates, showing date of entry, name and address of inmate, and expenses and receipts of inmates itemized daily. Arranged chronologically by dates entered. No index. Handwritten on printed forms. Average 150 pages. 12 x 8 x 1.5. Superintendent's office.

427. REGISTER, ADMISSIONS
1896—. 1 vol.

Record of admissions to county infirmary, showing date admitted, name, age, sex, race, nativity, physical and mental condition, from what township, town, and county admitted, date and place of birth, complete family history, and date Apprentice or absconded, or date of death. Arranged chronologically by dates of admissions. No index. Handwritten. 275 pages. 16 x 12 x 2. Superintendent's office.

428. COMMITMENT PAPERS
1865—. 1 file drawer.

Original papers, showing date and name of person committed to county home, address, reason, and remarks. Correspondence filed with each case in manila folders. Arranged alphabetically by names of persons committed. No index. Handwritten on printed forms. 11 x 16 x 24. Superintendent's office.

Financial Records

429. DUPLICATE REPORT OF MEDINA COUNTY HOME EXPENDITURES AND AMOUNTS TO DIVISION OF CHARITIES, DEPARTMENT OF PUBLIC WELFARE
1928—. 1 file drawer.

Copies of monthly and annual reports by county home superintendent to commissioners and state division of charities, showing date of report, number of inmates in home, number of inmates admitted, number discharged, number of deaths, and total. Arranged chronologically by dates of reports. No index. Handwritten on printed forms. 11 x 16 x 24. Superintendent's office.

431. EXPENDITURES AND RECEIPTS, MEDINA COUNTY INFIRMARY
1908—. 3 vols. (1-3).

Record of expenditures and receipts of the county infirmary, showing date entered, to whom paid, for what purpose including salaries, groceries, stock, feed, machinery, and nursing and medical care; receipts, showing date entered, from whom, for what purpose, including farm produce, stock, and told. Arranged chronologically by date centered. No index. Handwritten on printed forms. 2 volumes average 400 pages. 17 x 15 x 2; 1 volume, 600 pages. 18 x 16 x 3. 1 volume, 1908-1923, North storeroom; 1 volume, 1924-1937, Auditor's office; 1 volume, 1938—, Superintendent's office.

432. PETTY CASH
1900—. 4 vols.

Daily accounts of cash on hand, showing date of entry, amount received, amount expended each day, and total for each day. Arranged chronologically by dates entered. No index. Handwritten. Average 200 pages. 9.5 x 8 x 1. Superintendent's office.

Miscellaneous

433. VISITORS' REGISTER
1920—. 1 vol.
Register of visitors at the institution showing date registered, name and address of visitors, day and time visiting county home, and remarks. Arranged chronologically by dates of registrations. No index. Handwritten. 400 pages. 13 x 8.5 x 2. Superintendent's office.

434. REGISTRATION CARDS [Of Employees]
1907—. 3 file drawers.
Registration on cards for civil service positions, showing name and address of employee, grades on examination, date of appointment, age, position, and salary. Duplicate copy sent to civil service commission, Columbus, Ohio. Arranged alphabetically by names of employees. No index. Handwritten on printed forms. 18 x 28 x 45. Superintendent's office.

CHILDREN'S HOME

There is no children's home in Medina County.

The board of county visitors, and agency for the examination and inspection of county institutions supported wholly or in part by county or municipal taxation, was created by an act of the general assembly in 1882. Under this act, the judge of the court of common pleas was authorized to appoint five persons, three of whom were to be women, who were to visit periodically such county institution as the county jail, municipal prisons, and children's home, and file annually a report of their proceedings and recommendations for changes with the clerk of courts, and to forward a copy to the state board of charities. The members, appointed for an indefinite period were to serve without compensation.[1]

By the act of 1892, the personnel of the board was increased to six persons, three of whom were to be women, and not more than three to have the same political affiliations. Furthermore, the act made it the duty of the probate judge, whenever proceedings were instituted in his court to commit a child under 16 years of age to the boys' industrial home or to the girls' industrial home, to have notice given to the board of such proceedings; and it was the duty of the board of visitors to attend the meeting of the court, as a body or as a committee, to protect the interest of the child.[2] The power of appointment of board members was given to the probate judge.

While the provisions of the act of 1892 were redefined by the acts of 1898 and 1900, these acts did not, in the main, affect the duties of the board.[3] The latter act, however, made the board a continuous body with two members serving for one year, two members serving for two years, and two members serving for three years. In addition to this, the board was allowed a minimum expense schedule for their services.[4]

---

1. *Laws of Ohio,* LXXXIX, 107.
2. *Ibid.,* LXXXIX, 161.
3. *Ibid.,* XCIII, 57; XCIV, 70.
4. *Ibid.,* LXIV, 70.

Six years later the board was authorized to recommend to the county commissioners measures for the more economical administration of county institutions. Their report, together with their recommendations, was to be filed each year with the judge of the probate court and with the county prosecuting attorney.[5]

Under an act of 1913 the juvenile judge, like the probate judge under the act of 1892, was authorized to notify the visitors when any proceedings were instituted in his court for the commitment of any child to a state institution for correction.[6] The practice of annually filing reports of the board with the probate judge, prosecuting attorney, and state board of charities has been continued.[7]

In Medina County the board makes its inspections of the county institutions at intervals of three months, and makes its annual report according to the requirements of state law.

The board of county visitors keeps no separate records; for record of appointments, see Probate Journal, entry 154, and for Reports of Board of County Visitors, see entry 193.

---

5. *Ibid.,* XCVIII, 28.
6. *Ibid.,* CIII, 173, 888.
7. G. C. sec. 2976.

The soldiers' relief commission was established by an act of the legislation passed May 19, 1886, entitled "An act to provide for the relief of indigent Union soldiers, sailors, and marines, and the indigent wives, widows, and minor children of indigent or deceased Union soldiers, sailors, and marines." Under provisions of this act the commissioners of each county were authorized to levy a specified tax for the purpose of creating a fund for the relief of such beneficiaries; and the judge of the court of common pleas was authorized to appoint three county residents, at least two of whom were honorably discharged Union soldiers, to serve for a term of three years as members of the commission, which was organized by the selection of a chairman and a secretary and was known as the soldiers' relief commission.[1]

An amendment passed on March 4, 1887, provided that councilmen of city wards, as well as the board of trustees of the townships, certify to the soldiers' relief commission the names of those requiring and entitled to aid under the act.[2]

By the act of the legislature, passed April 28, 1890 the soldiers' relief commission was required to appoint annually a committee of three in each township and in each ward in any city in the county, whose duty it was to receive all applications for aid and to certify them to the soldiers' relief commission.[3]

Sections 2930 and 2933-4 of the general code were amended, March 6, 1917, to provide for the appointment to each county commission of one member who is the wife, widow, son, or daughter of an honorably discharged soldier, sailor, or marine of the Civil War or of the Spanish-American War, the other two members to be honorably discharged soldiers, sailors, or marines of the United States; and for the appointment to each township and ward committee of a wife or widow of a soldier, sailor, or marine of the United States.[4]

---

1. *Laws of Ohio,* LXXXIII, 232.
2. *Ibid.,* LXXXIV, 100.
3. *Ibid.,* LXXXVII, 352.
4. *Ibid.,* CVII, 27.

Two years later, in 1919, the provisions of the act were extended to include indigent veterans of the World War or indigent parents, wives, widows, or minor children of such veterans.[5]

Sections 2930 and 2934 of the general code were amended on April 6, 1929, to provide for the appointment by the court of common pleas in each county of a soldiers' relief commission, to consist of three members, one to be the wife, widow, son, or daughter of an honorably discharged soldier, sailor, or marine of the Civil War, the Spanish-American War, or of the World War, the other two members to be honorably discharged soldiers, sailors, or marines of the United States, one of whom should, if possible, be a member of the Spanish-American War Veterans, the other a member of the American Legion.[6]

The Medina County commissioners make appropriations each year for this commission each member is allowed $60 annually for compensation.[7] The aid granted varies from year to year. In 1938, the average monthly output was $4,112.40, in 1940 it dropped to $2,970.14 and in 1941 it was still further reduced to $2,7 00.[8]

---

5. *Ibid.,* CVIII, pt. i, 633.
6. *Laws of Ohio,* CXIII, 466.
7. General Appropriation Ledger, 1940, *see* entry 277
8. Soldiers' Relief Commission Report to County Auditor, 1938-1941, *see* entry 293.

Minutes

435. SOLDIERS' RELIEF COMMISSION RECORD
1902—. 2 vols.

Minutes of the meetings of the soldiers' relief commission, showing date and place of meeting, names of members present and absent, and subjects discussed, including applications, showing name of soldier, sailor, or marine, address, rank, number in family, amount granted, and signatures of president and clerk of commission; also includes a copy of commissioners' monthly report to county auditor for payments, showing date of payment, list of names and addresses, monthly allowance, and date allowed. Arranged chronologically by dates of meetings. No index. Handwritten on printed forms. Average 200 pages. 14 x 9 x 2. Soldier's Relief Commission, Second Floor, Princess Block, Medina, Ohio.

Applications

436. APPLICATIONS
1931—. 1 file box.
Original applications for relief by ex-soldiers, sailors, and marines, their widows, mothers, and dependent children, showing date of application, name of applicant, age, occupation, physical condition, number of dependents, length of service, company, regiment, or ship affiliation, and certification of discharge papers. Arranged chronologically by dates of application. No index. Handwritten on printed forms. 10 x 4.5 x 14.5. Auditor's main office.

437. SOLDIERS' AND SAILORS' RELIEF
1938—. 1 file box.
Record of applications and statements for relief by soldiers, sailors, marines, and their dependents, and approved by the commission showing name of applicant, date of application, name of county, amount of relief recommended, amount allowed, and signatures of the soldiers' relief commission. Arranged chronologically by years and alphabetically thereunder by names of applicants. No index. Typed on printed forms. 14 x 10 x 5. Auditor's office.

438. AUDITOR'S RECORD OF SOLDIERS' RELIEF
1882—. 2 vols. (1, 2).
Record of indigent soldiers, sailors, marines, and their dependents entitled to relief, showing name of recipient, amount and date of monthly award, and by total of awards granted for year. Arranged chronologically by years and alphabetically thereunder by names of recipients. No index. Handwritten on printed forms. Average 150 pages. 18 x 11 x 2. 1 volume, 1886-1916, North storeroom; 1 volume, 1917—, Auditor's office.

In 1884, the legislature made provision for soldiers' burial commission in each county, to consist of three persons in each township, appointed by the county commissioners, which was directed to defray the expense incurred in the interment of any honorably discharged union soldier, sailor, or marine who died in poverty. The commission, serving at the pleasure of the appointing power, was required to report to the county commissioners the name, rank, and command of the decedent, which report was transcribed by the county commissioners in a book kept for that purpose.[1] The original act, amended in 1891, extended the provisions of the act to include the interment of the wives or widows of Union soldiers.[2] In 1893, the act was again amended to provide for the internment of mothers of Union soldiers, sailors, marines, and army nurses.[3] In 1908, the personnel of the commission was reduced to two.[4]

Under the present law which became effective in 1921, the county commissioners are authorized to appoint two suitable persons in each township and ward in the county, who are directed to contract with the undertaker selected by the family or friends of the deceased, and to direct the burial in a respectable manner of the body of any honorably discharged soldier, sailor, or marine having at any time served in the army or navy of the United States, or the mother, wife, or widow of any soldier, sailor, or marine, or that of any war nurse who served at any time in the army of the United States who died in poverty.[5]

---

1. *Laws of Ohio,* LXXXI, 146-147.
2. *Ibid.,* LXXXVIII, 330-331.
3. *Ibid.,* XC, 177.
4. *Ibid.,* XCIX, 99.
5. G. C. sec. 2950; *Laws of Ohio,* CVIII, pt. i, 34; CIX, 211.

The burial commission is instructed to enforce all laws relative to the burial of indigent veterans, investigate the financial status of the decedents' family, and report its finding to the county commissioners, together with the name, rank, and command to which the deceased belonged, date of death, place of burial, occupation while living, and an itemized statement of the cost of burial.[6]

Upon receiving this report of the burial commission, the county commissioners transcribe the information in a book kept for that purpose, and certify the expense to the county auditor who draws his warrant for payment to the person or persons specified by the county commissioners.[7]

The amount contributed by the county for the burial of an indigent veteran set by the legislature at $35 in 1884, was increased to $75 in 1908, and to $100 in 1921.[8] Since 1908, each member of the burial commission has been allowed one dollar for each service performed.[9]

In Medina County, the commission has very few burials to supervise. It conducted only four in 1899, six in 1925, and four in 1940, with the average expenditure of $50 for each.[10]

The soldiers' burial commission keeps no separate records; for applications for soldiers' burial, see entry one, and Burial Record of Indigent Soldiers', entry 11.

---

6. *Laws of Ohio,* XCIX, 100.
7. *Ibid.,* XCIX, 101.
8. *Laws of Ohio,* LXXXI, 146, 147; XCIX, 99; CIX, 212; G. C. sec. 2951.
9. *Laws of Ohio,* XCIX, 99; G, C. sec. 2951.
10. Commissioners' Journal, XVII, [1935-1940], 509.

Provision for the relief of the indigent was made in 1805, but it was not until 1898 that the legislature provided separate relief for the indigent blind. The act authorizing the township trustees to certify to the county commissioners an amount not to exceed $100 a person yearly for such relief, the certification to be made a record listing the name of the beneficiary and the amount required; and directed the county commissioners to levy on the townships to the amount certified, this amount to be paid and to the county treasury and thence to the township treasurer to be used for blind relief.[1]

Six years later, in 1904, certification authority was transferred from the township trustees to the probate judge, who was required to register the names and address of beneficiaries and to issue to each a certificate giving his name, address, and the amount to be drawn. Persons eligible for relief were blind males over 21 and blind females over 18 years of age, without property or means of support. Not less than two county citizens, one a physician selected by the court, were required to testify that the applicant had been a resident of the state for five years and a resident of the county for one year immediately preceding the filing of an application for relief as a condition for granting aid.[2]

The act of 1904 was declared unconstitutional on the ground that it required the spending of public funds raised by taxation for a private purpose.[3] Hence, in 1908, an act was passed authorizing the county commissioners to levy a stipulated tax to create a fund for relief of the needy blind, the maximum benefits

---

1. *Laws of Ohio*, XCII, 270.
2. *Ibid.*, XCVII, 392-394.
3. *Auditor of Lucas County* v. *The State, Ohio State Reports*, LXXV, 114-137.

not to exceed $150 a person yearly to be paid quarterly; and authorizing the probate judge to appoint a blind relief commission consisting of three members to serve for a three-year term, directed to meet annually in the office of the county commissioners to examine applications recorded in order of their receipt in a book furnished by the county commissioners. This record was required to be kept open for public inspection.[4]

The blind relief commission was abolished by the legislature in 1913 and its powers and duties were transferred to the county commissioners.[5]

---

4. *Laws of Ohio,* XCIX, 56-58
5. *Ibid.* CIII, 60.

439. RECORD, BLIND RELIEF COMMISSION [Minutes]
1908-1927. 1 vol. (1).

Record of minutes of meetings and proceedings including list of claims presented to the blind relief commission, 1908-1913 and of the county commissioners acting in the same capacity, 1913-1927; first half, showing case number, name and address of claimant, date filed, date of action, annual amount of grant, amount payable quarterly, and date order issued to auditor; second half, record of proceedings, showing date of meeting, action upon claims made, increases or decreases of existing pensions, and all resolutions before the board. Arranged chronologically by dates of meetings. Indexed alphabetically by names of claimants. Handwritten on printed forms. 280 pages. 14 x 9 x 2. North storeroom.

440. BLIND RELIEF COMMISSION
1908-1913. 1 file box. Discontinued.

Record of application to the blind relief commission including brief case history, showing case number, date of application, name and address of applicant, affidavit proving need of assistance amount of claim granted, approval of county commissioners for payment, number rejected (if any), and reason. Arranged chronologically by years and alphabetically thereunder by names of applicants. No index. Handwritten on printed forms. 10 x 4.5 x 14.5. Auditor's main office.

The "Old Age Pension" law proposed by initiative petition, was adopted by the people of Ohio in the general election of 1933.[1] The act, as amended in 1936, provided that any person 65 or more years of age may upon certain stipulated conditions, receive a pension, providing his total income does not exceed $360 annually. The applicant must be a citizen of the United States, and must have resided in Ohio not less than five years of the nine prior to making application for aid, nor less than four years continuously in the county in which application is made. He must be unable to support himself, and have no claim on any legally responsible person who is able to support him. In addition, the net value of all unencumbered property of the unmarried applicant must not exceed $3,000; if the applicant is married, the combined property of husband and wife must not exceed $4,000 in value.[2]

Such property may be transferred to the division of aid for the aged to be held in trust. An amendment in 1937[3] made this transfer of property optional, and (illegible) as originally ruled, as required to be complied with before aid might be granted. Upon the death of the recipient of aid, this property, as well as life insurance over $250, less deductions for funeral expenses, claims of administrators, doctors, widow, and children, is used to defray in part or holy expense of the state of such aid as has been allowed.[4] A bill for the amount of the aid is presented to the estate. If no funds are available for funeral expenses, the state allows $100 for the funeral, and $25 for a burial lot.

The division of aid for the aged was set up as a part of the state department of public welfare in 1933 for the purpose of administering the old age pension law.

---

1. *Laws of Ohio*, CXV, pt. ii, 431-439.
2. *Ibid.,* CXVI, pt. ii, 216-221.
3. G. C. sec. 1359-6.
4. *Ibid.*

In each county, however, the commissioners might operate as a local board if they so desired. If they declined to serve in this capacity, the chief of the division of aid for the aged was authorized to appoint, with the consent of the director of public welfare, a board of three or five members of the community who served without compensation. The board was required to keep complete records, and might employ, subject to the approval of the division, such agents and other assistance as proper administration of the act required.[5] Since 1937 the chief of the division has been required to appoint such a board in any county.[6]

Each case is thoroughly investigated, but the board is advised to make its inquiries not in a strictly formal way, but in the manner "which seems best calculated to conform to substantial justice." Its decisions maybe appealed to the division.[7] After a case has been investigated, the applicant, is considered eligible is granted a certificate of relief which is then passed on by the division,[8] and once accepted by the division, need not be renewed.

Under the social security act, the federal government contributes all administrative expenses and 50 percent of the amount contributed as aid to the age, Within a minimum of $20 a month for each person aided.[9] The remainder of the money is supplied by the state.

The local board has been operating since May 1934. A subdivision manager is appointed directly by the (illegible) welfare department and works under the supervision of a district supervisor who directs work in several other counties.

---

5. *Laws of Ohio*, CXV, pt. ii, 431-439.
6. G. C. sec. 1359-12.
7. *Laws of Ohio*, CXV, pt. ii, 431-439.
8. *Laws of Ohio*, CXV, pt. ii. 435.
9. U. S. C. A., XLII, 303.

The administrator is appointed by the chief of Oho Division of Aid for the Aged.[10] The manager has a staff of three. In 1941, there were 605 persons receiving aid from this agency,[11] the grant for that year being $156,000.[12]

All records are located in board office, in the Princess Block, Public Square, Medina, Ohio.

---

10. *Laws of Ohio*, CXV, pt. ii, 431-439.
11. [Progress Book], 1940, *see* entry 443.
12. *Ibid.*

441. PENDING CASES.

1936—. 1 file box.

Record of pending cases, showing case number, name, age, place and date of birth, and residents of applicant, date of application, correspondence relative to application, and complete family history. Arranged alphabetically by names of applicants. No index. Handwritten on printed forms. 12 x 16 x 24.

442. CASH RECORD

1934—. 12 file boxes.

And record of applications for aid for the agent, showing case number, name, address, age, and date and place of birth of applicant, liability of relatives, complete family history, amount of grant (if any), reason for denial of aid, cases withdrawn or deceased after applying for aid, and amounts of insurance and property owned (if any). Arranged alphabetically by names of applicants and chronologically thereunder by dates of applications. No index. Handwritten on printed forms. 12 x 16 x 24.

443. [PROGRESS BOOK]

1935——. 1 vol.

Records of persons who have applied for aid, showing date of entry, name and address of applicant, date of application, and whether repeated or granted, also if canceled, discharged, reopened, transferred to another county and date of same, amount of each grant per month, and total amounts for year. Arranged chronologically by dates entered. No index. Handwritten on printed forms. 50 pages. 14 x 11 x 2.5.

The office of county surveyor, another English institution transplanted to America during the colonial period, became an important office in frontier Ohio where land titles and boundary lines were often in dispute. The office is purely a creature of statute, there being no constitutional provision for its establishment.

The first act of the general assembly pertaining to the surveyor was passed during the first legislative session of 1803. Under this act the court of common pleas was authorized to appoint a person well qualified to act as county surveyor. He received his commission from the governor, was required to give bond conditioned for the faithful performance of the duties of his office, and was directed to survey all lands which were sold or were to be sold for taxes, and was authorized to appoint chainmen or markers whose function it was to establish corners. The surveys made by the surveyor or his deputies were the only ones to be accepted as legal evidence in any court of law or equity. For remuneration, the surveyor was permitted to retain all fees collected by him in the operation of his office.[1]

Although it made no fundamental change in the duties of the surveyor, the act of 1816 fixed his term of office at five years; authorized him to appoint deputies, and made him responsible for their official acts; and made him liable to removal by the court for negligence or incompetency, and liable to suit by persons believing themselves damaged by his negligence or that of his deputies.[2] A year later, in 1817, provision was made for the appointment of a successor in the event the office became vacant because of death, resignation, or removal.[3]

---

1. *Laws of Ohio,* I, 90-93.
2. *Ibid.,* XIV, 424-431.
3. *Ibid.,* XV, 64.

The act of 1831 consolidated the previous acts, redefined the duties of the surveyor, increased the amount of his bond, and authorized him, when directed by the county commissioners, to procure from the surveyor general's office a "certified plat, together with the field notes of corners, bearing trees to each section, quarter section, lot, or original survey in his county, and cause the same to be preserved in a book by him provided for that purpose; which shall be deposited in the county auditor's office, for the use of the land holders in the county." It provides further, that the surveyor shall keep "fair and accurate record of all official surveys made by himself or by his deputies," in a suitable book to be kept by him for that purpose, and that he should number his surveys progressively. More significant, however, was the fact that the office was made elected for a three-year term by the act of 1831. The term remained at three years until 1906 when it was reduced to a two-year period; and by the act of 1927, beginning with the term of surveyor elected in 1928, the term was increased to four years.[4]

During the years of the development of the office other duties have been delegated to the surveyor. In 1842 he was given the duty of ascertaining and reporting trespassing of public lands.[5] Twelve years later he was given the same powers as the justices of the peace to take and certify deeds, mortgages, powers of attorney, and other instruments affecting real estate, to administer oaths, and to take and certify affidavits.[6] In 1867 he was given authority, when directed by the county commissioners, to transcribe any and all dilapidated maps, records of plats, and field notes of surveys of other counties.[7]

---

4. *Laws of Ohio,* XXIX, 399; XCVIII, 245-247; CXII, 178.
5. *Ibid.,* XL, 57.
6. *Ibid.,* LII, 70.
7. *Ibid.,* LXIV, 216-217; LXXVIII, 285.

Similarly, in 1881, he was authorized to procure for any office in the state a certified plat together with the field notes of corners, quarter sections, lots, or original surveys and place them in a book provided for that purpose. Certified copies from his book were to be taken as *prima facie* evidence.[8]

With the increase in modern means of transportation, there developed a growing need for more efficient methods of road construction and maintenance. Accordingly in 1906, the surveyor was directed to act, whenever the services of an engineer were required, in the capacity of an engineer with respect to roads, turnpike, bridges, or ditches, except in cities of the first grade.[9] He was directed by statute to perform all duties in his county which would be done by a civil engineer or surveyor, to prepare all plans, specifications, and estimates of cost, and to submit forms or contracts for the construction and repairs of all bridges, culverts, roads, draws, ditches, and other public improvements (except buildings) over which the county commissioners had authority. At the same time, he was made responsible for the inspection of all public improvements, and was directed to keep a complete list of all estimates and bids received for such work, as well as of contracts awarded for improvements.[10]

Similarly, another measure enacted in 1919 increased the duties of the surveyor regarding road construction and road maintenance. Under this act the surveyor was authorized to designate one of his deputies as maintenance engineer. This engineer, under the direction of the surveyor, was to have charge of all "road maintenance and repair work" in his county. Furthermore, when authorized by the county commissioners, the surveyor was to appoint a maintenance supervisor or supervisors to have charge of the maintenance of improved highways within

---

8. *Ibid.*, XXIX, 399; LXXVIII, 285.
9. *Ibid.*, XCVIII, 245-247.
10. *Ibid.*, XCVIII, 245-247.

a district or districts established by the commissioners or the surveyor, and containing not less than ten miles of improved county roads.[11] In 1923 the surveyor was delegated to assist the county planning commission wherever such commission was established.[12]

Thus, the general responsibility of planning and directing county road construction is vested in the county surveyor. Because of the increased responsibility placed on this office there has been an attempt to raise the general qualifications of those seeking election to it.

Accordingly, in 1935, an act was passed changing the title of the office to that of "county engineer," and eligibility to the office was restricted to "registered professional engineer and registered surveyor licensed to practice in the State of Ohio."[13] This act was amended, in 1936, to permit the incumbent to continue in office upon re-election, even if he lacked these qualifications.[14]

In Medina County, the staff of the engineer's office includes, in addition to the engineer himself, a deputy engineer, a maintenance supervisor, one highway engineer, and a tax map draftsman. There is a permanent maintenance force of 30 men, which in the summer season is enlarged with temporary workers.[5] This staff maintains 626 miles of county and township roads, and about 3000 bridges and culverts.[16] In 1940, expenditures for construction, maintenance, and repair amounted to $223, 327; in 1941 this sum decreased to $168,702.[17] Funds are appropriated by the commissioners entirely from the county's income in gasoline and motor vehicle taxes.

---

11. *Laws of Ohio,* CVIII, pt. i, 497.
12. *Ibid.,* CX, 312.
13. *Laws of Ohio*, CXVI, pt. i, 283.
14. *Ibid.*, CXVI, pt. ii, 152.
15. Pay Rolls and Miscellaneous, 1940, *see* entry 479.
16. Rural Road Mileage Report, 1940, *see* entry 180.
17. Road Contract Record, 1940, *see* entry 464.

Surveys, Maps, and Plats
(See also entry 454)

444. INDEX [Record] TO SURVEYS
1843—. 1 vol.

Index record to surveys, showing names of persons for whom
property was surveyed, name of surveyor, date and number of
survey, range and section numbers, name of township, and volume
and page numbers of records also contains Index to Surveys
[Village], 1843-1879, entry 445. This serves as an index to entries
446 and 447 by showing survey number, volume letter and number,
and page numbers of records. Arranged by names of townships and
numerically thereunder by survey numbers. No index. Handwritten
on printed forms. 168 pages. 24 15 x2. Engineer's vault.

445. INDEX TO SURVEYS [Villages]
1880—. 1 vol. 1843-1879 in Index [Record] To Surveys,
entry 444.

Index to Record of Surveys, entry 446 and Revised Numbers,
Towns, and Villages, entry 447, showing village sections with
streets and lot numbers, range, township, and survey numbers, and
volume letter or number and page numbers of records. Arranged
numerically by lot numbers. Handwritten. 290 pages. 19 x 18 x 2.
Engineers' vault.

446. RECORD OF SURVEYS
1834—. 12 vols. (A-K; 1).

Record of surveys and plats made by county surveyor, deputies,
and other surveyors, showing survey bill, date and number of
survey, name of township, section and lot numbers, distances,
angles, and original stakes or posts including plats; also contains
Revised Numbers, Towns, and Villages, 1881—, entry 447.
Arranged alphabetically by name of townships and numerically
thereunder by survey numbers. 1834-1842, no index; for index

1843—, see entry 444, and 1880—, see entry 445. Average 200 pages. 23 x 18.5 x 1. Engineer's vault.

447. REVISED NUMBERS, TOWNS, AND VILLAGES
1880. 1 vol. (1).

Surveyor's record of all identification number changes made of lots in towns and villages where subdivisions and additions have been made, showing date of entry, names of town or village, corporation, and owner, identification of property, and old and new lot number assigned; also includes plats, showing old and new lot numbers, name of addition, tract, range or section numbers, name of township, and boundaries. Prepared by county engineer. Arranged chronologically by dates entered. For separate indexes, see entries 444 and 445. Surveys, handwritten; plats, hand drawn, black on white. Scales vary. 398 pages. 18 x 12 x 2.5. Engineer's vault.

448. ENGINEER'S FIELD NOTES
1863—. 458 notebooks. 420 subtitled Road Records; 8, Nill Fill-ins; 30, Bridges and Culverts.

Record of surveyor's field notes made in surveys conducted on hills, roads, ditches, bridges, and culverts, showing measurements, curved degrees, elevations, grades, ground levels, direction of water flow, type of soil, names of abutting property owners, cubic yards of excavation or fills, consecutive survey numbers, date of entry, and name of surveyor. Arranged numerically by consecutive survey numbers and also arrange chronologically by dates entered. For separate indexes, see entries 452 and 458. Hand sketched. Average 80 pages. 8 x 5 x .5. Engineer's vault.

449. PLATS OF TOWNSHIPS AND MUNICIPALITIES [1817], 1880, 1900, 1910, 1923. 86 vols. Title varies: Original Survey of Medina County [1817], 1 vol.; Villages [1817], 2 vols.; Real Estate Plat Books, 1880, 2 vols.; Plats of Townships (includes Municipalities), 1910, 19 vols. and duplicate set.

General record of surveys of land tracts made by county surveyors, showing names of townships and villages, date of survey, survey, section, tract, and lot numbers, description of tract surveyed, and name of owner of tract; also includes a plat sketch of surveyed tract, showing boundary lines, length of each boundary line, area of tract, streams, roads, and location of landmarks. One volume, 1817, includes plats of the sections of Medina County later given to Lorain and Summit Counties. The year 1900, includes assessments of real property, showing valuation and totals of lands and buildings on left hand page and map of townships and municipalities on right hand page; 1817, arranged by names of townships and villages; 1880, arranged numerically by section numbers; 1900, arranged by names of townships; 1910, 1923, arranged numerically by tract numbers and numerically thereunder by lot numbers. 1817, 1880, 1900, no index; 1910, indexed numerically by lot numbers; 1923, indexed numerically by lot numbers placed on reference map in front of each volume. Handwritten and hand drawn. Duplicate 19 volumes, 1910, photostatic copies. 1817, 1880, average 150 pages. 24 x 20 x2Semicolon 1900, 1910, average 40 pages. 17.5 x16.5 x11923, average 30 pages. 34 x 24 x 1. 24 volumes [1817], 1880, 1910 (Photostatic copies), Engineer's vault; 62 volumes, 1900, 1910, 1923, Engineer's map and plat room.

450. ATLAS OF MEDINA COUNTY TOWNSHIPS 1897. 1 vol.

Maps of the county, showing names of townships and corporations with roads, streets, alleys, railroads, streams, section and range lines and numbers, boundary lines of land tracts with area, and name of owner; corporations or hamlets, showing boundary lines of corporation or hamlets, lot lines with lot numbers, street names, and location of public buildings; also contains county directory, showing brief summary of industrial pursuits of each township and town with short biography and photographs of prominent citizens. Contains 17 maps, one for each of the 17 townships, extra pages contain a combination history of each township and township map. Compiled by county engineers. Arranged alphabetically by names of townships or towns. Alphabetical table of contents. No index. Printed and colored. Scale 2.5 inches equal 1 mile. 143 pages. 19 x 15 x 1. Engineer's office.

451. [BLUEPRINTS, TRACINGS, AND MAP NEGATIVES]
1910—. 21 pigeon holes. (1-21).
Blueprints, Tracy's, map negatives, having names of township and taxing district, tract number, and names of roads, intersections, culverts and bridges. Prepared by county engineer. No systematic arrangement. Indexed alphabetically by names of townships. Handwritten and hand drawn. Scle varies. 14 x 17 x 44. Engineer's vault.

Public Improvement

Roads (See also entries 465, 467, 481)

452. INDEX [Record] TO ROADS AND DITCHES
[1863—]. 1 glass-covered wall case.
Index record of roads and ditches, showing road numbers, names of roads and ditches, and volume and page number of records. This serves as an index to Road Records [Including Petitions], entry 454 and Engineer's Field Notes, entry 448, by showing road numbers and volume and page numbers of record. Arranged numerically by road numbers. Handwritten. 26 x 32 x 4. Engineer's vault.

453. PLAT BOOK, INDEX TO ROADS
1890—. 1 vol.

Plat book index record to road records [Including petitions], entry 454, showing name of township, volume, page, and entry numbers referring to petitions or resolutions of county commissioners, report of reviewing committee, surveyor's findings on county roads, names of roads in each township, tract and lot numbers, and names of owners. Arranged alphabetically by names of townships. No index. Handwritten. 36 pages. 23.5 x 15 x 1.5. Engineer's vault.

454. ROAD RECORDS [Including Petitions]
1818—. 2 vols. (1, 2).

Record of petitions presented to the county commissioners to establish and extend roads and highways, showing name of circulator, name of proposed roads, description of route of proposed road, names of other petitioners, copies of notice of petition filed, affidavit of posting notice, bond filed by petitioners, report of viewers to commissioners recommending or rejecting establishment of road, surveyors report on survey of proposed road with sketches of road and survey date on elevation and grade, and commissioners approval or rejection of petition; also surveyor's drawings to scale of proposed new roads, showing location, length, width, line, intersections, abutments for stream crossings, and publisher sworn statement of publication of notice of bond issues. Arranged alphabetically by names of circulators. 1818-1862, no index; 1863— indexed by entries 452, 453. Handwritten on printed forms. Average 600 pages. 17 x 15 x 3.5. Engineer's vault.

For other records of road petitions, see entry 1.

455. COUNTY ROAD JOURNAL
1930—. 1 vol. 1 bdl.

Record of county roads, showing expense of road construction and repairs regarding materials, supplies, and labor, date expense incurred, name, location and number of road, total amount of labor, total amount of supplies and materials, and cost; also contains surveyors identification symbol known as a key. Arranged numerically by road numbers and key (meaning county surveyor's key system). No index. Handwritten and typed, some on printed forms. Volume 300 pages. 16 x 14 x 2.5; Bundle, 16 x 14 x 24. Engineer's office.

456. ROAD DATA [Construction and Maintenance]
1921—. 1 wooden box, 8 file drawers.

Record of road construction and repairs to roads, ditches, bridges, culverts, showing estimates, name, location, and number of road or improvements, commissioners resolution on bonds issue, requisitions, contractors bonds, copies of contracts, inspection reports, shipping bills on material, gasoline tickets, and data, work orders, records of Work Projects Administration projects, property assessments, ditch reports, time sheets, payrolls, and miscellaneous expense data with itemized cost. Arranged numerically by road numbers. No index. Typed on printed forms. Box, 18 x 17 x 12; file drawer, 16.5, x 11.5 x 26. 1 wooden box, 1921-1930 Engineer's storeroom; 8 file drawers, 1930—, Engineer's office.

For other records of road construction and maintenance, see entry 8.

Bridges

457. BRIDGE AND CULVERT REPORTS
1920—. 66 vols. 24, subtitled Bridge Reports; 42, Culvert Reports.

Reports on bridges and culverts, showing date of report, name of township, location, road and section numbers, name of stream or ditch, name and distance to nearest railroad, name and address of individual or firm by whom built, description of materials used, price, span, dimensions, width and depth of streams, superstructure, floor system, floor joist, truss, plate girder, and other details; also inspection of culverts, showing date of report, date of inspection, condition of culvert, new parts required, and remarks. Arranged chronologically by dates of reports. For separate index, see entry 458. Handwritten on printed forms. Average 100 pages. 10 x 8 x 2.5. Engineer's vault.

458. INDEX [Record] TO BRIDGES AND CULVERTS
1863—. 1 pasteboard wall chart.
Index record to bridges and culverts, showing road, culvert, and bridge numbers, and page numbers and volume letter or number of record. This serves as an index to Bridge and Culvert Reports, entry 458; Engineer's Field Notes, entry 448, by showing road, bridge, or culvert number, and volume and page numbers of records. Arranged numerically by road numbers with bridges and culverts arranged the same in opposite columns. Handwritten. 26 x 21. Engineer's vault.

459. COST CARDS [Bridges and Culverts]
1923—. 2 file drawers.
Card record of costs of building and repairing bridges or culverts, including top abutments, approaches, and wings, showing road number, section letter, date and number of bill, road bed and surface, name of township, and type and length of road. Arranged at numerically by road numbers. No index. Handwritten. 6 x 9 x 13. Engineer's office.

Ditches (See also entries 452, 476)

460. DITCH RECORD [Petitions]
1886-1928. 6 vols. (2 unlabeled; 1, 2, 2, 4). 1925— in [Journal Road District #1], entry 6.
Record of petitions to county commissioners for deepening, widening, and straightening ditches or construction of new ditches, including auditor's notice to landowners that such petitions have been filed, showing copy and date of petitions, date of hearing, notice to file for compensation or damages, report of commissioners' findings at hearings, followed by order to auditor to record findings, and order to surveyor to make necessary survey; surveyor's report county commissioners, showing date of report

name of ditch, surface and grade elevation each 100 feet, total fall, depth and width of ditch to top and bottom, number of cubic yards, and price of yard, also bond of contractors with approval of bond. Arranged chronologically by dates of reports on petition. Indexed alphabetically by name of ditches. Handwritten. Average 215 pages. 16.5 x 11 x 1.5. Engineer's office.

Estimates, Bids, and Contracts

461.   SPECIFICATIONS,   AGREEMENTS,   AND
CONTRACT BONDS
1929-1930. 17 vols.
Record of specifications to cover all types of road building, one copy each for the 17 townships, showing date of contract, names of road and township, particulars covered by contract; includes in back of volume, auditor's certificate of funds available for contract, signed agreement between commissioners and contractor, and contractor's bond filled out and signed by surety. Arranged chronologically by dates of contracts. Indexed alphabetically by names of townships. Typed on printed forms. Average 152 pages. 10 x 8 x .5. Engineer's office.

462. RECORDS AND SPECIFICATIONS OF BRIDGE
CONSTRUCTION
1920-1925. 1 bundle (labeled by names of bridges).
Discontinued.
Original record of specifications, contracts, and bonds, covering the building, repairing, and replacing bridges throughout the county; contracts, showing names and addresses of contractors, name a bridge, and name of surety; bonds showing amount of bond and name and address of surety. Arranged alphabetically by names of bridges. No index. Typed. 9 x 12 x 15. Engineer's storeroom.

463. SURVEYOR'S CONTRACT RECORD
1906—. 11 bdls., 3 vols.
Record of commissioners resolution authorizing the improvement

or repair of county roads and bridges, including copies of advertisements for bids, record of bids received, and copy of contract entered into by county commissioners with approved bidder, showing date of improvement or repair, name and number of road or bridge, specifications and amount of contract, date contract to be completed, record of payment to contractor on account, actual cost, and distribution of cost between township, county, villages, and property owners. Arranged numerically by road numbers. No index. Handwritten on printed forms. Bundles 12 x 12 x 18; volumes average 300 loose leaf pages 18.5 x 12.5 x 2.5. 11 bundles, 1908-1918, Engineer's storeroom; 3 volumes, 1919—. Engineers office.

464. ROAD CONTRACT RECORD
1919—. 2 vols. (1, 2).

Record contracts of road maintenance and repairs, showing name and number of road, name of township, date of entry, contract number, name of contractor, length width, and type of road, material to be used, itemized proposals, names of bidders, summary of cost, including payroll, amounts of materials and supplies used, inspections, and repair. Arranged chronologically by dates entered. Indexed numerically by road numbers. Handwritten on printed forms. Average 300 pages. 18.5 x 13 x 2.25. Engineers' office.

465. CONTRACT RECORD (Bridges and Culverts)
1903—. 3 vols. (1-3).

Contract records entered into by county engineer by authority of county commissioners with individuals or firms, for construction or repair of county bridges and culverts, showing culvert or bridge contract number, road section, name of township, estimated quantities and costs, names of bidders, contract awarded by commissioners, quantity used and cost of same, date and amount approved, fund, and total amounts; also contains Expense Account, Bridge Fund [and Culverts], 1903—, entry 471. Arranged chronologically by date approved. Indexed numerically by bridge and culvert contract numbers showing road section and name of township. Handwritten on printed forms. Average 350 pages. 18 x 12 x 3. Engineer's office.

466. SURVEYOR'S ROAD AND SECTION RECORD
1927—. 1 vol.
Record of road contracts and construction by county force where township and property owners bear entire cost, showing name and number of road, length of road, section letter, name of township, type of construction, preliminary detail, estimate of unit and total cost, roadway, surface, miscellaneous costs, names of bidders, unit price, and total bid. Arranged numerically by road numbers. No index. Handwritten. 300 pages. 14 x 17.5 x 4. Engineer's office.

Financial Records

467. INDEX TO BILLS
1916—. 8 vols. (1-8).
Index record to vouchers and invoices showing date and number of invoice or voucher, to whom payable, description of purchase, whether for material, fuel, or light, miscellaneous items, and payrolls for the department. The serves as a numerical index to Bills approved, entry 468; Bill Records and Employees Cards, entry 469; and Pay Rolls and Miscellaneous entry 479, by showing invoice or voucher numbers. Arranged numerically by invoice or voucher numbers. Handwritten on printed forms. Average 180 pages. 9 x 14 x 1. Engineer's office.

468. BILLS APPROVED
1932—. 10 file boxes (labeled by contained bill numbers).
Vouchers and invoices for all county building and repairing roads, ditches, culverts, and bridges, materials, and pay rolls, showing voucher number, name of payee, supplies and services rendered, date of payment, and signature of recipient. Arranged alphabetically by subjects and alphabetically thereunder by names

of payees. For index, see entry 467. Handwritten on printed forms.
11 x 4.5 x 12. Engineers office.

469. BILL RECORDS AND EMPLOYEE'S CARDS
1929—. 1 file box.

Record of invoices covering material, freight, and expense for
maintenance and repairing of roads, showing name of payee,
invoice number, date and amount of invoice, and description; also
includes a record of employees under road department, showing
name, address, age, nativity, and marital status of employee,
number of dependents, records of education and previous
employment, date of employment, and rate of pay. Arranged
alphabetically by subjects in alphabetically thereunder by names
of (illegible). For index, see entry 467. Typed on printed forms. 6
x 9 x 13. Engineer's vault.

470. RECEIPTS JOURNAL
1935. 1 vol. Discontinued.

Record of receipts, showing date of receipt, name of payer, date
covering pay, bill number, amount received, and amount credited
to accounts receivable; appropriation section of volume, showing
date of payment, name of payee, purpose, purchase order number,
amount and number of warrant, debit amount to appropriation,
(illegible) in appropriation, and names of funds debited and
credited. Arranged chronologically by date of receipts. No index.
Handwritten. 40 pages. 18.5 x 14 x 1. Engineer's vault.

471.EXPENSE ACCOUNT, BRIDGE BOND [and Culverts]
1907-1921. 1 vol.

Record of expenses for culverts and bridges, with original
estimates and specifications cor county surveyor on construction
and repair of county bridges and culverts as filed with county
commissioners, showing date filed, name of improvement, record
of amount of material, hours of labor, grade of material, contracts
entered, and name of firm or individual; expense account, showing

date of bill, date filed, name of creditor, for what purpose, total amount, names of townships, bridge or culvert, and landowner, and amount of assessment against landowner (if any), 1933—, entry 465. Arranged alphabetically by names of townships and chronologically thereunder by date filed. No index. Handwritten on printed forms. 248 pages. 20 x 25 x 2.5. Engineer's vault.

472. SURVEYOR'S BRIDGE AND ROAD REPAIR EXPENSE RECORD
1910-1913. 1 vol. (1).
Record of expenses of repairs to roads and bridges, showing date of entry, name, (illegible), and measurements of bridges, cost of construction and bills approved by commissioners for cost. Arranged chronologically by dates entered. No index. Handwritten. 289 pages. 20 x 15 x 2.5. Engineer's vault.

473. SURVEYOR'S AND ASSISTANTS' (illegible) ROAD AND HILL ACCOUNT
1912-1915. 2 vols.
Surveyor's and assistants' expense accounts of work on bridges, roads, and hills and fills, including estimating, inspecting, refilling, and various kinds of field work, showing date of entry, amount allotted for transportation by livery, food, incidentals, regular salary, improvement on county line, and inter-county road (illegible) to adjoining (illegible) of one-half total cost. Arranged chronologically by dates entered. Indexed alphabetically by (illegible). Handwritten on printed forms. Average 100 pages. 18 x 12 x 1.5. Engineer's office.

474. TIME BOOKS [Construction of Westfield Free Pike]
1882-1885. 3 vols.
Daily account of workers' time in grading and hauling (illegible), gravel and sand, for the construction of the Westfield Free Pike, showing date of labor, name of workman, number of labor hours (illegible), rate an hour, total for day, grand totals, and date of settlement. Arranged chronologically by dates of labor. No index.

Handwritten. Average 150 pages. 18 x 6 x .5. Engineer's storeroom.

475. ENGINEER'S LABOR AND EXPENSE RECORD
1916-1923. 2 vols.
Record of (illegible) of improvement repair costs, showing date of entry, cost of engineering, maintenance of equipment, material, transportation, names of assistant chainmen and rodmen, and total county, state, and township apportionment. Arranged by dates entered. No index. Handwritten on printed forms. Average 91 pages. 12.5 x 19.5 x 2. Engineer's office.

476. DITCH EXPENSE ACCOUNTS,
1912-1923. 1 vol. (1).
Record of expenditures for dishes of Medina County, showing date of entry, name and location of ditch in township, name and bond of contractor, time allotted for the work, and county and township share of cost. Arranged chronologically by dates entered. Indexed alphabetically by name of contractors. Handwritten on printed forms. 150 pages. 21 x 15 x 2. Engineer's vault.

Miscellaneous

477. INVENTORIES, TOWNSHIP EQUIPMENT
1925—. 2 vols.
Annual inventories of road equipment owned by each township, showing date of inventory, name of township, itemized list and value of equipment, and date filed with county commissioners. Arranged by dates of inventories and alphabetically thereunder by names and type. No index. Typed on printed forms. Average 50 pages. 12 x 15 x 1.5. Engineer's vault.

478. CORRESPONDENCE
1913-1916. 3 bdls., 13 letter files, 1 file box.
Originals and copies of letters from engineer's office to State Highway Department regarding highway property frontage

improvements, instructions to bidders for contracts, way bills on
shipment of materials, and miscellaneous items, showing date of
correspondence, name of correspondent, subject discussed,
pertinent date. Arranged alphabetically by subjects. No index.
Handwritten and typed some on printed forms. Bundles 19 x 12 x4;
letter files, 12 x 12 x 3; file box. 10 x 15 x 23. 3 bundles, 1925-
1928, North storeroom; 13 letter files, 1 file box, 1913-1916,
1928—, Engineer's office.

479. PAY ROLLS AND MISCELLANEOUS
1928—. 18 file boxes.

Original payrolls and time slips of roadmen, 1930 - 1937, showing
names of employees, voucher number, position, job number,
number of hours, rate of pay, total and date due; requisition to the
county commissioners for the purchase of material for building and
repairing roads, ditches, culverts, and bridges, 1928-1935, showing
date requisition, date needed, quantity, quality, date approved,
from whom purchased, cost, and job number; also includes daily
reports of gasoline consumption and cost of same to operate road
machinery, 1933-1937, showing job and equipment numbers,
number of gallons of gasoline used, time on job, time idle, cost.
Arranged by invoice or voucher numbers and alphabetically
thereunder by names of employees or pays. For index see entry
467. Handwritten and typed, some on printed forms, 4.5 x 10.5 x
25. Engineer's vault.

480. RURAL ROADS MILEAGE REPORT
1933—. 1 folder.

Annual report to state highway department, showing date of report,
number of miles of rural road actually in use of public highways,
mileage of various types of roads, including Portland cement,
concrete, or gravel, type of soil, reported mileage at beginning of
year, mileage built, replaced, or abandoned during year with a total
mileage at close of year, and certification and signature of
engineer. Arranged chronologically by dates of reports. No index.
Typed on printed forms. 14 x 8 x .5. Engineer's office.

Metropolitan Park District Boards in Ohio were formed on the basis of the state Metropolitan Park District Law of 1917, which authorized every county or part thereof to form such a district on the petition of the people of the county or of any local governing body therein. The governing body of these districts is a board of park commissioners and usually consists of three members, who serve without pay and who are appointed by the probate judge. They serve three years and one term expires every year. A director is appointed by the board.[1]

Medina County's Metropolitan Park is part of the Cleveland Metropolitan Park District, and is known as the Hinckley Reservation. It has an area of 1154 acres, and is noted for its scenic beauty and rock formations.

The reservation is administered by the Board of Park Commissioners of the Cleveland Metropolitan Park District, who house all records in the Cleveland office, with the exception of the minutes of the meetings, which are kept in the Medina County auditor's office, entry 351.

---

1. *Laws of Ohio,* CVII, 65-69.

The agricultural conservation association was organized in Medina County by the secretary of agriculture by authority vested in him under section 7d(2) of the Soil Conservation and Domestic Allotment Act as amended February 29, 1936. This section provides for such participation by county committees or associations of producers in the administration of the federal conservation program as the secretary finds necessary.[1]

The county committee of three members is selected by delegates to a County Convention attended by elective delegates from the various townships who are selected by community committees. The county committee includes a chairman and two members. The members of the committee receive compensation only for the days employed.

The county agricultural agent meets with the county committee in an advisory capacity but does not have a vote in its proceedings.

Medina County is in District 11 of Ohio. The three committeemen appointed by each of its 17 townships constitute a large and representative group of the farmers of the county, who meet together under the direction and guidance of the county chairman. They are paid for the time they give to these meetings. The work of the association is conducted by the agency office, the staff of which consists of the county chairman, the vice-chairman, a third member appointed by the township committeemen, and three clerical workers.

All records located in Agricultural Conservation Association Office, Second Floor, Gazette Block, Medina, Ohio.

481.   RECORD OF FARMS
1936—. 24 file boxes.
Report on crop production and soil conservation of county farms, showing name of farmer, sketched map, waste section, number of fields, disposition of crops planted or land used, and assign record of seeding, location of farm, number of acres, and total crop production. All office records and expense vouchers are kept in the

same file. Arranged alphabetically by names of farmers. No index. Handwritten on printed forms. 11.5 x 13 x 22.

482. [Arial] MAPS OF TOWNSHIPS
1936—. 17 file drawers (Labeled by townships).
Arial maps of township farmlands, including forest coverage, crop distribution, pasture lands, waterways, varieties of soil, and waste lands, showing name of township, date of map, acreage, and location of each classification. Acreage measured by planimeters, four of which are kept running in the office of the association, and added to the maps in red ink together with location notes. Maps are made by arial photography from 1500 feet on clear October days by the United States Department of Agriculture in cooperation with United States Army (regulars and reserves). Arranged alphabetically by names of townships and chronologically thereunder by dates of maps. Scales vary. No index. Photographs, white on black. 350 maps. 50 x 48 in file drawer, 53 x 1.5 x 50.

483. CORN-HOG CONTRACTS
1933-1935. 4 file boxes.
Applications of farmers for federal grants and statements of reduction in the annual production of corn and hogs, showing date of application, names of township, county, and farmer, also feeder's report, compliance certificates, and proof of compliance. Arranged alphabetically by names of townships and alphabetically thereunder by names of farmers. Typed on printed forms. 11.5 x 13 x 22.

484. CORN AND WHEAT CONTRACTS
1936—. 12 file drawers.

Record of crop control, showing contracts between county farmers or landlords and the United States Department of Agriculture to limit the acreage of corn and wheat, showing names of farm and township, name and address of farmer or landlord, map of farm, acreage for corn, acreage for wheat, until land, division of crops or proceeds, and other land owned or operated in this county for production of corn or wheat. All data pertaining to each farm including compliance certificate and proof of compliance in large envelope labeled by name of farm, farmer, or landlord. Arranged alphabetically by names of townships and thereunder by names of farmers or landlords. No index. Handwritten and typed on printed forms. 11.5 x 13 x 24.

County Agricultural Societies in Ohio were provided for by Statute as early as 1846. On February 28th of that year the legislature passed an act authorizing the forming of such societies and making provisions for their aid by the counties.[1] On February 15, 1853, the legislature declared such societies to be bodies corporate and politic, capable of suing and being sued, and capable of holding in fee simple such real estate as they might purchase for sites where on to hold fairs, the same to be paid for by the county commissioners.[2]

By an act of the legislature passed February 20, 1861, county agricultural societies were required to report annually to the state board of agriculture, and to send a delegate to meet with the state board at Columbus once each year.[3] In 1883 the legislature provided for the organization of district or county agricultural societies. The act making this provision stipulated that when 30 or more persons, residents of any county or district embracing two counties, organized themselves into an agricultural society, under the rules and regulations of the state board of agriculture, the county might aid such society with a grant not to exceed $400 per year.[4] By act of April 21, 1896, provision was made for representation in a county society of 30 or more residents of any county or district embracing two or more counties.[5] In 1900 the legislature extended the amount of county aid to $800 per year.[6] Later, on May 6, 1902, the legislature passed an act authorizing 30 or more residents of a county or of a district embracing one or more counties, to organize themselves into an agricultural society.[7]

----

1. *Laws of Ohio,* XLIV, 70.
2. *Ibid.,* LI, 333.
3. *Ibid.,* LVIII, 22.
4. *Ibid.,* LXXX, 142.
5. *Ibid.,* XCII, 205.
6. *Ibid.,* XCIV, 395.
7. *Ibid.,* XCV, 403.

On April 17, 1919, the legislature provided for the organization of county and independent agricultural societies, the payment class premiums; define the duties of persons competing for premiums; prescribed the publication of treasurers' accounts and the list of awards by societies; designated conditions of membership in a county agricultural society; authorized the society to elect a board of directors consisting of eight members, and prescribed their term of office and the manner of their election. The acts further stipulated how such societies might obtain state aid, and authorized the county commissioners to ensure all buildings belonging to agricultural societies.[8]

The legislature, in 1921, passed an act stipulating that the total amount of county aid to the county agricultural societies should equal 100 percent of the amount paid by the society in regular class premiums but should not exceed $800.[9] By act of March 27, 1925, the county commissioners were authorized to purchase or to lease, for a term of not less than 20 years, real estate whereon to hold fairs under the management of county agricultural societies, and to erect thereon suitable buildings.[10] On March 10, 1927, the legislature authorized the county commissioners to appropriate annually on the request of the agricultural society a sum not less than $1500 or more than $2000 from the general fund for the purpose of "encouraging agricultural affairs."[11]

---

8. *Ibid.*, CVIII, pt. i, 381-385.
9. *Laws of Ohio*, CIX, 240.
10. *Ibid.*, CXX, 238.
11. *Ibid.*, CXII, 84.

The most recent legislation affecting agricultural societies was that of March 19, 1935. This act provides that where no duly organized county agricultural society existed, and when no fair was held by a duly organized county agricultural society which had held an annual exposition for three years previous to January 1, 1933, the county commissioners should, on the request of an independent society, appropriate annually from the general fund are some not more than $2000 nor less than $500 for the encouragement of independent agricultural fairs.[12]

In Medina County interest in agricultural society activities was shown very early, and a society was formed at Medina in 1846, the same year the legislature first authorized such organizations. The first fair was held at Medina in 1848, and others have been held there each year since. The society has been a vital organization, and in recent years has increased the scope and interest of its fairs. Improvements and new buildings, including the grandstand and a special junior fair building, have increased the attractiveness of the fair site. Further evidence of revived interest is found in the fact that all townships in the county are now represented among the 26 members of the society's board of directors. A junior fair board which conducts its own phase of the annual three-day program now enlists participation of the youth of the county in the society's activities.

---

12. *Ibid.,* CXVI, 47.

485. MINUTES–MEDINA AGRICULTURAL SOCIETY

1894—. 4 vols. Title varies: Record, 1894-1918. 2 vols.

Minutes of Medina County fair association, showing date of meeting and record of business transacted, including discussions, motions, votes, and final decisions on subjects, date affair, premiums to be offered, printing up premium book, entrance charges, appointments of superintendents for the departments of entries and races, and supervisors of the grounds and exhibition buildings. Arranged chronologically by dates of meetings. No index. Handwritten on printed forms. Average 500 pages.8 x 12.5 x 2.5. In custody of Jay V. Einhart, Secretary-Treasurer, Medina County Agricultural Fair Association, R. D. 6, Medina, Ohio.

486. WARRANTS
1936—. 2 vols.

Copies of warrants issued on the treasurer of the Agricultural Society for County Fair or Agricultural Society expenditures, showing date and amount of warrant issued for construction and upkeep of buildings, grounds, and race track, also rent and utility expense together with a certification of the secretary and treasurer. Arranged chronologically by dates of warrants. No index. Handwritten on printed forms. Average 200 pages. 9 x 9 x 1. In custody of Jay V. Einhart, Secretary-Treasurer, Medina County Agricultural Fair Association, R. D. 6, Medina, Ohio.

487. RECEIPTS AND EXPENDITURES
1901—. 25 vols. Title varies: Journal, 1901-1918. 1 vol.

Record of receipts and expenditures of Medina County Fair association, showing funds received from contributions and county, date of entry, total amount, to whom paid, for what purpose, and balance also includes a record of expenditures for the year. Arranged chronologically by dates entered. No index. Handwritten one volume 600 pages. 12 x 8 x 2.5. In custody of Jay V. Einhart, Secretary-Treasurer, Medina County Agricultural Fair Association, R. D. 6, Medina, Ohio.

488. REPORT TO THE STATE BOARD OF
AGRICULTURE
1918—. 23 vols.
Duplicate copies of the annual Medina County Fair board report to
state board of agriculture, showing opening and closing dates of
annual fair; detailed financial statement, showing receipts from
gate admission fees, space rentals and other miscellaneous items;
expenditures, showing amount of premiums paid, salaries of
officials, utility and advertising expenses, cost of construction and
upkeep of buildings, grounds and race track. Arranged by subject
headings. No index. Handwritten on printed forms. Average 12
pages.8 x 6 x (illegible). In custody of Jay V. Einhart, Secretary-
Treasurer, Medina County Agricultural Fair Association, R. D. 6,
Medina, Ohio.

In 1914, the federal government passed an act providing for cooperative agricultural extension service between the state agricultural colleges and the United States Department of Agriculture. The purpose of the extension service was to give instructions and practical demonstrations in agricultural and home economics to persons not attending college, and to give such information through field demonstrations, publications, and other means. The funds for such work were to be supplied in part by the federal government and in part by the state.[1]

A year following the federal legislation, the Ohio legislature accepted the provisions of the act by providing that 120 or more residents of a county organize themselves into a "farmers institute society for the purpose of teaching better methods of farming, stock racing, fruit culture and business connected with agriculture," accepted a constitution and bylaws conforming to the rules and regulations prescribed by the trustees of Ohio State University, and elected proper officers, the institute could be a corporate body. Ohio State University was required to furnish speakers for their annual meeting. At the close of the session the trustees are authorized to publish the lectures in pamphlet or book form.

Besides maintaining an institute, the society was authorized to maintain a county's experimental farm. Furthermore, the county commissioners were authorized to select a county agent subject to the approval of the Dean of the College of Agriculture of Ohio State University. It is the duty of the agent to inspect and study the agricultural conditions in the county, distribute agricultural literature, cooperate with the United States Department of Agriculture and College of Agriculture of Ohio State University. In the event the commissioners failed to make such an appointment, the electorate could require them to do so on a referendum vote.[2]

---

1. *United States Statutes at Large* ,XXXVIII, pt. i, 372-374.
2. *Laws of Ohio*, CVI, 356-359.

In 1919, the original legislation was amended so as to authorize the employment of a home demonstration agent. The act of 1929, which is still effective, empowered the trustees of Ohio State University to employ boys' and girls' club agents as well as agricultural and home demonstration agents. The county extension agent was given the additional duty of carrying the teachings of the College of Agriculture of Ohio State University in agriculture and home economics to the residents of the county through personal visits, bulletins, and practical demonstrations. Furthermore, it was his duty to render educational service not only relating to agricultural productions, but also relating to economic problems including marketing, distribution, and the utilization of farm products.[3]

The initial legislation contained a clause which required the county commissioners to appropriate annually $1,000 if they wished to obtain the services of an agricultural agent. This amount was to be matched by the state. Under the present system the commissioners are empowered to levy attacks and to appropriate money from the proceeds thereof or from the general fund of the county an amount not to exceed $3000 for each agent to be paid to the state treasury to the credit of the agricultural fund. Amounts in excess must have the unanimous consent of the commissioners.[4]

The extension service began in Medina County in 1918, and in its early years was closely related to and financially supported by the Farm Bureau. At the present time the county commissioners make it annual appropriation of 2300, while other funds are derived from federal and state sources. The agency has sponsored and assisted the organization of various county 40-H clubs, the membership of these clubs in Medina been about 925 boys and girls.

---

3. *Laws of Ohio* CVIII, 364; CXIII, 82-83.
4. *Ibid.,* CXIII, 82-83.

489. 4-H CLUB
1918—. 5 file boxes.
Reports of 4-H Clubs, showing date of report, names of members, present enrollment, grades, and accomplishments of each club, also individual progress record for each member, dates of meetings, record of subjects, including camps, roadside markets, field days, honor club, and health winners. Also contains a yearly resume of all club activities. Arranged alphabetically by subjects and chronologically thereunder by dates of reports. No index. Typed on printed forms. 11.25 x 13 x 22. Agricultural extension agents' office.

490. CORRESPONDENCE AND MISCELLANEOUS
1926—. 7 File boxes.
Miscellaneous correspondence between counties regarding developments and experiments in agriculture and new developments regarding extension service, including bulletins and data concerning agricultural economics, conservation, engineering, extension methods, animal husbandry, budgets, circular letters, district conference records, contracts with cooperating agencies and county agents association, crop data, hybrid crop data, entomology and plant pathology, forestry, home economics, horticulture, institute data, instructions from United States government and state agencies, laws and regulations, mailing lists, dairy herd improvements, office management, personnel lists, photographs, poultry projects data, game, and wildlife, and United States Department of Agriculture bulletins and soil management and weed control, showing date of correspondence, to whom, from whom, subject covered, and signature of correspondent, also includes annual reports of local supervisors. Arranged alphabetically by subjects. No index. Handwritten typed, and mimeographed some on printed forms. 11.5 x 13 x 22. Agricultural extension agents' office.

Laws and Ordinances

Baldwin, William E., ed., *Throckmorton's Ohio Code Annotated* (certified ed., Cleveland, 1936).
Carter, Clarence Edwin, ed. and comp., *The Territorial Papers of the United States* (4 volumes, Washington, 1934).
Chase, Salmon P., comp., *The Statutes of Ohio and the Northwestern Territory, 1788-1833* (3 volumes, Cincinnati, 1833-1835).
Constitution of the State of Ohio, 1802.
Constitution of the State of Ohio, 1851.
Curwen, Markell E., comp., *Public Statutes at Large of the State of Ohio* (3 volumes, Cincinnati, 1853-1854).
Laws of the Territory of the United States Northwest of the River Ohio (3 volumes, Philadelphia and Cincinnati, 1792-1796).
Page, William H., *New Annotated Ohio General Code* (3 volumes, Cincinnati, 1926; supplement 1 volume, 1926-1935, Cincinnati, 1935; supplements to date).
Sayler, J. R., comp., *The Statutes of the State of Ohio* (4 volumes, Cincinnati, 1876).
State of Ohio Legislative Acts, 1803-1939 (118 volumes, published under State authority).
United States Code Annotated (50 volumes, New York and St. Paul, 1871).
United States Statutes at Large, 1789-1940 (53 volumes, United States Government Printing Office).

Public Records

Annual Reports, entry 323.
Annual Statistical Report, entry 410.
Appearance and Execution Docket, entry 121.
Auditor's Annual Financial Report, entry 322.
Auditor's Appropriation Ledger, entry 282.
Board of Revision [Minutes], entry 395.

Public Records (continued)

Bond Register, entry 319.
Cash Book, entry 108.
Civil Docket, entry 150.
Commissioners; Journal, entry 1.
Common Pleas Journal, entry 124.
Contract Record [Bridges and Culverts], entry 466.
[Coroner's] Inquests, entry 113.
Criminal Appearance and Execution Docket, entry 119.
Court of Appeals Appearance Docket, entry 144.
Expenditures and Receipts, entry 379.
General Appropriation Ledger, entry 279.
Jail Register, entry 223.
Judicial Statistics to Secy. [Secretary] of State, entry 114.
Miscellaneous Report, entry 232.
Pay Rolls, entry 290.
Pay Rolls and Miscellaneous, entry 480.
Poll Books and Tally Sheets, entry 399.
Probate Court Journal, entry 154.
[Progress Book], entry 444.
Receipts Journal, entry 284.
Record, Common Pleas, entry 126.
Record of Minutes and Proceedings, entry 405.
Record of Official Bonds, entry 316.
Registered Lands, entry 53.
Register of Conveyances, entry 34.
[Relief Encumbrance Register], entry 27.
Road Contract Record, entry 465.
Rural Road Mileage Report, entry 481.
Sheriff's Cash Book, entry 225.
Sheriff's Foreign Execution Docket, entry 219.
Treasurer's Cash Book, entry 380.

Official Reports

Digest of Statutes Relating to County Government in Ohio: Report of the Governor's Commission on County Government (mimeographed, Columbus, 1934).

McCook, G. W., and others, eds. *Reports of Cases Argued and Determined in the Supreme Court of Ohio* . . .(132 volumes, Cincinnati, 1852—).
Also known as *Ohio State Reports.*

Ohio Auditor of State, *Annual Report,* 1836-1939. (75 volumes, published under state authority).

Ohio Attorney General, *Opinions,* 1846— (69 volumes, published under state authority).

Ohio Secretary of State, Annual Report, 1836-1938 (90 volumes, published under state authority). Some volumes titled: *Ohio Statistics.*

Ohio Tax Commission, *Financing State and Local Government in Ohio.* 1900-1932 (mimeographed, Columbus, 1934).

The Reorganization of County Government in Ohio: Report of the Governor's Commission on County Government (n. p., n. d.). Submitted to the Governor, December 1934.

Report of the Geological Survey of Ohio, series ii (10 volumes, Columbus, 1873.

Smith, J. V., rep., *Official Reports of the Debates and Proceedings of the Ohio State Convention . . . held at Columbus, Commencing May 6, 1850, and at Cincinnati, Commencing December 2, 1859* (Columbus, 1851).

Shepard, Vinton B., ed., *The Ohio Nisi Prius Reports* (32 volumes, Columbus and Cincinnati, 1894-1934. Cases decided by the common pleas, probate and municipal courts of the State of Ohio.

U. S. Bureau of the Census, *Fifteenth Census of the United States, 1930* (United States Government Printing Office, Washington, D. C.).

—, *Sixteenth Census of the United States, 1940* (United States Government Printing Office, Washington, D. C.).

General Histories and Reference Works

Adams, George B., *Constitutional History of England* (New York, 1921).

Amer, Francis J. *The Development of the Judicial System in Ohio from 1788 to 1932.* (Johns Hopkins University, Baltimore, 1932 Institute of Law Bulletin No. 8).

Ayer, W. W., and Sons, *Directory of Newspapers and Periodicals* (Philadelphia, 1937).

Bond, Beverly, W., Jr., *The civilization of the Old Northwest: A Study of Political, Social, and Economic Development, 1788-1812.* (New York, 1934).

Burnet [Jacob], *Notes on the Early Settlement of the Northwestern Territory* (Cincinnati, 1847).

Channing, Edward, *A History of the United States* (6 volumes, New York, 1905-1925).

Duff, William A., *History of North Central Ohio* (Topeka and Indianapolis, 1931).

Estrich, William A., *et al.*, eds. *Ohio Jurisprudence* (43 volumes, Rochester, 1928-1938). Henry P. Farnham was editor-in-chief, 1928-1929.

Fess, Simon D., *Ohio Reference Library* (4 volumes, New York and Chicago, 1937).

Gwynne, A. E., *A Practical Treatise on the Law of Sheriff and Coroner with Forms and References to the Statutes of Ohio, Indiana, and Kentucky* (Cincinnati, 1849).

Heigen, R. E., *The Office of Sheriff in the Rural Counties of Ohio* (Findlay, 1933).

Howe, Henry, *Historical Collections of Ohio* (3 volumes, Norwalk, Ohio).

Karraker, Cyrus H. *The Seventeenth Century Sheriff. . .*(Chapel Hill, 1930).

Kennedy, Elizabeth A. *The Ohio Poor Law and its Administration* (Sophonisba P. Breckenridge, ed., Social Service Monographs, No. 22, University of Chicago Press, Chicago, 1934).

McCarty, Dwight G., *The Territorial Governors of the Old Northwest: A Study in Territorial Administration* (Iowa City, 1910).

Moley, Raymond, *The Sheriff and the Coroner* (New York, 1926. The Missouri Crime Survey, pt. ii).

Pollock, Frederick, and William Maitland, *The History of English Law Before the Time of Edward I* (Cambridge, 1895).

Sutherland, Edwin H., *Principles of Criminology* (Chicago,1934

Upton, Harriet T., *History of the Western Reserve* (Chicago and New York, 1910).

Van Waters, Miriam, *Youth in Conflict* (New York, 1925).

Willoughby, W. F., *Principles of Judicial Administration* (Washington, 1929).

Local Histories

Northrop, N. B. *Pioneer History of Medina County* (Medina, 1861).

Perrin, W. H., J. H. Battle, and W. A. Goodspeed, *History of Medina County and Ohio* (Chicago, 1881).

Webber, A. R., *History of Hinckley Township* (Elyria, Ohio, 1933).

Articles Published in Periodicals

Atkinson, E. C., "County Home Rule Developments in Ohio." *National Municipal Review,* XXIII (1934), 238.

—, "Ohio–County Charter Elections," *National Municipal Review*, XXIV (1935), 702-703.

—, "Ohio–Optional County Legislation," *National Municipal Review*, XXIV (1939), 235.

Downes, Randolph Chandler, "Evolution of Ohio County Boundaries," *Ohio State Archaeological and Historical Quarterly*, XXXVI (1927), 340-477.

Dykstra, C. A., "Cleveland's Effort for City-County Consolidation," *National Municipal Review*, VIII (1919), 551-556.

Gates, Charles M., "The Administration of State Archives." *The Pacific Northwest Quarterly,* XXIX (January 1938), no. 1.

Kaplan, H. Eliot, "A Personnel Program for County Service," *National Municipal Review,* XXV (1936), 596-600.

Moorehead, W. K., Report of the Field Work in Various Portions of Ohio," *Ohio Archaeological and Historical Quarterly,* XI, (1899), 197.

Morris, William A., "The Office of Sheriff in the Anglo-Saxon Period," *English Historical Review,* XXXI (1916), 20-40.

Price, Robert, "The OhioAnti-Slavery Convention of 1836," *Ohio Archaeological and Historical Quarterly,* LV (1936), 173-187.

Commissioners**

Miles Clark	1818-1819	Solomon Halliday	1849-1852
Timothy Doan	1818-1820	Jonathan Simmons	1850-1853
Andrew Deming	1818-1820	Carr C. Rounds	1851-1854
John Bigelow	1819-1822	James Henderson	1852-1855
Stephen Sibley	1820-1824	James S. Redfield	1853-1856
Ebenezer Harris	1820-1823	William Crane	1854-1857
William Eyles	1822-1828	Thomas S. Seeley	1855-1858
Wiley Hamilton	1823-1826	Samuel Miller	1856-1859
John Codding	1824-1830	Jacob H. Welcher	1857-1860
Seth Warden	1826-1829	Arza Pearson	1858-1861
Rufus Vaughn	1828-1834	John W. Stowe	1859-1862
John Newton	1829-1832	George W. Wise	1860-1863
Jonathan Starr	1830-1836	Russell B. Smith	1861-1862
Samuel Stoddard	1832-1835	Joshua Bernard	1862-1862
Alexander Forbes	1834-1837	(Part of year)	
Henry Hosmer	1835-1838	Wilson Mahan	1862-1871
James F. Leonard	1836-1839	Joseph Fitch	1862-1863
Curtiss Bullard	1837-1840	(Died in office)	
Elisha Hinsdale	1838-1839	E. A. Tillotson	1863-1870
Timothy Burr	1839-1842	(Vice J. Fitch)	
Richard Warner	1840-1840	Leonard J. Parker	1863-1869
(Part of year)		Nathan W. Whedon	1866-1868
Alexander Forbes	1840-1843	Joseph S. Boise	1869-1875
Sheldon W. Johnson	1814-1844	Joseph P. Wyman	1870-1871
John Tanner	1842-1845	(Died in office)	
Jabish Castle	1843-1846	Alexander R. Whitesides	
Sherman Loomis	1844-1847		1871-1871
William Packard	1845-1848	(Part of year,	
Lucius Warner	1846-1849	vise J. P. Wyman)	
Joseph Overholt	1847-1850	William Kennedy	1871-1879
Francis Young	1848-1851	Benjamin Burt	1871-1877
		F. M. Ashley	1875-1881

*Compiled from: Ohio Governor's Office, General Record, 1803-1854; Ohio Secretary of State, County Officers [Commission Registers], 1858-1940; Judicial Commission Register, 1810-1915; Baskin & Battey, *History of Medina County, Ohio,* Chicago, 1881, 222-224, 238-242.

Commissioners (continued)

Spencer F. Codding	1877-1883	B. M. Fenn	1911-1913
Frank Mills	1879-1885	F. A. Strong	1911-191
Sherman B. Rogers	1881-1887	George Starr	1913-1917
George W. Ganyard	1883-1889	D. L. Towslee	1913-1917
John Pearson	1885-1891	H. J. Vandermark	1913-1917
Richard Freeman	1887-1893	R. M. Albert	1919-1921
Noah N. Yoder	1889-1895	C. H. Scanlon	1917-1921
Albert Evans	1891-1897	R. M. Baughman	1917-1919
HarveyE. Leach	1893-1899	William Leach	1919-1923
Arthur Bradley	1895-1901	John Ewing	1921-1929
William H. Hobart	1896-1899	J. E. Gault	1921-1925
James Lowe	1897-1903	John Dunn	1923-1931
Irving H. Kennedy	1899-1905	S. M. Overholt	1925-1933
L. O. Brown	1901-1907	George Zeigler	1929-1933
W. H. Ripley	1903-1906	R. A. Auble	1931-1939
Fremont A. Branch	1905-1911	Arthur Mong	1933-1941
James F. Brittain	1906-1911	R. S. Hartman	1933-1941
Mahlon D. Fretz	1907-1911	Grant G. Chidsey	1939—
J. F. Andrew	1911-1913	Elno R. Stauffer	1941—
		Charles F. Fuller	1941—

**The board of county commissioners, with three members each serving a three-year term was established in 1804 (*Laws of Ohio*, II, 150). In 1906, the term of office was changed to two years (*Laws of Ohio*, XCVIII, 271); in 1920, it was increased to four years and so remains (*Laws of Ohio*, CVIII, pt. ii, 1300).

Recorders*

John Freese	1818-1823	James Newton	1897-1900
Timothy Hudson	1823-1836	Frederick Beck	1900-1906
Oviatt Cole	1836-1842	H. J. Barnabee	1906-1911
David H. Simmons	1842-1848	F. Eugene Clark	1911-1915
Samuel J. Hayslip	1848-1857	M. F. Bailey	1915-1917
Earle Moulton	1857-1864	C. S. Rice	1917-1919
Ashael Boswick	1864-1870	J. Frank Styer	1919-1923
M. Irvine Nash	1870-1876	Jennie Styer Bowman	
Franklin R. Mantz	1876-1882		1923-1927
Lester A. Lewis	1882-1888	Edna T. Loomis	1927-1933
Jacob Long	1888-1894	Eugennia Beck Gage	
Romain B. Hart	1894-1897		1933-1937
		Dorotha L. Pearson	1937—

*Under the law of 1803, the associate judges of the court of common pleas appointed the recorder for a seven-year term (*Laws of Ohio*, I, 136). The office became elective for a three-year term in 1829, a two-year term in 1905, and a four-year term in 1936 (*Laws of Ohio*, XXVII, 65; *Laws of Ohio*, CXCVI, pt. ii, 184; *Ohio Const.* 1851, Art. XVII, sec. 2).

Clerk of the Court of Common Pleas**

John Freese	1818-1823	William N. Pardee	1837-1842
Timothy Hudson	1823-1837	Edward L. Warner	1842-1849

**Called prothonotary under the laws of the Northwest Territory and appointed by the governor. Under the Ohio Constitution of 1802, the court appointed its own clerk for a seven-year term (Art. III, sec. 9). The constitution of 1851, made the office elective for a three-year term (Art. IV, sec. 16). Under the constitutional amendment of 1905, the term was changed to two years and to four in 1936 (*Laws of Ohio*, XCVII, 641; *Laws of Ohio*, CXVI, pt. ii, 184).

Clerk of the Court of Common Pleas (continued)

Harman Canfield	1849-1852	Omar C. Van Dusen	1895-1897
John B. Young	1852-1855	Lester B. Ganyard	1897-1900
Oscar S. Codding	1855-1861	William C. Smith	1900-1906
Asaph Severance, Jr.	1861-1864	J. A. Koons	1906-1911
(Died in office)		Claud Hatch	1911-1915
W. H. Hayslip	1864-1871	Lakey J. Flickinger	1915-1919
(Vice A. Severance, Jr.)		G. C. Frazier	1919-1923
Joseph Andrew	1871-1877	L. Earl Richard	1923-1927
George Hayden	1877-1883	Marion E. Garver	1927-1933
Charles D. Neil	1883-1889	B. A. Davenport	1933-1937
Nicholas Van Epp	1889-1895	Cloyd W. Derhammer	1937—

Judges of the Court of Common Pleas*

President judges under the constitution of 10802 for the several districts which included Medina County

George Tod	1816-1830	Ezra Dean	1834-1841
Reuben Wood	1830-1833	Jacob Parker	1841-1848
Mathew Burchard	1833-1834	Levi Cox	1848-1852

     *The president and associate judges under the first constitution were appointed for seven-year terms by joint ballot of both houses of the general assembly (*Ohio Const., 1802*, Art. III, sec. 8). The cosntitution of 1851, made the office elective for five-year periods and required the incumbent to be a resident of the district in which elected (*Ohio Const., 1851*, Art. IV, sec. 12). The amendment of 1912 changed the term to six years, required the election of at least one judge for each county, who must be a resident of the county in which elected (Art. IV, srec. 12, as amended September 3, 1912).

*Associate judges under the constitution of 1802 for the several districts
which included Medina County*

Joseph Harris	1818-1830	Orson M. Oviatt	1834-1839
Izaak Walton	1818-1825	Benjamin Lindsley	1836-1837
Frederick Brown	1818-1832	(Vice R. Smith)	
Noah M. Bronson	1823-1830	Philo Welton	1837-1840
John Freese	1825-1832	Stephen N. Sargent	1839-1847
Reuben Smith	1830-1836	William Eyles	1840-1847
(Resigned August)		Jesse L. Hinman	1842-1849
John Newton	1832-1834	John L. Clark	1844-1851
(Resigned October)		Charles Castle	1846-1853
Allen Pardee	1832-1833	Henry Horner	1847-1854
(Vice John Newton)		Josiah Piper	1847-1854
Allen Pardee	1833-1847		

*Judges under the constitution of 1851 for District IV which included
Medina County*

Samuel Humphreville		George W. Lewis	1883-1884
	1852-1857	(Vice John C. Hale)	
James S. Carpenter	1857-1862	Georg e W. Lewis	1884-1892
Wm. H. Canfield	1859-1864	Edwin P. Green	1883-1890
Stephen Burke	1862-1869	(Resigned December)	
(Resigned January)		Alvin C. Voris	1890-1891
Washington W. Boynton		(Vice Edwin P. Green)	
	1869-1870	Alvin C. Voris	1891-1896
(Vice Stephen Burke)		(Unexpired term)	
Washington W. Boynton		David J. Nye	1892-1902
	1870-1877	Jacob A. Kohler	1896-1906
Samuel W. McClure	1871-1876	George Hayden	1901-1911
Newell D. Tibbals	1876-1883	Amos R. Webber	1902-1904
(Resigned May)		(Resigned November)	
John C. Hale	1876-1883	Clarence G. Washburn	
(Resigned February)			1904-1907
Ulysses L. Marvin	1883-1885	(Vice Amos R. Webber)	
(May - October, vice		Reuben M. Wanamaker	
Newell D. Tibbals)			1906-1912
		(Resigned December)	

Judges under the constitution of 1851 for District IV which included Medina County (continued)

Clarence G. Washburn		S. G. Rogers	1913-1914
	1907-1914	William J. Ahern, Jr.	1912-1922
Dayton A. Doyle	1907-1919	(Vice R. M. Wanamaker)	
Lee Stroup	1911-1914	Horace G. Redington	1914-1915
(Resigned September)		(Vice Lee Stroup)	

Resident judges under the constitutional amendment of 1912
Judges of the Probate Court

Nathan H. McClure   1915-1933   John D. Owen   1933—

Judges of the Probate Court*

Calvin B. Prentiss	1852-1855	George A. Richards	1897-1897
Henry Warner	1855-1861	(Part of year)	
Samuel C. Barnard	1861-1867	George A. Richards	1897-1903
George W. Lewis	1867-1873	F. M. Plank	1903-1909
Charles G. Codding	1873-1879	J. R. Kennan	1909-1917
Albert Munson	1879-1885	C. C. VanDeusen	1917-1925
John T. Graves	1885-1891	Fremont O. Phillips	1925-1933
Fremont O. Phillips	1891-1897	George M. Benton	1933-1941
		Windsor E. Kellogg	1941—

*The probate court, established under the laws of the Northwest Territory in 1788, consisted of a probate judge and two judges of the court of common pleas (Pease, *op. cit.*, 9). Under the constitution of 1802, it lost its identity completely in the court of common pleas. It emerged with its present form and functions in 1852, with a single judge serving a three-year term, under the constitution of 1851 (Art. IV, secs. 1, 8). On September 3, 1912, the term was changed to four years (Art. IV, sec. 8, amendment, 1912) as at present.

Prosecuting Attorneys*

Luther Blodget	1819-1820	William W. Pancoast	1872-1874
Reuben Wood	1820-1820	Edmund B. King	1874-1876
(Part of year)		J. Thurman Graves	1876-1880
Boaz M. Atherton	1820-1826	Stephen B. Woodward	
Jonathan Sloan	1826-1826		1880-1884
(Part of year)		Joseph Andrew	1884-1888
Charles Olcott	1826-1830	Jesse W. Seymour	1888-1894
Edward Avery	1830-1831	Charley D. Wightman	1894-1897
George Tod	1831-1832	(Resigned)	
William H. Hanfield	1832-1834	Frank Heath	1897-1899
Charles Olcott	1834-1838	(Vice C. D. Wightman)	
Israel Camp	1838-1842	Frank W. Woods	1899-1905
Henry Smith	1842-1844	N. B. McClure	1905-1911
Whitman Mead	1844-1846	Arthur Van Epp	1911-1915
Chester T. Hills	1846-1850	Aldrich B. Underwood	
Francis B. Kimball	1850-1854		1915-1919
Henry McElheiney	1854-1856	Floyd E. Stine	1919-1921
Charles Castle	1856-1858	Joseph Seymour	1921-1923
Nathaniel H. Bostwick		John A. Weber	1823-1925
	1858-1862	Joseph Seymour	1925-1927
Stephen B. Woodward		Raymond B. Bennett	1927-1931
	1862-1866	David Porter	1931-1933
Charles G. Codding	1866-1870	L. Ashley Pelton	1933-1935
Chester T. Hills	1870-1871	Ralph E. Snedden	1935-1941
Charles G. Codding	1871-1872	William G. Batchelder	1941—

*At first appointed by the supreme court and later (1805) by the court of common pleas, a law passed January 23, 1833, made theoffice of prosecuting attorney elective for a term of two years (*Laws of Ohio,* XXXIX, 13). In 1881 the term was increased to three years, in 1906 reduced to two, and in 1936 increased to four (*Laws of Ohio,* LXXVIII, 260; *Laws of Ohio,* XCVIII, 271; *Laws of Ohio,* CXVI, pt. ii, 184).

Coroners*

Moses Deming	1818-1820	John McCormick	1867-1871
Abraham Scott	1820-1822	William H. Bradway	1871-1874
John Hickox	1822-1826	Alexander Whitesides	1874-1875
Henry Hosmer	1826-1832	Hiram Goodwin	1875–1883
H. R. Chicester	1832-1834	Aaron -anders	1883-1891
William Paull	1834-1836	Charles F. Freeman	1891-1897
Jonathan Denning	1836-1838	George Hasel	1897-1899
H. R. Chicester	1838-1841	Charles B. Freeman	1899-1901
Earl Moulton	1841-1842	H. H. Bard	1901-1909
Abraham Morton	1842-1843	H. L. Johnson	1909-1911
Silas Judson	1843-1844	H. F. H. Robinson	1911-1913
Ransom Clark	1844-1846	Roy G. Strong	1913-1915
Lewis C. Chatfield	1846-1850	Roy A. Brintnall	1915-1919
Joseph Whitmore	1850-1852	E. L. Crum	1919-1933
Addison Alcott	1852-1856	H. F. H. Robinson	1933-1940
Morgan Andrews	1856-1858	(Resigned)	
Josiah B. Beckwith	1858-1865	John L. Jones	1940-1941
William M. Alden	1865-1867	R. Graham Johnston	1941—

*Established in 1788, the county coroner was appointed for a two-year term by the territorial governor Pease, *op. cit.*, 24, 25). The Ohio Constitution of1802 (Art. VI, sec. 1) made the office elective without changing the term, which remained at two years until 1936, when it was increased to four years (*Laws of Ohio*, CXVI,. pt. ii, 184).

Sheriffs**

Lathrop Seymour	1818–1822	William H. Alden	1840-1842
Samuel Y. Potter	1822-1825	William T. Welling	1842-1844
(Died in office)		John L. Clark	1844-1846
Gustavus V. Willard	1825-1826	Allen R. Burr	1846-1852
(Vice Samuel Y. Potter)		George R. Jordan	1850-1854
Gustavus V. Willard	1826-1828	John Rounds	1854-1858
Hiram Bronson	1828-1830	Morgan Andrews	1858-1862
Stephen N. Sargent	1830-1834	Jesse Seeley	1863-1865
William Root	1834-1836	Lucius M. Sturges	1865-1869
John L. Clark	1836-1840	Nelson W. Piper	1869-1873

*Sheriffs** (continued)

Oscar P. Phillips	1873-1875	Edwin D. Parent	1899-1903
Samuel Scott	1875-1877	H. W. Orr	1903-1907
Charles R. Parmelee	1877-1881	Pat Hutchinson	1907-1911
Jonathan D. Stow	1881-1885	R. E. Young	1911-1915
O. S. Dealing	1885-1889	R. L. Gehman	1915-1919
Herman F. Nicholas	1889-1893	Park C. Bigelow	1919-1923
Benjamin L. Wells	1893-1897	Fred O. Roshon	1923-1927
C. L. Van Deusen	1897-1899	Neal D. Roshon	1927-1929
Edwin J. Gilbert	1899-1899	L. H. Buffington	1929-1933
(Part of year, resigned)		Roy Kruggel	1933-1941
James D. Carpenter	1899-1899	Oliver Barry	1941—
(Part of year, vice Edwin J. Gilbert)			

*Under the territorial government the sheriff was appointed by the governor from the time the office was created in 1792 (Pease, *op. cit.,* 8). Under the first constitution the office was made elective for two-year terms (*Ohio Const. 1802* Art. VI, sec. 1) and was not changed until 1936, when the term was increased to four years. (*Laws of Ohio*, CXVI., pt. ii, 184).

*Treasurers**

Rufus Ferris	1818-1832	Samuel J. Hayslip	1870-1874
Gustavus V. Willard	1832-1839	Hosea P. Boskett	1874-1878
Isaac R. Henry	1839-1840	Francis B. Clark	1878-1882
James W. Weld	1840-1842	J. H. Damon	1882-1886
Charles Castle	1842-1844	Joseph A. Stebel	1886-1890
Abraham Norton	1844-1846	Eldridge G. Hard	1890-1898
Eli Baldwin	1846-1848	Irvin Hard	1894-1898
William Root	1848-1850	(Resigned)	
Josiah B. Beckwith	1850-1852	James Newton	1898-1898
Robert Carr	1852-1856	(Part of year, vice I. Hard)	
Barney Daniels	1856-1858		
Samuel B. Curtiss	1858-1862	Irving H. Kennedy	1898-1900
William Shakespeare	1862-1866	James Newton	1900-1901
Joseph Andrew	1866-1870	Thomas Palmer	1901-1903

Treasurers* (continued)

P. H. Hickard	1903-1907	Elmer R. Lee	1923-1927
A. B. Aylord	1907-1911	Otto Harp	1927-1931
R. J. Hyde	1911-1915	P. N. Yoder	1931-1937
Charles Frank	1915-1919	Lloyd B. Leatherman	1937—
B. W. Moyer	1919-1923		

**Omitted from the constitution of 1802, the office of treasurer was created by legislative act in 1803 (1 O. L. 98). Appointive by the associate judges in 1803 (*Laws of Ohio,* I, 98). Appointive, by the associate judges in 1803 and, annually by the county commissioners from 1804 to 1827, when the office became elective for two-year terms (*Laws of Ohio,* I, 98; *Laws of Ohio,* II, 154; *Ilaws of Ohio,* XXV, 25-32). The constitution of 1851 provided that no person should hold the office for more than four years in any six (Art. X, sec. 3). In 1859 the general assembly made the term two years (*Laws of Ohio,* LVI, 105). In 1936, it was increased to four years, as at present (*Laws of Ohio,* pt. ii, 184).

Auditors**

Abraham Freese	1822-1824	Charles J. Chase	1881-1887
Peter Berdan	1824-1833	Alfred L. Corman	1887-1896
W. H. Canfield	1833-1841	George A. Richards	1896-1899
Isaac R. Henry	1841-1843	Christian R. Hoover	1899-1899
Charles Lum	1843-1845	(Part of year)	
W. H. Alden	1845-1849	William H. Hobart	1899-1905
Samuel H. Bradley	1849-1853	Ralph R. Randall	1905-1908
George A. L. Boult	1853-1855	Homer J. Hale	1908-1911
Gideon W. Tyler	1855-1859	R. R. Garver	1911-1915
John R. Stebbins	1859-1863	George L. McNeal	1915-1919
Alexander R. Whitesides		Ward S. Washburn	1919-1927
	1836-1867	Hobert Edwards	1927-1935
Thomas S. Shaw	1867-1871	Erwin G. Eastwood	1935-1939
Henry C. Pardee	1871-1875	Everett J. Wilson	1939—
Shepard L. Dyer	1875-1881		

Auditors** (continued)

**Office established by legislative act February 18, 1820 (*Laws of Ohio*, XCIII, 70). At first appointive, it was made elective annyally by an act of February 2, 1821, the person elected taking office March 1 each year (*Laws of Ohio,* XCX, 116). In 1831 the term was set at two years, in 1877 at three years, in 1906 at two years, and in 1919 at four years (*Laws of Ohio,* XXIX, 280; *Laws of Ohio,* LXXIV, 381; *Laws of Ohio,* XCVIII, 271; *Laws of Ohio,* CVIII, pt. ii, 1294.

Infirmary Directors*

H. A. Warner	1854-1855	Samuel H. Pomeroy	1883-1886
Henry H. Hibbard	1854-1855	Samuel B. Curtiss	1886-1892
Moses Hoskett	1854-1855	William F. Nye	1887-1890
John Albro	1855-1855	Henry A. Mills	1888-1894
(Part of year)		Ransom Vanderhoef	1890-1893
Joshua Hernard	1855-1859	William Ritter	1892-1898
Barrett Spitzer	1855-1860	Lewis Loehr	1894-1900
Pemberton Randall	1855-1862	Frank W. Woods	1896-1896
James R. Newton	1860-1863	(Part of year)	
Charles Eddy	1861-1867	George Hasel	1896-1902
William D. Prouty	1862-1865	John Handyside	1989-1904
Henry H. Noble	1863-1866	Thomas C. Woodward	
Roswell Williams	1865-1871		1900-1906
Albert Rounds	1866-1875	W. R. Fitch	1902-1911
Lyman Pritchard	1867-1873	John Randall	1904-1911
Samuel H. Pomeroy	1871-1877	J. F. Shumaker	1906-1909
G. B. Chase	1875-1882	W. H. Zimmerman	1909-1913
Abraham Depew	1875-1878	C. F. Parmelee	1911-1913
Samuel B. Curtiss	1876-1883	J. H. Rickard	1911-1913
Amos Gardner	1878-1887	John B. Ewing	1913-1919
Waylord Thomas	1882-1886	J. Platte Foskett	1919—

*Infirmary Directors** (continued)

*This office was authorized by a legislative act in 1816, providing for the appointment by the commissioners of seven directors, to have charge of the county infirmary and choose its superintendent (*Laws of Ohio,* XIV, 248, 249). By an act of 1831, the membership of the board was reduced to three, and in 1865 the members were made elective for terms of three years (*Laws of Ohio,* XXIX, 319; *Laws of Ohio,* LXII, 24, 25). The board was abolished by law in 1913, its powers and duties were transferred to the board of county commissioners and the infirmary superintendent (*Laws of Ohio,* CII, 433),

*Surveyors***

James Moore	1820-1826	Amos D. Sheldon	1875-1893
Nathaniel Bell	1826-1837	Lester B. Ganyard	1893-1896
Whitman Mead	1837-1838	Romain B. Hart	1896-1899
Abel Dickinson	1838-1839	Lester B. Ganyard	1899-1902
Abraham Fresse	1839-1847	A. D. Sheldon	1902-1908
William F. Moore	1844-1847	Clyde Harvey	1908-1913
Whitman Mead	1847-1850	William F. Peters	1913-1917
Zachery Dean	1850-1856	Walter R. Bibbins	1917-1923
Alonzo Beebe	1856–1863	Fremont E. Tanner	1923-1925
William P. Clark	1863-1869	W. W. Anderson	1925-1929
Flavious J. Wheatley	1869-1875	R. E. House	1929-1935

**From 1803 to 1831, the surveyor was appointed by the court of common pleas and commissioned by the governor (*Laws of Ohio,* I, 90, 93). From 1831 to 1906 he was elected for a three-year term, from 1906 to 1928, for a two-year term, and since 1928, for a four-year term(*Laws of Ohio, XXIX, 399; Laws of Ohio*, XCVIII, 245-247; *Laws of Ohio,* CXII, 179).

*Engineers**

R. E. House	1935-1937	Wayne W. Anderson	1937-1941
		C. Homer Bricker	1941—

*An act, of 1935, changed the title of surveyor to engineer (*Laws of Ohio,* CXVI, 287).

All addresses refer to Medina unless otherwise noted

Auditor
https://www.medinacountyauditor.org/
144 North Broadway Street

Board of Elections
https://www.boe.ohio.gov/medina/
3800 Stonegate Drive, Suite C

Clerk of Courts
https://medinacountyclerk.org/
225 East Washington Street

Commissioners
https://www.medinaco.org/county-commissioners/
144 North Broadway Street
Room 201

Common Pleas Court
https://www.medinaco.org/judge-hutson/
225 East Washington Street

Coroner
https://www.medinaco.org/coroner/
144 North Broadway Street
Room 110

County Home
https://www.medinaco.org/medina-county-home
6144 Wedgewood Road

Dog Shelter
https://www.medinaco.org/dog-shelter/
6334 Deerview Lane

Health Department
https://medinahealth.org/
4800 Ledgewood Drive

Juvenile Court
https://medinaprobate.org/
225 East Washington Street
4th Floor

Prosecutor
https://medinacountyprosecutor.weebly.com/
60 Public Square

Recorder
https://recorder.co.medina.oh.us
144North Broadway Street
Suite 117

Sanitary
https://www.medinaco.org/sanitary/
791 West Smith Road

Sheriff
https://medinasheriff.org/
555 Independence Drive

Treasurer
https://www.medinacountytax.com#/
144 North Broadway Street

Veterans
https://www.medinacountyveterans.org/
210 Northland Drive

Non-governmental websites and locations

FamilySearch
https://www.familysearch.org/search/catalog
FamilySearch is a free website with digitized records. Records located for Medina County include Probate, Supreme, Common Pleas, Recorder, and Auditor. Each of these headings has further information. Ohio Birth and Death Records from 1867-1909, as well as marriage records are available

Medina County District Library
https://www.mcdl.info
210 South Broadway Street
This library houses the Virginia Wheeler Martin Family History & Learning Center. The library offers numerous online databases from the Ohio Memory Project, Periodical Source Index (PERSI), Heritage Quest, Fold3, Find My Past, as well as being a FamilySearch Affiliate Library and Ancestry.com's Library Edition. A large collection of Medina County newspapers are available from 1830-1977.

Ancestry
Ancestry.com
Ancestry is a pay site, but can be used at the Medina County District Library. Searching may lead to records such *as Ohio Wills and Probate Records 1786-1998*; and *Indexed Early Land Ownership and Township Plats, 1785-1898.*

Western Reserve Historical Society
https://www.wrhs.org
10825 East Blvd., Cleveland, Ohio
See website for hours of operation.
Located in the Cleveland History Center, WRHS has an extensive collection of works pertaining to Medina County in their books and manuscript collections.

ADDRESSES AND WEBSITES

Well worth investigating for your family history

FamilySearch

myscouch

FamilySearch is a free website with digitized records ...

As the *Inventory* for Medina County contain no index to the entries, a smaller, concise index has been developed. In many instances, this index gave a range of pages to find the precise entry within a specific office.

Agricultural conservation association, 481, 482, 483, 484
Agricultural extension service, 489, 490
Agricultural society, 485, 486, 487, 488
Auditor
 Maps and Plats,238
 Property transfers, 264, 234, 236, 237
 Taxes
 Real property, 239, 240, 241, 242, 243, 244
 Tax duplicate and abstracts, 245, 246, 247, 248, 249, 250, 251
 Special assessments, 252
 Personal property, 253, 254, 255, 256, 257, 258, 259, 260
 Delinquent, 261, 262, 263, 264, 265, 266, 267, 268, 269
 Inheritance, 270, 271, 272
 Utility, 273
 Excise, 274, 275, 276
 Fiscal Accounts
 Budgets and appropriations, 277
 Settlements, 278, 279
 General accounts, 280, 281, 282, 283, 284, 285, 286, 287, 288, 289, 290, 291
 Bills and claims, 302

Auditor (continued)
 Vouchers, orders, and warrants, 303, 304, 305, 306, 307, 308, 309, 310, 311, 312
 Licenses and Permits
 Enumerations and statistics, 313, 314, 315, 316, 317, 318, 319, 320, 321
 Bonds, 325, 326, 327, 328, 329, 330
 Weights and measures, 331
 Miscellaneous, 332, 333, 334, 335, 336, 337, 338, 339, 340, 341, 342, 343, 344, 345, 346, 347, 348, 349, 350, 351
Board of education
 Minutes, 407
 Pupils, 408, 409
 Statistics, 410, 411
 Financial records, 412
 Miscellaneous, 413
Board of Elections
 Minutes, 397
 Elections, 398, 399, 400, 401, 402
 Miscellaneous, 403, 404, 405, 406
Board of health
 Minutes, 414, 415
 Immunizations, 416
 Communicable diseases, 417

Board of health (continued)
Inspections, 418
Vital statistics, 419, 420, 421
Tuberculosis hospital, 422
Blind relief, 439, 440
Board of revisions, 394
Additions and deductions, 395
Budget commission, 393
Clerk of courts,
Court proceedings, 77, 78, 79, 80, 81, 82, 83, 84
Jury and witness records, 85, 86, 87, 88
Motor vehicles, 89, 90, 91, 92
Commissions, 93, 94, 95
Licenses and certifications, 96, 97, 98, 99, 100, 101
Partnerships, 101, 103, 104
Elections, 105
Coroner inquest, 106
Financial records, 107, 108, 109, 110, 111
Miscellaneous, 112, 113, 114
County commissioners
Proceedings, 1, 2, 3, 4, 5
Public Improvements
Roads, 6, 7, 8, 9, 10, 11
Institutions and relief, 11
Financial records, 12, 13
Claims, 14
Miscellaneous, 15, 16
Aid for the blind, 17, 18, 19, 20, 21, 22

County Commissioners (continued)
Relief administration, 23, 24, 25, 26, 27
County engineer
Survey, maps and plats, 444, 445, 446, 477, 448, 449, 450, 451
Public Improvement, 452, 453, 454, 455, 456
Bridges, 457, 458, 459
Ditches, 460
Estimates, bids, and contracts, 461, 462, 463, 464, 465, 466
Financial records, 467, 468, 469, 470, 471, 472, 473, 474, 475, 476
Miscellaneous, 477, 478, 479, 480
Court of appeals
District court, 133, 134, 135, 136, 137, 138, 139
Circuit court, 140, 141, 142, 143
Court of appeals, 144, 145, 146, 147, 148
Court of common pleas
Civil cases, 115, 116
Naturalization, 117, 118
Criminal cases, 119, 120, 121, 122, 123, 124, 125, 126, 127, 128, 129
Division of aid for the aged, 441, 442, 443
Dog warden, 233
Juvenile court
General court proceedings, 194, 195, 196, 197

Juvenile Court (continued)
Financial records, 198
Probation Department, 203, 204,
205, 206
Aid to dependent
children, 207, 208, 209,
210, 211, 212, 213
Probate Court,
Civil cases, 149, 150,
151, 152
Criminal cases, 153
General court
proceedings, 154, 155,
156, 157, 158, 159
Criminal document, 161
Estates and guardianships
Wills, 161, 162, 163,
164, 165, 166
Inventories and
appraisements, 167, 168,
169
Schedule of debt, 170
Cost bills, 171
Settlements and
accounts, 172
Inheritance tax record,
173, 174
Assignments, 175
Departments, 176
Naturalization, 177, 178
Vital statistics
Births and deaths, 179,
180, 181, 182, 183, 184
Licenses, certificates and
permits, 185, 186
Financial records, 187,
188, 189, 190, 191
Miscellaneous, 192, 193
Prosecuting attorney, 214, 215,
216, 217, 218

Recorder
Real property transfers
Deeds, 28, 29, 30, 31 32,
33 34, 35, 36
Leases, 37, 38, 39, 40,
41, 42
Mortgages, 43, 44, 45,
46, 47
Liens, 48, 49, 50, 51, 52
Registered lands, 53, 54,
55, 56, 57
Plats and maps, 58, 59,
60, 61, 62
Personal property
transfers, 63, 64
Corporations and
partnerships, 65, 66
Grants of authority, 67,
68, 69
Fiscal accounts, 70, 71,
72
Miscellaneous, 73, 74,
75, 76
Sheriff
Court orders, 219, 220,
221, 222
Jail records, 223, 224
Financial records, 225,
226, 227
Miscellaneous, 228, 229,
230, 231, 232
Soldiers relief commission
Minutes, 435
Applications, 436, 437,
438
Superintendent of the county home
Minutes, 423
Case records, 424, 425,
426, 427, 428

Superintendent of the county
home (continued)
        Fiscal records, 429, 430,
        431, 432
        Miscellaneous, 433, 434
Supreme court, 130, 131, 132
Treasurer
        Taxes
        Real property, 352, 353,
        354, 355, 356, 357
        Special assessments, 358
        Personal property, 359,
        360, 361, 362, 363
        Delinquent, 364, 365,
        366
        Adjustments, 367, 368
        Inheritance, 369, 370
        Excise, 371, 372, 373,
        374, 375, 376
        Fiscal accounts
        General accounts, 377,
        378, 379, 380
        Special accounts, 381
        Warrants and orders,
        382, 383, 384, 385, 386
        Bonds, 387, 389
        Miscellaneous, 390, 391,
        392
Trustees of the sinking fund, 396

Heritage Books by Jana Sloan Broglin:

Additions and Corrections to the W.P.A. Inventory of Adams County, Ohio: West Union

Additions and Corrections to the W.P.A. Inventory of Allen County, Ohio: Lima

Additions and Corrections to the W.P.A. Inventory of Ashland County, Ohio: Ashland

Additions and Corrections to the W.P.A. Inventory of Athens County, Ohio: Athens

Additions and Corrections to the W.P.A. Inventory of Belmont County, Ohio: St. Clairsville

Additions and Corrections to the W.P.A. Inventory of Fulton County, Ohio: Wauseon

Additions and Corrections to the W.P.A. Inventory of Geauga County, Ohio: Chardon

Additions and Corrections to the W.P.A. Inventory of Hancock County, Ohio: Findlay

Additions and Corrections to the W.P.A. Inventory of Lorain County, Ohio: Elyria

Additions and Corrections to the W.P.A. Inventory of Lucas County, Ohio: Toledo

Additions and Corrections to the W.P.A. Inventory of Medina County, Ohio: Medina

Additions and Corrections to the W.P.A. Inventory of Muskingum County, Ohio: Zanesville

Additions and Corrections to the W.P.A. Inventory of Wayne County, Ohio: Wooster

Hookers, Crooks and Kooks, Part I: Hookers

Hookers, Crooks and Kooks, Part II: Crooks and Kooks

Lucas County, Ohio, Index to Deaths, 1867–1908

Mason County, Kentucky Wills and Estates, 1791–1832, Second Edition

www.ingramcontent.com/pod-product-compliance
Lightning Source LLC
Chambersburg PA
CBHW060132280326
41932CB00012B/1490